“Struggle a Hard Battle”

“Struggle

Essays on Working-Class Immigrants

a Hard Battle"

Edited by Dirk Hoerder

N·I·U PRESS
Northern Illinois University Press
DeKalb, Illinois 1986

Published by the Northern Illinois University Press,
DeKalb, Illinois 60115
Manufactured in the United States of America

Library of Congress Cataloging-in-Publication Data

Main entry under title:
"Struggle a hard battle."
(Explorations in the history of American radicalism)

Includes bibliographies and index.
1. Alien labor—United States—History—Addresses, essays, lectures.
2. Labor and laboring classes—United States—History—Addresses, essays, lectures.
3. Labor and laboring classes—United States—Political activity—History—Addresses, essays, lectures.
4. Radicalism—United States—History—Addresses, essays, lectures.
I. Hoerder, Dirk. II. Series.
HD8081.A5E87 1986 304.8'00973 85-25894
ISBN 0-87580-112-9 ISBN 0-87580-533-7 (pbk.)

Contents

"Struggle a Hard Battle"

DIRK HOERDER

Introduction

This collection of original essays explores aspects of immigrant workers' radicalism and direct action. We have not attempted to cover all ethnic groups, but we have tried to deal with the whole lives of the migrants: the work sphere, including strikes and other forms of resistance and organization, as well as the everyday life in the community. These are closely related subjects, hardly separable at times; but the scholarly emphasis on work (labor history) or ethnic groups (immigration history) has obscured this relatedness. The "class and community" approach of the last decade has overcome the artificial dichotomy between work and "leisure." Though it was often not easy within the constraints of the essay format, all the authors in this collection have tried to include in their analyses the cultural backgrounds of the migrants. Only studies of migrants which take into consideration their primary socialization in the culture of origin can provide meaningful answers about the North American experience.

The paradigms of the history of immigration and of labor migration are changing fast, and some of the essays in this volume have been selected because they contribute to this reorientation. The customary distinction between the old immigration and the new is being replaced by a distinction between a settlers' migration and a labor migration overlapping in time. Only the latter is our concern in this volume, though an immigrant (and native) farmer radicalism, which frequently was close to labor radicalisms, did develop.

Labor migrants began to come early in the century, mainly British laborers and artisans as well as impoverished Germans. They continued to come—as did Scandinavian, Irish, and German labor migrants—in the years after 1880 when, according to a simplified version of immigration history, mainly unskilled Eastern and Southern European workers migrated. To be quite explicit: those Western and Northern European newcomers customarily considered "old immigrants" moving to the agrarian areas of the North American West often, in fact, stayed in the cities as workers or artisans. After the Civil War these groups included an increasing number of unskilled industrial workers.

Second, the immigration paradigm is being replaced by a model of international, often temporary, migrations in the framework of a segmented labor market comprising various areas of the Atlantic economies. These labor migrations involved larger numbers within Europe than in the cross-Atlantic move. However, because of the high visibility and comparatively reliable statistical data of the cross-Atlantic move, it received more attention from contemporaries and historians than justified. Only an analysis of the whole complex network of migrations in the European and the North American nations yields an adequate picture. In a conceptualization that has received less attention than it deserved, the statisticians Wilcox and Ferenczi spoke in 1931 of the "proletarian mass migration."

Many of the migrants, however, were not class-conscious proletarians but peasant-workers. They came from a rural background and they moved to industry, but most of them intended to go back to the land or at least to their culture of origin. At the turn of the century even German and Jewish in-migrants left the United States in considerable numbers. An estimated one-third of all migrants returned or went to other industrializing areas. Perhaps as many were "involuntary immigrants": they came as temporary migrants but postponed the decision to leave the receiving culture again and again.

According to established historiography, these peasant-workers were fragmented into ethnic groups and therefore did not and could not develop a common class consciousness. The strike activities of the Industrial Workers of the World, whose mass meetings were sometimes held with simultaneous translation into some five to twelve languages, are often mentioned as important but short-lived attempts to overcome this fragmentation. Multi-ethnic organization and solidarity certainly were not easy to achieve, but migrants could often rely on previous experience. In their old countries, many members of these ethnic groups had lived in ethnically mixed areas. Nor did the ghettos in the industrial cities consist of isolated ethnic enclaves; they were mixed by street. Because of settlement patterns and hegemonial languages, considerable parts of the population in the Austro-Hungarian empire were bi- or multilingual. In addition to their own language, people had to know the administrative language, German or Hungarian (or both), and the languages of their ethnic neighbors. Before the turn of the century, strike announcements in Budapest were printed in four languages; the German federation of trade unions published newspapers in Italian and Polish for labor migrants; Paris and London had Yiddish labor periodicals and Vienna, Czech ones. The fragmentation paradigm, therefore, also stands in need of revision.

It is in this context that the writers of this book analyze the labor migrants in the United States and Canada. When we talk about immigrant militancy, we do not assume that the migrants rejected acculturation. Certainly only few assimilated in the sense that they took over the cultural tenets, work ethos, and customs of the Anglo/prior-migrant majority. Acculturation means the adjustment of old beliefs, values, and patterns of behavior to new societal surroundings. But at the same time the process of acculturation to some degree involves adaptation of the new institutions and customs to fit old values and life-styles. Militancy and radicalism are, then, particular approaches to the new society, which, if it fails to measure up to preconceived standards, has got to be changed.

The history of the United States began with a revolutionary change that took much of its inspiration from European customs of popular ritual and resistance. In turn it inspired the European political debate during the Age of Revolution up to 1848. The popular or plebian forms of direct action in the 1760s and 1780s were followed by the struggle over who should rule at home once home rule had been achieved, and aspects of this struggle are the theme of the present volume.

Artisans and workers struggled for their rights throughout the first century of the new republic. Working-class militancy—which is not only reactive, as the term *resistance* implies, but proactive—drew on the American revolutionary tradition. The rhetoric of the Knights of Labor made this abundantly clear from the beginning of the nineteenth century. It also drew on the European revolutionary and anti-colonial traditions carried over by immigrant artisans and workers. Under the impact of industrialization and in the process of interaction with each other, the American and the immigrant traditions were transformed. The basis for such militancy was the cooperation and solidarity of different ethnic communities and the shared work experience. By World War I this movement for "industrial democracy" crested, became intensely political, national, and international, and seemed to collapse. But did it? Several essays in the volume point to new departures. A reorganization of protest movements and forms began. The ethnic community declined in importance, multi-ethnic party and union organizations assumed leadership functions in a new working-class culture. Allen Seager analyzes these developments among coalminers. Their result, the industrial unionism of the 1930s, is well known. While the immigrant workers in the United States are the main subject of these essays, it is also made clear that national boundaries often do not coincide with class experience. Cigar workers in Cuba and Florida had similar experiences (Mormino/Pozetta), so had immigrant miners in both North American nations (Seager). Accordingly, most United States-American unions became international unions that included Canadians, Puerto Ricans, and workers from other neighboring countries and areas.

The first international organization of the lower classes, artisans and workers, began with the sympathies of the Democratic-Republican societies for the French Revolution. The top echelons of society reacted with the Alien and Sedition Laws. Next came the British connection and the conspiracy trials. British artisans and skilled workers came to live in the United States but kept their connections first with the French-inspired Jacobin movement in their home country and later with the Chartists. In the United States they became Jeffersonians and, in the 1830s, labor militants. After the revolutions of 1830 and 1848 the often-ridiculed German "Latin Farmers" and show-case liberals, for example, Carl Schurz, were not the only ones to come. Radical craftsmen and poor laborers also came. Their hopes for a free and just society not fulfilled by the American system, they continued to criticize and to struggle in their adopted country as they had done in their native country. *Bruce Levine* points out that Jacobinism, the plebeian radicalism in the age of bourgeois-democratic revolutions, was a reaction to changes of the social and economic structures. The ancien regimes were being swept away, but the development, or "modernization," toward a capitalist society and the exploitation of labor was not what craftsmen and skilled workers were struggling for. Other essays in the volume continue this theme into the 1880s: Czech Fortyeighters and lumberworkers combined to form a freethought community that moved to socialism (R. Schneirov); Slovak labor migrants celebrated the Fourth of July with references to their own struggles in 1848 (P. Krause).

Impoverished Irish migrants carried a different tradition over the Atlantic. Not only the temporary potato blight but the far worse and persistent British colonial domination forced them to leave their plots. Accordingly, they brought with them a strong anti-colonial radicalism and could not find ultimate satisfaction with the achievement of positions on the local police force. Irish workers were in the forefront of many labor struggles in a number of working-class organizations. *David Brundage* describes the connections between the Irish struggles for independence and a republican government. The Land League, founded to support tenant farmers in Ireland, denounced monopoly and inequality in the United States. Many of its members became active Knights of Labor.

British, German, and Irish artisanal and plebeian radicalism was the connecting link between the American popular radicalism of the 1770s and the migrant working-class struggles of the 1870s. At first this radicalism was on leave from the European situation: German radicals hoped to return, Irish radicals hoped to free Ireland from British domination. But the radicalism became genuinely American in that it was adapted to the needs of the migrants in their new surroundings. Even if European and American social structures were deeply divergent—a widespread but unproved assumption—the rhetoric and the underlying value system that led to a critique of an aristocracy of birth could easily be applied to an aristocracy of wealth. Being forced off the land by British, East Elbian, Austrian, or Hungarian landlords was in some respects very different from being forced out of an artisanal or industrial job. In other respects it was very similar: peasants and workers had to provide for their families and had to bring opportunities, however severely limited, into line with their expectations. Thus needs, and often values, did not change; and the way they were expressed in the old country frequently proved a valid background for their expression in the new country.

Hartmut Keil uses the German mass migration of East Elbian agricultural workers, skilled industrial workers as well as artisans, to show how the broad spectrum of German social-democratic, socialist and anarchist thought became an integral element of American, temporarily German-American, unions and parties. Broadening his research from Germans in Chicago to the whole of the German labor migrants in the United States in this essay, he argues that the old-culture "multiplicity of class and cultural experiences" was subjected to an American experience, which the German-American socialists called "the mightiest and ultimate teacher." While thus destroying the cliché of isolated German Marxist émigrés in an alien environment, he logically arrives at revising a further standard interpretation. It has been common to point to a decline of German-American ethnic institutions in general during World War I. But Keil shows that the German immigrant labor militants had become part of the English-speaking mainstream by the 1890s, shaping that mainstream in the process of entering it.

While Keil is concerned with militant industrial workers and artisans trying to influence their immigrant fellow workers of agrarian background, *Donna Gabaccia* approaches similar questions through the experience of Sicilian artisans and peasants. Like other authors in this volume she revises the widely held notion that migration meant a decline in militancy in both the old culture and the new. The agrarian experiences of peasant-workers often provided a useful background for industrial strife, particularly when connected to artisanal radicalism. Sicilian day laborers with a history of occupation of the land of their employers could transfer forms of resistance to industrial settings. East European migrant workers in mines and mills kept gardens and raised pigs to augment their wages and support their strikes. Old culture ways of living and of struggling in agrarian villages made cooperation with the movements of American-born workers in some respects a creative fusion of traditions.

Such solidarity could be avoided, capitalist entrepreneurs reasoned, by moving away. Steelworks were transfered to Gary, cigar making to Ybor City. But on arrival they found no new workers with empty minds to be molded and rolled according to the needs of steel and cigar bosses. The workers—men, women, and children—followed, and their beliefs and hopes became rooted in clean company towns just as they had once been in festering ghettos. Capital, with the assistance of the engineering sciences, reacted with task division and mechanization. From the viewpoint of labor economists, this meant a homogenization of the labor force: after the interchangeable parts came the interchangeable workers. The consequent and intended breakdown of craft consciousness destroyed many craft unions. But in the dialectics of moves and countermoves between capital and labor the new mode of production brought about new forms of resistance, new possibilities for common action.

Community support provided the resources for such struggles. It permitted the weathering of strikes and deprivations, physically and mentally. Workplace communication provided the opportunity to unify particular ethnic groups with common grievances. In particular, jobs and factory departments became common experience and turned out to be similar enough that common, united action could be taken. Both furnished a means of acculturation even for temporary migrants, who were not uprooted and did not usually enter into a strange new culture, though the workplace, at least for peasants, meant a break with the past. Rather, they migrated within an Atlantic segmented labor market from an ethnic or multi-ethnic village community to an ethnic or multi-ethnic community in a city, company town, or mining location. Individuals moved from one community and workplace to another—but within the framework of shared ideas and experiences. From the security of these supportive institutions they looked toward the larger society.

In the new industrial and mining locations, community building took many forms. Some institutions were specific to one ethnic group, like the socialist building and loan associations of the Czech lumbershovers, the socialist halls of the Finns, the cultural and health-care centers of the Latin groups in Ybor City. Other arrangements were common to many ethnic cultures but organized on a mono-ethnic basis: boardinghouses, Turnvereine-Sokols-Falcons, singing societies. Special events such as commemorations of the Paris Commune and the Haymarket martyrs; burials of strikers, work-maimed miners, or respected union activists; festivities like picnics and excursions—but also the meetings of some labor organizations—were genuinely multi-ethnic. For each community the interaction—solidarity as well as hostility—among ethnic groups, crafts, and industries has to be understood separately. In Ybor City three Latin groups built a common community but clashed on the labor market. In the Mesabi range, Slavic, Scandinavian, and Finnish (at that time considered Russian) immigrants shared the work experience but were slow to build common institutions, while an Alberta mining community of extremely heterogeneous ethnicity united in labor and political organizations. A temporary solidarity was also achieved in the Chicago stockyards and in Pennsylvania's Homestead steelmills. The predominance of unifying or dividing factors when specific issues were at stake depended on local circumstances and prior experiences. The essays on ethnic communities, their solidarity and the limits of their cooperation, reveal that changing the focus from British, Irish, and German immigrant radicalism to that of Latin or Eastern immigrants does not reveal deeply rooted differences. The work and reproductive experience in the new society was similar though cultural backgrounds varied.

Richard Schneirov points out that the Catholic Czech lumbershovers came into a community of Czech fortyeighters in Chicago, found their free thought a suitable frame of reference for the work experience and moved to socialism when conditions and struggles changed. Schneirov describes the inseparable relationship between ideological and economic viewpoints, a relationship which may also serve for a better understanding of business unionism. These Czech workers remained organizationally tied to the Church, though ideologically removed from it, because they needed the ceremonial services of the priests for certain stages in their lives. Once benevolent societies began to provide just these services in secularized form, the tie to the religious organization could finally be cut completely. Obviously ideological and practical needs had to be fulfilled at the same time, preferably in closely linked institutions but if necessary in widely differing ones: free-thought societies for ideological comfort, benevolent societies for material comfort, the church for ceremonial services.

The essay on the Chicago lumbershovers also takes up the question of nationalism, which surfaces in several other studies in this volume. It has begun to be recognized as an important topic for a new synthesis of this period of the North American labor movements. A few historians have argued that the peasant masses flooding through Ellis Island began to think of their nationality and ethnicity only when queried by the immigration officials where they came from. As anyone with some background in Eastern and Southern European history knows, nationalism had surfaced decades before it found intense political expression in the revolutions of 1848. These national traditions, which in some aspects add up to both a bourgeois and a Jacobin internationalism, could be appropriated by the labor movement to its own purposes, as is demonstrated by the parallels Slavic workers saw between the American Revolution of 1776 and the East European revolutions of 1848 and their own struggles against capital in the 1870s and 1880s.

This merging of historical traditions is explored by *Paul Krause* and other authors. The celebration of the American independence and the achievement of a republican form of government was, for Slavic workers, a reason to wish "Live Forever the United States." This may indicate happiness with and gratitude to their new culture. It may also be a reference to an idealized republican government and to a national independence, both of which were aims of the East European fortyeighter movements. The achievements of the American and French revolutions had dominated the political discourse in the Western world, and by the 1870s they were taken over and adopted by industrial workers and their organizations. The class dominance of capitalists (plutocrats) and of feudal exploiters (aristocrats) could also be attacked in a common rhetoric. Western Canadian immigrant miners called their employers Kaisers, immigrant miners in the western United States and in the Pennsylvania coalfields called the notorious Coal and Iron Police and state militia Cossacks. An aspect that needs further exploration is the emphasis of American-born militants among the Homestead workers on the distinction between free men and chattel, as well as wage, slaves. When Slavic speakers translated their speeches, how did they translate the word *slavery?* The East European/Ottoman meaning of the term was different from Anglo-American meaning. Would they use the term *serfdom,* which few of them but most of the generation of their parents had experienced? Personal freedom and the right to organize in a society dominated neither by large and hereditary landowners nor by capital or capitalists were the preconditions to achieve fair wages or "to get bread." Economic and political discourse merged.

When Homestead workers took over the town's administration and keeping of order, they felt they protected the law—and the ideal—from being further sullied. Middle-class observers from the press, the government, and the factory owners interpreted the situation differently. "Where law is an open fraud, public life a chimera, and politics the personification of corruption, the [anarchist] organization of 'No Law!' [or the return to 'first principles' in the American tradition] is a logical and natural answer." *Gary R. Mormino* and *George E. Pozetta* use this (unamended) statement to explain the background of Spanish cigar workers' radicalism, but it could well have been said of the Homesteaders. Once again, experiences in the old world and the new were similar. Still, these continuities, which have been emphasized to counter wrong or incomplete views of the ethnic working-class communities, could not overcome internal divisions and capital and state repression. Cigar workers in Tampa were Spanish, Cuban, and Italian, with a clear hierarchy at the workplace. A pan-ethnic union existed only for a few years. The Cubans struggling for independence from Spain and the Spanish internationally minded anarchist minority formed an alliance against Spanish imperialist-minded workers. A local union, multi-ethnic in composition, was opposed by the Cigar Makers International Union of the AFL. Out of this ethnic, organizational, occupational, and political diversity city authorities and manufacturers created a unified "dangerous class," the members of which had to be repressed as workers, as Cuban nationalists, as radicals, during the wars as enemy aliens, and generally as volatile "Latins."

What the anarchist clubs, the cultural *centros,* and the cooperative medical and benevolent facilities were to the Latin cigar workers, the socialist halls, the theaters, and the cooperative stores were to the Finnish mineworkers, as *Michael G. Karni* demonstrates. Their rural background in the culture of origin was similar to that of most unskilled agrarian migrants—poverty, oppression, lack of enough to support oneself, not to mention a family. Ethnic rivalries were similar to the experience of many other groups in the new culture: Experienced Cornish miners held top positions, the American-born were promoted to machine operators, Scandinavians were foremen. The Finns and East European migrants held the lowest-paying jobs. Other obstacles to Finnish acculturation were the particular language problems and perhaps the old-country struggle to preserve a Finnish culture. Would people who fled Russification programs and economic deprivation readily submit to Americanization programs? Was there a political meaning in the charge of one Finnish immigrant woman that U.S. Steel "claimed our lives, our thoughts, our allegiances"? Finns tried to escape military service in the Russian empire, and some fled to Canada to avoid U.S. conscription during World War I. But through constant struggles the Finnish migrants did move closer to American society.

They also moved through various forms of militancy and socialisms. In this respect the Finns resemble the Germans and the Spanish migrants, as well as others. Probably historians should be less concerned with doctrinal differences and view the emergence of different parties and movements of the Left as responses to changed circumstances, just as platforms of the Democratic and Republican parties represented responses to changing social and economic demands.

The essays on work, organization, and strikes revolve around the same issues as those placing more emphasis on the community. *James R. Barrett* analyzes multi-ethnic solidarity and unionization as well as inter-ethnic hostility among Chicago packinghouse workers. Employer policy, governmental intervention, technological change, and hiring practices induced skilled, Americanized butchers to reach out to an internal and an international unskilled group—U.S. Blacks and Slavic migrants. The garment trades' mainly Jewish and Italian immigrant workers had to understand each other's cultural backgrounds. In her essay on the shirtwaist makers, *Maxine Schwartz Seller* suggests that women workers "were more likely to become engaged in the labor movement if their ethnic backgrounds supported such activism and if they were relatively unburdened with domestic responsibilities." *Steve Fraser* is concerned with the social trade unionism of the Amalgamated Clothing Workers of America. This quasi-industrial, polyglot organization steered a middle course between business and revolutionary unionism and gave workers some stability and continuity in their relations with employers. The decline of ethnicity as a divisive factor in the 1920s and the possibility of socialist-communist splits in the same period marked the labor movement's transition to the 1930s. External influences—for example, the rise of fascism in Italy—could still disrupt the movement through immigrant sympathizers, but the acculturation process and union loyalty prevented lasting damage. The change from pre- to post–World War I labor activities is further illustrated by *Allen Seager*'s analysis of Canadian immigrant miners whose ethnic organizations recede in importance in favor of unions like the United Mine Workers of America and parties, particularly the Communist party. The multi-ethnic red unionism of the 1930s led to a pragmatic industrial one in the 1940s. Ethnicity was still a factor in labor militancy, but by the 1930s and 1940s it was of secondary importance. The integration of particular ethnic forms of militancy that began in the 1890s with the demise of a separate German-American labor movement came to a conclusion in the industrial unionism of the 1930s when the "new immigration" had achieved accommodation with the hegemonial culture.

In addition to the process of acculturation and the new organizational forms of militancy, one further aspect merits attention, the intense European-centered nationalism of recently arrived ethnic groups from the three large but dissolving empires: Russia, Prussia-Germany, and Austria-Hungary. The radicalism of the labor migrants in the second and third quarter of the nineteenth century has been described as "on leave" from Europe. The short-term militancy of the "new migrants" who came for a temporary work stint was transformed to the persistent militancy of the working masses. Its ethnic aspect assumed new dimensions when the distinct possibility of creating nation-states in East and South Central Europe emerged. Migrant, or perhaps immigrant, workers—together with middle-class sections of their group—perceived the chance of becoming active on the international scene. War slogans, such as Make the World Safe for Democracy, received enthusiastic support in the new and for the old culture. Class and national interests, both of them radical (though sometimes supportive of each other, sometimes in opposition), led to an unparalleled strike intensity after 1916. Once again, as *David Montgomery* demonstrates, the economic and political demands and discourses merged. Since all ethnic groups were concerned, as were Anglo and acculturated immigrant workers, the debate over whether this was a war among capitalists subsided so that the opportunity of restructuring European and North American societies could be seized. But the militancy seems to have ended in defeat. Once the nation-states had been carved out of the collapsed empires, the slow process of building new social, political, and economic structures began. In North America the organizational changes toward industrial unionism continued, as did the process of acculturation. The ideological strife between the new communist, socialist, and social-democratic parties sometimes prevented united action—or even mere reaction—to employer inroads on unionization. State intervention, in the form of the so-called Red Scare, destroyed some militant working-class organizations, caused the deportation of some leftist leaders, and spread a climate of fear. More important were probably the integrative capacities of imperialist capitalism moving to its corporate phase and the unresolved dilemma of working-class culture between pragmatic business unionism and struggles for deep societal change.

We have chosen to deal with the struggles of working-class immigrants. Some of them have to be rescued from oblivion, others have to be rescued from one-sided interpretations that cast them as alien subversives and un-American radicals of unassimilable peoples. In recent years ethnic and labor historians have come a long way toward this rescue. But what about the quiet workers? To take one example, only one fourth of the Finnish immigrant workers espoused radicalism. The others, the quiet ones, are present in all essays. While they did not overtly join the battles, they benefitted from the struggles. Every wage increase, every improvement in working conditions fought for by many were steps toward the acculturation of all. And the quiet workers certainly shared the exploitation, the miserable living conditions—and the rewards—of the particular American form of capitalism.

One such worker was a young nurse in New York City who addressed herself to the question of "What America Means," raised by a "prize competition" sponsored by the *Immigrants in America Review* in January of 1916 (pp. 70–71). From her essay, we borrowed the title of this book. To her, a young Rusian Jewess coming out of a "fear-mood" brought on by massacres and the hatreds of "teachers who offend us, calling 'zudovka' (dirty jew)," remembering painfully the suffering in her life ("What can be worse a sight than a child with a frightened and hating soul? And that what I was."), the North American continent represented a place that "wellkomed us," a place with a meaning for immigrants that "is new and holly and wonderfully dear to us."

Writing of leaving home, she says,

My way was hard, . . . no help from any one could I expect, and I was not very big, never worked before. I had just graduate from high school when

> decided to go away. What made me take the hardships of the long way? Not the looking forward made me go, but the looking backward made me search a new life and struggle a hard battle.

But this young woman also tells us of the trials of learning her new country: "the children of Americans [who] call the immigrants 'pollack' and 'Diego' and only torment their Americanising, because they loose their confidence in Americans." But she prevails:

> America opened to me through my patients. There were immigrants unable to speak, even to each other because of the mixture of all different nationalities and languages, Americans of all ranks who were sometimes cross and impatient to the little foreighn nurse. America opened to me through the Irishmen and Italians hurt in a saloon fight and others their countrymen who were sick because they worked a whole day at hard labor in factories and outside and then went to school to study civics in night school, for their ambition told them, that they ought know their civil duties to a country in which they worke with a shovel diging sewers and laying tracks.

The anonymous young nurse, a lover of America but a clear critic of its hardness to newcomers, refers finally to the other battle, the battle of working-class immigrants to improve their lives. And she speaks to those Americans who would help immigrants: "teach their . . . children to respect those people that struggle such a hard battle."

I am grateful for the advice of many colleagues: Paul Buhle, Leon Fink, Herbert Gutman, Gregory Kealey, Harmut Keil, David Montgomery, and others suggested contributors and have helped to form this book. Alfred F. Young of Northern Illinois University has been a very supportive series editor. Mary Lincoln, director of the NIU Press, discussed the volume with me in its early stages and encouraged the work. Wanda H. Giles as copy editor contributed a sensitive understanding of immigrants' lives. Without the diligent help of my editorial assistant, Christiane Harzig, this anthology would never have seen the light of day—my thanks to her.

Old Immigrants and Early Radicals

BRUCE C. LEVINE

In the Heat of Two Revolutions: The Forging of German-American Radicalism

This [civil war] is essentially a people's war. On the side of the Union it is a struggle for maintaining in the world that form and substance of government whose leading object is to elevate the condition of men—to lift artificial weights from all shoulders; to clear the paths of laudable pursuits for all; to afford all an unfettered start, and a fair chance in the race of life.

Abraham Lincoln, 1861

The American people . . . are still fighting the same battle in which the European nations are engaged. . . . Yes! The conflict now on the eve of decision in the United States is neither more nor less than one of the manifold phases of the struggle between aristocracy and democracy.

Friedrich Kapp, 1861

For nearly a century following the signing of the Declaration of Independence, revolutionary conflicts repeatedly shook societies on both sides of the North Atlantic: the American, French, Haitian, and (abortive) Irish revolutions of the eighteenth century, the manifold European oubreaks of 1830 and 1848, the United States Civil War and Reconstruction. As contemporaries like Lincoln and Kapp often observed, these upheavals had much in common. Each outbreak, moreover, directly influenced subsequent ones.[1]

Reflecting this kinship, scholars have often grouped these revolutions under common adjectives and labels—liberal, democratic, modernizing, middle-class, bourgeois—depending on one's particular standpoint.[2] Useful in emphasizing the revolutions' official programs or leaders, principal beneficiaries, or long-term structural impact, such labels may obscure the highly complex and contradictory internal dynamics of these revolutions. Most of them mobilized very heterogeneous popular forces, with some of the most active and enthusiastic of these elements displaying as little love for the forces of capitalist development (or "modernism") as for the despised ancien regime. Like the sans-culottes supporters of France's Jacobin party, they gravitated toward radical democratic creeds resonant with familiar values, hopes, and fears. "Their common ideal," as Albert Soboul wrote of the French prototype,

> was a society of small independent producers, peasants and artisans, each owning his own field, shop or workshop and capable of providing for his family without having to fall back on working for a wage. It was an ideal that reflected the condition of people's lives in France at the end of the eighteenth century, conforming to the aspirations of the small peasants and agricultural labourer, the artisan and the journeymen, or, indeed, the shopkeeper.[3]

And (as E. P. Thompson observed of their contemporary English counterparts) the attraction of this social ideal for small producers increased as capitalism undermined their real status, confronting them with ruin and proletarianization.[4]

This sociopolitical tradition (which historians have generically named Jacobinism) put its stamp on plebeian culture and politics in Europe and the United States during the first half of the nineteenth century and even after. The strength of the Jacobin outlook reflected two facts. First, the countries involved were all experiencing related changes in their socioeconomic structures. Second, the ideas themselves were regularly revived and reinforced through a continuous process of intellectual cross-fertilization among plebeian democrats on both sides of the Atlantic. The career of former artisan and Jacobin publicist Thomas Paine in England, North America, and France represents only the best-known instance of this trans-Atlantic phenomenon.

This essay explores an important but often neglected phase of this ongoing international exchange—a phase marked by the German revolution of 1848–1849 and the tumultuous years leading up to it, the migration to America of large numbers of German craft workers influenced by those events, and the ways in which those workers, and their European memories and ideas, reacted to life, work, and politics in the new world. Special attention is given to German-American craft workers of New York City and their response to the escalating struggle over chattel slavery, a struggle which culminated in the Civil War, "America's Second Fight for Freedom."[5] These people constituted a key link between European and American politics as well as a source of continuity *within* the evolving tradition of American plebeian radicalism. In important but usually neglected ways, they carried forward the traditions of earlier generations of American artisans.

Emigration and Revolution

Between the 1840s and the end of the nineteenth century, more Germans landed on the shores of the United States than any other national group. Between 1840 and 1860 alone, almost a million and a half Germans left their homes, bound for the United States. By the 1850s, when the antebellum *Auswanderung* (emigration) reached its peak, nine out of every ten continental European immigrants to the United States originated in the states of the later German Empire. As a result, German-born residents in the United States increased in number by 123 percent between 1850 and 1860, more than triple the 35 percent growth rate of the U.S. population as a whole.[6]

All German social strata took part in this massive *Auswanderung,* from impoverished farm laborers, craft workers, and peasants through wealthy merchants, manufacturers, and even some landed aristocrats. Reflecting Germany's overwhelmingly agricultural character at that time, the agrarian population predominated among the emigrants. But especially during the late 1840s and 1850s, urban working people—and particularly skilled artisans—departed in steeply rising numbers. Craft workers especially composed a far larger proportion of the *Auswanderer* than they did of German society as a whole. In Hesse-Darmstadt, for example, artisans represented only about 6 percent of the total population but in 1846 made up nearly 40 percent of the grand duchy's total emigrants.[7]

This mass migration was one symptom of a general systemic crisis then wracking German society, a crisis born of tensions between still strong semi-feudal classes and institutions and the new forces unleashed by an expanding European capitalism. Shrinking incomes, deteriorating working conditions, mass unemployment, and the specter of pauperism and proletarianization plagued artisans, especially those in the garment, shoe, and furniture-making trades. Land hunger, crop disease and poor harvests, onerous rents and taxes pressed down on much of the agricultural population. Frustrated merchants and manufacturers fretted over the sluggish growth or stagnation of their investments. Other symptoms of the crisis included strikes, food riots, social banditry, religious dissidence and disaffection, the spread of subversive doctrines among the populace, and finally the revolutionary events of 1848–1849.[8]

The 1848 revolution roused all these discontented social strata. In Germany's urban centers, where issues and conflicts were most sharply posed and fought out, liberal businessmen and their political representatives provided formal leadership and controlled the insurgent governments. Their aims were specific and limited. As one liberal leader put it, they sought "to assure for the middle class a preponderant influence over the state." They found the appropriate political formula for this in a constitutional monarchy based on a limited suffrage. Nor did social leveling arouse much enthusiasm among these new men of money. "Human nature being what it is," another explained philosophically, "we will always have an aristocracy of wealth and . . . an aristocracy of intellect" if not necessarily one of birth.[9]

But the program and leadership of the liberals encountered persistent challenge from the more radical urban craft workers who provided the revolutionary coalition's shock troops and from the democratic intellectuals supported by them. "You are right when you maintain that it was essentially the workers who decided the revolution," explained a discerning Berlin physician to his father, adding that consequently "this revolution is not simply political but fundamentally social."[10] For the liberals, the social question was explosive, for by mid-century Germany's small producers were suffering at the hands not only of the old regime but of the nascent new one as well. They bore the weight of the landed aristocracy, its established churches, state bureaucracies, and armies and that of merchants and employers who profited by squeezing producers and consumers. For the artisans above all, 1848 was a two-front war waged to defend or regain incomes and social independence in the face of forces threatening to pauperize or permanently proletarianize them. Obtaining "a preponderant influence over the state" for a bourgeois "aristocracy of wealth and intellect" hardly satisfied their concerns.[11]

The Communist Manifesto appeared in January of 1848, but its viewpoint found little support. At this early stage of Germany's industrial development, few as yet blamed private property in general for their misery. It was, rather, property's increasingly unequal distribution which preoccupied them, along with the government policies and unequal political privileges which seemed to aid and abet it. "At that time," Friedrich Engels remembered decades later, "one had to seek out one by one the workers who had an understanding of their position as workers and their historico-economic antagonism to capital, because this antagonism itself was only just beginning to develop."[12] Most politically conscious artisans subscribed to some variation of a general radical democratic creed which envisioned a republic based firmly upon small agricultural and craft producers' sharing equal liberties and social rights. Such a republic was expected not to dissolve social classes but to allow an amicable and just cooperation among them. Democratic leaders like Baden's Gustav Struve demanded for his plebeian constituency "a share in the profits of labor" that they might realize "prosperity, education, and freedom for all." Struve urged his program on the Frankfurt pre-Parliament as the best way to guarantee the "security of property." "I do not wish to destroy individual property rights," agreed Struve's sometime ally Karl Heinzen. "I only wish to see that they are safeguarded for all."[13]

Jacobin ideas current in the rest of Europe reached German craftsmen in a number of ways. Guild rules requiring journeymen to spend at least one year (the *Wanderjahr*) traveling led many to the radical hothouses of Paris and Geneva; they returned to Germany with broadened perspectives. Thomas Paine's own works were available in German translation throughout the nineteenth century. Democratic leaders like Struve and Friedrich Hecker (the latter the most prominent figure associated with the 1848 Left) were so stirred by Paine's exposition of democratic values and goals that each published his own German translation of Paine's works.[14]

In this and many other ways, intellectuals like Struve and Hecker played important roles in the political lives of their plebeian supporters, but only because—and only so long as—their words and deeds struck a responsive chord among the latter. Once again, the appropriate parallels point to other plebeians and radical democrats of Europe and America "whose spokesmen and leaders," noted E. J. Hobsbawm, "were intellectuals, especially young and marginal ones." Such intellectuals "helped the sans-culottes to realize their true political aims and to identify their social grievances," wrote Soboul. "But they did not cause these aims or grievances." Gwynn Williams has made the same point: "[F]or all the credulity with which the sans-culottes accepted the word of men they trusted, there was a certain natural selection of ideas. . . . Their reception of Rousseau was very much like the British artisans' reception of Paine—it was a 'shock of recognition.' " In Germany, the same natural selection of ideas attracted artisans and others similarly situated to the democratic intellectuals, and vice versa. Discovering each other, both sides felt this "shock of recognition." Neither Marxist nor liberal intellectuals got the same reception in that quarter.[15]

Indeed, the plebeian democracy deeply antagonized liberal spokesmen and their well-to-do patrons, who labored to curb the mobilization and demands of those social layers beneath them. When plebeians rebuffed this attempt, liberal governments responded with repression, opening the door to counterrevolution.[16] That counterrevolution, in turn, accelerated the emigration of hundreds of thousands—particularly from Germany's conflict-ridden south and west, artisans prominent among them—unable or unwilling to remain under those economic and political conditions. The early 1850s thus saw the emigrant river swell into a flood.[17] Many carried the causes, programs, and vivid memories of 1848 into their exile.

Nearly all set out for North America, a destination easy to understand. To the dissatisfied German craftsman, the United States appeared a near paradise. Its burgeoning economy, plentiful land, and shortage of labor promised personal independence and prosperity, a chance to retain or regain self-employed status. Politically, the United States was the most democratic republic of the early nineteenth century, a fact well known in Germany. In 1848, Friedrich Hecker had proposed replacing Germany's monarchical system with a republic modeled on the U.S. constitution. Symbolizing the same attitude, two flags dominated the first congress of plebeian democratic societies held at Frankfurt-am-Main in June 1848. Pride of place went to the black-red-gold banner, symbol of German unity and freedom, but right beside it hung the Stars and Stripes.[18] Departing for the States, seventy-five natives of Baden typically declared, "We have reached the decision, since Capital so commands Labor in the Fatherland, to find a new home . . . where the reverse relationship prevails." A shoemaker leaving Württemberg agreed. In Germany, he complained, "The aristocracy of money is unrestrained now. Reliance on the honest working man has declined; the capitalist and the rich have little or no heart for the destitute . . . their hearts beat only for Mammon. Therefore I preferred to go to a land where . . . a worker is worth his wage."[19]

Life and Labor in America

In the United States, the Germans concentrated both geographically and occupationally. Some two-thirds of them took up residence in just seven mid-Atlantic and midwestern states (New York, New Jersey, Pennsylvania, Illinois, Ohio, Indiana, and Michigan), and there primarily in the growing urban centers. This settlement pattern transformed entire sections of these towns and cities into enclaves of immigrant popular culture.[20] Although factory production was beginning to develop in this era, Germans rarely worked in such settings. They tended instead to pick up the traditional handicrafts with which they were already familiar. As a result, Germans filled these economically and politically strategic occupations in disproportionate and sometimes preponderant numbers.[21]

Most German-American working people found life in the United States a definite improvement, but the country's very economic growth and development doomed hopes of finding there a place where labor commanded capital. For at least a generation, an expanding home market had paced a parallel expansion and rationalization in craft production. As the volume, scale, and rate of production increased, so did the division of labor. So, too, did the number of skilled working people forced to work for wages. Working conditions declined, the working day lengthened, and pay rates fell. As in Europe, the journeyman's hopes of one day joining the ranks of independent masters grew daily dimmer. Deteriorating conditions repelled native-born youth, who increasingly left the debased handicrafts to less occupationally and geographically mobile immigrants.[22]

Nowhere was this ethnic-occupational shift more evident than in New York, the country's principal manufacturing city, largest immigrant center, and the de facto cultural and political capital of all German America. The heart of New York's German residential district was called *Kleindeutschland* (Little Germany). Roughly bordered by the Bowery, Division Street, Fourteenth Street, and the East River, it comprised most of the city's tenth, eleventh, thirteenth, and seventeenth wards. The vast majority of its 1860 residents arrived after 1845, when the city's German-born residents numbered 25,000. In just five years that figure more than doubled. By the mid-1850s it lapped at the 100,000 mark, and only Berlin and Vienna boasted more German-speaking residents. By the time of the Civil War, New York's German-born numbered about 120,000, some 15 percent of the city's total population (Table 1).[23]

Once again, however, the Germans' effective social weight outstripped even their sheer numbers because of their great occupa-

Table 1 Germans in the New York City Population, 1845–1860

	1845	1850	1855	1860
Total NYC	371,223	515,547	629,904	813,669
German-born	24,416	56,141	97,572	119,004
Percent German-born	6.6%	10.9%	15.5%	14.5%

SOURCE: Ira Rosenwaike, *The Population History of New York City* (Syracuse, N.Y.: Syracuse University Press, 1972), table 9.

tional concentration. According to the 1855 state census, fewer than 800 Germans in the city—less than 2 percent of all the gainfully employed German-born—made their living as merchants, financiers, agents, traders, speculators, and salesmen. Composed primarily of small entrepreneurs, this group nevertheless included some of the most prosperous German-born businessmen in the nation, among them John Jacob and William B. Astor, August Belmont, Caspar Meier, Frederick Gebhard, Charles Hallgarten, and the Seligman brothers. They derived their fortunes from banking, speculation, insurance, real estate, domestic and international trade, railroads, and other lucrative fields of enterprise.[24]

The overwhelming majority of the immigrants lived and worked under very different circumstances. Fifteen percent of the total German labor force made their living in unskilled, low-paid, usually arduous and low-status work—as laborers and porters, domestic servants, janitors, and laundresses. More than half of all gainfully employed Germans worked in the crafts, fully 30 percent in just three industries; garment (tailors, dressmakers, and seamstresses); shoes; and furniture (cabinetmakers and upholsterers). In the United States as in Germany, these were precisely the trades which first succumbed to the notorious sweating system. They were also the first to reflect these pressures in mounting labor conflict and growing worker receptivity to radical social doctrines.[25]

The Germans' occupational concentration, in turn, transformed the makeup of New York's artisanry. By 1855, German immigrants accounted for more than half of all tailors, cabinetmakers, and shoemakers in the city (Table 2). With the simultaneous influx of rural Irish into the ranks of unskilled manual and domestic labor, this Germanization of many of the most hard-pressed and hard-driven trades signaled a major change in the national and cultural composition of the urban work force.

In 1845, when the truly massive immigration was just beginning, the *New York Daily Tribune* offered its readers a glimpse of conditions in some of these sweated trades. Although organized on a comparatively decentralized basis, New York's boot and shoe industry employed some two thousand journeymen of various nationalities at an average wage of four to six dollars a week (a pay rate comparable to that of an unskilled laborer). In general, "the manner in which the different classes of the Shoe-makers live varies according to the nation," the *Tribune* discovered. "Comparatively few" journeymen were native- or English-born, and that minority generally enjoyed better working conditions than the rest.

Table 2 Germans in Selected New York City Occupations, 1855

Occupation	Total number employed	Proportion German-born
Tobacconists	1,996	61.4%
Cabinetmakers, upholsterers	3,517	61.0
Shoemakers	6,745	55.0
Bakers, confectioners	3,692	54.0
Tailors	12,609	53.2
Brewers, distillers	360	53.0
Turners, carvers, gilders	1,126	52.0
Peddlers, traders	1,915	49.0
Textile workers (various)	210	47.6
Food dealers	8,300	36.6
Clothiers	403	34.4
Hatters	1,422	30.0
Carpenters	7,531	22.0
Dressmakers, seamstresses	9,819	9.5

SOURCE: Calculated from numerical data in Robert Ernst, *Immigrant Life in New York City, 1825–1863* (New York: King's Crown Press, 1949), 214–17.

"The Germans," on the other hand, "are generally found occupying basements and cellars." A description of a typical basement dwelling/workshop followed:

> The floor is made of rough planks laid loosely down, and the ceiling is not quite so high as a tall man. The walls are dark and damp, and a wide, desolate fireplace yawns in the center to the right of the entrance. . . . In one corner is a squalid bed, and the room elsewhere is occupied by a work bench, a cradle made from a dry goods box, two or three broken and scattered chairs, a stewpan, and a kettle.

"There is no outlet [in the] back," the report added, "and of course no yard privileges of any kind. The miserable room is lighted only by a shallow sash [window], partly projecting above the surface of the ground, and by the light that struggles down the steep and rotting stairs." Into such quarters three generations might crowd—husband and wife, five or six children, and one or more grandparents. "Here they work," the reporter concluded, "here they cook, they eat, they sleep, they pray."[26] Similar conditions prevailed among many immigrant tailors and cabinetmakers.[27]

But these conditions did not immediately engage the attention or organized efforts of most radical immigrant leaders. Most initially preoccupied themselves with unfinished work in Europe, closely following the news from that continent, thronging to greet exiled leaders of the Old World's democratic and national struggles (including Hecker, Gottfried Kinkel, and the Hungarian Louis Kossuth) when the latter toured the United States. Commentators and participants alike noted that immigrant working people displayed much greater support for those causes than did their better-off fellow countrymen. The 1853 American tour of a papal nuncio implicated in the Italian counterrevolution of 1849 called forth vigorous and at times bloody protests. Nationalist and revolutionary-democratic German societies sprang up in most of the major cities of the North and the West.[28]

Eventually, however, the obvious consolidation of reaction in Germany dissolved prospects for an early triumphal return home; what many thought would be a brief exile, a mere interlude, began to look like a new life. Meanwhile, naive initial expectations about life and work in the New World were also collapsing before hard realities encountered. "The newly arrived European democrat," Carl Schurz later recalled, "having lived in a world of theories and imaginings without having had any practical experience of a democracy at work, beholding it for the first time, ask[s] himself: 'Is this really a people living in freedom? Is this the realization of my ideal?' " Shielded from personal adversity by a wealthy wife and a successful career, Schurz viewed the grimmer aspects of American life calmly; they merely revealed "a democracy in full operation on a large scale."[29] Less comfortably situated, some of his countryfolk were also less Panglossian in their reactions. One Pittsburgh German, for example, elaborating a critique begun earlier by native- and English-born antecedents, penned this harsh indictment of American society and the social and political inequalities discovered here:

> The rich and distinguished stand here higher above the law than in any other country. The poor are held in more contempt, and nowhere in the world is poverty a greater crime than in America. In the land which boasts of its humanity, which claims to be at the very top of civilization, society does far less for the poor than anywhere else. The laboring masses are treated in as shameful a manner as in Europe, with all its ancient prejudices.[30]

Protested the Pittsburgh German Workingmen's Congress:

> The earth and all the elements necessary for the happiness and well-being of the race belong alike to the whole of mankind; and there can be no just or natural right existing on the part of a select few to monopolize that which by right belongs equally to all for use.[31]

If in America such basic principles were more and more being ignored, believed the Amerikanische Arbeiterbund (American Workers' League), this was because

> social relations are no longer the same as when the Republic was founded. The introduction and development of large-scale industry has produced a

new revolution, dissolved the old classes, and above all, created *our* class, the class of propertyless workers. . . . So long as industry serves only capital, our position must of necessity worsen with each passing day.[32]

Equally unwelcome were attempts by native-born employers and others preoccupied with industrial discipline and social control to impose puritanical cultural norms upon immigrant workers. Proliferating statutes forbidding the manufacture, sale, or consumption of alcoholic beverages and strictly limiting social intercourse on the Sabbath were roundly denounced as the work of a "money aristocracy." Newark immigrant leader Fritz Anneke voiced the anger of many:

This money aristocracy, which has the time and means to take care of its body through the whole week, and which in spite of its hypocritical laws, knows how to serve all worldly desires on the holy Sabbath, strives zealously to deprive the working man of every means of escape from his drudgery. In the opinion of this money aristocracy, the most wholesome thing for the working man is to drudge day after day the whole week through and on the holy Sabbath to pervert [his thinking] with clerical quirks and to dine on sermons relating to the other world

"on high
where the angels enjoy
bliss without flesh."[33]

The Amerikanische Arbeiterbund's program likewise demanded "abrogation of all laws, such as Sunday laws, temperance laws and the like, which encroach on the workers' enjoyment of their liberty."[34]

As immigrants gave up their self-image as but temporary exiles in the United States, they paid increasing collective attention to these economic, political, and cultural issues. At the same time, the discovery in America of problems first confronted in Europe lent new life to some old ideas. More than a few doctrines, programs, and methods of Old World vintage proved unexpectedly appropriate in the New World as well. "We must not look upon ourselves as refugees in America," wrote one immigrant journalist from Illinois. "This nation is not our land of exile. Here one can fight as vigorously as in Europe for our highest and most sacred ideals, and the battle for the realization of those ideals is rightly ours."[35]

As in Germany, a minority took Marxist ground. The Proletarian League, a small communist educational and propaganda circle, arose in 1852 in New York City at the behest of fortyeighter journalist and engineer Joseph Weydemeyer. Five years later, in the throes of unemployed demonstrations in that city, some thirty

German Marxists formed a New York Communist Club united by belief in the inevitability and irreconcilable nature of class conflict under capitalism. Only by abolishing "so-called bourgeois property, whether inherited or acquired," declared the club's constitution, could the "equality of all human beings—irrespective of color or sex" be achieved. Only collective ownership of the means of production would permit all "a reasonable share in the natural and spiritual riches of the earth."[36]

Even more than in Europe, however, such views were in these years still confined to small numbers of the most extreme radicals. Far more common was the kind of broad plebeian democracy manifested in 1848, which sought simply to narrow differences in wealth and political rights among the classes. Along with some small shopkeepers, laborers, and sympathetic members of the intelligentsia, those craft workers attracted to Jacobin doctrines constituted a hard core of radical democrats. Though still a definite minority of the immigrant plebeians as a whole, under the right circumstances this core could draw much larger numbers into joint action around specific issues and elicit the sympathies of still broader layers.

In these decades, German craft workers often took the lead in organizing trade unions and producer cooperatives, and the fervor with which they did so deeply impressed native-born contemporaries like Horace Greeley. Reporting in 1850 that "the organization of the Trades into Protective Associations proceeds unabated," his *New York Daily Tribune* added, "No class of our population goes more effectively to work than our German artisans, who have held meetings nearly every evening during the past week, and have succeeded in uniting many of the trades into Unions."[37] Some twenty New York trades were soon organized in this way. In April of 1850, German craftsmen met in New York to form the Central Committee of the United Trades (CCUT). The initiative came largely from Germany's first major artisan leader, the journeyman tailor and self-taught utopian socialist Wilhelm Weitling. Claiming over two thousand members in New York, the CCUT attracted delegates from many trades to its first meeting. Most heavily represented were cabinetmakers, upholsterers, bakers, shoemakers, and tailors—the main strongholds of immigrant German craftworkers. This movement viewed cooperatives not as a temporary convenience but as a fundamental alternative to the developing capitalist mode of production. As envisioned in the 1850 constitutions of New York's German tailor, carpenter, and cordwainer societies, cooperatives would offer a refuge from the wild and destructive fluctuations of the open market.[38]

Similar associations arose in Buffalo, Detroit, Cincinnati, Philadelphia, Pittsburgh, St. Louis, Milwaukee, Louisville, Newark, Cleveland, and New Orleans, allowing Weitling successfully to convene the first national German craft worker congress in Philadelphia six months later. Representatives of 4,400 working people attended. The delegates' Jacobin concerns shone through the platform they adopted, which demanded the distribution of western lands among working farmers rather than speculators, increased taxation of privately owned but uncultivated land, the further democratization of government and the defense and extension of democratic rights (particularly those of the immigrants), and an end to the forced sale of homesteads for reasons of debt. The congress summed up its outlook with the motto, Equal Rights and Duties, a phrase simultaneously invoking the traditions and values of both the Workingmen's movement of Jacksonian America and the plebeian democratic currents of 1848 Europe.[39] When Weitling's organization declined a few years later, the Amerikanische Arbeiterbund, founded by the Marxist Joseph Weydemeyer on a broad, noncommunist platform, arose to replace it. Later in the decade, in turn, Gustav Struve assumed leadership of the New York craft worker movement. In its name, Struve edited a paper called *Die Soziale Republik* whose masthead featured the same motto Struve had popularized in the Old World: Welfare, Education, and Freedom for All.[40]

Jacobin demands and sentiments momentarily united and mobilized much larger and more diverse forces during the economic crises of 1854–1855 and 1857. Trapped between inflated prices and staggering unemployment, a public meeting of eight thousand German, Irish, and native-born New York workers in January 1855 angrily insisted "that the labouring classes are in no way answerable for the condition in which they are found" and demanded laws forbidding eviction of tenants unable to pay rent, providing employment for the jobless on public-works projects, and giving free land to the landless. In 1857 similar scenes were reenacted in New York, Newark, Philadelphia, Chicago, and elsewhere.[41]

German labor organizations usually maintained close ties and shared memberships with a broad range of social, cultural, and political *Vereine* (associations) also based in the immigrant population. One of the most important, well known, and durable of these associations was the Turnverein. Founded as an athletic association at the start of the century, the Turner movement by the 1840s combined physical culture, nationalism, and democratic principles and served as one locus of artisanal organization in 1848. In America, transplanted Turners celebrated Thomas Paine's birthday and paraded through the streets of New York City carrying banners inscribed with the familiar motto, Liberty, Welfare, and Education. In 1850 a national Turner convention founded the Gymnastics Union of North America, and the growing movement changed its name the next year to the Sozialistischer Turnerbund (Socialist Gymnastics Union). Firmly rooted in the artisan radicalism of two continents, the Turner concept of socialism defined it as "a democratic-republican society, one guaranteeing everyone prosperity, free quality education to maximize the capacities of each, the elimination of all hierarchical and privileged centers of power." The Turners later elaborated the idea as follows:

> The socialism of today, in which we Turners believe, aims to remove the pernicious antagonism between labor and capital. It endeavors to effect a reconciliation between these two and to try to establish a peace by which the rights of the former are fully protected against the encroachments of the latter.[42]

Overwhelmingly plebeian in composition, New York's Turners had over 500 members by 1853. By decade's end the national organization claimed a membership of about ten thousand.[43]

Emigré Karl Heinzen and his associates founded a kindred organization called the Freimännerverein (known in English as the League of German Freemen), pledged to democracy and religious free thought. Launched in 1854 in Louisville, Kentucky, the Freemen and groups like it quickly spread throughout the 1848-era German immigration, especially in the Midwest. In Cincinnati alone, the Freimännerverein soon boasted upwards of one thousand members and close supporters, male and female alike. The Freemen platform contained one of the most complete and characteristic catechisms of mainstream fortyeighter values, concerns, and demands. Once again, the motto adopted by the Verein sounded the tocsin of 1848: Liberty, Welfare, and Education for All.[44]

The immigrant Jacobin outlook also found expression in a spate of new German-American newspapers. In New York City, such papers at one time or another included the *Abendzeitung*, published on a cooperative basis by journeymen typesetters and edited by Friedrich Kapp; the *Turnzeitung;* the *New Yorker Demokrat;* Weitling's *Republik der Arbeiter;* Hermann Kriege's *Volkstribun;* Struve's *Soziale Republik;* the New York *Criminal Zeitung und Belletristisches Journal*, edited by the cousins Rudolf and Friedrich Lexow, both fortyeighters (the latter having served an eight-year prison term in Germany for subversive activities); *Die Reform,* published by Weydemeyer in association with emigré democrat Dr. Gottlieb Kellner; Karl Heinzen's *Schnellpost;* and the rationalist *Hahnruf,* "edited in the interest of the laboring classes" (so its masthead announced) by two other veterans of European politics, G. Scheibel and J. A. Försch.[45]

Of all the issues and demands in the radical-democratic lexicon, few found a more receptive audience or had a more lasting long-term significance than the call for land reform. Since the beginning of European settlement of North America, the promise of land for homesteads had drawn millions across the Atlantic in search of alternatives to economic dependence. The Workingmen's movements of the 1820 and 1830s regularly returned to this issue. The calamitous depression of 1837–1843; the expansion of immigration, wage labor, and agrarian tenancy during the subsequent business revival; and later the wresting of great chunks of territory from Mexico and American Indians—all these developments intensified interest in western lands. Federal land-disposition policy favoring railroad companies and land speculators over small homesteaders stimulated popular demands for reform. "Where shall we go," asked a Lynn, Massachusetts, shoemaker in 1844, "but to the land? Deprive us of this and you reduce us to the condition of the serfs of Europe."[46]

In 1845, former New York Workingmen's leader George Henry Evans convened a group of veteran artisans and other activists to launch the National Reform Association to carry on vigorous agitation around the land issue. "If any man has a right on the earth," Evans held, "he has a right to land enough to raise a habitation on. If he has *a right to live,* he has a right to land enough for sustenance. Deprive anyone of these rights, and you place him at the mercy of those who possess them."[47] His message appealed not only to the native-born but also to many who left the Old World precisely to escape poverty and proletarianization there. The difficult industrial conditions encountered by these immigrants in America's eastern cities strengthened their interest in westward migration, whether to take up farming per se or simply to reach the booming and still labor-scarce urban centers of the West. Evans's efforts thus won him the support of exiled Chartists like Thomas Devyr of Ireland, earlier active in the Hudson Valley rent wars; John Cluer of Scotland, a leading ten-hours advocate in New England; and James Pyne of England, another former leader of New York's Workingmen's Party.[48]

Hermann Kriege, once a collaborator of Marx, launched his own Sozialreformverein (Social Reform Association) to bring the word to German immigrants. To the foreign-born, he believed, land reform would bring special benefits. By making it easier to obtain a homestead, land reform would relax competition for both jobs and farmland and so ease native-born resentment of immigrants. "If once the soil is free," Kriege's *Volkstribun* promised, "then every honest workingman who leaves his old home in order to lead a happier life in the free air on this side of the ocean, becomes a blessing to our republic . . . [for] the more producing hands, the more wealth."[49] We have already observed the way land-reform themes reverberated through various immigrant associations and demands. Independent German-American land-reform societies sprang up in Milwaukee, Cincinnati, Boston, Newark, Philadelphia, Chicago, St. Louis, and New York. So strongly, in fact, did these immigrants embrace the cause that opponents of homestead legislation were soon denouncing it as the "offspring of the German school of socialism."[50]

Germans and Slavery

From the Jacobin standpoint, the North American republic suffered from one defect more obvious than all others—the existence of chattel slavery. Slavery clashed head-on with all the democratic ideals of 1848 and inevitably stirred bitter memories of the European aristocracy, whose culture American planters mimicked, and the whole system of unfree labor upon which that class rested.[51] "Instead of ensuring Liberty to all," stormed the Freemen in their founding manifesto, "more than three million human beings have been condemned to Slavery, and they [the slaveowners] try to increase their number daily."[52] When the national Turner organization added the word "socialistic" to its name it also endorsed "the principles underlying the Free-Soil Party [founded in 1848] and urge[d] all members to support that party in every way possible."[53] On Christmas Eve, 1851, members of Kriege's Social Reform Association and New York's Sozialistischer Turnverein met under the leadership of J. A. Försch and Erhard Richter in *Kleindeutschland*'s Shakespear Hotel to found a German branch of the local Free Soil Party. "Strictly opposed to Slavery in whatever shape it might be seen," the new body aimed "to carry out land reform measures in the most radical manner."[54]

But so long as it seemed possible to separate the matter of slavery's containment in the South from the issue of its immediate abolition—and so long as abolition itself could be depicted as a preordained if long-range certainty—most German democrats, plebeian and intellectual alike, refrained from active involvement in the issue. Pending the anticipated demise of the South's peculiar institution, most immigrants would simply settle elsewhere; plenty of open land was available. Their initial preoccupation with European developments, moreover, and with the immediate pressures of daily life also diverted most northern immigrants' attention from the southern planters. Indeed, the planters' allies, the northern Democrats, regularly received overwhelming German-born suppport, not only because of their apparently friendly attitude to the immigrants but also because they presented themselves as the champions of suffering labor against overbearing capital, a performance in which Hermann Kriege himself played a role.

The Kansas-Nebraska Act of 1854 finally transformed widespread but generally passive antislavery sentiments among the German immigrants into overt and effective action. Introduced by Senator Stephen A. Douglas, Democrat of Illinois, this single law annulled the Missouri Compromise and all existing federal barriers to the westward spread of slavery. The Douglas bill thus exploded the widespread and comforting assumption that anachronistic slavery was headed for automatic extinction. More importantly, by openly planning to preempt the West for the slave-labor system, the planters now directly threatened the interests and aspirations of many German-born northerners. Their concerns were astutely addressed in a manifesto issued by free-soil congressmen entitled "The Appeal of the Independent Democrats." Previously, the Appeal recalled, the West had been considered a haven for "freedom loving emigrants from Europe and energetic and intelligent laborers from our own land." The Nebraska bill, however, would turn this huge territory "into a dreary region of despotism, inhabited by masters and slaves." That alone would exclude free labor, since "freemen, unless pressed by a hard and cruel necessity, will not, and should not work beside slaves. Labor cannot be respected where any class of laborers is held in abject bondage."[55]

This Appeal (and a German translation) was widely reprinted and even more widely paraphrased. The response deeply gratified the authors. Douglas's bill shocked the North generally and its German-American population in particular, triggering a tidal wave of protest. The American and Foreign Antislavery Society, meeting in New York in May, "rejoice[d] in the great unanimity manifested by the German presses, and our German fellow-citizens throughout the country, in opposition to the Nebraska scheme." Horace Greeley's *New York Daily Tribune* likewise exulted, "The Germans are moving all over the North and West. They feel even more deeply than the native citizens."[56]

While capturing something of the drama and ardor of German anti-Nebraska feeling, such sweeping declarations exaggerated the unanimity of immigrant sentiment. Radical democrats threw themselves into the fight against slavery's expansion. The small but powerful German business elite, on the other hand, along with the immigrant Lutheran and Catholic hierarchies, Democratic party stalwarts, and allied newspapers, reacted very differently. Catering to the wealthiest German-American merchants, the *New Yorker Staats-Zeitung* had long fought its Jacobin countrymen over virtually every issue of the day. In 1854, it staunchly defended Douglas's bill and flayed those agitating against the extension of slavery.[57] Gustav Neumann (editor of the *Staatz-Zeitung* and, as an officer in the local customs house, a powerful dispenser of Democratic party patronage) and the Democrats' United German Central Committee called a public meeting for 23 February 1854 to demonstrate support for the Kansas-Nebraska bill. Publicity for the meeting strove to identify Douglas's "popular sovereignty" formula with German democratic ideals while linking anti-Nebraska forces with the disunionism and evangelical fanaticism ascribed to native-born abolitionists.[58]

The dramatic proceedings that evening revealed the depth and intensity of feeling that animated both sides of the Nebraska conflict.[59] Between one and two thousand Germans came to the meeting in Washington Hall, located near the corner of Grand and Elizabeth streets, in the heart of *Kleindeutschland.* Pro-Douglas Democrats controlled the podium, but most of the audience proved unsympathetic. Led by the city's Turnverein, a *Demokrat* editor named Hartmann, and free-soil activists Erhard Richter and J. A. Försch, the majority promptly demanded a new chairman. When the regular Democrats rejected the demand and physically attacked opposition speakers, a bloody two-hour brawl ensued, waged on the floor and tabletops alike with fists, canes, and clubs made from shattered furniture. At last, a well-drilled paramilitary squad of Turners routed the most die-hard Douglas forces and physically drove them from the premises. Two-thirds of the original crowd remained to cheer and ratify strong anti-Nebraska resolutions.

Five days later, the residents of *Kleindeutschland* awoke to find the streets posted with a new call, issued by the Amerikanische Arbeiterbund, this one to an *anti*-Nebraska meeting. Despite the short notice, five hundred people met the following evening in a Forsyth Street tavern in the German section of the tenth ward.

Speakers including Weydemeyer, Kellner, Richter, Försch, Kapp, Scheibel, and other Jacobin figures roundly denounced the bill and its sponsor. The resolution endorsed that night exemplified the approach taken by most German democrats in 1854, fusing hostility to both wage labor and chattel slavery. It blamed "capitalism and land speculation" for a law which "withdraws from or makes unavailable in a future homestead bill vast tracts of land," declared its opposition to "both white and black slavery," and called for the creation of a "general organization of working men" to oppose slavery's westward expansion.[60]

In the wake of the Arbeiterverein's initiative, the city's anti-Nebraska Germans held a larger meeting two days later, once again in Washington Hall, the scene of the recent Turner-led coup.[61] Even the pro-Douglas *New York Herald* counted three thousand in attendance. Mostly "working men," according to the *Times,* they filled the hall to overflowing, and their banners symbolized the values with which these immigrant Jacobins confronted the slavery question in America: the red flag of plebeian radicalism,, the Stars and Stripes, and the black-red-gold. The meeting's first order of business—the singing of "The Marseillaise," the nineteenth century's international anthem of insurgent democracy—also asserted the propriety of fighting for European democratic principles in America. The *Times* reported that "the whole throng joined [in the singing] with a chorus, repeated cheers, and a tremendous stamping of feet beating time to the music."

Though speakers ranged from moderate to radical, the audience's sympathies proved less catholic. A liberal immigrant of the 1830s drew sentimental applause when he identified German nativity with the love of freedom. But when the same speaker, trying to confine the day's protest merely to slavery's further expansion, asserted that "none of us wants to take away their slaves from the South," members of his audience angrily dissented. "Oh, yes! Oh, yes!" they shouted; they did indeed want to carry freedom southward. Equally instructive was the reception accorded J. A. Försch, one of the meeting's presiding officers. Försch won lusty cheers by declaring, "In this country as in the Old World, we have to start the cry, 'Revolution!' " Earlier that week, Försch recalled, the Turners and their allies had dealt the pro-Douglas "loafers" the "sore heads" they deserved. Let that kind of bold action become our model, he urged, for

> nothing can be effected now by forebearance. Therefore let us send men to congress who will revolutionize—who will dare to tell the slave breeders

to their faces who they are. Let us stand together firmly and faithfully, and the loafers at Washington will [also] get their "sore heads."

At the meeting's close, the crowd flowed out of doors. With banners flying, three bands playing, and their ranks eventually swelling to five thousand, they marched downtown to jeer at Douglas's political allies in Tammany and City hall.

The passage of Douglas's bill initiated a major reorganization of American political life that finally destroyed the Whigs, split the Democrats, and called to life a Republican Party which swept the North two years later and captured the White House in 1860. Immigrant German radicals were intimately involved in this political reorganization. Turner, Freemen, and Arbeiterverein leaders alike campaigned vigorously for Fremont and Lincoln, regularly invoking parallels between German republicanism and the U.S.'s Republicans.[62]

A huge rally in New York City in the fall of 1856 illustrates this point.[63] Between eight and ten thousand German-Americans converged on the Academy of Music on Tuesday, 7 October, at the call of the new German Republican Executive Committee. Friedrich Kapp, *Abendzeitung* editor and committee chairman, called the meeting to order. "Most of the Germans here," he said, had "taken part in the late struggle" in Europe and "followed the republican baner in the old country." The same people would be "its true followers in their adopted home." Gustav Struve declared it "a day of rejoicing for thousands who, driven from their native soil and suffering here in exile, assemble in this free soil to greet the rising of a new day of freedom." Bracketing the fortunes of American slaveholders with those of "the despots of Europe," Struve asserted the living interdependence of democratic causes on both continents. "If freedom shall be restored in America," he promised, "the oppressed of Europe will look confidently to this hemisphere as a new area of liberty." These speeches and a similar one by Friedrich Hecker drew repeated, enthusiastic cheers from the crowd.

For a number of reasons, however, New York's Republican organization found it difficult to translate the antislavery sentiment reflected that day into ballots. Mistrust of the city's nativist-tainted, upper-class Republican leadership combined with fears of losing crucial southern markets and the thousands of craft-work jobs dependent upon them to contain the German Republican vote.[64] Even so, when the Republican Party in 1856 received less than a fourth of all the votes cast in the city, the *New York Daily Times* reported that "in several of the strong German wards of this

City probably full one-third of all Germans voted with the Republicans." Some German Republicans claimed still greater success in mobilizing their constituents.[65] In 1860 the total New York vote for Lincoln reached 35 percent of the total—and the three wards containing the strongest concentrations of Germans gave Lincoln up to 42 percent, with individual precincts registering still greater gains.[66] In cities whose Republican leaders were less tied to nativism and whose craft workers were less reliant upon southern markets for employment, Lincoln swept the main German wards.[67]

The 1860 election proved a decisive turning point for American society. The protracted era of compromise over chattel slavery now came to an explosive close in the second American revolution. Germans took part in great numbers. Turnverein members and supporters alone supplied from seven to eight thousand troops and organized entire units for the Union army, including New York's Twentieth (United Turner) Regiment. All told, one-tenth of the Union army was German-born, and 36,000 of these soldiers served in all-German units under German (often enough fortyeighter) commanders.[68] In and out of uniform, immigrant radicals pressed for an aggressive military policy and a militantly antislavery program for reconstructing southern society, repeatedly demanding the confiscation and division of plantations owned by Confederate leaders.[69]

That this civil war was an extension of the nation's founding democratic revolution was a common view at the time. But for many, that second revolutionary conflict also rang with words and ideals first encountered on another continent in an earlier decade. In this as in other respects, German-American Jacobins constituted a political bridge joining European and North American experiences and outlooks. At the same time, they linked the American democratic radicalism of earlier decades with that of the Civil War era. When, in the spring of 1861, the new president called for volunteers to suppress the slaveholder rebellion, one of New York's fortyeighter editors typically replied, "In the conflict between liberty and slavery, civilization and barbarism, loyalty and treason, the Germans will play not a subordinate, but a leading role. The spirit of 1848 is abroad again."[70]

Notes

The Abraham Lincoln quotation that heads this essay comes from his 4 July message to congress in 1861. The accompanying quotation from Friedrich Kapp is from *Geschichte der Sklaverei in den Vereinigten Staaten von Amerika* (Hamburg: Otto Meisner, 1861), xi.

1. See R. R. Palmer, *The Age of the Democratic Revolution: A Political History of Europe and America, 1760–1800*, 2 vols. (Princeton: Princeton University Press, 1969), 1:4–11, 22–23; George Rudé, *Debate on Europe, 1815–1850* (New York: Harper and Row, 1972); Charles Breunig, *The Age of Revolution and Reaction, 1789–1850* (New York: W. W. Norton & Co., 1970); Eric J. Hobsbawm, *The Age of Revolution, 1789–1848* (New York: New American Library, 1962); and idem, *The Age of Capital, 1848–1875* (New York: New American Library, 1975); Alfred F. Young, ed., *The American Revolution: Explorations in the History of American Radicalism* (DeKalb: Northern Illinois University Press, 1976); David Montgomery, *Beyond Equality: Labor and the Radical Republicans, 1862–1872* (New York: Knopf, 1967). On the Haitian revolution in its international setting and resonance, see C. L. R. James's classic *The Black Jacobins: Toussaint L'Ouverture and the San Domingo Revolution*, 2d rev. ed. (New York: Vintage Books, 1963); and Eugene D. Genovese, *From Rebellion to Revolution: Afro-American Slave Revolts in the Making of the Modern World* (Baton Rouge: Louisiana State University Press, 1979), 48–49, 90–97.

2. In addition to the works cited in the previous note, see Lewis B. Namier, *1848: The Revolution of the Intellectuals* (Oxford: Oxford University Press, 1946); Charles Morazé, *The Triumph of the Middle Classes: A Political and Social History of Europe in the Nineteenth Century* (Garden City, N.Y.: Anchor Books, 1968), esp. x, 291; Staughton Lynd, *Intellectual Origins of American Radicalism* (New York: Vintage Books, 1969), esp. 3; Barrington Moore, Jr., *Social Origins of Dictatorship and Democracy: Lord and Peasant in the Making of the Modern World* (Boston: Beacon Press, 1967), xv, 112; Richard D. Brown, *Modernization: The Transformation of American Life, 1600–1865* (New York: Hill and Wang, 1976), 160–61, 183, 185; Theodore S. Hamerow, "History and the German Revolution of 1848," *American Historical Review* 55 (1954–1955): 27–44; Andreas Dorpalen, "Revolutions of 1848," in *Marxism, Communism, and Western Society*, ed. C. D. Kerring, 8 vols. (New York: Herder and Herder, 1973), 7:244–53; Donald J. Mattheisen, "History as Current Events: Recent Works on the German Revolution of 1848," *American Historical Review* 88 (1983): 1219–37; and Dieter Langewiesche, "Einleitung," in *Die deutsche Revolution von 1848/49* (Darmstadt: Wissenschaftliche Buchgesellschaft, 1983).

3. Albert Soboul, *The French Revolution, 1787–1799: From the Storming of the Bastille to Napoleon* (New York: Vintage Books, 1975), 394. On the general point, see Rudé, *Debate on Europe*, p. 134; idem, *Ideology and Popular Protest* (New York: Harper and Row, 1980), 82, 85, 91.

4. E. P. Thompson, *The Making of the English Working Class* (New York: Vintage Books, 1963), 262. See also Margaret Jacob and James Jacob, eds., *The Origins of Anglo-American Radicalism* (London: Allen & Unwin, 1984).

5. The quoted phrase comes from fortyeighter Friedrich Anneke, *Der zweite Freiheitskampf der Vereinigten Staaten von Nordamerika: Ursachen, Entstehung und Entwicklung des Kampfes bis zum Fall des Fort Sumter* (Frankfurt-am-Main: J. D. Sauderlander's Verlag, 1861). I have discussed the experience of other cities in "Free Soil, Free Labor, and *Freimänner:* German Chicago in the Civil War Era," in *German Workers in Industrial Chicago, 1850–1910*, ed. Hartmut Keil and John B. Jentz (DeKalb: Northern Illinois University Press, 1983), 163–82, and "Immigrant Workers, 'Equal Rights,' and Antislavery: The Germans of Newark, New Jersey," *Labor History* 25 (Winter 1984): 26–52.

6. U.S. Bureau of the Census, *Historical Statistics of the United States, Colonial Times to 1970*, 2 vols. (Washington, D.C.: Government Printing Office, 1975), 1:8–9 and 117–18.

7. Statistics from other regions reveal a similar pattern: Mack Walker, *Germany and the Emigration, 1816–1885* (Cambridge, Mass.: Harvard University Press, 1964), 74, 77, 155, 160n, 165–67; Theodore S. Hamerow, *Restoration, Revolution, Reaction: Economics and Politics in Germany, 1815–1871* (Princeton, N.J.: Princeton University Press, 1966), 36–37; Wolfgang Köllmann and Peter Marschalck,

"German Emigration to the United States," *Perspectives in American History* 7 (1973): 523–24, 530–31; Carl Wittke, *Refugees of Revolution: The German Forty-Eighters in America* (Westport, Conn.: Greenwood Press, 1970), 44; Clifford Neal Smith, *Emigrants from Saxony (Grandduchy of Sachsen-Weimar-Eisenach) to America, 1854, 1859* (DeKalb, Ill.: Westland Publications, 1974).

8. Hamerow, *Restoration, Revolution, Reaction;* Walker, *Germany and the Emigration;* Frederick D. Marquardt, "*Pauperismus* in Germany during the *Vormärz*," *Central European History* 2 (1969): 77–88; idem, "A Working Class in Berlin in the 1840s?" in *Sozialgeschichte Heute,* ed. Hans-Ulrich Wehler (Göttingen: Vandenhoeck & Ruprecht, 1974), 191–210; P. H. Noyes, *Organization and Revolution: Working-Class Associations in the German Revolutions of 1848–1849* (Princeton, N.J.: Princeton University Press, 1966); Rudolf Stadelmann, *Social and Political History of the German 1848 Revolution* (1948; Eng. ed., Athens, Ohio: Ohio University Press, 1975); J. F. Bergier, "The Industrial Bourgeoisie and the Rise of the Working Class, 1700–1914," in *The Industrial Revolution,* vol. 3 of *The Fontana Economic History of Europe* (London: Fontana Books, 1973), 444–45; and Knut Borchardt, "The Industrial Revolution in Germany, 1700–1914," in *The Emergence of Industrial Societies,* vol. 4 of *The Fontana Economic History of Europe,* pt. 1, 76–160; and Jürgen Kocka, *Lohnarbeit und Klassenbildung: Arbeiter und Arbeiterbewegung in Deutschland, 1800–1875* (Berlin: J. H. W. Dietz, 1983), 51–69, 96–110.

9. Hamerow, *Restoration, Revolution, Reaction,* pp. 127–28; Erich Hahn, "German Parliamentary and National Aims in 1848–49: A Legacy Reassessed," *Central European History* 13 (1980): 287–293. See also Carl Schurz, *The Reminiscences of Carl Schurz,* 2 vols. (New York: Doubleday, Page and Co., 1909), 1:142–43.

10. Hamerow, *Restoration, Revolution, Reaction,* pp. 84–85, 102, 107–11. See also Rudé, *Debate on Europe,* p. 202; and Dorpalen, "Revolutions of 1848," pp. 248, 252.

11. Noyes, *Organization and Revolution,* pp. 25–33; Hamerow, *Restoration, Revolution, Reaction,* pp. 79, 88, 119, 141–46; Marquardt, "Working Class."

12. "On the History of the Communist League" (1885), in Karl Marx and Frederick Engels, *Selected Works,* 2 vols. (Moscow: Progress Publishers, 1962), 2:356.

13. Hamerow, *Restoration, Revolution, Reaction,* p. 119; Carl Wittke, *Against the Current: The Life of Karl Heinzen (1809–1880)* (Chicago: University of Chicago Press, 1945), 65. Even the Communist League was saturated with this Jacobin outlook. "The social doctrine of the League," Engels later recalled, had been extremely "indefinite," a weakness he attributed to its social composition. "The members, insofar as they were workers at all, were almost exclusively artisans"—i.e., "not yet full proletarians" but independent producers only then "passing into the modern proletariat." It was therefore inevitable, Engels concluded, "that their old handicraft prejudices should be a stumbling block to them at every moment" and that in their eyes "for the time being 'equality,' 'brotherhood,' and 'justice' helped them surmount every theoretical obstacle," "Communist League," pp. 343–44 (144).

14. Hermann Schlüter, *Die Anfänge der deutschen Arbeiterbewegung in Amerika* (Stuttgart: Verlag von J. H. W. Dietz, 1907), 18; Noyes, *Organization and Revolution,* pp. 50–53; William Howitt, *The Rural and Domestic Life of Germany* (Philadelphia: Carey and Hart, 1843), 54–61; Mark O. Kistler, "German-American Liberalism and Thomas Paine," *American Quarterly* 14 (1962): 81–83.

15. Hobsbawm, *Age of Capital,* p. 16; Soboul, *French Revolution,* pp. 8, 331–32; Gwynn A. Williams, *Artisans and Sans-Culottes: Popular Movements in France and Britain during the French Revolution* (New York: W. W. Norton and Co., 1969), 18, 32; see Kocka, *Lohnarbeit,* pp. 167–77. Thompson, *Making,* pp. 20–21, 122, 145, 157.

16. Hamerow, *Restoration, Revolution, Reaction,* pp. 92–94, 92ff., 111–16, 127; Noyes, *Organization and Revolution,* pp. 71, 379; Dorpalen, "Revolutions of 1848," pp. 246, 250–52; Oscar J. Hammen, "Economic and Social Factors in the Prussian Rhineland in 1848," *American Historical Review* 54 (1949): 825–40.

17. Walker, *Germany and the Emigration*, pp. 160–65; Günter Moltmann, "Die deutsche Amerikaauswanderung im 19. Jahrhundert," in "*. . . nach Amerika!" Auswanderung in die Vereinigten Staaten* (Hamburg: Museum für Hamburgische Geschichte, 1976), 13–15; Peter Marschalck, *Deutsche Überseewanderung im 19. Jahrhundert: Ein Beitrag zur soziologischen Theorie der Bevölkerung* (Stuttgart: Ernst Klett Verlag, 1973), 38–41, 50, 74. As Hildegard Binder Johnson noted more than thirty years ago, nearly nine out of every ten German immigrants between 1848 and 1854 came from "the very regions which were the scenes of memorable revolutionary events" ("Adjustment to the United States," in *The Forty-eighters: Political Refugees in the German Revolution of 1848*, ed. A. E. Zucker [1950; reprint, New York: Russell and Russell, 1967], 46).

18. Karl Obermann, *Joseph Weydemeyer: Pioneer of American Socialism* (New York: International Publishers, 1947), 33; Walker, *Germany*, 50, 63, 161; Thomas Stockham Baker, *Lenau and Young Germany in America* (Philadelphia: P. C. Stockhausen, 1897), 47–48, 52.

19. Walker, *Germany and the Emigration*, p. 155.

20. Thomas W. Page, "The Distribution of Immigrants in the United States before 1870," *Journal of Political Economy* 20 (1912): 683. Although the *Auswanderung* is often depicted as a basically farm-to-farm migration, by 1870 only 27 percent of all gainfully employed German-born Americans worked in agriculture while 50 percent made their living in manufacturing, mechanical, mining, trade, and transportation occupations. These percentages are calculated from the numerical data in E. P. Hutchinson, *Immigrants and Their Children* (New York: John Wiley, 1956), 79, 81.

21. Theodore Hershberg, Michael Katz, Stuart Blumin, Laurence Glasco, and Clyde Griffen, "Occupation and Ethnicity in Five Nineteenth-Century Cities: A Collaborative Inquiry," *Historical Methods Newsletter* 7 (1974): 174–216; Nora Faires, "Occupational Patterns of German-Americans in Nineteenth-Century Cities," in *German Workers in Industrial Chicago*, ed. Keil and Jentz, pp. 37–51.

22. The literature on the decline of the crafts has become too voluminous to require or permit citation here. Studies correlating that decline with the rising immigrant composition of these trades include Robert Ernst, *Immigrant Life in New York City: 1825–1863* (New York: King's Crown Press, 1949); Laurence Glasco, "Ethnicity and Occupation in the Mid-Nineteenth Century: Irish, Germans, and Native-Born Whites in Buffalo, New York," and Clyde Griffen, "The 'Old' Immigration and Industrialization: A Case Study," both in *Immigrants in Industrial America, 1850–1920*, ed. Richard L. Ehrlich (Charlottesville: University Press of Virginia, 1977), 152–155, 174; Bruce Laurie, Theodore Hershberg, and George Alter, "Immigrants and Industry; The Philadelphia Experience, 1850–1880," *Journal of Social History* 9 (1975): 233–34; and Amy Bridges, *A City in the Republic: Antebellum New York and the Origins of Machine Politics* (Cambridge: Cambridge University Press, 1983), chap. 3.

23. Schlüter, *Die Anfänge*, pp. ix–x; Ernst, *Immigrant Life in New York City*, pp. 41–42; Stanley Nadel, "Kleindeutschland: New York City's Germans, 1845–1880" (Ph.D. diss., Columbia University, 1981), pp. 1, 58–59.

24. Ernst, *Immigrant Life in New York City*, pp. 33, 92, 94–95, 257n; *Caspar Meier and His Successors* (New York: Oelrich's & Co., 1898); [Herman Julius Ruetnik], *Berühmte deutsche Vorkämpfer für Fortschritt, Freiheit und Friede in Nord Amerika, von 1626 bis 1888* (Cleveland: Forest City Bookbinding Co., 1888), 134–44, 181–85, 417–20; Gustav Koerner, *Das deutsche Element in den Vereinigten Staaten von Nordamerika, 1818–1848* (Cincinnati: A. G. Wilde & Co., 1880), 96–103, 112–13, 148–49; Theodore Lemke, *Geschichte des Deutschthums von New York von 1848 auf die Gegenwart* (New York: Theodore Lemke Verlag, 1891), 11–17, 33–41, 99–103, 107–12, 116–24; Theodor Griesinger, *Freiheit und Sclaverei unter dem Sternenbanner oder Land und Leute in Amerika* (Stuttgart: A. Kroner, 1862), 261–66.

25. Howard B. Rock, *Artisans of the New Republic: The Tradesmen of New*

York City in the Age of Jefferson (New York: New York University Press, 1979), esp. chaps. 9 and 10; John Barkley Jentz, "Artisans, Evangelicals, and the City: A Social History of Abolition and Labor Reform in Jacksonian New York," Ph.D. diss., City University of New York, 1977; Ernst, *Immigrant Life in New York City*, pp. 214–17; Sean Wilentz, *Chants Democratic: New York City and the Rise of the American Working Class, 1788–1850* (New York: Oxford University Press, 1984), 119–29.

26. *New York Daily Tribune*, 5 and 9 September 1845.

27. Karl Buechele, *Land und Volk der Vereinigten Staaten von Nord Amerika* (Stuttgart, 1855), 478–81; Ernst, *Immigrant Life in New York City*, pp. 77, 80, 83, 102–3.

28. E. Schlaeger, *Die sociale und politische Stellung der Deutschen in den Vereinigten Staaten: Ein Beitrag zu der Geschichte des Deutsch-Amerikanerthums der letzten 25 Jahre* (Berlin: Puttkamer & Muhlbrecht, 1874), 7–14; Baker, *Lenau*, pp. 57–58, 71–72; *New Yorker Staats-zeitung*, 25 March 1848, 21 April 1849; Wittke, *Refugees*, pp. 199–200; Ernest Bruncken, *German Political Refugees in the United States during the Period from 1815–1860* (pamphlet reprint from the *Deutsch-Amerikanische Geschichtsblätter*, 3 [1903]), 42.

29. Schurz, *Reminiscences*, 2:16.

30. Reprinted in John P. Sanderson, *Republican Landmarks: The Views and Opinions of American Statesmen on Foreign Immigration* (Philadelphia, 1856), 223–24.

31. *New York Daily Tribune*, 31 July 1850.

32. Schlüter, *Die Anfänge*, p. 136.

33. *Newarker Zeitung* reprinted in the *Newark Daily Mercury*, November 8, 1853.

34. Schlüter, *Die Anfänge*, p. 140–41.

35. Christian Esselin, quoted in Wittke, *Refugees*, p. 108. In 1848, the republican Esselin had helped lead the Frankfurt workers' association, which in turn played a leadership role among artisans throughout southwestern Germany. See Noyes, *Organization and Revolution*, p. 154.

36. Obermann, *Weydemeyer*, pp. 55, 91–92; Schlüter, *Die Anfänge*, pp. 160–62. See "Statuten des Kommunisten Klubs in New York," *Science & Society* 41 (1977): 334–37.

37. *New York Daily Tribune*, 23 April 1850; Schlüter, *Die Anfänge*, p. 17.

38. Carl Wittke, *The Utopian Communist: A Biography of Wilhelm Weitling, Nineteenth-Century Reformer* (Baton Rouge: Louisiana State University Press, 1950), 200–213; Ernst, *Immigrant Life in New York City*, pp. 99, 107–12; Schlüter, *Die Anfänge*, p. 80; John R. Commons and Associates, *History of Labour in the United States*, 4 vols. (New York: Macmillan, 1918), 1:567–68; Wilentz, *Chants Democratic*, pp. 372–86.

39. Schlüter, *Die Anfänge*, pp. 83–86.

40. Schlüter, *Die Anfänge*, pp. 135–44, 164–67.

41. *New York Herald*, 16 January 1855; 6, 7, 10, 11, and 13 November 1857; *New York Daily Tribune*, 6, 11, and 12 November 1857.

42. "Sozialismus und Turnerei," *Jahrbücher der Deutsch-Amerikanischen Turnerei*, vol. 1, pt. 4 (1892–1894), 147; Henry Metzner, *A Brief History of the American Turnerbund* (Pittsburgh: American Turnerbund, 1924), 7–17; Augustus J. Prahl, "The Turner," in *The Forty-Eighters*, ed. Zucker, pp. 98–99; Schlüter, *Die Anfänge*, pp. 199–203; Wittke, *Utopian Communist*, p. 14.

43. Hugo Gollmer, *Namensliste der Pionere des Nord-Amerik. Turnerbundes der Jahre 1848–1862* (St. Louis: Im Auftrag des Bundesvororts zusammengestellt, 1885); Nadel, "Kleindeutschland," p. 246; Wittke, *Refugees*, p. 225.

44. The Freemen Manifesto was widely reprinted, as in *The Free West* (Chicago), 18 May 1854. On the movement itself see E. Schlaeger, "Das Freidenkerthum in den Vereinigten Staaten," *Internationale Monatsschrift. Zeitschrift für allgemeine und nationale Kultur und deren Litteratur*, vol. 1, pt. 1 (Chemnitz: Verlag von Ernst

Schmeitzner, 1882), 52–54; William F. Kamman, *Socialism in German American Literature* (Philadelphia: Americana Germanica Press, 1917), 51–64.

45. Carl Wittke, *The German-Language Press in America* (Lexington: University Press of Kentucky, 1957), 77–81, 107, 170; Schlüter, *Die Anfänge*, pp. 130–31; Ernst, *Immigrant Life in New York City*, pp. 153–54.

46. Paul G. Faler, *Mechanics and Manufacturers in the Early Industrial Revolution: Lynn, Massachusetts, 1780–1860* (Albany: State University of New York Press, 1981), 121.

47. Helene Sara Zahler, *Eastern Workingmen and National Land Policy, 1829–1862* (New York: Columbia University Press, 1941), 30–37, 46–56; Commons, *History of Labour in the United States*, 1:522–34.

48. Zahler, *Eastern Workingmen*, pp. 36–37.

49. Hermann Kriege, "Die Zunehmende Einwanderung aus Deutschland," *Volkstribun*, 9 May 1846, reproduced in John R. Commons and associates, *Documentary History of American Industrial Society*, 10 vols. (New York: Russell and Russell, 1958), 7:91–93; Schlüter, *Die Anfänge*, pp. 19–48.

50. Arthur C. Cole, *The Irrepressible Conflict, 1850–1865* (Chicago: Quadrangle Press, 1971), 137.

51. In this connection see Shearer Davis Bowman's interesting "Antebellum Planters and *Vormärz* Junkers in Comparative Perspective," *American Historical Review* 85 (1980): 779–808.

52. *The Free West*, 18 May 1854.

53. Prahl, "The Turner," in *The Forty-Eighters*, ed. Zucker, p. 99.

54. Other characteristically Jacobin platform planks included calls for educational reform, expanded rights for craft associations, and an aggressively prodemocratic foreign policy (*New York Daily Tribune*, 26 October 1851).

55. "Appeal of the Independent Democrats in Congress to the People of the United States," *The Congressional Globe*, 33d Cong., 1st sess., 1854, pp. 281–82.

56. William Vocke, "The Germans and the German Press," McLean County Historical Society, *Transactions* 3 (1900): 54; *New York Daily Tribune*, February 28, 1854.

57. See issues of the *Staats-Zeitung* for 23 February, 13 July, and 21 September (on Kriege), 1850; 21 January, 4, 18, and 25 February, and 11 March (on the Appeal of the Independent Democrats), 1 April (on Kossuth's visit) and 6 and 8 April, and 30 December 1854. Oswald Ottendorfer, editor of the *Staats-Zeitung* in the 1850s, had also participated in the 1848 revolution. But, as a fellow fortyeighter recalled, Ottendorfer became quite wealthy in the United States, and his political sympathies quickly shifted rightward. See M. J. Becker, *Germans of 1849 in America* (Mt. Vernon, Ohio: Republican Printing House, 1887), 28, 43. See also Ernst, *Immigrant Life in New York City*, p. 280n.

58. *New York Daily Tribune*, 24 February 1854.

59. This account is based on the following newspaper reports: *New Yorker Demokrat*, reprinted in the *New York Evening Post* of 24 February 1854, along with the *Post*'s own account; *New York Daily Tribune*, February 24; *New York Herald*, February 24.

60. *New York Daily Times*, 2 March 1854; *Newark Daily Mercury*, 3 March 1854.

61. This account is based on the following newspaper reports: *New York Herald*, 4 March 1854; *New York Daily Times*, 4 March; *New York Daily Tribune*, 6 and 7 March 1854; *New York Evening Post*, 4 and 7 March 1854.

62. See, for example, Wittke, *Refugees*, pp. 206–7.

63. Accounts of this rally appeared in the *New York Daily Tribune* and the *New York Daily Times* of 8 October 1856.

64. Obermann, *Weydemeyer*, pp. 109–12; Eric Foner, *Free Soil, Free Labor, Free Men: The Ideology of the Republican Party before the Civil War* (New York: Oxford University Press, 1971), 197, 238, 242–55.

65. *New York Daily Times*, 7 November 1856.

66. See the 7 November 1860 editions of the *New York Daily Tribune*, the *Times*, and the *Herald*, as well as Ernst, *Immigrant Life in New York City*, p. 193.

67. This was the case, for example, in urban Illinois, Minnesota, Missouri (St. Louis), and Ohio (Cleveland, Cincinnati).

68. *Jahrbücher der Deutsch-Amerikanischen Turnerei*, 1:62–71, 81–82; 97–100; and 3:141–44, 170; Ella Lonn, *Foreigners in the Union Army and Navy* (Westport, Conn.: Greenwood Press, 1969), pp. 576–78.

69. See Levine, "Free Soil, Free Labor, and *Freimänner*," in *German Workers in Industrial Chicago*, ed. Keil and Jentz, pp. 175–78; Herman Belz, *Reconstructing the Union: Theory and Policy during the Civil War* (Ithaca, N.Y.: Cornell University Press, 1967), 68. On the contrasting behavior of a key figure in New York's German-American elite and his circle, see Irving Katz, *August Belmont: A Political Biography* (New York: Columbia University Press, 1968), 43–89, 139; and Joel H. Silbey, *A Respectable Minority: The Democratic Party in the Civil War Era, 1860–1868* (New York: W. W. Norton, 1977), pp. 63–64, 92–93, 113, 126, 130, 208.

70. *New Yorker Criminal Zeitung und Belletristiches Journal*, 26 April 1861.

DAVID BRUNDAGE

Irish Land and American Workers: Class and Ethnicity in Denver, Colorado

The relationship of Irish-American workers to nineteenth-century labor radicalism has turned out to be more complex than it once appeared. Not long ago, historians pictured Irish workers as overwhelmingly conservative, led by their church and their "lace curtain" middle class to shun socialism, anarchism, and the like. Today, by way of contrast, most historians would agree that the Irish were central actors in the building of American labor radicalism in the 1870s and 1880s, putting a distinctive stamp on the Knights of Labor in particular.[1]

Irish nationalism played a crucial role in this. From the mid-nineteenth century on, the Irish in America have given generous support to their nation's struggle against British domination. Their enthusiastic nationalism has in turn affected the political situation in this country. In the 1860s, for example, many Irish-Americans joined the Irish Republican Brotherhood, a secret revolutionary organization popularly known as the Fenians. The Fenians fought not only for Irish independence but also for the establishment of an Irish republic. Not surprisingly, Irish-Americans who embraced the republican doctrines of Fenianism also tended to back the Republican party, the Union, and the war against the southern slaveholders.[2]

At no time was the trans-Atlantic connection more important than in the early 1880s. It was then that the American Land League, an organization formed to support the struggles of tenant farmers in Ireland, ended up denouncing monopoly and social inequality in America. The Land League eventually provided the Knights of Labor with much of their anti-monopoly language and some of their most enthusiastic members.[3] This essay will trace the impact of the Land League on the working-class movement in a single community, that of Denver, Colorado. Such a case study should enable us to understand more precisely the relationship between class and ethnicity in late nineteenth-century America.

Denver was a classic example of urban growth in the age of industry. Founded in 1859 as the "commercial emporium" of the

Colorado goldfields, the town stagnated through much of the 1860s and early 1870s. But the 1878 discovery of silver at nearby Leadville had a powerful effect on Denver. The city quickly developed as the transport and processing center of the Rocky Mountains, with smelters, railroad shops, and mining equipment manufacturers creating a powerful demand for industrial labor. From 1880 to 1890, Denver's population nearly tripled, rising from 35,629 to 106,713, while distinct working-class neighborhoods took shape to the north and the west of the business district. By the latter date, more than 46 percent of the city's labor force was composed of first- or second-generation immigrants, with the Irish, English, and Germans representing the largest contingents.[4]

Denver became a major stronghold of the Knights of Labor after a successful strike of railroad shop workers in May 1884. Prior to this time, working-class organizational life in the city had revolved around two different types of institutions, both of which were limited in different ways. The first was craft unionism, a major force in the lives of many skilled male workers. Although important, craft unions excluded a large proportion of the city's unskilled working people. Exclusive in a different sense were the various immigrant voluntary organizations which had proliferated in Denver over the course of the 1870s. While these organizations provided essential social and cultural services, they tended to divide Denver's working people along ethnic and religious lines. The rise of the Knights of Labor marked a sharp departure from both of these organizational forms. Above all, the Knights sought to unite those they called the "producing classes" in a movement that cut across the lines of skill, gender, race, and ethnicity.

This kind of solidarity did not happen automatically. Rather, it was the product of a long and conscious struggle on the part of labor activists to instill and cultivate a set of mutualistic values among laboring people. In Denver, this struggle began before the rise of the Knights in 1884. It was triggered primarily by the emergence of Irish-American radicalism in the city in the years from 1880 to 1883.

The organization that expressed this radicalism, the Denver branch of the American Land League, commanded considerable attention throughout the community and played a significant role in city politics. More importantly, the Land League bequeathed an impressive ideological legacy to the Knights of Labor and the Denver labor movement as a whole. Its attempt to ameliorate the bitter religious antagonism within the Irish community and its criticism of the traditionally subservient role of Irish women were themes the Knights would take up and develop further. The League's denunciation of Irish landlords and its defense of Ireland's rural poor, moreover, provided an implicit justification for the labor movement's critique of monopoly and wage labor.

Yet the Land League in Denver was led not by wage workers, but by members of the Irish-American middle class. Their opposition to trade unionism and the Knights and their efforts to lead their countrymen into an alliance with Colorado's anti-labor Republican party tended to obscure the full implications of their radicalism. Only when Denver's labor activists began to intervene in discussions of "the Irish question" in 1883 did the situation begin to change. Then it changed rapidly. An interethnic solidarity quickly emerged among the city's working people, an essential condition for the rapid growth of the Knights of Labor in the mid-1880s and ultimately for the flowering of working-class radicalism in the early twentieth century.

Unions

The struggle to build effective craft unions in Denver had been an arduous one, but by the end of 1882 a small group of trade unions had emerged among the city's skilled workers. All of Denver's three large immigrant groups—the English, the Germans, and the Irish—had participated in the building of the trade union movement. Furthermore, the unions represented a powerful form of solidarity that could be broadened substantially as the city's labor movement grew. But hindering such growth was a central feature of the nineteenth-century craft union: it drew a rigid line between the skilled and the unskilled worker, between the craftsman and the laborer.

Many of Denver's most important industries, such as building, tailoring, printing, and the manufacture of mining equipment, were dominated by highly skilled craftsmen. Such craftsmen formed the backbone of the early labor movement in cities throughout America, and Denver was no exception. In April 1860, printers at the recently founded *Rocky Mountain News* organized the Denver Typographical Union, the first labor organization in Colorado. During the 1870s, tailors, iron molders, and stonecutters established trade unions in Denver; and railroad engineers, firemen, and conductors organized lodges of their respective brotherhoods. The early 1880s saw increasing activity. Carpenters, machinists, and bakers began to organize, and two Knights of Labor assemblies appeared in the city.[5] The most important development of the early 1880s occurred in November 1882, when the printers and four other unions came together to form the Denver Trades and Labor Assembly. One month later, printer Joseph R. Buchanan began publishing a weekly newspaper, the Denver *Labor Enquirer,* which served as the official organ of both the Trades Assembly and the fledgling Knights of Labor.[6]

Although conditions in each trade varied considerably in the late 1870s and early 1880s, certain common problems confronted all skilled workers in the city, problems which encouraged their moves toward organization. Most pressing were the attempts of Denver employers to introduce various incentive pay schemes, especially piecework. While employers favored piecework as a way of increasing productivity, skilled craftsmen, who had been accustomed to a certain amount of workplace autonomy, saw it as a direct attack on their established traditions of work. While it might lead to higher wages for some workers in the short run, the long-run effect of the piece system was to create competition among workers that would lead to a decline in pay. By connecting wages to measurable output, the new system also greatly enhanced the power of the foreman, at the expense of the craftsman. Thus the abolition of piecework became a central objective for a number of trade unions in Denver and provided impetus for the organization of new ones.[7]

Piecework became a major issue in three of Denver's most important trades: printing, tailoring, and the manufacture of mining machinery. When Joseph Buchanan arrived in Denver in the late 1870s, he found that in nonunion printing establishments the piece system had created "many opportunities for the practice of favoritism." "Some workmen were frequently enabled, through favors shown them by foremen, to make larger bills than men greatly their superiors as compositers," Buchanan later recalled.[8] Piecework in Denver's mining machinery foundries encouraged a spirit of competition among workmen which, as one Denver iron molder put it, was "the most expeditious route to hell for the human race." "Both molder and boss help in this competition, this cutting of each other's throats," he proclaimed. "Both are criminals and both are victims."[9] In the manufacture of men's clothing the system assumed its most vicious form: since Denver employers provided no workshops for their employees, tailors worked at home and were thus pushed to exploit the labor of their wives and children.[10]

The fight against piecework was crucial to the development of the Denver labor movement because it necessitated the assertion of a mutualistic ethos against the competitive individualism enshrined in middle-class ideology. Craftsmen built this ethos into the fabric of their union rules, rules which attempted to fix terms of apprenticeship, limit foremen's rights, and put journeymen on "an equal footing as to wages and other conditions."[11]

Enforcing these rules was not always easy. In the Denver printers' union, mutuality meant the expulsion of "rat" printers who broke the union's "laws" regarding work practices. Even those who supported such laws sometimes found the union's discipline harsh. In 1882, for example, Joseph Buchanan argued that the Denver Typographical Union should grant a pardon to a rat printer who sought readmission. "I believed the union's treatment of him was cruel and uncalled for," Buchanan later recalled, "but men older than I in the union said that his offense could not be condoned."[12] Associated with this harsh discipline, on the other hand, was an intense, almost family-like solidarity. "I look to the welfare of the Union as I would that of my children," said one printer at a union meeting in 1884.[13]

The establishment of the Denver Trades Assembly in 1882 marked the extension of this group solidarity from the individual craft to the community of skilled workers as a whole. The Trades Assembly was the consequence of the increasing use of the boycott in Denver labor disputes. The boycotting of recalcitrant employers was used mainly by Denver tailors, but in principle it was a tactic open to all who worked in trades that served a working-class market. Since boycotts required funds and coordination beyond the resources of the individual trade union and demanded solidarity beyond the ranks of its members, craftsmen formed the Trades Assembly mainly to coordinate boycotts (and less frequently strikes) and to enforce interunion support. According to the Trades Assembly's constitution, when a decision had been made to endorse a boycott or strike, "a call shall be made on all trades and labor organizations to assist the one in difficulty. . . . Any union failing to assist another when called upon by the Assembly shall forfeit its right in a similar emergency."[14]

Immigrant craftsmen in Denver took active roles in the struggle to build trade unions. In 1882, English carpenters and machinists organized Denver branches of British unions, the Amalgamated Society of Engineers, and the Amalgamated Society of Carpenters, which preceded unions among American workers in these trades.[15] In the same year, German bakers in the city established a union which helped found the Trades Assembly, although it collapsed shortly thereafter in the face of strong employer hostility.[16] While there are no conclusive data on the ethnic composition of other early labor organizations in Denver, the fact that the Iron Molders, the Stonecutters, and the first local assembly of the Knights of Labor held their regular meetings at Mitchel Guard Hall, an Irish community center, suggests a significant presence of Irish-Americans in these organizations.[17] The Knights of Labor, led nationally by the Irish Catholic machinist, Terence V. Powderly, attracted early Irish-American support in the city. Four out of the seven pioneer organizers for the Denver Knights were first- or second-generation Irishmen, a figure far exceeding their proportion in the city's working class as a whole.[18]

Black craftsmen found the early Denver trade unions considerably less sympathetic to their aspirations. In 1869, the Denver Typographical Union refused to admit Henry Wagoner, a leader in the struggle for Black voting rights in Reconstruction Colorado.[19] Lewis H. Douglass, the son of Frederick Douglass, launched sharp attacks on "the folly, tyranny, and wickedness of labor unions" in the mid-1870s, partly as a result of his experience with the Denver labor movement. Douglass had come to Denver seeking work as a typographer but was unable to find employment, apparently as a result of his exclusion by the Denver Typographical Union.[20]

Attitudes toward the admission of women to trade unions varied in Denver. The printers allowed the admission of women members as early as 1869.[21] Iron molders, on the other hand, remained implacably hostile to the idea of women entering either their trade or their trade union.[22] The tailors' position fell between these two poles. Although one of their "cardinal principles" was "to procure for female workers the highest possible wages," the Denver Journeymen Tailors Union never actually tried to organize women workers.[23]

Racism and a firm belief that woman's "place" was in the home undoubtedly accounted for the attitudes of trade unionists towards Black and female workers. The exclusive position of trade unions toward unskilled workers generally, however, sprang from a different source. It was built into the very nature of craft unions, which derived their strength from the scarce skills possessed by their members. Despite the growing mutuality of the early Denver labor movement, the movement remained essentially one of skilled workers. On occasion it even expressed a deep-rooted belief in the craftsman's superiority to the common laborer.

The railroad brotherhoods, especially those of engineers and firemen which held aloof from the broader labor movement throughout the late nineteenth century, were famous for this. "The idea of an engineer associating with section men and wipers" was unthinkable for one Denver brotherhood member in the mid-1880s. "Do you consider a man getting a dollar per day equal to [one] who gets four dollars per day?" he reportedly asked a Knights of Labor organizer. "As for me, I consider myself four times better." Although the account of the conversation may have been apocryphal, it illustrates values widely held among what contemporaries called the "aristocracy of labor."[24] Such sentiments were not widely voiced in the Denver Trades Assembly. Its stated intention "to secure united action on the part of *skilled* labor" in the city, however, reveals the limits of its ambitions.[25] Even the early Knights of Labor assemblies were restricted in practice to skilled craftsmen. The first, founded in May 1881, was composed of plasterers, plumbers, and other skilled building tradesmen. The second, organized in November 1882, was made up entirely of printers.[26]

Denver's early labor movement, then, was pulled in different directions. On the one hand, in the course of its growth before 1884—and particularly in its struggles against piecework—the trade union movement developed an ethos of mutuality which ran directly counter to the individualism of the day. Denver's labor activists would later broaden this ethos into a sweeping denunciation of "the selfishness and deadening effects of competition" generally.[27] On the other hand, the early trade unions excluded women, Blacks, and unskilled workers from their ranks. This exclusiveness effectively blocked the growth of a broad working-class movement in the city.

Immigrant Societies

The trade union was not the only organizational expression of working-class life in this period. For immigrant working people, the ethnic fraternal or benevolent society was a much more important institution in the 1870s and early 1880s. Unlike trade unions, immigrant societies drew no occupational line among their members and often included women in their activities, if not in their active membership. Although serving a working-class constituency, Denver's ethnic societies also included middle-class members, who frequently provided organizational leadership. Nonetheless, in its own way the ethnic society was just as exclusive as the trade union, for it deepened the divisions of nativity and religion among the city's working people.

The pioneering ethnic organization in Denver was the Turnverein, founded by German immigrants in 1865. As the city's population grew in the 1870s, increasing numbers of Irish, English, and German immigrants provided the basis for a rich organizational life. In 1872, the first English society, the St. George's Protective Association, was founded, followed in 1874 by the Mitchel Guards, a semimilitary Irish social club. In the mid-1870s, an inclusive German-American Association was added to the Turnverein in the German community.[28]

These societies provided a number of important economic and social services to immigrant working people in the city. In the absence of governmental social insurance, ethnic societies provided sickness, death, and burial benefits to working-class families, many of them on the margins of poverty. In the absence of any urban recreational facilities save the saloon, they provided a major focus of working-class leisure.[29]

Above all, ethnic organizations provided a sense of community for immigrants frequently on the move. Railroad construction and mining in Denver's hinterland offered employment opportunities that drew large numbers of workers in and out of the city. As a result, Denver's inhabitants were even more mobile than the restless nineteenth-century American population as a whole.[30] Immigrant societies helped ease the loneliness that accompanied high geographic mobility.

The absence of stable immigrant neighborhoods in the city also gave the ethnic organization considerable importance. Denver's small Chinese population occupied a distinct neighborhood in the 1880s, and by the early twentieth century Black residents were increasingly segregated in the Five Points section of the city.[31] But among the large immigrant groups of the late nineteenth century no such patterns emerged. English, Germans, Irish, and Scandinavians were scattered widely throughout the city's neighborhoods.[32] This meant that a sense of ethnic community could not readily develop through the informal institutions of the immigrant neighborhood; the burden thus fell upon the formal immigrant organization.

"We are all very clannish," wrote the printer Joseph Buchanan, describing Denver's working class in 1883, "and each clan must have its own club or society to keep us from identifying with the people among whom we have come to live."[33] There had indeed been a proliferation of ethnic organizations in the city. By the early 1880s, the Irish maintained chapters of the Ancient Order of Hibernians and the Irish-American Progressive Society along with the Mitchel Guards; and the English, Welsh, and Scots had organized branches of the Albion, Cambrian, and Caledonian clubs. Denver's Germans, known for their tendency toward insularity, had even organized a separate German-speaking branch of the Odd Fellows. The German and Irish communities of the city also supported their own newspapers, the *Colorado Journal* and the *Rocky Mountain Celt.* [34]

Despite the strength of these identifications, Buchanan's view that these societies divided the working class—a view echoed by many later historians—probably exaggerates the problem.[35] They did encourage ethnic cohesiveness, and they united working-class people with their middle-class countrymen, functions that may have served to block the emergence of a broad working-class movement. But the fraternal and collective spirit that was the central tendency of the immigrant society posed an implicit challenge to the individualist ethos of the times which paralleled that of the trade unions. Like the trade union, the ethnic organization was pulled in different directions.

Religion, rather than ethnicity, provided the most important line of conflict among Denver's working people. Tensions between Protestant and Catholic were paramount, affecting several immigrant groups. Germans, for example, were divided between Lutherans and Catholics, each with their own organizations.[36] The division took on an especially bitter character among immigrants from the British Isles. The Catholic Ancient Order of Hibernians, for example, expressed hostility toward the Protestant Scotch-Irish while anti-Catholic sentiments flourished among immigrants from northern Ireland, Scotland, and Wales.[37]

Denver's political parties also gave expression to the conflict between Catholics and Protestants. Although party alignments based on religion were not as pronounced in Colorado as in the Midwest, it was generally true that the Democrats were the party of Catholic cultural groups while the Republicans spoke for the Protestants. During the 1870s, religion entered the political arena more directly. In 1876, a group of Catholics struggled to obtain public aid for parochial schools, triggering intense opposition from Protestants. Two years later, Colorado's bishop Joseph Machebeuf brought the church into politics again, taking a strong stand against women's suffrage.[38]

Women's suffrage was one of the most important reform issues of the Gilded Age, and Machebeuf's position reflected what some Denver reformers perceived as Catholicism's implacable hostility to the nineteenth-century reform tradition. Caroline Churchill, Denver's leading feminist and prohibitionist, for example, frequently used her weekly newspaper to denounce the church as an opponent of reform. Churchill also ridiculed Irish immigrants, the largest contingent of American Catholics, as a class made up wholly of "criminals" and "paupers." Reform, it would appear, was for Protestants only.[39]

From the abolitionist crusade to the feminist movement of the early twentieth century, the American reform tradition had indeed been shaped by the powerful forces of perfectionist Protestantism. But the mercurial rise of the American Land League among Irish-Americans in the early 1880s marked, as a recent historian has noted, "a conjunction of Irish America with the Protestant reform tradition.[40] In Denver, the rise of the Land League also prepared the way for the emergence of a broad working-class movement, a movement which could finally overcome the limitations of both the trade unions and the immigrant organizations.

The Land League

Organized in Ireland by Michael Davitt and John Devoy in the summer of 1879, the Land League heralded what has come to be known as the "New Departure" in Irish politics. Although the League put forward the historic demand for national independence from British rule, its greater significance lay in its efforts to redress the grievances of Ireland's rural poor. Specifically, it waged political war against oppressive Irish landlords and raised the slogan, "The Land for the People." Under the leadership of Charles Stewart Parnell, the organization built an enormous following over the next few years and represented the first genuine mass movement of the Irish poor.[41]

The Land League soon began to play a major role on this side of the Atlantic as well. In 1880, Parnell and Davitt toured the United States to raise funds for their struggle in the Irish-American community. They met with immediate success, and in the same year the American Land League was founded. By September 1881, there were 1,500 branches of the League in towns and cities across the nation. Michael Davitt himself organized Denver's branch of the Land League on his cross-country tour of 1880.[42]

The impact of the Land League on divisions among Denver's working people was profound and unexpected. Even the traditionally bitter conflict between Irish Protestants and Catholics was challenged by the city's Land League. The signal on this issue came from the struggle in Ireland itself. As one activist from Ireland told a Denver League meeting in 1882, "Catholics and Protestants in Ireland feel that upon this question of land reform they have one common ground to stand upon; one common cause to fight for, and one common enemy to oppose."[43] In the spirit of this proclamation, the Denver League opened its doors to Protestant members and even elected a Northern Irish Protestant, Robert Morris, as its first president. At a demonstration in 1882, Denver Land Leaguers carried banners reading "North and South" and "Orange and Green." In 1883, the Denver League went so far as to oppose the celebration of St. Patrick's Day. After considerable debate, its members decided that this essentially religious holiday was divisive in a community that included many non-Catholics. Denver saw no celebration of St. Patrick's Day until 1887, when it was revived by the Ancient Order of Hibernians.[44]

The Denver Land League also launched an attack on the traditionally subservient role of Irish-American women, with the cue again coming from events in the Emerald Isle. In what was generally regarded as "the most important step since the start of the movement," Anna Parnell organized the Ladies Land League in Ireland in 1881. As an early historian of the movement noted, "the Land League was the one national movement that availed themselves of their [women's] services as citizens, instead of shutting them out like children from the conduct of political business."[45] By April 1881, men in the Denver branch of the League were voicing support for "working with the Ladies," and by December of that year the Ladies Land League of Denver had organized itself and elected officers.[46] In Denver, as in Ireland, this marked a massive rupture with the deeply embedded conservatism of Irish culture regarding the public roles of women.

The organization of women and Protestants in the Land League was also related to a growing anticlericalism among Denver's Irish Catholics, for a vocal sector of the church hierarchy had expressed strong opposition to both of these moves. Anticlerical sentiments in Denver had been latent for some time. Although the city's Catholic population was overwhelmingly Irish, its bishop, Machebeuf, was French. In the 1870s, Machebeuf had aroused opposition from Denver's Irish for his pro-British political views and his alleged discrimination against Irish priests.[47] The Denver Land League was able to activate a critical spirit that Irish Catholics had already expressed toward their local church hierarchy.

The conflict with the church had ramifications far beyond the local situation. It came to a head in June 1882, when Bishop Gilmour of Cleveland censured the Ladies Land League of that city, ostensibly because "he had heard bad reports about their character." The Denver Land League went into a long and argumentative session to determine a response to Gilmour's action. Although some members believed that "if you open a breach by criticizing the conduct of Bishop Gilmour you will bring nothing but harm and will awaken prejudice against the League," sentiment generally ran toward strong condemnation. The Irish Catholic Judge John (J. W.) Mullahey, for example, did not favor the denunciation of Gilmour "as a man or as a Catholic, but he would denounce the action of any man, whether priest, bishop, or pope, who opposed the Irish people in their struggle for liberty." A formal resolution of denunciation carried the day. As one Land Leaguer put it in a statement reflecting both the deeply rooted republicanism and the growing anticlericalism of the Denver organization, "it was not for kings or priests to dictate to the Land League."[48]

The Denver Land League's openness regarding women's participation, its attempt to put aside the traditional animosity between Catholics and Protestants, and its growing independence from the Catholic hierarchy established an ideological legacy of tremendous importance for the city's working-class movement, the Knights of Labor in particular. In 1883, for example, Joseph Buchanan began calling for the organization of Denver working women into the Knights, thus breaking decisively with the notion of the labor movement as the special preserve of highly skilled males. In support of his position, he argued that "in the Irish Land League cause the best men were the women, and . . . they would prove to be in every emancipatory cause, if they were given the opportunity."[49] Buchanan's weekly, the *Labor Enquirer,* also carried through with the Land League's efforts to overcome religious differences among Denver's working people. Although the columns of the newspaper were strongly influenced by the rhetoric of Protestant perfectionism, it showed none of the anti-Catholicism characteristic of reformers like Caroline Churchill. Indeed, Buchanan frequently praised individual Catholic priests like Father Brennan, who was deeply concerned about the plight of the city's poor and who was "unostentatious" in his personal life.[50]

But if Denver's labor activists treated individual priests with sympathy, they shared with the Land Leaguers an antipathy toward the meddling of the Catholic hierarchy in the affairs of their movement. The Land League had prepared the way. When Bishop Gilmour turned his attacks from the Ladies Land League to the Knights of Labor in the mid-1880s, Denver labor leaders could respond effectively, without fear of alienating their substantial Irish Catholic constituency. Burnette G. Haskell, who took over the editorship of the *Labor Enquirer* in 1887, could even proclaim that the Catholic hierarchy had become "part of the machinery of oppression" and so naturally opposed the Knights.[51] This perspective undoubtedly went beyond the feelings of Denver's Irish Catholic Knights but, according to Buchanan at any rate, "most of these hold the opinion that the Church has no right to interfere in the matter."[52]

Middle-Class Leaders

Despite the important ideological legacy of the Land League for Denver's labor movement, the meaning of the Irish land struggle for the city's working people was not entirely clear. It emerged only after months of intense conflict between labor activists and the leaders of the Land League. In Denver, as in the nation as a whole, there were two distinct centers of power within the Irish nationalist movement. The first revolved around the Irish-American middle class and the political machine. In spite of their support for the agrarian and national struggle in Ireland, individuals associated with this wing of the movement were not particularly sympathetic to workers' struggles in America. There was also, however, a radical working-class tendency within the Land League, represented by the Irish-American newspaper editor Patrick Ford.

From New York, Ford edited a widely circulated weekly, the *Irish World and Industrial Liberator.* As the paper's title indicates, Ford sought to draw connections between the land struggle in Ireland and the labor struggle in the United States. "The cause of the poor in Donegal," he proclaimed, "is the cause of the factory slave in Fall River."[53] In some areas of the country, particularly the anthracite region of Pennsylvania and the industrial belt of New England, working-class branches of the Land League arose which adhered closely to Ford's position, in some cases virtually merging with the Knights of Labor. In these areas, the Land League and the Knights together shaped what some historians have termed a "producer ideology," which posited a fundamental conflict between the producing classes (workers, farmers, small businessmen) and monopolists. The latter were seen as posing a fundamental threat to society, controlling not only the land of Ireland, but increasingly American industry and finance as well.[54]

But social patterns within Denver's Irish-American community differed in important ways from those of the mining towns and industrial cities of the East. In the early 1870s, Irish-Americans in the town were heavily concentrated in unskilled occupations but, following the Leadville mining boom of 1878, the situation changed dramatically. Denver's rapid growth in the late 1870s and early 1880s provided opportunities for occupational mobility not present in more settled eastern cities. Thus, although the city's Irish-American population was small by eastern standards, its occupational structure exhibited considerable diversity. In 1890, nearly 30 percent of Irish-born males in the work force held occupations in the skilled trades, a figure roughly comparable to that for the native-born. Even more important was the emergence of an Irish-American middle class. By 1890, nearly 15 percent of the Irish-born in Denver's work force occupied positions in business, the professions, and the white-collar trades.[55]

When Michael Davitt organized Denver's Land League branch in 1880, it was this nascent Irish-American middle class, not the city's working people, who answered his call. Denver's Land League activists from 1881 to 1883 were overwhelmingly middle class. Lawyers, judges, politicians, newspaper editors, and building contractors formed the active core of the organization, while Colorado's wealthiest Irishman, flour mill owner John K. Mullen, served as the League's treasurer.[56]

Not surprisingly, this Land League branch expressed little sympathy with Patrick Ford's radical producer ideology. Explicitly rejecting Ford's attempt to draw parallels between social conditions in the United States and Ireland, the Denver organization was much more impressed with the contrasts. Denver Land Leaguers applauded enthusiastically, for example, when a speaker argued that unlike "feudal" Ireland, "America is the hope of every enslaved nation . . . a land of promise in which the ark of freedom shall securely and forever rest."[57] As Robert Morris, the president of the Denver organization observed, "the Land League was not a revolutionary organization."[58]

This stance was reflected in the hostility expressed by the Land League's leadership toward the labor movement. The epitome of the self-made man, Land League treasurer John K. Mullen denounced labor radicalism wherever it appeared.[59] C. E. McSheehy, an important figure in the Irish movement and the editor of the Irish Catholic weekly, the *Rocky Mountain Celt,* used the editorial columns of his paper for a running attack on trade unionism, the Knights of Labor, and labor activism generally.[60] Connections with the most anti-labor sector of Denver's native-American elite were cemented by the liberal contributions to the Land League treasury by Republican governor Frederick Pitkin. Pitkin had called out the state militia to crush a strike of miners in Leadville in 1880.[61]

Pitkin's association with the Land League also illustrates the role of party politics in its development. Throughout the early 1880s, the Denver League maintained a close working relationship with Colorado's dominant Republican party. This relationship was furthered by the arrival of Michael Boland in the city in August 1883. According to the Irish leader John Devoy, Boland, along with several other leaders of the Fenian Brotherhood, was attempting to turn the Irish nationalist movement into "an American political machine to secure jobs" for Irishmen with the Republican party. Whether or not one accepts Devoy's characterization of Boland as "a crooked lawyer who fleeced his clients in Louisville and had to get out because no one there would trust him," his analysis of the latter's political inclinations was on the mark.[62] One month after his arrival in Denver, Boland and Judge J. W. Mullahey, an officer of the Land League, organized an Irish-American Republican Club to orchestrate support for the GOP within the Irish-American community.[63]

The basis for this strategy had actually been worked out earlier, in the Denver municipal election of 1881. Robert Morris, president of the Land League, ran for mayor of the city on the Republican ticket and won the election. Although he had been born in Ireland, Morris was both a well-to-do businessman and a Protestant; nevertheless, his candidacy drew wide support among Denver's Irish Catholic workers. Despite their traditional allegiance to the Democratic party, an estimated four-fifths of Irish voters supported Morris, according to the *Rocky Mountain News*, "because of his relations to the various national organizations of his countrymen."[64] Middle-class members of the Land League, of course, were delighted with the election returns. Immediately following the election, John K. Mullen praised Morris and the Land League for "creating a bond of sympathy which has united Irishmen as they have never been before."[65]

Working-Class Critics

By 1883, the ethnic unity so carefully cultivated by the Land League was foundering. The attack on the Land League's connections with the Republicans and its anti-labor stance came not from a working-class tendency within the League itself, but rather from the outside, from the nascent Denver labor movement. The local labor press played an essential role in shaping this attack. As noted earlier, in 1882, the typographer Joseph Buchanan founded the Denver *Labor Enquirer*. With a stated mission "to educate, elevate, and advance the laboring classes" of the city, the *Labor Enquirer* appeared every Saturday until 1888 at a subscription rate of $1.50 a year.[66] One of the most interesting characteristics of Buchanan's paper was its total identification with the Irish cause. Although native-born and raised as a Protestant, Buchanan held that "the downtrodden people of Ireland" had been "subjected to wrongs which entitle them to the sympathy of every man and woman in the world, of whatever nationality or belief."[67] The columns of his paper were filled with news of both the Denver and the national Land Leagues and with the progress of the struggle in Ireland itself. By mid-1883, it was a rare Denver gathering for the Irish cause which did not find Buchanan in a prominent place in the hall.[68]

Yet it was Buchanan who led the initial attack on Denver's Irish-American middle class. Throughout the 1880s, the labor editor sought to construct an independent "anti-monopoly" political challenge to the two-party system in Colorado. This led him to denounce in no uncertain terms the Republican activities of the Land League—particularly Judge Mullahey, whose "disgraceful conduct . . . should be a lesson to the working men and should teach them that it is best not to be swayed by feelings of compassion and personal friendship when selecting men for positions of prominence and responsibility."[69] When Mullahey and Boland organized the Irish-American Republican Club, Buchanan warned "all workingmen, and particularly the sons of Erin" to beware; as for himself, he was "sick and tired of party 'clubs.' "[70]

The challenge to Denver's Irish political leaders was extended to the Irish press. In 1883, Buchanan began a series of diatribes against the "hypocrisy" of the *Rocky Mountain Celt.* While denying any personal animosity toward its editor, he sought "to call attention of the patriotic printed-in-green advocate of the oppressed poor that its policy of crying out against existing wrongs and urging their overthrow [in Ireland] don't jibe very well with the long and prevaricating tirades upon trade unionists." In Buchanan's view, "the editor of the *Celt* knows about as much of what are labor's rights as he does of the 'make up' of a newspaper."[71]

The position Buchanan counterposed to that of Denver's Irish elite was, logically enough, Patrick Ford's notion of the struggle between "producing classes" and "monopolists." Throughout 1833, excerpts from Ford's *Irish World* appeared *in every issue* of the *Enquirer,* and the paper was made available to Denver's working people in a reading room that Buchanan maintained in his editorial offices.[72] It was one thing to advance an ideology, however, and quite another to transmit it effectively. In this regard, the pages of the *Labor Enquirer* reveal an important dimension of the nineteenth-century labor press, a dimension that has received little notice from historians.

While using his editorial pages to attack the *Rocky Mountain Celt,* Buchanan simultaneously attempted to take over the necessary functions of the ethnic press. Thus the *Labor Enquirer* reported at length on the meetings, picnics, and social gatherings of organizations such as the Mitchel Guards and the Irish-American Progressive Society.[73] In September 1883, the *Enquirer* devoted a full column on page two to the marriage of a "well-known" Irish iron molder and his bride at the Stout Street Church.[74] Buchanan reported at equal length on the social and cultural activities of the German and Scandinavian communities in Denver. The *Enquirer*'s attack on the ethnic middle class, then, was not an attack on ethnicity per se. Rather, Buchanan sought to shift the center of gravity within these ethnic communities, to make the labor press and the labor movement a pole around which a series of ethnic cultural activities would revolve. It was this approach to the cultural world of Denver's immigrant workers that enabled Buchanan to transmit an ideology which in substance asserted the primacy of class over ethnicity.

By November 1883, Buchanan reported that subscriptions to the *Enquirer* were growing rapidly among Denver's Irish workers.[75] Buchanan was not alone in his struggle, however. The Irish-born Joseph Murray, a local labor leader of equal stature to Buchanan, was an even more important voice among Irish workers. "Plain and substantial in his language, as well as in his apparel and his life," Murray provided Buchanan with an indispensable ally.[76]

Murray had lived a life worlds apart from the lawyers, politicians, and businessmen who dominated Denver's Land League. Born in poverty near Dublin in 1843, he emigrated to Manchester with his family, where he worked in the mills and acquired the rudiments of an education in a night school. As a youth, Murray became active in the Irish nationalist movement in Manchester. But he also became a corresponding member of Garibaldi's Carbonari and in 1859 left the English mill city to fight with the Redshirts for Italian independence. He returned to Manchester in 1860 but in the following year enlisted in Thomas Francis Meagher's famous "Irish Brigade" of the Union Army to aid in the defeat of the southern "slave power." In 1869, after several years as a bookkeeper in New York, Murray moved to Colorado as a founding member of the Greeley agricultural colony. Although he remained a working farmer for the rest of his life, in the late 1870s he began to take an active part in Colorado's young labor movement. In 1878, Murray left the Republican party to stand for Congress on the Greenback ticket and in the same year helped found the first local assembly of the Knights of Labor in the state.[77]

Murray's life illuminates two important points. First, although his origins lay in the working class, his political career reveals a clear shift from middle-class republicanism to working-class radicalism, the turning point coming in his 1878 decision to leave the Republican Party. Second, there was also an important element of consistency in Murray's career. "A soldier of liberty on the battlefields of two continents," Murray was an internationalist throughout his life.[78] Although his internationalism was expressed through support for various national struggles, the very breadth of these struggles indicates Murray's commitment to a *global* vision of "human liberty."

An event at Denver's Tabor Opera House in the winter of 1883 illustrates both strands of Murray's political outlook and serves as a measure of his growing influence among the city's Irish-American workers. The house was packed for a speech by Thomas Brennan, an important figure in the Land League in Ireland, who was received with enthusiasm by the audience. At the conclusion of Brennan's speech, however, "a unanimous cry" went up for a response by Murray, who had been discovered in the dress circle. As the *Labor Enquirer* reported it, Murray disagreed with Brennan "that the struggle in Ireland is one of race," arguing instead that "it is a *class* war." As Murray saw it, "it was not only the poor of Ireland who were suffering from the tyranny of despotic and capitalist rule but that the poor of *all countries* were enslaved thereby; and that the cry would soon be—is now, in fact—for the equality of all mankind."[79]

The divisions of class and ideology that were beginning to undermine the ethnic unity of Denver's Irish-American community were revealed in the audience's response to these observations. Half of those present followed the example of the members of the Land League ("the specialistic liberators," Buchanan called them) in walking out of the hall. Those remaining, however, broke into loud and steady applause. The struggle Murray and Buchanan had been waging for the past year was beginning to show results.

The Knights of Labor

On 1 May 1884, less than five months after the Tabor Opera House incident, the entire work force of six hundred men at

Denver's Union Pacific shops put down their tools in response to a 10 percent wage cut. The Union Pacific management rescinded the wage cut three days later, and the shop workers organized a local assembly of the Knights of Labor that would stand at the heart of the Denver labor movement through the early 1890s. While precise statistics are unavailable, accounts indicate that Irish-Americans constituted a large proportion of the railroad's shop workers.[80]

"The producers here are awakening from their sleep and are organizing very fast," a Denver labor leader declared in the fall of 1884.[81] The Knights of Labor in the city grew particularly rapidly, leaping from two assemblies with a total of 180 members in 1883 to thirteen assemblies representing 2,447 members in 1885.[82] In 1888, Cornelius J. Driscoll, Deputy Commissioner of the new Colorado Bureau of Labor Statistics, put forth an explanation for this impressive growth. Denver's workers, he observed, "perceiving the benefits derived from organized efforts on the part of the Union Pacific employees, began to unite, and assemblies of the Knights of Labor sprang rapidly into existence."[83] Although statistics are again lacking, evidence points toward the widespread participation of Irish-American workers in the Knights. Indeed the Irish-American Driscoll had himself been active in the Order prior to his appointment as deputy labor commissioner.[84]

Changing economic conditions played an important role in the working-class "awakening" of 1884 and 1885. As business conditions deteriorated in these years, employers began to lay off workers and reduced wages substantially. These attacks on their living standards prompted first resistance and then organization among Denver's working people.

But that was not the whole story. While economic conditions can explain the existence of working-class militance, they cannot explain the form that militance took. This form was set by the example of the Union Pacific shop workers whose organization included both skilled and unskilled workers and embraced English, Irish, and native-born Americans.[85] Both the early craft unions and the ethnic fraternal societies had pointed in this direction by encouraging the growth of a sense of mutuality among the city's working people. But neither type of organization could lead directly to the broad working-class solidarity the Denver Knights would uphold during the middle years of the 1880s. It was rather the Denver Land League, and the struggle between the Land League and the nascent labor movement over the meaning of Irish radicalism, that prepared the way for the Knights.

Notes

1. See Robert Sean Wilentz, "Industrializing America and the Irish: Towards the New Departure," *Labor History* 20 (1979): 579–95.

2. David Montgomery, *Beyond Equality: Labor and the Radical Republicans, 1862–1872* (New York: Alfred A. Knopf, 1967), 126–34.

3. See Eric Foner, "Class, Ethnicity, and Radicalism in the Gilded Age: The Land League and Irish-America," in his *Politics and Ideology in the Age of the Civil War* (Oxford and New York: Oxford University Press, 1980), 150–200.

4. David Brundage, "The Making of Working-Class Radicalism in the Mountain West: Denver, Colorado, 1880–1903" (Ph.D. diss., University of California, Los Angeles, 1982), pp. 14–43.

5. Colorado, Bureau of Labor Statistics, *First Biennial Report of the Colorado Bureau of Labor Statistics, 1887–1888* (Denver: Collier & Cleaveland, 1888), 86–87, 102–5; Jonathan Ezra Garlock, "A Structural Analysis of the Knights of Labor: A Prolegomenon to the History of the Producing Classes" (Ph.D. diss., University of Rochester, 1974), p. 255.

6. *Rocky Mountain News*, Denver, Colorado, 13 November 1882; and, also in Denver, *Labor Enquirer*, 16 December 1882.

7. See David Montgomery, *Workers' Control in America: Studies in the History of Work, Technology, and Labor Struggles* (New York and London: Cambridge University Press, 1979), 9–31.

8. Joseph R. Buchanan, *The Story of a Labor Agitator* (New York: Outlook Co., 1903), 41.

9. *Iron Molders' Journal*, August 1887, p. 2.

10. Colorado, Bureau of Labor Statistics, *First Biennial Report, 1887–1888*, p. 89.

11. Buchanan, *Labor Agitator*, p. 41; Montgomery, *Workers' Control*, pp. 15–18. On apprenticeship rules and the restriction of foremen's rights among printers, see minutes of Denver Typographical Union, No. 49, 7 July 1884, 11 March 1885, Denver Typographical Union Records, Norlin Library, University of Colorado, Boulder.

12. Buchanan, *Labor Agitator*, pp. 42–43.

13. Minutes of Denver Typographical Union, 7 July 1884.

14. Quoted in ibid. See also Colorado, Bureau of Labor Statistics, *First Biennial Report, 1887–1888*, pp. 90–91; and on the boycott generally, Michael A. Gordon, "The Labor Boycott in New York City, 1880–1886," *Labor History* 16 (1975): 184–229.

15. Colorado, Bureau of Labor Statistics, *First Biennial Report, 1887–1888*, pp. 73–74, 76–77.

16. Ibid., pp. 70–71.

17. Stephen J. Leonard, "Denver's Foreign Born Immigrants, 1859–1900," Ph.D. diss., Claremont Graduate School, 1971, pp. 150–51.

18. *Journal of United Labor*, 15 May and 15 July 1881, 15 May 1882, November 1882 and August 1883.

19. Minutes of Denver Typographical Union, 3 November 1869; Eugene H. Berwanger, "Reconstruction on the Frontier: The Equal Rights Struggle in Colorado, 1865–1867," *Pacific Historical Review* 44 (1975): 313–29.

20. Philip S. Foner, *Organized Labor and the Black Worker, 1619–1973* (New York and Washington: Praeger Publishers, 1974), 43–44; Berwanger, "Reconstruction on the Frontier," pp. 325–26, 328.

21. Philip S. Foner, *Women and the American Labor Movement: From Colonial Times to the Eve of World War I* (New York and London: Macmillan, 1979), 148–50; Minutes of Denver Typographical Union, 4 October 1885.

22. *Iron Molders' Journal*, March 1885, p. 8.

23. Colorado, Bureau of Labor Statistics, *First Biennial Report, 1887–1888*, pp. 88–89.

24. *Union Pacific Employees' Magazine*, May 1886, p. 106. For other references to engineers and firemen as "labor aristocrats," see ibid., January 1886, p. 21, and June 1886, p. 130.

25. *Rocky Mountain News,* 13 November 1882 (my emphasis).

26. *Journal of United Labor,* 15 May 1881, 15 May 1882, November 1882, and December 1882; *Corbett and Ballenger's Denver City Directory* (Denver: Corbett and Ballenger, 1881, 1882).

27. *Union Pacific Employees' Magazine,* January 1886, p. 1.

28. Leonard, "The Irish, English, and Germans in Denver, 1860–1890," *Colorado Magazine* 54 (1977): 131–32.

29. See David Brundage, "The Producing Classes and the Saloon: Denver in the 1880s," *Labor History* 26 (1985): 29–52.

30. Robert M. Tank, "Mobility and Occupational Structure on the Late Nineteenth Century Urban Frontier: The Case of Denver, Colorado," *Pacific Historical Review* 47 (1978): 210–14; see also Stephan Thernstrom and Peter R. Knights, "Men and Motion: Some Data and Speculations about Urban Population Mobility in Nineteenth-Century America," in *Anonymous Americans: Explorations in Nineteenth-Century Social History,* ed. Tamara K. Hareven (Englewood Cliffs, N.J.: Prentice-Hall, 1971), 210–14.

31. Carl Abbott, "Boom State and Boom City: Stages in Denver's Growth," *Colorado Magazine* 50 (1973): 219; Daniel Doeppers, "The Globeville Neighborhood in Denver," *Geographical Review* 57 (1967): 506–11.

32. Leonard, "Irish, English, and Germans," p. 151. For a study of the comparable situation in Omaha, see Howard P. Chudacoff, "A New Look at Ethnic Neighborhoods: Residential Dispersion and the Concept of Visibility in a Medium-Sized City," *Journal of American History* 60 (1973): 76–93.

33. Quoted in Leonard, "Denver's Foreign Born," p. 151.

34. See ibid., pp. 117–46.

35. For a recent example, see Clyde Griffen, "Workers Divided: The Effect of Craft and Ethnic Differences in Poughkeepsie, New York, 1850–1880," in *Nineteenth-Century Cities: Essays in the New Urban History,* ed. Stephan Thernstrom and Richard Sennett (New Haven, Conn.: Yale University Press, 1969), 49–93.

36. Leonard, "Irish, English, and Germans," pp. 150–51.

37. *Report of a Lecture by a Dynamite Fiend and How it Strikes the Average American Citizen* (Denver: Times Print, 1884), 11–13, provides evidence on the close relationship between Scottish and Welsh social clubs and the virulently anti-Catholic organization, the Patriotic Order of the Sons of America.

38. James Edward Wright, *The Politics of Populism: Dissent in Colorado* (New Haven and London: Yale University Press, 1974), 80–83; Paul Kleppner, *The Cross of Culture: A Social Analysis of Midwestern Politics, 1850–1900* (New York: Free Press, 1970).

39. *Colorado Antelope,* Denver, December 1879 and January 1880.

40. Eric Foner, "Class, Ethnicity, and Radicalism," p. 151.

41. Ibid., pp. 154–155.

42. Ibid., p. 156; Michael Davitt, *The Fall of Feudalism in Ireland or the Story of the Land League Revolution* (London and New York: Harper and Brothers Publishers, 1904), 252.

43. *Rocky Mountain News,* 9 June 1882.

44. Leonard, "Denver's Foreign Born," pp. 143–45, 163.

45. F. Sheehy-Skeffington, *Michael Davitt: Revolutionary, Agitator and Labor Leader* (London and Leipsig: T. Fisher Unwin, 1908), 114–16. See also Hasia R. Diner, *Erin's Daughters in America: Irish Immigrant Women in the Nineteenth Century* (Baltimore, Md.: Johns Hopkins University Press, 1983).

46. *Rocky Mountain News,* 1 April and 4 December 1881.

47. Leonard, "Irish, English, and Germans," pp. 143–44.

48. *Rocky Mountain News,* 12 June 1882.

49. *Labor Enquirer,* 11 August 1883, quoting Henry George. See also Susan Levine, "Labor's True Woman: Domesticity and Equal Rights in the Knights of Labor," *Journal of American History* 70 (1983): 323–39.

50. *Labor Enquirer,* 1 September 1883; Herbert G. Gutman, "Protestantism and

the American Labor Movement: The Christian Spirit in the Gilded Age," in his *Work, Culture, and Society in Industrializing America* (New York: Random House, 1976), 89.

51. Quoted in Henry J. Browne, *The Catholic Church and the Knights of Labor* (Washington, D.C.: Catholic University of America Press, 1949), 232–33.

52. Quoted in ibid., p. 276.

53. Quoted in Thomas N. Brown, *Irish-American Nationalism, 1870–1890* (Philadelphia: J.B. Lippincott, 1966), 108.

54. Eric Foner, "Class, Ethnicity, and Radicalism," pp. 158–60, 168–79.

55. Calculated from U.S., Department of the Interior, Census Office, *Eleventh Census of the United States, 1890,* vol. 1, pt. 2 (Washington, D.C.: Government Printing Office, 1897), 660–61; for categories, see Brundage, "Working-Class Radicalism," pp. 267–69.

56. *Rocky Mountain News,* 1881–1883, selected issues; *Denver City Directory,* 1881, 1882, 1883.

57. *Rocky Mountain News,* 9 June 1882.

58. Ibid., 19 February 1883; Leonard, "Denver's Foreign Born," p. 154.

59. C. W. Hurd, "J. K. Mullen, Milling Magnate of Colorado," *Colorado Magazine* 29 (1952): 104–18.

60. *Labor Enquirer,* 24 March 1883.

61. Leonard, "Denver's Foreign Born," pp. 121, 142, 168; Wright, *Politics of Populism,* p. 24.

62. William O'Brien and Desmond Ryan, eds., *Devoy's Post Bag, 1871–1928,* 2 vols. (Dublin: C. J. Fallon, 1953), 2:233–35.

63. *Labor Enquirer,* 1 September 1883.

64. Quoted in Leonard, "Denver's Foreign Born," p. 164.

65. Quoted in ibid., p. 165.

66. *Labor Enquirer,* 16 December 1883.

67. Ibid., 3 November 1883; Gary M. Fink, ed., *Biographical Dictionary of American Labor Leaders* (Westport, Conn.: Greenwood Press, 1974), 42–43.

68. *Report of a Lecture by a Dynamite Fiend,* p. 3.

69. *Labor Enquirer,* 4 August 1883.

70. Ibid., 1 September 1883.

71. Ibid., 24 March 1883.

72. Ibid., 1883.

73. Ibid., 23 December 1882, 4 August 1883, and 1883–1884, passim.

74. Ibid., 8 September 1883.

75. Ibid., 3 November 1883.

76. Ibid., 15 December 1883.

77. James MacCarthey, *Political Portraits by Fitz-Mac* (Colorado Springs: Gazette Printing Co., 1888), 201–6; Leah M. Bird, "The History of Third Parties in Colorado," M.A. thesis, University of Denver, 1942, p. 30; *Journal of United Labor,* 15 July 1881.

78. MacCarthey, *Political Portraits,* p. 201.

79. *Labor Enquirer,* 15 December 1883 (my emphasis).

80. Buchanan, *Labor Agitator,* pp. 70–100; Leonard, "Denver's Foreign Born," p. 148.

81. John B. Lennon to *John Swinton's Paper,* 14 September 1884.

82. Garlock, "Knights of Labor," p. 255.

83. Colorado, Bureau of Labor Statistics, *First Biennial Report, 1887–1888,* p. 80.

84. Leonard, "Denver's Foreign Born," pp. 150, 160.

85. Buchanan, *Labor Agitator,* pp. 70–78; see also Shelton Stromquist, "Enginemen and Shopmen: Technological Change and the Organization of Labor in an Era of Railroad Expansion," *Labor History* 24 (1983): 485–99.

Old World Radicalism in Transition

HARTMUT KEIL

German Working-Class Radicalism in the United States from the 1870s to World War I

The Civil War marked a decisive turning point both for the American labor movement and German-American radicalism. "It was of great advantage," wrote Friedrich Sorge in his history of the American labor movement, "that the slavery issue had been solved and the ground prepared for the labor question. The . . . 'irrepressible conflict' between bound labor and free labor was fought out and its place was taken by the 'irrepressible conflict' between labor and capital."[1] The forces of industrial progress now became fully unleashed as capitalism was about to conquer the South as well as to expand in unprecedented ways. The competition for material rewards and the seemingly total disregard for social and cultural values were appropriately branded by Mark Twain with the metaphorical phrase the Gilded Age. Resumed immigration after the end of the Civil War contributed over and above proportion to the increasing working-class population, as it had even before the war; the largest immigrant group until the beginning of the depression of the 1890s continued to be the Germans.

Because the capitalist system required ever larger capital stock for the establishment and expansion of enterprises, the rampant economic individualism of this period was increasingly channeled into horizontal and vertical business concentration as represented by mergers, monopolies, and corporations. To answer the growing challenge of entrepreneurial expansion and consolidation, the trade union movement stepped beyond local and regional boundaries to organize on a national scale. The eight-hour agitation took on the dimensions of a mass movement; it demonstrated the organizing potential of the working class, protesting the inequities and injustices of the capitalist system of production while yet groping for adequate ways of making its demands heard and accepted. Although the depression years of the 1870s decimated the labor unions, the lessons that labor had learned were not lost.[2]

The ideological openness that characterized the American labor movement of the 1860s established a general climate of receptiveness to new ideas, including those introduced by German immigrants. What is the yardstick to be applied when evaluating their successes and failures? By and large, the prevalent emphasis of conservative and radical critics alike has been on organizational success. This institutional perspective has primarily been applied to evaluating the impact of German immigrant radicals in political (socialist) movements, whereas the economic (trade union) movement has been passed over rather lightly. It has tended to reinforce the traditional view of the sectarian and foreign character of the socialist movement in the United States by equating that movement with the political party only.[3]

The impact of the radical tradition brought over by immigrant workers and intellectuals from Germany and tested in, as well as adapted to, a characteristic American environment extends well beyond such limited institutional activities, however. German-American members of the Socialist Labor Party (SLP) readily conceded that many convinced socialists remained outside the party.[4] Since the impact of German socialists was significant, despite the limited range of the SLP, it is necessary to widen the scope of inquiry.

Most important of all, the social composition of German lower-class immigrants has to be reassessed. Since the German mass immigration extended over a period of roughly fifty years, beginning in the late 1830s and continuing until the depression of the 1890s, immigrants of similar ethnic background brought with them varying social, political, cultural, and work experiences.[5] They entered the United States at different stages of the nation's industrialization and settled in areas differently affected by the Industrial Revolution. Throughout the formative period of German social democracy, from the mid-1860s until its suppression by law in 1878, many German workers and intellectuals active in the movement emigrated to the United States, propagating such political principles as were being discussed at the time of their departure. And German socialism at this time was no homogeneous movement, not even after the Gotha congress in 1875 united the Lassalleans and Marxists.[6] Socialist immigrants in the German-American labor movement had to reckon with the many German immigrant workers who had emigrated from agrarian regions and who had not yet been exposed to the labor movement. Their efforts at reaching these masses of inexperienced workers were similar to the organizational tasks of socialists back home. Ties between the emerging socialist movements of the two countries continued to be close.[7] The German radical culture trying to gain a foothold in

America had many faces, and it was reflected in a diversity of traditions and groups, such as freethinkers and radical republicans, communitarians and land reformers, Lassallean and Marxist socialists, social democrats and anarchists.[8] The result of the extended migration was a multiplicity of class and cultural experiences that defies easy categorization.

How did these various groups fare in the American context? This question raises the issue of their ability to adapt their strategies, if not their goals, to American conditions. This was not simply an institutional and ideological problem; it had far-reaching social and cultural ramifications. The development and integration of a radical movement depended upon the people supporting it, upon their social and cultural position in American society. Was German-American labor radicalism grounded in an artisan community threatened by mechanization or in an industrial proletariat matured under the new system of mass production? At what periods were German immigrant workers in the center of production, and when was their position eroded? What was the numerical impact of German workers in certain cities, industries, and occupations at specific periods? Was there a generational succession of occupations from the immigrant to the second generation? What changes did these relationships undergo, and how did the gradual erosion of the ethnic heritage affect the visibility of German-American workers as well as the degree of their involvement in the American labor movement? On the basis of previous research on these questions[9] and in the context of institutions and issues of German-American radicalism in the last third of the nineteenth century, this essay will confine itself to pointing out continuities of development toward a multiethnic American labor movement—continuities that have been lost sight of among the diversity of movements and ideologies.

The Impact of the German-American Working Class

Mass immigration from Germany, which had ebbed in the depression of the late 1850s and come to a halt during the Civil War years, resumed on the prewar scale in the second half of the 1860s and continued at high levels until the end of the century, curtailed only by the depression years of the 1870s and 1890s. Worsening economic and political conditions at home, at the end of the 1870s and the beginning of the 1880s, increased the volume of emigration to an all-time record. The emigration areas had by this time decisively shifted from the regions of Southwest and Central Germany to the agrarian Prussian provinces east of the river Elbe, indicating the social shocks and population displacements triggered by the Industrial Revolution in Germany.[10]

While immigrants continued to be recruited from the laboring classes, this regional change also meant a decisive shift in social composition. Craftsmen and independent artisans still made up a goodly portion of those leaving their villages and small towns, but now unskilled farm laborers were a substantial proportion of those emigrants who became industrial workers. They were joined by many skilled workers who had migrated from the countryside to Germany's rising industrial towns before they crossed the Atlantic, often forced into this decision by depressed conditions in certain trades, like the textile, tobacco, or furniture industries.[11]

As a result, throughout the second half of the nineteenth century, the German population, in comparison to native-born Americans, was greatly overrepresented in urban areas. As early as 1870 and 1880, 39.3 percent of all German immigrants lived in the fifty principal cities of the United States.[12] Since the census included only towns with a population of over 35,000, a large proportion of the urban German population is excluded from this calculation. Herbert Gutman's findings that the proportion of foreign-born, even in smaller industrial towns, was continuously high,[13] reinforce the impression that the proportion of the urban German immigrant population was much higher.

An examination of the occupational distribution of German immigrants in 1880 and 1890 (first generation) shows that the relative number of German immigrants employed in agriculture had already declined by more than two percentage points in the 1880s to 27.5 percent in 1890; trade and transportation had increased by 1.1 percent to 13.9. The manufacturing and mechanical industries had decreased slightly (from 35.2 to 34.2 percent) but remained by far the largest sector. This category would be even larger if those listed as unskilled laborers (10.3 percent in 1890) could be properly assigned to industries. German-American industrial workers were the most substantial class of the German immigrant population throughout the second half of the nineteenth century, with 40 to 45 percent of all gainfully employed. This holds true even if American-born children of German immigrants are included: more second-generation than first-generation Germans were listed in manufacturing (36.5 as against 34.2 percent), while the percentage of unskilled laborers had dropped dramatically to 5.8 percent. The most significant developments with respect to the second generation were the simultaneous decline of agricultural pursuits and the sharp rise of the trade and transportation sector (20.0 percent in 1890) which includes clerks, salesmen, saleswomen, and other white-collar occupations. Since German immigrants were not evenly distributed among all the regions and in all the cities of the country but were concentrated in mid-Atlantic and midwestern states and cities, the German-American working class had a much greater impact regionally and locally than the figures for the United States as a whole suggest. Thus, at the turn of the century, two-thirds of all German households in Chicago were working-class households.[14] It was in such urban industrial centers that German immigrant radicalism secured its strongest foothold.

In spite of the increasing number of farm laborers among German immigrants, the backbone of German-American radicalism was still made up of skilled workers, and among these certain trades which had been central to the German labor movement also predominated in the United States. Thus the printing and the building trades, as well as the furniture workers, groups who had been among the first to organize in the 1850s, led the renewed efforts at organization after the Civil War, while other trades like the cigarmakers, tailors, bakers, butchers, and metalworkers joined them in the late 1860s and 1870s. In the United States, just as in Germany, the artisan tradition was still the indispensable basis of organization as late as the 1880s, although mass production and the reorganization of industries had already been initiated, even if unequally, depending upon the branch of industry affected.[15] However, the majority of skilled workers still worked in small and medium-sized shops, where the tradition of craft organization could be best transferred and applied. It was here that unions had their strongest support. On the other hand, the increasing competition between traditional artisan shops and modern large-scale production units forced skilled workers to accept lower wages and worse working conditions or displacement to lower-grade jobs in the larger industrial plants. The combination of depression and degradation of work fostered social unrest and receptiveness to the radical criticism of capitalist society, especially among the privileged class of craft-conscious workers proud of their skills and fighting to retain control of the production process.[16] But this unrest also spread to those new industrial workers whose ranks had been swollen by displaced skilled workers from Germany. Industrial reorganization and increasing mechanization and technological innovation during the Gilded Age thus coincided with the influx of a diverse immigrant labor force flooding the urban-industrial centers of the United States, often clinging to outdated hopes of rising to the rank of independent businessman or small entrepreneur that was no longer attainable in their country of origin. Economic and social displacement, resulting in frustrated illusions, thus served as an indigenous breeding ground for a working-class radicalism stimulated by the European socialist tradition.[17]

Organizational Multiplicity and Succession

The development of German-American working-class organizations involved a more complicated process of overcoming social and ideological differentiations than was the case in Germany. In the United States, on top of existing ideological cleavages within the German radicals' own ranks, a wide spectrum of offers by American organizations supplemented the options available. National and cultural characteristics further added to this diversity. At the same time, pressure to conform was great in a society boastful of its openness to all political creeds while in fact demanding unequivocal acceptance of its political and social system, and quick at branding nonconformist views as alien and un-American.[18] In this climate, it was not only necessary for German workers' organizations to head off repeated attacks from established quarters but also to convince their followers that belonging to such organizations was not a contradiction to integration into and acceptance by American society. It is evident that it was easier under such conditions to join unions, whose activities could be justified under the existing economic system, than to affiliate with a socialist party which openly propagated its abolishment.

Freedom of association not only meant the coexistence of the political and economic labor movement but in fact led to the predominance of the latter—a situation quite unfamiliar to those German socialists coming out of the Lassallean tradition. On the other hand, the unequal economic development of different regions of the United States, the frontier and large, unsettled, or thinly populated areas also provided the social base for agrarian and land reform solutions to social problems, so that the backward-oriented republican ideal of small independent producers could easily be reconciled with Lassallean versions of the good society and amalgamated with European guild traditions and artisanal aspirations.[19]

As a consequence, no single tradition, no ready-made formula existed to furnish organizational unity to German workers' organizations in the United States. Into this vacuum, Marxist socialists, especially through the activities of the International Workingmen's Association (IWA) introduced what was to serve as both a guideline to action and a test for radical working-class goals: the conviction that the emancipation of the working class could only be accomplished by the workers themselves.[20] This tenet implied the strategy of reaching America's working masses by identifying with immediate and practical problems while gradually educating them to become a class conscious of its condition and potential. Throughout the remainder of the nineteenth century, this proved for all practical purposes to be the only viable access to America's multi-ethnic working class. However, this is not to say that the ultimate goal was accomplished; rather, the course of events proved that it was as difficult to develop the labor movement beyond the bread-and-butter British-style unionism under the entrenched leadership of Samuel Gompers, P. J. McGuire, and Adolph Strasser as it was to free the labor movement from middle-class reform and co-optation.

If future strategies were therefore to be guided by unshakeable principles, the daily routine of implementing them proved to be a recurrent practical problem so that no permanent solution to the issue of how best to straddle the fine line between compromise and purity was found. German radicals were faced with a recurrent dilemma: In order to reach out beyond their limited circle, they needed to join and work through existing labor organizations as well as found new ones themselves. This procedure was justified only if sufficient influence could be gained to eventually ensure the priorities of working-class objectives. But what if these organizations proved too resistant? What were German radicals to do if their goals were watered down beyond recognition into an acquiescence approaching a loss of political identity?

An answer to such questions evolved gradually in the course of the 1870s and 1880s in connection with a number of test cases involving issues such as money and land, middle-class reform measures, the eight-hour day, and the appropriate structure for a labor organization. Marxian socialists within the International in New York City (led by Section 1) made great—and often successful—efforts to cooperate with labor bodies like the National Labor Union and the Workingmen's Assembly of New York, and with New England labor leaders, as long as such organizations pursued workers' issues. The eight-hour movement was therefore strongly supported by the IWA, as was the fight for the unemployed when the depression hit in 1873.[21] But these same Marxian socialists relentlessly opposed Section 12 in the North American Federation of the IWA once they became convinced that its American middle-class reformers and intellectuals set priorities unreconcilable with the objectives of the International, which "is and ought to be a *Workingmen's* organization."[22] The New York Central Committee defended its position in a letter to the London General Council, writing in no uncertain terms: "We want to keep it [the IWA] pure and unpolluted for the future affiliation of the organized Trades-Unions, who will never connect with organizations tainted by adventurous ideas and actions."[23] And it adopted a resolution whereby two-thirds of a section's members had to be wage earners.

Greenbackism was another issue that led to serious differences within the Socialist Labor Party, the successor to the IWA, finally splitting the movement into two opposing factions for years to come. One faction within the SLP, anxious to free itself of the taint of ethnic isolation of an organization overwhelmingly made up of German immigrants, wished to jump on the bandwagon of the Greenback Party. In the opinion of this faction, the Greenback Party was an indigenous movement apparently uniting farmers and workers and showing sympathy to socialist objectives. It would be only a matter of time until these would be fully accepted. Thus, socialism would finally relate to a mass base, the lack of which had been so painfully felt.[24] The faction vehemently opposing such a move had its stronghold in Chicago, and it had learned from experience. Having successfully engaged in local and state elections for some years, the Chicago socialists had faced corruption and fraud at the polls, defections and betrayals by labor politicians selling out to the old parties, and violence and suppression exerted by the police and the courts as the faithful guardians of the established order. The lesson to be learned from these experiences was twofold: not to coalesce with a reform party throwing out some bait to the workers simply to gain additional votes and not to participate in elections at all, since these tended to detract from solid working-class organization and issues.[25]

Developments in the 1880s forced the Chicago anarchists and the New York socialists to reconsider their positions. After the Haymarket tragedy in May 1886, all the feuding Chicago labor factions, including the anarchists, joined the United Labor Party in an attempt to defeat business at the polls, and the German socialists of New York, despite basic reservations about his program, plunged into a vigorous campaign for Henry George. The *New Yorker Volkszeitung* supported his nomination, although his social and political views were not totally compatible with socialism. However, "he has done inestimable good for the social enlightenment of the Anglo-Saxon people, and he is the representative of what this people aspires to at the present time."[26] Since the United Labor Party (ULP) was "going in the right direction," Alexander Jonas explained in another editorial, it would be "foolish and presumptuous" to stay aloof. Instead, socialists should seek to assume leadership in the ULP as far as possible.[27] Another veteran German socialist offered the opinion that Henry George was called upon to further the movement "not *because*, but *in spite of*, his theory."[28] As relations between the socialists and party leaders deteriorated in the spring of 1887, finally leading to the split at the Syracuse Convention of the ULP in August 1887, comments on George's political position became more outspoken and critical, while the line between cooperation and basic socialist principles was again more clearly defined. In its article "The Position of the Socialists toward Labor Politics," the leading German-language socialist paper in the country declared that socialists did not want to participate in an independent labor ticket in each and every election. The issue was a tactical one and had to be decided on the basis of the specific conditions prevailing at a certain point in time.[29] Another editorial half a year later pursued the same line of argument, pointing out that socialists had to participate in any mass labor movement, even if they did not yet follow socialist principles. Socialists were to be its most progressive element, "the pushing and purifying factor." However, there were also situations when a genuine labor party did not exist, when boodlerism, corruption, and minor issues dominated instead. Abstention in such cases was not equal to peevishness, however, but had to be accompanied by redoubled and relentless criticism.[30]

Thus, socialists in the 1870s and 1880s, including the SLP, which has often been branded as sectarian,[31] were far from dogmatic with respect to appropriate tactics and strategies. Their primary concern was to clarify the so-called typically American conditions that an evolving labor movement had to reckon with and determine which tactics had to be adopted accordingly. German-American socialists at the end of the 1880s, looking back on a history of more than twenty years of organizational activity, had come to the conclusion that experience was "the mightiest and ultimate teacher" and that socialists, too, had "to appeal to it under any circumstance and on any issue."[32] Above all, experience taught that a socialist movement in the United States depended for its success on a vital trade union movement.

Trade Unionism and the Flowering of the German-American Labor Movement in the 1880s

German socialists had no easy solution concerning their relationship to trade unionism in the United States. On the one hand, they had participated in the discussions on the same issue in Germany and knew the theoretical problems involved. But conditions in America obviously required a different approach. From the perspective of radicals concerned above all with revolutionary goals, the disquieting fact was, however, that this discussion lagged behind the actual degree and direction of organization among German immigrant workers. Whereas Marxian socialists in the IWA had unwaveringly supported the trade unions as the necessary basis of the American labor movement, they met with opposition from several quarters, foremost from Lassalleans and American socialists who wanted to take advantage of the free access to the ballot as offered by the American political system. However, slighting the growth of the trade unions among German immigrant workers would have meant isolating the radical movement from the very membership base on whose support it was primarily dependent. Radicals who understood the importance of trade unionism and who acted accordingly, were able to exert considerable leadership in the unions. Hermann Schlüter, a leading figure in the German-American labor movement well beyond the turn of the century, was not exaggerating when he pointed out that members of the First International had done inestimable service in organizing German workers into unions.[33] When, however, political socialists refused to deal with organizations not up to their own theoretical level, they kept trying in vain to catch up with the development of a working class whose primary concern was, of course, its own economic condition.

The views of two labor leaders among Chicago German workers may serve as appropriate examples of the developing attitude toward trade unions. In the case of Conrad Conzett, owner and editor of the *Vorbote* and the *Chicagoer Arbeiter-Zeitung* in the 1870s, the American experience was apparently decisive for his change of position.[34] Conzett, a printer from Switzerland, had first learned of the IWA while working in Leipzig in 1867. Having emigrated to the United States in 1869, he helped found the German typographer's union in Chicago in 1873.[35] His first editorials in the *Vorbote* supported participation in elections of the newly founded Labor Party of Illinois.[36] But the lack of electoral success and fraud at the polls soon made him set other priorities. Trade unionism became the issue most thoroughly discussed in the pages of the *Vorbote.* In a polemic against Gustav Lyser, the editor of the *Milwaukee'r Socialist,* Conzett expanded on his views. To Lyser's charge that "in America where more political freedoms are guaranteed it is nonsense to found several thousand trade unions beside the socialist workers party,"[37] he replied that his experience revealed the exclusively political movement to be impracticable in the United States. In Germany, there were numerous examples of trade unions under the strong influence of socialists, like the cigarmakers' union, the bricklayers' and stonemasons' union, and the furniture makers' union. In the United States, too, German trade unions were instrumental in founding socialist papers—for example, in New York, where the *Arbeiter-Union* was published by the German trade unions, and in Chicago, where the *Vorbote* was mainly supported by German unions. It was such "conservative" unions as the Chicago Typographical Union No. 9 that elected socialists like himself as delegates to the national union convention. Even if the trade unions were still apolitical self-interest groups, it was easier to work through them and educate their members than to deal with an "unorganized mass" of workers. Unions had a clear edge over reaching workers, since they touched their immediate, practical interests:

> Workers can be more easily organized in unions, which . . . offer immediate material advantages. . . . If we help unions in their material and ideal goals, they will help us in our ideal and political aims. Unions will soon be forced by conditions to centralize, to unite nationally and internationally, and to enter the political arena beside the economic fight in order to get laws passed that are indispensable for the working class. The fight for wages, etc., without the fight in the political field is foolish, as would be the exclusively political struggle.[38]

Not to organize workers into unions would mean to leave them at the mercy of capitalists who would exploit them even more and cause them even greater misery. Such a lumpenproletariat would not be amenable to socialist propaganda at all. Citing Friedrich Albert Lange's well-known tract on the "labor question," Conzett pointed out that even the English trade unions were favorably mentioned as the "preschools of cooperative labor."[39] Socialists had the duty, however, to educate and enlighten unions, for this was the only way to reach the masses and lead them to support socialist principles and the socialist political party. It is worth pointing out again that Conzett, even while still advocating participation in elections, was an active member of his union.[40] For him, both kinds of organization and activity were closely interrelated, and his changing position reflected above all a clearer understanding of the tactics necessary in an atmosphere so favorable to union growth.

The *Vorbote* staff could enlist a well-known political refugee from Germany early in 1878, when Paul Grottkau, who had escaped arrest in Berlin, settled in Chicago.[41] Although well aware that he was a greenhorn, he nevertheless continued his activities in the labor movement exactly where he had been forced to leave off in Germany, i.e., as an agitator for the trade unions and as an editor of a labor paper. Grottkau had belonged to the Lassallean wing of the German labor movement, but contrary to the prevalent notions of the antagonism of Lassalleans to the unions, his views fit in exactly with Conzett's. This was no coincidence, since Grottkau had been one of the foremost union organizers and supporters in Berlin, despite his Lassallean leanings. He was therefore well prepared for a situation in which trade unionism (in his opinion) seemed to be the right and only practicable form of organization in the United States, where political rights had already been granted and political equality secured. Instead, the extension and enforcement of property rights were at issue in this country, and therefore the political fight was inseparably connected with the economic struggle. Since Grottkau held the economic dependence of the working class to be much greater in America than in Europe, he concluded: "Political freedom in the face of economic dependence and servitude does not make sense. Political action of the workers without a strong organization and without real means of power in this country is equal to fighting windmills."[42] Throwing overboard Lassallean traditions as he had already done in Germany, Grottkau felt even more justified in this shift when he confronted American conditions. His was a conclusion that German radicals found inescapable, unless they wished to remain isolated from the mainstream of the American labor movement.

They were also agreed that while English trade unions were a point of departure, they should by no means be uncritically emulated but instead developed into strong class organizations also furthering the eventual transformation of society. As the trade unions gained strength during the 1880s, concern was voiced repeatedly in the German-American labor press that such ultimate goals should not be forgotten in the face of the immediate task of organization. When tendencies toward bureaucratization and hierarchization became stronger, unions with a sizable radical membership grew more restless over the slow progress of political awareness or the total disregard of professed goals. How much longer should principles be sacrificed on the altar of expediency, and what were the utmost limits of compromise?

German-American socialists were agreed that they should not stay aloof from existing trade unions but instead use them as an instrument of education and agitation. Therefore, socialists were urged to join the unions of their respective trades and work to win others over to their side. It was "the duty of socialists to retain friendly contact to the unions and, wherever possible, to participate in labor conventions."[43] Whereas trade unions formerly did not want to associate with the SLP at all for fear of being denounced as socialists and communists, wrote the *New Yorker Volkszeitung,* relationships had much improved since members of the SLP had themselves founded "many and numerous" unions.[44] The SLP National Executive Committee, in its report for the year 1880, proudly stated that "in almost all towns unions are headed by socialists."[45]

It was especially in the trades dominated by, or containing a high percentage of, German workers that this claim was accurate. Unions founded by members of the International in the late 1860s and before the depression in the early 1870s, like the Cigar Makers Union, the Furniture Workers Union, and the German-American Typographical Union, were able to survive the lean years because they had been placed on solid organizational grounds. Other trades, although not retaining their union form of organization, were able to weather the storm through mutual benefit societies. While the Cigar Makers Union is the best known example of a union introducing benefit features to attract workers, thus consolidating the membership and the organization, other German unions led by socialists undertook similar efforts at the same time. The Typographical Union and the Furniture Workers both established unemployment, sickness, life insurance, and strike funds. In order to provide for the specific needs of their trades, the furniture workers also supplied tool insurance, whereas the typographers paid advance travel money to itinerant members. Like the Cigar Makers Union, the other two unions succeeded in founding their own papers, the typographers in 1873, the furniture workers ten years later.[46]

Other trades organizing into unions at the end of the depression in the late 1870s learned from such experiences. Unions themselves were urged to make thorough investigations into the condition of their respective trades and to collect statistics on which to found their demands and strategy. They were, as well, to ask for sufficient dues to tie together self-interest and solidarity as the best guarantee of organizational permanence. The *New Yorker Volkszeitung* summed up the pertinent arguments when it editorialized that organization as such did not matter so much as a specific kind of organization. Unions asking for low membership dues could not be successful:

> The peaceful and legal fight of unions against usurpations by entrepreneurs is solely a power issue. Workers with empty pockets and empty stomachs, however, are no force in this fight. Unless their unions can adequately support them, the verdict is spoken in advance—that is docile

submission to the dictate of the entrepreneurs, and work for starvation wages. . . . But it is even more important that the workers are not deprived of their gains in bad times. . . . Let us therefore pay high dues![47]

Unions had a task distinct from that of a socialist party. They must not be misused as political instruments but serve as class organizations, including workers irrespective of their political beliefs. Socialists were to voice their convictions as union members inside their trade unions and thereby help speed the gradual development of the unions into progressive bodies.[48]

Thus the support of the material base of trade unionism was coupled in a matter-of-course way with larger social and political aims in the case of German-American unions, where socialists exerted a strong influence, or with the expectation of the visible development of other unions in the right direction. German radical workers became increasingly restless as such high hopes failed to materialize. Complaints about an exclusive craft orientation and political apathy, especially of English-speaking workers and their unions, grew louder toward the end of the 1880s. Whereas German socialists had participated in, and hailed the founding of, the American Federation of Labor as "the mightiest and most intelligent federation of workers,"[49] they became more and more critical of its hostility to socialist principles. In 1889, the *New Yorker Volkszeitung* pointed toward the "pitch-black darkness" that characterized most affiliated unions[50] but kept defending AFL's strategy of first attracting as many members as possible. But one year later, it openly attacked Gompers for slighting socialist trade union principles; however, since the convention had for the first time openly debated the issue of socialism, this in itself was believed to be a success.[51]

On the local level, German radical workers were not so diplomatic and patient as such editorials urged them to be. From the late 1870s until the end of the century, German unions repeatedly left local federated bodies to form their separate unions or federations because they no longer wanted to suffer what they judged to be the corrupt influence of politicians and leaders deviating from the path of true labor concerns. Chicago's German unions founded a Central Labor Union in 1884, and in New York delegates of thirty-two organizations left the central body early in 1889, dissatisfied with the disregard of its progressive principles by a conservative majority.[52] Support of the Socialist Trade & Labor Alliance by German unions at the end of the 1890s can be explained in similar terms.[53] Defections of union members and the formation of separate unions in the same trade on the local level originated mostly from the discontent of those rank-and-file members who believed original radical goals were being sacrificed for bread-and-butter expediency. It would thus be an oversimplification to interpret such moves as dual unionism only, when they usually occurred after years of tireless, but frustrating, work in existing organizations. They can instead be seen as efforts at stemming the fossilization of organizations that in the view of their radical members should have reached out to all workers but instead took on the appearance of privileged interest groups.

It is therefore not surprising that German radicals also looked for other forms of organization. The International Labor Union, founded by former members of the IWA in conjunction with New England labor leaders of the eight-hour movement, was one such short-lived effort to include unskilled workers on a national scale, as was the founding of laborers' unions on the local level, for example, in Chicago.[54] Criticism of the AFL for being too limited in scope was coupled with the demand to represent all industrial workers, and legislation was suggested as one such possibility.[55] Several unions took first steps away from their craft orientation toward industrial unionism as the only viable response to the debasing effects of industrialization, like the cigarmakers in the 1870s, the furniture workers a decade later, and the brewery workers around 1890.

This search for alternatives could not overlook the Knights of Labor, of course. On the one hand, this organization attracted German radicals for the all-inclusiveness it propagated. Until the mid-1880s the Order proved beyond doubt that it was indeed able to appeal to the mass of unorganized and semiskilled workers on the railroads and in the big industrial plants. In addition, some of its principles were identical with socialist conceptions. On the other hand, German radical trade unionists were suspicious of the Order's leadership, organizational structure, disregard of well-tried mechanisms of labor solidarity, and inroads into established unions of skilled workers. German skilled workers were especially unwilling to give up the discipline of organization involving material sacrifices and benefits which had been proven to be the strongest protections against weakness and dissolution. They had been educated in a democratic union tradition that stood in stark contrast to the high-handed hierarchical leadership of the Order, to its insistence on secrecy and ritual. While centralization on a national scale was zealously fought for by German-American unions, they resented giving up their local autonomy to a body controlled by a group of people more in conformity with middle-class than with working-class values, at least as German workers saw them. In such attitudes they also detected traces of nativism and pressure toward cultural conformity that struck at the very foundation of organization successes.[56] Thus German socialists were once more facing the choice of joining a broad mass movement of workers but running the risk of losing their identity in the process or of staying aloof from the movement and, thereby, running the risk of missing what Friedrich Engels had enthusiastically greeted as the American labor organization of the future.[57] This dilemma seems to have been a perennial one; was it symptomatic of an inherent unwillingness of German radicals in the United States to face the consequences of living in another society?

The Americanization of German Working-Class Radicalism

German-American radicals by the end of the 1880s were confronted with the indisputable fact that years of ceaseless agitation and efforts at organization had brought only meager results. Promising beginnings all too often had failed to translate into lasting successes. Frustrated socialists tried to find explanations for this disappointing lack of organizational progress. The several answers they offered revealed both the sincerity of their concern and their feeling of helplessness in the face of social and economic circumstances which, according to their understanding, should have made for a powerful working-class movement but instead had eroded it time and again. They held themselves responsible for this outcome, but they also blamed the specific conditions of American society for it.

In his article, "Nationality and Socialism," in the *New Yorker Volkszeitung,* Sergej Schewitsch explained that socialism stood above any nationality.[58] However, the "national character" could influence the form of organization and the plan of agitation, and socialism had to adapt to such national peculiarities. In a follow-up article, "Theory and Life," Schewitsch stated that the mentality of the Anglo-Saxon people was a priori averse to any abstract theory.[59] Others shared his observation; in a letter to the same paper, one writer voiced the opinion that "it was much easier to agitate among the immigrant element of the population than among those born in this country," because French and German immigrants seemed to be "intellectually more enlightened"[60] than the "practical-minded" American workers who had inherited this characteristic from England.[61] Johann Most's *Freiheit,* still published in

London during this time, agreed that Americans devoted all their energy to physical work and were therefore behind "in intellectual matters"; their "fundamental trait" was "a most blatant instinct of acquisition."[62]

Americans, in turn, had their difficulties with German socialism, as Henry George readily conceded before the Syracuse Convention of the United Labor Party in 1887. Individualism was so "strongly rooted in all the habits of thought of the peoples of English language" that "socialism of the German school can never make the headway here that it has on the continent of Europe."[63] In another editorial he complained: "German socialism is so confused and confusing in its terminology, so illogical in its methods; it contains such a mixture of important truths with superficial generalizations and unwarranted assumptions, that it is difficult—at least for people of English speech—to readily understand its real meaning and purpose."[64] For him "state socialism" was "an exotic born of European conditions that cannot take root and flourish in American soil."[65]

Such a conclusion implied a failure on the part of German socialists to adapt themselves to American conditions. Many German radicals agreed with this indictment. All too often, socialist immigrants haughtily conceived of America as an industrializing country that awaited only their missionary zeal to be made over in the German image. Despairing soon of the ineffectiveness of such an approach, many socialists then confined themselves to supporting the Social Democratic Party in Germany and identifying with its obvious advances rather than with the SLP which suffered repeated setbacks. They thereby reinforced their self-imposed isolation.[66] German-American labor papers, however, kept reminding their readers that actual developments were distinct from "notions conceived in the heads of German socialists in the United States who apply German standards to the completely different conditions here."[67] It was wrong to keep principles untainted by staying away from unfamiliar social movements; instead, the motto should be: "Go ye into all the world and preach the Gospel among the Gentiles."[68]

One indispensable requirement was knowledge of the English language. Workers could not content themselves with the claim of middle-class papers that it was "the mission of German-Americans" to preserve German traditions and the German language, wrote the *New Yorker Volkszeitung*. Learning English thoroughly was not equivalent to a betrayal of one's mother tongue but an opening of the way to more effective agitation. There was no sharper weapon than colloquial English. The paper admonished its readers to attend a language course offered in the numerous evening schools.[69] Wilhelm Liebknecht also addressed this burning issue during his American journey. In a speech in Brooklyn he exhorted his listeners to learn the language of their adopted country: "I tell you, study, and learn English above all else. It's a mistake that my fellow countrymen learn so little English. They must know the ways of Americans and therefore I tell you learn."[70]

English-language socialist papers were badly missed, and German socialists repeatedly made efforts at remedy. Thus the Chicago *Socialist* was financed by the overwhelmingly German membership of the SLP, as were the *Leader*, the *Workmen's Advocate*, and the *People* in later years. Likewise, Albert Parsons published his *Alarm* in the offices of the *Chicagoer Arbeiter-Zeitung*. From early on, German socialists also tried to reach workers through leaflets and pamphlets written in English—an undertaking impeded by the lack of native speakers. German-Americans who were relatively fluent in English, like Friedrich A. Sorge, Alexander Jonas, Adolf Douai, Adolph Hepner, and later Gustav A. Hoehn, therefore filled the gap.[71] Since these pamphlets explicitly referred to American conditions, they were preferred for agitational purposes over translations of German tracts reflecting German conditions.

Such praiseworthy activities could not hide the fact, however, that it was among the ethnic group of German immigrants that German radicals could score their most important organizational successes. Given the large concentrations of German skilled workers in specific branches of industry and in certain regions and cities, this comes as no surprise. Here were the natural starting points of a common national and cultural heritage upon which radicals could draw continually for more than three decades. The labor movement made no exception to using such traditions; they proved, in fact, to be a very powerful cement that brought workers together on the basis of a common craft and common skills. Reaching out from here, the English language was an important medium not only for the purpose of communicating with American workers but also to use in finding common ground with immigrant workers of other nationalities who, like the Germans, used their own cultural and work traditions for establishing effective organizational forms. Overcoming language barriers was therefore a problem faced by all immigrant groups except perhaps those from the British Isles, and the eventual acceptance of the English language may have had more to do with demographic changes, especially the replacement of the immigrant generation by the American-born children of immigrants, than with conscious efforts as described above.

Generational changes among German workers and overall shifts in the composition of the American working class lie at the bottom of a mellowed German-American radicalism as the century came to a close. The increasing tempo of industrial reorganization since the 1880s and the restructuring of work toward homogenization[72] had displaced German skilled workers, and especially traditional craftsmen, from the center of the production process, while second-generation sons and daughters also left aside outworn occupational prospects, instead looking for jobs in new-growth industries. Thus, at the very time that strong union organization had been effected after years of tireless struggle on the craft basis as propagated by the AFL, industrial development toward mass production and the reception of the new immigrants into the working class had already outmoded such forms of organization. German radicals who had matured in the 1870s and 1880s had grown old, while the membership for whom they could speak was decreasing. Those who were left in their ranks often represented the outlook of the "labor aristocracy," although they were not necessarily grounded in an economically and socially elevated status. The new labor radicalism after 1900, as expressed in new forms of organization like the Industrial Workers of the World, was carried by other population groups. German radicals instead tended to identify themselves with the Socialist Party in which they saw the culmination of their search for the close cooperation between the party and the trade unions.[73] Ironically, the radical tradition scored its most visible organizational successes in places like Milwaukee, where it discarded revolutionary goals for a self-complacent reform radicalism along the lines of German reform socialism, thus becoming almost indistinguishable from progressive local reform groups. It was only able to do so, however, because it had finally joined together the trade unions and the party in a common municipal program.[74] In this context, "Americanization" was almost equivalent to giving up the radical goals of the 1880s. Thus German radicalism was curbed even before the restrictive internal measures accompanying the entry of the United States into World War I were put into effect by the government.[75] Whatever heritage and traditions it had contributed to an American radicalism had either been transferred to multiethnic organizations before the war years or had become lost as German working-class organizations gradually thinned out.

German radical leaders welcomed this development, seeing in it the overcoming of ethnic and cultural isolation for which they had worked with so little apparent success for decades. When the Socialist Unity Congress finally assembled at Indianapolis in 1901, German socialists representing a conglomerate of radical groups rejoiced over the fact that this was no longer a "German" convention. Even if Eugene Dietzgen, the son of the venerated labor philosopher Joseph Dietzgen, had been influential in drawing up the platform of the new party, it was highly significant to Julius Vahlteich—former secretary of Ferdinand Lassalle and member of the German Reichstag, now a resident of Chicago and still active as a labor journalist—that young Americans had dominated the discussions and proven their substantial organizational skills.[76] Alexander Jonas also was proud of the new membership base of the Socialist Party, and he strongly urged Morris Hillquit to emphasize this subject in his report to the International Socialist Congress in Amsterdam in 1904.[77]

Even if such Americanization could be interpreted by German radicals as the culmination of their own struggles during the last third of the nineteenth century, it took on significance at this point in time for the "old" immigrants only; it disregarded the continuing and rapid changes within the American working class. Making the Socialist Party over into an American organization in this sense meant isolating it again from the mainstream of the working class by excluding, like the AFL, the millions of new immigrant workers who could be reached only in their own language. To the credit of the Socialist Party it must be said that it did not shun this task, even if it proved to be overwhelming. When the German leader Philipp Scheidemann visited the United States in 1914, he voiced his respect for the American comrades who faced so many more odds than the party in Germany, mentioning especially the heterogeneous national origins of the masses making up the American working class.[78] In this context German radicals, even though outnumbered after 1900 by new groups, still were able to contribute their past experiences toward solving what seems to have been a perennial American problem: to unite a multiethnic working class continually changing its composition into a powerful organizational body.

Notes

1. F. A. Sorge, "Die Arbeiterbewegung in den Vereinigten Staaten, 1860–1866," *Die Neue Zeit*, 9, no. 2 (1891): 398. This quotation and all following quotations from German-language sources were translated by this author.

2. For an overview of the period, see Ray Ginger, *Age of Excess: The United States from 1877 to 1914* (New York: Macmillan, 1965); for histories of the labor movement, see John R. Commons et al., *History of Labour in the United States,* vol. 2 (New York: Macmillan, 1918; repr. John A. Commons, 1946); Philip S. Foner, *From Colonial Times to the Founding of the American Federation of Labor,* vol. 1 of *History of the Labor Movement in the United States* (New York: International Publishers, 1947); David Montgomery, *Beyond Equality: Labor and the Radical Republicans, 1862–1872* (New York: Vintage Books, 1967).

3. For histories of German immigrant workers by German-Americans active in the labor movement, see Sorge, "Arbeiterbewegung"; Herman Schlüter, *Die Anfänge der deutschen Arbeiterbewegung in Amerika* (Stuttgart: J. H. V. Dietz, 1907); Hermann Schlüter, *Die Internationale in Amerika: Ein Beitrag zur Geschichte der Arbeiterbewegung in den Vereinigten Staaten* (Chicago: Deutsche Sprachgruppe der Sozialistischen Partei der Vereinigten Staaten, 1918); the respective chapters in Foner, *From Colonial Times,* and in Philip S. Foner, *From the Founding of the American Federation of Labor to the Emergence of American Imperialism,* vol. 2 of *History of the Labor Movement in the United States* (New York: International Publishers, 1955); for histories of the socialist party, see Morris Hillquit, *History of Socialism in the United States* (New York: Dover Publications, 1971); Howard H. Quint, *The Forging of American Socialism: Origins of the Modern Movement* (Indianapolis: Bobbs-Merrill, 1964); Daniel Bell, *Marxian Socialism in the United States* (Princeton, N.J.: Princeton University Press, 1967); Karl Marx and Friedrich Engels, *Letters to Americans, 1848–1895* (New York: International Publishers, 1953).

4. For examples see "SAP, Board of Supervision," *New Yorker Volkszeitung* (journal cited hereafter as *NYVZ*), 20 March 1881; "Ist der amerikanische Boden günstig für die Sozialdemokratie?" *NYVZ,* 4 August 1882; "Es nützt ja doch nichts," *Der Sozialist,* 29 September 1888; Adolf Douai to Richard T. Ely, 18 September 1886, Richard T. Ely Papers, Box 2, State Historical Society of Wisconsin, Madison.

5. Histories of German immigration are Mack Walker, *Germany and the Emigration, 1816–1885* (Cambridge, Mass.: Harvard University Press, 1964); Peter Marschalck, *Deutsche Überseewanderung im 19. Jahrhundert: Ein Beitrag zur soziologischen Theorie der Bevölkerung* (Stuttgart: Ernst Klett Verlag, 1973); Wolfgang Köllmann and Peter Marschalck, "German Emigration to the United States," trans. Thomas C. Childers, *Perspectives in American History* 7 (1973): 499–554. For a thorough review of the literature on German-Americans see Kathleen Neils Conzen, "Die Assimilierung der Deutschen in Amerika: zum Stand der Forschung in den Vereinigten Staaten," in *Die deutschsprachige Auswanderung in die Vereinigten Staaten: Berichte über Forschungsstand und Quellenbestände,* ed. Willi Paul Adams (Berlin: John F. Kennedy Institut, 1980), 33–64; and Conzen, "Germans," in *Harvard Encyclopedia of American Ethnic Groups* (Cambridge, Mass.: Harvard University Press, 1980), 405–25.

6. See Guenther Roth, *The Social Democrats in Imperial Germany: A Study in Working-Class Isolation and National Integration* (Totowa, N.J.: Bedminster Press, 1963); Franz Mehring, *Geschichte der Deutschen Sozialdemokratie II: Von Lassalles "Offenem Antwortschreiben" bis zum Erfurter Programm 1863 bis 1891,* (Berlin: Dietz Verlag, 1960); Werner Ettelt and Hans-Dieter Krause, *Der Kampf um eine marxistische Gewerkschaftspolitik in der deutschen Arbeiterbewegung 1868 bis 1878* (Berlin: Verlag Tribüne, 1975).

7. See Dirk Hoerder and Hartmut Keil, "The American Case and German Social Democracy at the Turn of the Twentieth Century, 1878–1907" (Paper presented at the conference "Why Is There No Socialism in the United States?", Centre d'Etudes Nord-Américaines, Ecole des Hautes Etudes en Sciences Sociales, Paris, 25–27 May 1983).

8. See Schlüter, *Die Anfänge;* Sorge, "Arbeiterbewegung." The standard books on the liberals escaping to the United States after the failure of the revolution in 1848 are Carl Wittke, *Refugees of the Revolution: The German Forty-Eighters in*

America (Philadelphia: University of Pennsylvania Press, 1952); and A. E. Zucker, ed., *The Forty-Eighters: Political Refugees of the German Revolution of 1848* (New York: Columbia University Press, 1950).

9. For some answers to these questions with respect to Chicago, see Hartmut Keil and John B. Jentz, eds., *German Workers in Industrial Chicago, 1850–1910: A Comparative Perspective* (De Kalb: Northern Illinois University Press, 1983).

10. See Walker, *Germany and the Emigration*; Köllmann and Marschalck, "German Emigration to the United States."

11. See John B. Jentz and Hartmut Keil, "From Immigrants to Urban Workers: Chicago's German Poor in the Gilded Age and Progressive Era, 1883–1908," *Vierteljahrschrift für Sozial- und Wirtschaftsgeschichte* 68, no. 1 (1981): 52–97.

12. Bureau of the Census, *U.S. Ninth Census, 1870, Population and Social Statistics* (Washington, D.C.: Government Printing Office, 1872), 386–89; and *Tenth Census, 1880, Population* (Washington, D.C.: Government Printing Office, 1883), 538–42. This is, of course, an extremely high limit for measuring the degree of urbanization; however, other data are not available for ethnic groups. See Walter Kamphoefner, *Westfalen in der Neuen Welt: eine Sozialgeschichte der Auswanderung im 19. Jahrhundert* (Münster: Coppenrath, 1982); and Conzen, "Germans," p. 413.

13. Herbert Gutman, "Working-Class Formation, Immigrants, and the Children of Immigrants, 1840–1890—Some Suggestions Concerning the Relations between Class and Ethnicity" (Paper given at the conference on the Chicago-Project, Munich, 18–21 June 1980).

14. Hartmut Keil, "Chicago's German Working Class in 1900," in *German Workers in Industrial Chicago*, ed. Keil and Jentz, p. 23.

15. Hartmut Keil, "Das Chicago-Project als sozial- und kulturgeschichtlicher Forschungsansatz," *Amerikastudien/American Studies* 24, no. 2 (1984): 113–32; John B. Jentz, "Artisan Culture and the Organization of Chicago's German Workers in the Gilded Age, 1860 to 1890," *Amerikastudien/American Studies* 24, no. 2 (1984): 133–48.

16. See Hanns-Theodor Fuß, "Arbeitswelt und Nachbarschaft. Die McCormick Harvesting Machine Company und die Arbeiterschaft der Südwestseite Chicagos während des Übergangs zur Massenproduktion, 1873–1886" (M.A. thesis, University of Munich, 1983); Hanns-Theodor Fuß, "Massenproduktion und Arbeiterbewußtsein. Deutsche Arbeiter in den McCormick Reaper Works, 1873–1886," *Amerikastudien/American Studies* 24, no. 2 (1984): 149–68. For a thorough historical discussion of the issue of workers' control from the end of the nineteenth century on, see David Montgomery, *Workers' Control in America: Studies in the History of Work, Technology, and Labor Struggles* (Cambridge, London: Cambridge University Press, 1980).

17. See Hartmut Keil and Heinz Ickstadt, "Elemente einer deutschen Arbeiterkultur in Chicago zwischen 1880 und 1890," *Geschichte und Gesellschaft* 5 (1979): 103–24.

18. See *NYVZ*'s quotation from Theodore Roosevelt's speech branding a class-conscious labor movement as un-American ("Theodore Roosevelt und die Arbeiterbewegung," 13 May 1887).

19. Schlüter, *Die Internationale in Amerika*, pp. 270–72.

20. See Samuel Bernstein, *The First International in America* (New York: August M. Kelley, 1965); Schlüter, *Internationale*; Sorge, "Arbeiterbewegung."

21. Bernstein, *The First International*; Schlüter, *Die Internationale in Amerika*; Herbert G. Gutman, "The Tompkins Square 'Riot' in New York City on January 13, 1874: A Re-examination of Its Causes and Its Aftermath," *Labor History* 6, no. 1 (Winter 1965): 44–70.

22. Quoted in Bernstein, *The First International*, p. 116.

23. Ibid.

24. See Foner, *From Colonial Times*, pp. 475–88; Commons et al., *History of Labour*, 2:284–86.

25. Hartmut Keil, "The German Immigrant Working Class of Chicago, 1875–90:

Workers, Labor Leaders, and the Labor Movement," in *American Labor and Immigration History, 1877–1920s: Recent European Research*, ed. Dirk Hoerder (Urbana: University of Illinois Press, 1983), 156–76.

26. *NYVZ*, 24 September 1886.

27. *NYVZ*, 5 December 1886.

28. Jakob Franz, "Die Entstehung der neuen Arbeiterpartei," *NYVZ*, 9 December 1886.

29. *NYVZ*, 21 April 1888.

30. *NYVZ*, 29 September 1888.

31. For a new approach to the SLP's role in the 1890s, see Hubert Perrier, "The Socialists and the Working Class in New York, 1890–1896," *Labor History* 22, no. 4 (Fall 1981): 485–511; this essay appears also in *American Labor and Immigration History*, ed. Hoerder, pp. 111–34.

32. *NYVZ*, 29 September 1888.

33. Schlüter, *Internationale*, 487–91.

34. Renate Kiesewetter, "Die Institution der deutsch-amerikanischen Arbeiterpresse in Chicago. Zur Geschichte des *Vorboten* und der *Chicagoer Arbeiter-Zeitung*, 1874–1886" (M.A. thesis, University of Munich, 1982), pp. 53–56.

35. *Vorbote*, 13 May 1876.

36. *Vorbote*, 6 June 1874.

37. *Vorbote*, 13 May 1876.

38. Ibid.

39. Ibid.

40. Hartmut Keil, "The Knights of Labor, the Trade Unions, and German Socialists in Chicago, 1870–1890," in *Impressions of a Gilded Age: The American Fin de Siècle*, ed. Marc Chénetier and Rob Kroes (Amsterdam: Amerika Institut, Universiteit van Amsterdam, 1983), 301–23.

41. Kiesewetter, "Institution der deutsch-amerikanischen Arbeiterpresse in Chicago," pp. 56–58; Keil, "German Immigrant Working Class of Chicago," in *American Labor and Immigration History*, ed. Hoerder.

42. *Vorbote*, 2 and 9 March 1878. The quotation is from 2 March, p. 4.

43. *NYVZ*, 2 February 1880.

44. *NYVZ*, 21 June 1880.

45. *NYVZ*, 22 May 1881.

46. Keil, "Knights of Labor," in *Impressions of a Gilded Age*, ed. Chénetier and Kroes.

47. *NYVZ*, 21 November 1881.

48. *NYVZ*, report on lecture by Jakob Franz, "Die Gewerkschaftsbewegung und die Politik," 14 August 1882.

49. *NYVZ*, 14 December 1886.

50. *NYVZ*, 10 December 1889.

51. *NYVZ*, 9 and 15 December 1890.

52. *NYVZ*, 18 February 1889; Henry David, *The History of the Haymarket Affair: A Study in the American Social-Revolutionary and Labor Movements* (New York: Crowell-Collier Publishing Company, 1963), 136f.

53. Perrier, "The Socialists."

54. See Foner, *From Colonial Times*, pp. 500–504; Keil, "Knights of Labor," in *Impressions of a Gilded Age*, ed. Chenétier and Kroes.

55. *NYVZ*, 14 December 1885, 11 January 1886.

56. See Keil, "Knights of Labor," in *Impressions of a Gilded Age*, Chénetier and Kroes.

57. Engels, "The Labor Movement in the United States," in Marx and Engels, *Letters to Americans*, pp. 285–91.

58. *NYVZ*, 4 August 1878.

59. *NYVZ*, 11 August 1878. The same arguments were taken up once more in a series of articles by the same author, "Socialism on Anglo-Saxon Ground," *NYVZ*, 8, 15, 22, and 29 August 1880.

60. *NYVZ,* 15 October 1879.
61. *NYVZ,* 15 August 1880.
62. *Freiheit,* 4 September 1880.
63. "The New Party," *Standard,* 30 July 1887.
64. "Socialism and the New Party," *Standard,* 6 August 1887.
65. "The United Labor Party and Socialism," *Standard,* 13 August 1887.
66. See Dirk Hoerder and Hartmut Keil, "The American Case."
67. Conrad Conzett, "Der Weg zum Ziele," *Vorbote,* 12 August 1876.
68. Alexander Jonas, "Die Socialdemokratie und die neue Arbeiterpartei," *NYVZ,* 5 December 1886.
69. Edward Thimme, "Die deutschen Arbeiter und die englische Sprache," *NYVZ* (tenth anniversary issue), 28 January 1888.
70. "Wilhelm Liebknecht in Brooklyn," *NYVZ,* 24 September 1886.
71. E.g., Sorge, "Socialism and the Worker"; Jonas, "Reporter and Socialist"; Douai, "Better Times"; Hepner, "Immoral and Unconstitutional: Our Accessory Laws. A Postscription to the Chicago Anarchists' Case"; Hoehn, "Labor and Capital."
72. See David M. Gordon, Richard Edwards, Michael Reich, *Segmented Work, Divided Workers: The Historical Transformation of Labor in the United States* (Cambridge: Cambridge University Press, 1982).
73. See Charles Leinenweber, "The Class and Ethnic Bases of New York City Socialism, 1904–1915," *Labor History* 22, no. 1 (Winter 1981): 31–56, for evidence of the composition of the Socialist Party in New York.
74. See Robert Mikkelsen, "The Social Democratic Party of Milwaukee, Wisconsin: A Study of Ethnic Composition and Political Development" (M.A. thesis, University of Oslo, 1976); Elmer A. Beck, *The Sewer Socialists: A History of the Socialist Party of Wisconsin 1897–1940,* 2 vols. (Fennimore, Wisc.: Westbury Associates Publishers, 1982); Joseph Anthony Kunkel III, "The Ideological Party in American Politics: The Case of the Milwaukee Social Democrats" (Ph.D. diss., University of Minnesota, 1980). For the close cooperation between party and trade unions that made electoral success possible, see the completely different situation in Reading, Pennsylvania, as analyzed by Henry G. Stetler, *The Socialist Movement in Reading, Pennsylvania, 1896–1936: A Study in Social Change* (1943; reprint, Philadelphia: Porcupine Press, 1974).
75. See Quint, *The Forging of American Socialism;* Hillquit, *History of Socialism in the U.S.;* Ira Kipnis, *The American Socialist Movement: 1897–1912* (New York, London: Monthly Review Press, 1952); James Weinstein, *The Decline of Socialism in America, 1912–1925* (New York: Vintage Books, 1969).
76. Julius Vahlteich, "Der Einigungskongreß der amerikanischen Sozialisten in Indianapolis," *Neue Zeit* 19, no. 2 (1900–1901): 663–66.
77. Alexander Jonas to Morris Hillquit, 23 June 1904, Morris Hillquit Papers, Correspondence, box 1, State Historical Society of Wisconsin, Madison.
78. Philipp Scheidemann, "Reiseskizzen über Amerika und amerkanische Verhältnisse," *Vorbote,* 8 April 1914.

DONNA GABACCIA

Neither Padrone Slaves nor Primitive Rebels: Sicilians on Two Continents

The old view of the Italian immigrant as either scabbing padrone slave or occasional spontaneous rebel is slowly being revised. It appears likely that at least a significant minority of the workers of south-Italian immigrant communities were labor militants, influenced by socialist, syndicalist, and anarchist thought and press, and, especially in the period 1905 to 1918, at least peripherally involved in radical Italian-language associations.[1] This was certainly the case among the Sicilians who are the topic of this essay.

Revision of old stereotypes is always welcome. In this instance, however, it poses an interpretive problem. Our understanding of south-Italian culture, influenced as it is by Edward Banfield's "amoral familism" and E. J. Hobsbawm's "primitive rebels," seems to rule out the extent of south-Italian radicalism that historians are now uncovering in the United States.[2] Familists and primitive rebels simply do not make ideal labor militants. Are we then to see labor militance only as evidence of Americanization, as, for example, did Edward Fenton or (more recently) Humbert Nelli?[3]

This essay argues instead that our understanding of south-Italian culture has been simplistic.[4] Italian immigrant labor militance very definitely had its roots in Europe, although not in the familism or spontaneous rebellions said to be characteristic of the region. The essay focuses on the relationship of culture, labor militance, and Sicilian migration on both sides of the Atlantic.[5] Residents of the provinces of Trapani, Agrigento, and Palermo, western Sicilians have often been classified as familists; Hobsbawm found among them many examples of primitive rebels—bandits, *mafia*, and millenarians.[6] Sicily, a diverse region, is representative of the equally diverse Italian south.[7] Western Sicily offered further advantages for a comparative study of this kind. Sicilians were one of every four Italian emigrants to the United States, but because American observers believed them more dangerous than southern Italians as a whole, Sicilians were more often identified and, thus, more visible than others. In addition, Sicily alone among south-Italian regions produced a major folklore collection in the nineteenth century, one that mirrors the social values of ordinary people more accurately than their behavior or the observations of outsiders might do.[8]

The essay is divided into three unequal parts. The first, and longest, describes how a tradition of labor militance emerged in Sicily in the years around 1890. Changing class dynamics, altering the place of the artisan in many towns, encouraged the creation of new cultural forms that linked explicitly artisanal traditions to widely held beliefs about the rich and the poor. Labor militance became popular, however, only where it also appealed to others, specifically to peasants. In Sicily, peasant response to labor militance varied considerably. The second section of the essay summarizes how immigrants in the United States responded to the ideas of militance carried to the United States by radicalized artisans. It describes artisans in immigrant communities facing new obstacles, which ultimately proved more crippling to the tradition of labor militance than did fascism in Italy. There, as section three relates, labor militants continued to attract a growing following among peasants despite heavy return migration and Fascist repressions.

The Origins of Sicilian Militance

To Italians arriving in the 1860s, western Sicily seemed a foreign land, "just two steps from Africa." Throughout the decade, revolution threatened: brigandage, tax protests, jacquerie, and draft evasion challenged the island's new administrators from a unified Italy.[9] Agriculturally, the island was in the throes of quite another revolution.[10] Western Sicily in 1860 still raised wheat for export on huge ranch-like estates, the *latifondi.* A new elite, the *civili,* acquired control over the *latifondi* at this time, but they also began extending grape and citrus cultivation, often on their own smaller estates, carved from former church and communal lands.[11] Most peasants depended on work as sharecroppers or wage laborers on *civile*-controlled lands.[12] This is not to say that no peasants owned land; many Sicilian peasants, in both wheat- and grape-raising areas possessed tiny parcels.[13] But few peasants could support themselves on their own holdings.

Its changing agriculture was important to Sicily; still, the island also housed a surprisingly large contingent of nonagriculturalists in the nineteenth century.[14] The largest single group were half petty capitalists and half artisanal craft workers: shoemakers, butchers, and the like. Sulfur miners lived in large numbers in twenty towns.[15] More generally throughout the island, cottage industry involved some men and many women in weaving, spinning, broommaking, and the like.[16] With the exception of the sulfur miners, industrial workers produced mainly for local consumption, both for *civile* agricultural enterprise and for socially ambitious *civili* emulating the ostentatious consumption styles of the old aristocracy.[17] Although early employment statistics are notoriously difficult to interpret, one study suggests that more than half of Sicily's active population earned its living outside agriculture.[18] These nonagriculturalists played a central role in the history of Sicilian labor militance and emigration.

For fifteen years after unification, Sicily enjoyed a period of rising expectations, the result of new agricultural investments and considerable *civile* expenditure on housing and urban amenities (theatres, gardens, paved streets for the carriages). Population grew rapidly, especially among nonagriculturalists.[19] Then, beginning in the 1870s, crisis rocked every sector of the island's economy. First affected were local industries and artisans, as imported manufactured goods reached frantically consuming island elites. By the mid-1880s, wheat prices and harvests dropped precipitously and simultaneously, followed rapidly thereafter by phylloxera in the vineyards, by the flooding of cheap Florida oranges into markets formerly dominated by Sicilian fruits and, finally, after 1900, by the collapse of the market for Sicilian sulfur.[20] These crises have rightly been seen as the origin of both Sicilian labor militance and mass migrations to the United States.[21]

Scholars agree that Sicilians confronted with economic crisis turned to labor militance, but they disagree about which islanders acted collectively in the long run. Throughout 1892 and 1893, Sicilian men and women struck, demonstrated in their piazzas, and attacked their city halls. Revolution was again a fear.[22] These were not spontaneous rebellions; when, for example, harvesters in the town of Prizzi struck for better wages in June of 1893, they did so not as primitive rebels but as members of a workers' organization called a Fascio. Fasci were organized in most Sicilian towns during these years; they lend their name to the unrest of the period—the Fasci Siciliani. Hobsbawm therefore rightly emphasized that the Sicilian revolts of 1892 and 1893, while millenarian in outlook, were organized, and "less primitive" than past rebellions. He argued further that the history of the Fasci demonstrated how easily primitive rebels became modern leftists—as did many Sicilians over the next twenty years.[23] But J. S. MacDonald (and others) have disagreed with Hobsbawm, stressing instead that most Sicilians abandoned labor militance after the decline of the Fasci, choosing instead to migrate in large numbers. MacDonald termed Sicily an area of declining militance—more likely to support the Socialist Party than the nonmilitant "Deep South," but less supportive of leftist politics than the rural militant provinces of Apulia and Emilia-Romagna.[24]

In order to analyze the history of Sicilian labor militance, I compiled chronologies of labor organizations and activity in 136 western Sicilian towns, excluding as atypical only the very large city of Palermo.[25]

Western Sicily's 136 towns fell into three categories: militant, declining-militant, and nonmilitant. Nonmilitant towns had no class-conscious organizations and no evidence of any kind of collective action, spontaneous or organized, at any time between 1890 and 1921. By contrast, in militant towns, peasants and/or artisans typically organized a Fascio and a Socialist Party section in the 1890s and a peasant cooperative or league in one or both of the subsequent two decades. (I considered a town militant if residents employed socialist slogans in their public protests, struck their employers or occupied land during at least two of the three decades, and if attacks on property led at least once to armed confrontations with the militia. Most towns experienced organization, action, and violence during all three decades.) Finally, the residents of towns I called "declining-militant" typically organized a Fascio and a single (often very violent) tax protest in 1892–1893 before apparently abandoning class-based organization and action after 1894. The results for western Sicily were 74 militant towns with 833,218 residents in 1901, 31 declining-militant towns with 252,952 residents in 1901 and 31 nonmilitant towns with 130,438 residents in 1901. Most Sicilians towns were militant, and the majority of western Sicilians lived in militant towns.

Within limits, western Sicily fit Hobsbawm's argument: millenarian rebels of the 1890s became "modern" political leftists after the turn of the century. Of course, even militant towns fell quiet when the Italian state violently repressed the Fasci in 1894; but after government pressures again eased, Socialist and (to a lesser extent) Catholic peasant leagues quickly reorganized: large numbers of peasants left work in a second wave of strikes between 1901 and 1904.[26] By 1913 enfranchised artisans and peasants supported socialists in many militant towns.[27] And, from 1919 through 1921, peasants again occupied lands, demanding collective leases or outright partition of large estates.[28] None of these events was as widespread as the revolts of the 1890s; labor militance did in fact decline, as MacDonald believed, at least in one group of towns. But it is certainly not the case that all Sicilians simply abandoned labor militance as they began to migrate in large numbers in the 1890s.

Western Sicilian peasant leagues and strikes raise troubling questions about the role of culture in the development of south-Italian militance. Although they are often characterized as familists, western Sicilians from 1890 through 1921 did not behave in ways we expect of amoral familists. According to Banfield, familists will "maximize the material short-run advantage of the nuclear family"; thus, "organization (i.e., deliberately concerted action) will be difficult to achieve and maintain," and "there will be no connection between abstract political principle and concrete behavior."[29]

I have been unable to find clear and unambiguous evidence of so-defined familism among western Sicilians. Familists, by Banfield's definition, do not form voluntary associations, yet mutual benefit societies were common in western Sicily.[30] Scores existed in the 1880s and by 1890, four of every five western Sicilians towns had at least one. Even in "familist" towns (those with no mutual benefit society), familism proved only a small obstacle to the growth of labor militance. While towns with no benefit society were found disproportionately among the nonmilitant, most did form a Fascio in the 1890s; and, of these, most then became militant towns. At best, familism seemed on the wane in western Sicily.

Similarly, Sicilian proverbs collected in the 1870s and 1880s by Giuseppe Pitrè provide few rules that much resemble the "predictive hypotheses" Banfield believed guided amoral familists. True, Sicilian proverbs emphasized the importance of nuclear family solidarity, and they hinted at the intense competition that existed among families. But they also demonstrated a strong desire for cooperation beyond the nuclear family; cooperation was praised as often as was the skill of competition. Cooperation, in fact, was an important measure of a person's position in the community, for it garnered "respect." A man without friends literally had no honor.[31]

Furthermore, in their own way, Sicilians were intensely class-conscious. The proverbs glorified no monarchs or aristocrats who understand or protect peasants. Instead, Sicilians—like Marx—divided the world starkly into two antagonistic classes—the rich and the poor. While enough proverbs expressed envy of the rich, most simply described the exploitative interdependence between the two groups.[32]

The concept of familism does not accurately delineate the cultural beliefs that shaped the development and appeal of labor militance in Sicily. A comparison of towns with differing patterns of labor militance indicates that the key to the success or failure of labor militance was the way that artisans, wheat raisers, and grape cultivators reacted to economic crisis in the late nineteenth century. Facing hardship, each occupational group seemed to draw different guidance from their shared social values.

Where many residents mined sulfur or worked as artisans or industrial employees or, alternatively, where most peasants depended upon the large wheat-raising estates, the *latifondi*, for work as sharecroppers and day laborers, towns typically became militant.[33] By contrast, declining-militant towns were overwhelmingly agricultural; peasants in these towns raised more grapes and citrus crops and less wheat for export. Nonmilitant towns resembled the declining-militant towns but were smaller (fewer than 5,000 residents) and more isolated.

With some modification, western Sicily's pattern of labor militance resembled the model elaborated twenty years ago by J. S. MacDonald.[34] MacDonald attributed regional variation in labor militance in Italy to differing forms of agricultural organization. Where small-scale household agriculture prevailed, labor militance was low; where large-scale capitalist or semicapitalist estates employed proletarianized cultivators, militance was high. MacDonald ignored the influence of crop raised and the role of nonagriculturalists in rural labor militance. In Sicily, however, the history of labor militance began among artisans in provincial towns: variation in agricultural organization (closely linked to the kind of crop raised) influenced the spread or decline of labor activism after the repression of the Fasci—that is, after the mid-1890s.

The relationship of artisan and peasant in southern Italy has been persistently misunderstood by historians of immigration, who describe the two as one class, with small-scale familist agriculturalists seeking supplemental income through artisanal or industrial work.[35] This was not at all the position of Sicily's artisans and industrial workers. The wives of peasants might engage in cottage industrial production, but mines and artisans excluded most peasants from apprenticeship, especially in smaller towns. Peasants and artisans were distinctive and clearly demarcated social groups in Sicily.

Take the case of one town, Sambuca di Sicilia, in the southwestern corner of Agrigento province.[36] There in 1880, artisans were small landowners who leased their lands to peasants while they worked and sold from their *bottega* workshops.[37] Artisans, who were townsmen, limited entrance to the trades to their sons; they wore "urban" clothing styles, lived on the second floor of substantial houses, achieved Sicilian family ideals, and sent their sons and daughters to school to learn reading and writing.[38] By contrast, peasants were illiterates who in many cases lived in houses that could hardly be differentiated from animal stalls; only rarely could they behave as "proper" husbands, wives, or children.[39] Like animals, too, they worked in the "uncivilized" and disparaged countryside.[40] Artisans did not often marry peasants; when they occasionally sought partners outside their own group, they also found them among *civili.*[41] In a very real sense, artisans were part of Sambuca's "rich." Although their incomes were low, their lives in almost any respect more closely resembled their *civili* patrons than those of the town "poor," the peasants.

Sicily's artisans were not familists. They identified proudly with their occupational group. Part of the social respect they enjoyed as "masters" (*mastru*) was the result of close cooperation with others in the trades. After their guilds were outlawed in the 1830s, artisans and miners organized religious confraternities; they also founded most of Sicily's first mutual benefit societies.[42] In fact, most western Sicilian mutual benefit societies in 1890 were still limited in membership to men in the skilled trades or to "honest workers," a term often used by journeymen to distinguish themselves from masters.[43]

As imported goods invaded local markets and found favor among local *civile* elites, artisans rejected potential political alliances with the *civile* elite to seek cooperation with town peasants. They switched their allegiance to "the poor," often within the space of a few years. To the poor, artisans had much to offer, especially a tradition of occupational solidarity missing among peasants.

Again, Sambuca provides an example of this transformation. In 1885, the town had two artisans' societies—the Unione Elettorale and the Società Franklyn.[44] Both of these societies were formed soon after reforms of 1882 gave most artisans electoral rights,[45] and at least one (and probably both) of them were vote-gathering "machines" for competing *civile* political bosses. By 1893, a socialist Fascio was noted in the town, and several of Sambuca's artisans were imprisoned in 1894, during the repression of the Fasci.[46] (In jail, one grew close to Nicola Barbato, the prominent early Sicilian Socialist.)[47] By 1900, Socialists—almost all artisans—displayed a red flag in their rooms above a shoemaker's shop. (Peasants reportedly crossed themselves when passing, since the place was surely inhabited by the devil.)[48] A major activity of Sambuca's Socialist artisans during these years was to educate peasants at their "workers' school," allowing them eventually to join artisans at the polls and to vote Socialist. When peasants were enfranchised for the 1913 election, the first Socialist artisans did enter a coalition municipal government in Sambuca.[49]

Sicilian artisans everywhere changed their loyalties and political strategies during the 1880s; their new consciousness shaped Sicilian labor militance beginning in the 1890s. Nonmilitant towns remained quiet mainly because these very small towns lacked a critical mass of artisan activists. Declining-militant towns differed from militant towns mainly in the success artisans enjoyed in incorporating peasants into their culture and organizations before, during, and after the Fasci.

Even before the 1890s, artisans in some towns that became militant attracted a peasant following. Artisans early convinced wheat-raising peasants of the *latifondo* of the advantages of occupational cooperation; mutual benefit societies exclusively for peasants existed before the Fasci in many *latifondo* towns—but not, curiously, in mining towns. During the years of the Fasci Siciliani, artisans in both militant and declining-militant towns played an active role, organizing the local fascio and proposing or leading peasant strikes or community-wide tax protests.[50] Again, however, there were differences in the two groups of towns: in towns where militance later declined, artisans and peasants protested high taxes and sacked town halls or the homes of tax collectors; in towns that became militant, wheat harvesters and miners instead protested in their workplaces, as strikers.[51]

After 1894, Sicilian peasants in particular faced a crossroads: either they listened to artisans' message that labor militance was a useful strategy for social and economic change, or they did not. Only where peasants organized extensively after the 1890s could a town become militant. (Even in sulfur towns, the typical disturbances of the twentieth century were peasants' strikes and land occupations, not miners' strikes.) In declining-militant towns, however, peasants did not become labor militants. I think we can safely reject the possibility that declining-militant towns were culturally "more familist" than others.[52] MacDonald believed instead that militance declined when peasants chose migration instead of militance as a solution to their grievances.[53] As I will show, emigration from declining-militant towns was indeed quite high in the twentieth century—but so was migration from many very militant towns. Migration did not inevitably undermine militance in western Sicily; it cannot alone explain declines in labor militance among the grape cultivators of declining-militant towns.

My own hypothesis is that the organization of grape and citrus cultivation discouraged peasant militance, in much the same way that MacDonald believed household agriculture undermined support for the Socialist Party. Comparing grape and wheat raising is instructive. Wheat cultivators typically owned and sharecropped marginal lands; as a result, they ate almost all of their potential cash crop—the wheat they raised—and thus needed to work as wage earners to pay rent or to buy additional food. The estate manager who claimed his own and the landlord's shares of the wheat harvest on the threshing floor literally cut into the peasant's food supply. When harvests were poor—as they consistently were in the 1880s and early 1890s—his demands had devastating consequences for the peasant family's food supply. This same man, the *gabelloto,* simultaneously granted or denied peasants access to the wage-labor jobs they desperately needed. Not surprisingly, few wheat raisers failed to recognize the landlord and his middlemen as oppressors, representatives of "the rich" and precisely the kind of grasping enemy that socialists described.[54] In contrast, grape cultivators raised much of their own food, either on lands they owned or sharecropped. Their tenure on the land was more secure; after paying their landlord in money or kind, they themselves marketed the cash crop they also raised.[55] These peasants faced a hard and changeable, but nevertheless impersonal, market. A drop in income from their cash crop threatened their ability to pay taxes (thus the importance of tax revolts in such towns) or, perhaps, land rents in the future, but not their food supply. Grape cultivators had to think abstractly in order to appreciate the economic struggle of rich and poor that socialists described; for them the enemy was the tax man or, more abstractly, the Italian State. Wheat cultivators hated their employers, as socialists believed they should.

The transformation of primitive into modern social movements, Hobsbawn noted, "does not take place, or takes place only very slowly and incompletely, if the matter is left to the peasants themselves."[56] In Sicily, the matter was not left to the peasants themselves. Artisans, suffering through their own crises, created a tradition of labor militance out of available social values; they were eager to share their insights with the peasants who formed the bulk of "the poor." Proletarianized wheat raisers were disposed to hear the artisans' message; their grape- and citrus-raising equivalents in other towns were not: differing work experiences conditioned both responses. The artisans' voice and the peasants' ear can be the starting place for explaining both immigrant labor radicalism and the politics of twentieth-century Sicily.

Sicilian Migration and Immigrant Labor Militance

One need not laboriously document thousands of individual cases to argue convincingly that labor militants and a tradition of labor militance were well represented among the Sicilians emigrating to the United States between 1880 and 1920. Overall, emigrants came from precisely those towns and those backgrounds where labor militance enjoyed its greatest appeal.

As many recent studies of immigrant origins show, nonagriculturalists left southern Italy in large numbers.[57] John Briggs found that artisans, construction workers, small shopkeepers, and fishermen actually outnumbered peasants emigrating from one Sicilian town.[58] Aggregate figures on Sicilian migrants suggest that nonagriculturalists were a substantial minority of those leaving the island as a whole.[59] Furthermore, Sicilian artisans and industrial workers, with the important exception of sulfur miners, were among the first to emigrate. They forged the first links in chains that would bring hundreds and even thousands of fellow villagers (*paesani*) to the United States.[60] By 1910, according to figures collected by the U.S. Immigration Commission, between 15 and 60 percent of the south-Italian migrants living in various American cities were of nonpeasant backgrounds.[61] Artisan voices there were in America's Sicilian communities.

Furthermore, most western Sicilians left behind towns that had recently experienced, or still were experiencing, considerable labor militance. Table 1 summarizes my estimates of the number of persons who permanently left militant, declining-militant, and nonmilitant towns between 1881 and 1910. These estimates are subject to the same weaknesses that plague all measures of net

Table 1 Migration from Sicilian Towns, According to Militancy

	Adjusted Population Losses[a]		Annual Migration Rates per 1,000[b]	
	1881–1900	1901–1910	1881–1900	1901–1910
Nonmilitant	−17,880	−15,491	−7.7	−11.9
Declining militant	−33,865	−44, 355	−4.2	−17.5
Militant	−65,981	−97,795	−4.8	−11.7

[a] Stefano Somogyi, *Bilanci Demografici dei Comuni Siciliani dal 1861 al 1961* (Palermo: Università di Palermo, Istituto di Scienze Demografiche, 1971).
[b] Computed from adjusted intercensal population balances in Somogyi.

migration rates; but since they coincided quite closely with published figures for passport applications during this period, I have some limited confidence in them.[62]

The western Sicilian case supports in part J. S. MacDonald's influential contention that Italian agriculturalists chose either to migrate or to fight. But it contradicts the related argument of immigrant historians who believe that southern Italians unfamiliar with labor militance came to the United States in overwhelming numbers.[63] Migration rates in western Sicily did vary roughly with levels of labor militance. Still, there were important exceptions to this general pattern. The single most important exception was that *latifondo* towns, the most militant towns in the area, had the highest average migration rates.[64] It was the extremely low rates of migration from sulfur-mining towns that depressed the overall migration rate of militant towns.

In any case, it was not the rate of migration but the representation of labor militants that would influence most the transfer of European experiences and ideas to the United States. At least half of Sicilian migrants came from towns where class conflict was recurring and serious. Both nationally known and locally active militants migrated: repressions of the Fasci in 1894 in particular spurred a regular migration of political exile from Sicily. Corleone resident Bernardino Verrò, a prominent Fascio and strike leader, worked for a time among Buffalo's Italians; Nicola Barbato, instrumental in encouraging Sambuca's artisans' turn leftward, did propaganda work for a time with the Italian Socialist Federation in New York; syndicalist Lorenzo Panepinto helped organize a workers' school among Tampa's Sicilians.[65] Perhaps more impressive is the fact that more than half of the founders of Sambuca's Socialist circle went at least temporarily to the United States before World War I.

It would be more surprising than not to find at least some evidence of labor militance among Sicilian immigrants living in the United States. In fact, Sicilians were instrumental in founding Socialist Party sections in Buffalo, Tampa, New York, and other cities.[66] Nicola Barbato's travels on behalf of the New York newspaper *Il Proletario* hint at something of a Sicilian radical network on the East Coast.[67] Scarcely a strike of immigrant Italians in any major American city lacked a contingent of local Sicilian leaders. Overall, I estimate that Sicilians eventually constituted about a third of the leftist Italian immigrant leaders working within various branches of the American labor movement.[68] The Amalgamated Clothing Workers claimed what was probably the most active group of Sicilians in the labor movement: Frank and August

Bellanca, Giuseppe Procopio, Giuseppe Salerno, and Vincenzo Messina all hailed from western Sicilian provinces.[69]

Still, the Sicilian record of labor militance in the United States was a mixed one. In New York, in some mining towns, and in Tampa, Sicilians built on labor militance traditions rooted in their European experiences. Boston, San Francisco and many other northern cities, however, never acquired the militant reputation of New York's Italian colony.[70] Elsewhere, new growth was completely stunted. For example, New Orleans, a city with a Little Italy populated almost exclusively by Sicilians from *latifondo* towns, claimed no more than a handful of radicals.[71] As in Sicily, the success of labor militance varied considerably.

Many obstacles besides familism have been cited as explanations for low levels of labor militance among south-Italians: high mobility rates, frequent returns to Italy, interethnic conflict, the timing of south-Italian migration, divisions resulting from fascism, and social fragmentation in Little Italies.[72] All of these factors undoubtedly played their roles. But none, I think, can adequately explain the variation we find between Tampa and Utica or between New York and San Francisco. Each of these communities faced the same structural problems, yet only some gained a reputation for immigrant radicalism.

The Sicilian history of labor militance can provide some guidance in explaining variation in immigrant radicalism in the United States. In Sicily, labor militance succeeded in towns where artisans spoke and peasants, influenced by distinctive work experiences, listened and responded. Rudolph J. Vecoli has argued similarly that in American Little Italies, artisans spoke, but peasants failed to respond: "They found it difficult to penetrate the *braccianti*" (day laborers).[73] Since artisans in Sicily faced the same challenge and sometimes succeeded, we need to understand why emigrated peasants, like grape cultivators, did not hear the message of labor militance.

The kind of work taken by peasant immigrants in the United States was of obvious importance. In New Orleans, Italian immigrants concentrated in petty trade and commerce; in militant Tampa emigrated Sicilians found work in cigar making. In San Francisco, Sicilians often became fishermen; in New York they crowded garment factories, excavation sites, and shoe factories. It seems reasonable to argue that peasants finding work as unskilled ditch-diggers or factory operators more closely resembled Sicily's wheat raisers, while the peddler of fish or lemons, like the cultivator of grapes or oranges, confronted a changeable market, not an exploitative employer.[74]

But even New York had its pushcart Sicilian markets, and Chicago and Boston had their Sicilian construction workers and factory operatives. Other factors were at work. The history of migration from Sambuca revealed another way that migration to these cities might have influenced artisans' efforts to reach peasants with their plea for class unity and action.[75] The most surprising finding in Sambuca's archives was the extent to which artisans and peasants from the town migrated to differing locations in the United States. Artisans preferred a single destination—the New York area—in overwhelming numbers. Thus, while more than two-thirds of artisans leaving Sambuca went to New York, Brooklyn, and Hoboken, only about a quarter of migrating peasants headed for New York. Peasants from Sambuca chose a wider variety of destinations than artisans. Many flocked first to Louisiana and, slightly later, to Chicago. They also went to the mining towns of Illinois, to Kansas City and—in small numbers—to Denver, Tampa, Boston, and Texas. Migration thus separated most peasants from the town's militant artisans. The artisans lived among themselves; in Brooklyn, for example, they formed a mutual benefit society, participated in shoemakers' strikes in the first decades of the twentieth century and continued to marry among themselves as they had in Sambuca.[76] Relatively few fellow villagers of peasant origin could hear their message.

Outside New York, Sambuca's colonies in the United States were dominated by peasants; in Chicago, for example, only one emigrant in seven was an artisan. The role of artisans in cities like Chicago and New Orleans differed fundamentally from that of artisans in Sicily or in New York. Both circumstantial and direct evidence suggest that artisans in these communities came as padroni (labor bosses) and became not labor militants but immigrant *prominenti* (the elite).

Artisans were among the first to leave their western Sicilian homes; this, and their literacy, suggest that they would become padroni, linking employers in the United States to eager new Sicilian recruits. Sambuca's local records preserve more direct evidence: throughout the 1890s, children were born to a local shoemaker who also sometimes gave his occupation as "sub-agent of emigration," a typical padrone title.[77] It is probably significant that artisans who migrated from Sambuca to Chicago, New Orleans, and other smaller cities were men who already had close occupational ties to peasants—they were carters, millers, and butchers. By contrast, the typical artisan emigrating to New York was a barber, a tailor, or a shoemaker.

Artisans became padroni because they were the most respected and financially secure of Sambuca's migrants. Sambuca's *civile* elite could scarcely have served as padroni; too few migrated and, when they did migrate, they went exclusively to New York. Since padroni typically formed the immigrant elite in cities and towns with peasant majorities, most immigrant *prominenti* probably were former artisans. John Briggs has described small-city *prominenti* as entrepreneurial and energetic, capable institution- and community-builders. He traced their culture to workers' mutual benefit societies and worker education projects in southern Italy.[78] In other words, artisan *prominenti* also built upon their European experiences—that of threatened "half petty capitalists." Unlike Sicily or artisan-crowded New York, peasant-dominated Little Sicilies provided ample opportunities for artisans again to become successful petty capitalists.[79] Furthermore, by migrating, they automatically became the social pinnacle of village-based immigrant communities. Unlike the men described by Briggs, many would clearly imitate the habits of the Sicilian *civile* elite, educating their sons as pharmacists and lawyers and dividing immigrant organizations with the kind of intense factional fighting that had also characterized *civile* "boss" politics in many Sicilian town halls in the 1880s.[80]

Sambuca's migration patterns have very clear implications for labor militance in American Little Sicilies. Where artisans concentrated, especially in New York, labor militance could prevail, as it did, of course, in that city. Elsewhere, however, where a few artisans lived among peasant majorities, Sicilian traditions might have a weaker echo, especially if peasants found work other than as industrial wage earners. The problem was not so much (as Vecoli believed) that peasants would not listen but rather that artisans themselves—the bankers, saloon owners, and storekeepers of the community—no longer had a message to broadcast. Peasant immigrants in Chicago and Tampa might become militants because their work experiences encouraged them to listen to labor militants outside their village-based communities. When fellow village artisans no longer linked the European tradition of militance to the immigrant community, then radicalization may, in fact, have had to await a kind of Americanization, or at least a decline in the local loyalties of *campanilismo*.

Migration: The Sicilian Consequences

Migration complicated the transference of Sicilian traditions of labor militance to the United States by restoring many artisans to their position as successful petty capitalists and by separating most artisans from most peasants. The impact of migration on Sicilian labor militance was quite different, however. In towns that were already militant, migration did not hinder and may have encouraged further labor militance. Again, the effect of migration and return migration on peasant-artisan ties was of utmost significance.

It is important to stress that migration was not a particularly effective long-term safety valve for Sicilian discontent. The link between migration rates and labor militance in the 1880 to 1921 period was not a simple one. Not only did *latifondo* residents fight and flee in above average proportions, residents of nonmilitant towns showed no extraordinary preference for migration, and migration rates from these towns were much lower than in MacDonald's nonmilitant "Deep South" (Abruzzi, Calabria, Basilicata). In wheat-raising towns without *latifondi* yet another pattern prevailed; there, emigration and militance developed together more slowly. Peasant strikes and a veritable migratory hemorrhage began around 1902 to 1904 in many of these towns. Thus western Sicily provides at least some evidence for any imaginable theoretical linkage between migration and labor militance.

Second, return migration did not push Sicilian political culture in a uniformly conservative direction, as is usually assumed. Return migration to Sicily was high. Returners, existing studies posit, used American savings to purchase small plots of land, thus entering the lower-middle class.[81] In good familist fashion, the *Americani* improved their families' economic position temporarily, undercutting the labor militants' insistence that only collective action and radical change could improve the lot of agriculturalists. Return migration has been mentioned as a factor important in explaining peasant support for fascism and especially for strong Christian Democratic support in southern Italy since World War II.[82]

Politically, return migration had none of these consequences in western Sicily. Support for fascism was nowhere particularly strong on the island; the nationalist appeal so important to Mussolini and his followers fell on deaf ears in Sicily.[83] It was not the lower-middle class, expanded by *Americani*, but the old elite, the *civili*, that supported Mussolini, and even the *civili* turned to Mussolini as a matter of expedience. (And many regretted their choice when il Duce attacked the *mafia* that had always provided *civili* with assistance in controlling peasant insurrections.)[84]

Similarly, in the years immediately after World War II, Sicily's support for the Christian Democrats was far from overwhelming. A significant group of towns had strong leftist electorates. If we define any town "red" that saw 40 percent of its electorate choose

Table 2 Leftist Vote, 1947, by Type of Town

	Proportion of Town Residents voting for Blocco del Popolo[a]
Nonmilitant towns	19%
Declining militant towns	17
Militant towns	44

SOURCE: Presidenza della Regione Siciliana, *Le Elezioni in Sicilia, Dati e Grafici dal 1946 al 1956* (Milan: A. Giuffrè, 1956).

[a]The Blocco del Popolo was a popular-front coalition of Socialist and Communist Party members in the regional elections of 1947.

leftists in the immediate postwar years, then a third of Sicilian towns were red towns. Fascism had not destroyed Sicilian traditions of labor militance. In fact, as Table 2 shows, it was precisely the militant towns of the early twentieth century that most strongly supported Socialist and Communist parties forty years later. In almost half of all western Sicilian "militant" towns, a coalition of leftists was in a position to govern locally. Concretely, this meant that long-time militants in these towns had successfully recruited both new adherents and a younger generation of supporters in the face of Fascist repressions.

Some of these new supporters undoubtedly were returned migrants and their children. Migrants returning to nonmilitant towns may have entered the ranks of the Christian Democrats. But in other towns, returning migrants—and ironically, most especially those achieving lower-middle-class status—were drawn to the local tradition of labor militance. That tradition originated, after all, in the lower-middle class, among artisans. Again, events in Sambuca demonstrate how this process occurred in one town.

The social basis for leftist politics in twentieth-century Sambuca was cooperation between town artisans and peasants. New ties between the two groups began in the 1880s but bore little political fruit before 1900, when the town's Socialist Party was still completely dominated by artisans. In 1913, however, enfranchised peasants helped elect the first Socialists to the town government and, in 1918, peasants acted decisively and collectively for the first time, occupying town lands.[85] Thus it seems that artisans in Sambuca successfully attracted peasants to their tradition of labor militance during the peak years of migration out of and back into the town. How did this happen?

Migration quickly undercut the sharp social distinctions that had separated Sicilian artisans from peasants in 1880. As new manufactured goods appeared in Sambuca, artisan sons left the town en masse.[86] Only a third returned permanently; half then became peasants farming family-owned land while the rest opened their own workshops or took over those of their fathers. Since few artisan daughters migrated, most had little choice but to marry peasant men.[87] These were some of the first recorded instances of intermarriage between artisans and peasants. The marriage records of the town attest to the status differences of the two parties—the scrawled X of the bridegroom next to the bride's careful signature.

Curiously, peasant boys clamored to replace emigrating artisans as apprentices in the *bottega* workshops. Even more curiously (given their undeniable familiarity with deteriorating local markets), older artisans took on peasant apprentices for the first time during the 1880s and 1890s.[88] It is impossible to know whether they feared that no son would return to take over the workshop, whether they trained peasants in order to provide appropriate bridegrooms for their daughters, or whether they consciously trained peasants with skills useful to emigrants. (Many peasants so trained did later migrate to New York.) Regardless of motivation, the effect was the same: the occupational boundary separating peasant from artisan was breached.

Returning peasant emigrants showed a similar enthusiasm for artisanal work. Only a minority of returned peasants actually succeeded in achieving lower-middle-class status, but of these upwardly mobile men, as many opened workshops as purchased land.[89] (Studies that emphasize the burning lust of the Italian "bird of passage" for land ownership conveniently ignore the disdain with which Sicilians of all classes looked on agricultural labor.) Returned peasants were also far more likely than others to train their sons as artisans or to arrange marriages between their daughters and artisan sons.[90] Thus, despite the competition of imported goods and the departure of so many artisans for the United States, artisanal work remained a desirable goal, and the numbers of artisans working in Sambuca remained quite stable.

The result was that by 1920 artisan and peasant families in Sambuca had kinship, marital, and occupational connections to each other. As Sambuca's artisans became land-owning peasants, it was their long-standing tradition of occupational solidarity and their more recent acceptance of labor militance that shaped the culture of Sambuca's lower-middle class. For peasants, any route to lower-middle-class status, whether land ownership or craft work, led to close and intimate contact with artisans. It was through these new peasant middlemen that socialist ideas finally entered the world of Sambuca's proletarianized peasants. As wheat growers, they listened.

The political expression of new ties between artisans and peasants was the formation of Sambuca's Communist Party. By 1921, when young Italian maximalists split from the Socialists to form the Communist Party, Sambuca already had peasant and shepherd leaders to follow their example.[91] Whereas only three of ten early Socialists had been of agricultural background, seven of thirteen early Communists were peasants or peasants' sons.[92] Many of these men had a seamstress mother and artisan maternal grandparents; they were the products of the first "mixed marriages" of the 1880s and 1890s. A handful of Sambuca's young Communists spent time in Fascist jails; many more went north and to Apulia to join the partisans.[93] In 1947, more than three-quarters of Sambuca's voters chose the Blocco del Popolo, and since that time Communists have controlled the municipal government. Sambuca today is one of Sicily's "red" towns. For the American descendants of Sambuca's earlier migrants, this divergence of immigrant and Sicilian political traditions often comes as a shock when they return to rekindle family ties and to seek their roots.

Labor Militance: Culture in Context

Very few studies of immigrant radicalism have chosen a transatlantic comparative approach. This is unfortunate, for the benefits of such a method are real.[94] The case of western Sicily easily demonstrates some of the advantages of a simultaneous view of events on both sides of the Atlantic. First, by examining one group in a variety of both Sicilian and American settings, the scholar can better "hold culture constant," treating it as an independent variable in the study of labor militance. Considerable variation on both sides of the Atlantic should serve as a firm reminder, however, that culture at best set very broad limits on Sicilian political and organizational behavior. Furthermore, the success of labor militants in differing contexts provided a unique opportunity to assess the relative importance of noncultural factors that influenced Sicilians' receptivity to labor militance. Artisan/peasant social relations and peasant work experiences emerged as key factors in the history of labor militance.

Finally, and most importantly, the development of labor militance among Sicilians on both sides of the Atlantic Ocean should remind us that modernization (or the transition from pre-industrial to industrial society) is not simply a tale of increasing cultural homogeneity.[95] Certainly culture varied from village to village in Sicily in 1880—but only in some respects. If we focus exclusively on such variables as marriage customs, on costume, or on language, then a trend from diversity to homogeneity can easily be demonstrated; for it was these aspects of Sicilian life that varied most in the years prior to mass migration. But a people's culture is not limited to the rituals and beliefs best loved by folklore preservationists. All over western Sicily, people shared one set of ideas about class, occupation, cooperation, and conflict; all over the region, artisans enjoyed a unified and strong tradition of occupational identification and voluntary association. From this set of shared ideas and experiences, Sicilians created many traditions as they moved through space and time. Sicilians in militant, nonmilitant, and declining-militant towns, as well as in New York and in San Francisco or in Sicilian "red" and Christian Democratic towns today, all shared roughly the same cultural starting place in their understanding of class relations. Culturally, however, they became more diverse as they moved into the twentieth century. Keeping that cultural dynamism at the center of future studies should lead to the firm rejection of portrayals of familist south Italians and of immigrant padrone slaves and primitive rebels. A better understanding of the uniqueness of the multiethnic American working classes will seem a less distant goal as a result.

Notes

I wish to thank Christiane Harzig, George Pozzetta, and Jane and Peter Schneider, who read earlier versions of this essay.

1. In 1976, Rudolph Vecoli could list only three authoritative English-language studies on Italians in the labor movement: Edward Fenton, "Italians in the Labor Movement," *Pennsylvania History* 26 (April 1954): 133–43; Fenton, "Italian Immigrants in the Stoneworkers' Union," *Labor History* 3 (Spring 1962): 188–92; and Samuel L. Baily, "The Italians and the Development of Organized Labor in Argentina, Brazil and the United States, 1880–1914," *Journal of Social History* 3 (Winter 1969): 123–34. See Vecoli's "*Pane e Giustizia:* A Brief History of the Italian-American Labor Movement," *La Parola del Popolo* 26 (September–October 1976): 55–61. Since then, Fenton's dissertation has been published, *Immigrants and Unions, A Case Study* (New York: Arno Press, 1975). See also Paul Buhle, "Italian-American Radicals and the Labor Movement, 1905–30," *Radical History Review* 17 (1978): 14–53; George E. Pozzetta, "Italian Radicals in Tampa, Fla., A Research Note," *International Labor and Working Class History* 22 (Fall 1982): 77–81; George E. Pozzetta, ed., *Pane e Lavoro* (Toronto: Multicultural History of Ontario, 1980).

2. Edward C. Banfield, *The Moral Basis of a Backward Society* (Chicago: The Free Press/Research Center in Economic Development and Cultural Change, University of Chicago, 1958), esp. 85–104; E. J. Hobsbawm, *Primitive Rebels* (New York: W. W. Norton, 1959), 1–5. The continued dependence of immigration historians on Banfield's and Hobsbawm's cultural analyses is significant. See, for example, Humbert S. Nelli, *From Immigrants to Ethnics: The Italian Americans* (Oxford and New York: Oxford University Press 1983), chap. 7.

3. Fenton, "Italians in the Labor Movement," pp. 133–35; Nelli, *From Immigrants to Ethnics*, p. 91.

4. Anthropologists in particular have long since rejected Banfield's work on south-Italian culture. See, for example, Jane Schneider and Peter Schneider, *Culture and Political Economy in Western Sicily* (New York: Academic Press, 1976). Among the revisionist historians are Carole White, *Patrons and Partisans: A Study of Politics in Two Southern Italian* Comuni (New York: Cambridge University Press, 1980); and John Briggs, *An Italian Passage* (New Haven: Yale University Press, 1978).

5. By "labor militance" I mean collective class-based action, in either the workplace or political arena, which has as its goal a new economic order.

6. Constance Cronin, *The Sting of Change* (Chicago: University of Chicago Press, 1971); Hobsbawm, *Primitive Rebels*, pp. 3–55, 74–104; E. J. Hobsbawm, *Bandits* (New York: Dell Publishing, 1969).

7. "Southern Italy"—the Mezzogiorno—was a conceptual product of social darwinist thinking in northern Italy and in the offices of the United States Immigration Commission; in the nineteenth century it was not a single unified culture area.

8. Giuseppe Pitrè, *Proverbi Siciliani*, vol. 8–11, Biblioteca delle Tradizioni Popolari Siciliane (Palermo: Luigi Pedone Lauriel, 1880).

9. Denis Mack Smith, *A History of Sicily: Modern Sicily after 1713* (London: Chatto and Windus, 1968), 445–50.

10. Schneider and Schneider, *Culture and Political Economy*, pp. 114–20.

11. Orazio Cancila, "Variazioni e Tendenze dell' Agricoltura Siciliana a Cavallo della Crisi Agraria," in *I Fasci Siciliani*, ed. C. Dollo et al. (Bari: De Donato, 1976).

12. Denis Mack Smith, "The Latifundia in Modern Sicilian History," *Proceedings of the British Academy* 6 (1965): 85–124; Emilio Sereni, *Il Captialismo nelle Campagne, 1860–1900* (Turin: Einaudi, 1968), 134–41.

13. *Atti della Giunta per l'Inchiesta Agraria e sulle Condizioni della Classe Agricola*, vol. 13, books 1 and 2, (Rome: Forzani Tip. del Senato, 1884–1885); *Inchiesta Parlamentare sulle Condizioni dei Contadini nelle Provincie Meridionale e nella Sicilia*, vol. 6, G. Lorenzoni, *Sicilia* (Rome: Tip. Naz. G. Bertero, 1910), 54.

14. This nonagricultural population has not yet received much scholarly attention from anthropologists or from historians of peasant society or emigration.

15. Ignazio Nigrelli, "La Crisi della Industria Zolfifera Siciliana in Relazione al Movimento dei Fasci," *Movimento Operaio* 6 (November–December 1954).

16. Jane Schneider, "Trousseau as Treasure: Some Contradictions of Late Nineteenth-Century Change in Sicily," in *Beyond the Myths of Culture*, ed. Eric Ross (New York: Academic Press, 1980), 333–37.

17. F. Brancato, *La Sicilia nel Primo Ventennio del Regno d'Italia* (Bologna: Dott. Cesare Zuffi, 1956), 54–55.

18. Jürg K. Siegenthaler, "Sicilian Economic Change since 1860," *Journal of European Economic History* 2 (1973): 363–415.

19. Jane Schneider and Peter Schneider, "The Demographic Transition in Sicily," *Journal of Family History* 9, no. 3 (Fall 1984): 245–72.

20. Cancila, "Variazioni e Tendenze" and Guiseppe Giarrizzo, "La Sicilia e la Crisi Agraria," in *I Fasci Siciliani*, ed. Dollo et al.

21. Francesco Renda, *L'Emigrazione in Sicilia* (Palermo: Tip. la Cartografica, 1963), 69; Renda, *I Fasci Siciliani, 1892–1894* (Turin: Einaudi, 1977), chap. 2.

22. There is a huge and growing Italian literature on the Fasci Siciliani; the best English introduction remains Hobsbawm, *Primitive Rebels*, chap. 6.

23. Ibid., p. 93.

24. J. S. MacDonald, "Agricultural Organization, Migration and Labour Militancy in Rural Italy," *The Economic History Review*, 2d. ser., no. 16 (1963): 61–75.

25. My approach to the study of workers' "collective action" will be familiar to readers of *The Rebellious Century*, Charles Tilly, Louise Tilly, and Richard Tilly (Cambridge, Mass.: Harvard University Press, 1975). National strike statistics for the period from 1884 to 1913 contained many and obvious omissions, but I was able to turn to a large literature by local Sicilian scholars to correct this problem. The only period for which no systematic evidence was available were the important

years 1919 to 1921: national summaries of strikes gave no local breakdowns, and local historians have unfortunately not yet mined newspapers and local archives for this period of unrest. Thus, if there is a bias in the reporting, it would be in the direction of overestimating declines in labor militance.

26. Giuseppe Carlo Marino, *Movimento Contadino e Blocco Agraria nella Sicilia Giolittiana* (Palermo: S. F. Flaccovio, 1979), 28–48; Francesco Renda, *Socialisti e Cattolici in Sicilia, 1900–1904* (Caltanissetta-Roma: Ed. Salvatore Sciascia, 1972).

27. Ministero di Agricoltura, Industria e Commercio, Direzione Generale della Statistica e del Lavoro, *Statistica delle Elezioni Generali Politiche* (Rome: Tip. Naz. di G. Bertero, 1914).

28. See note 25. Angelo Tasca, *Nascità e Avvento del Fascismo, l'Italia dal 1918 al 1922* (Florence: La Nuova Italia, 1950), 174–75; Giorgio Alberto Chiurco, *Storia della Rivoluzione Fascista*, 5 vol. (Florence: Vallecchi, 1929); Roberto Vivarelli, *Il Dopoguerra in Italia e l'Avvento del Fascismo, 1918–1922*, vol. 1 (Naples: Istituto Italiano per gli Studi Storici in Napoli, 1967).

29. Banfield, *The Moral Basis of a Backward Society*, pp. 85, 89, 99.

30. Christian Giordano, *Handwerker und Bauernverbände in der Sizilianischen Gesellschaft*, Heiderberger Sociologica 14 (Tübingen: J. C. B. Mohr, 1975), app. 1.

31. Donna Gabaccia, *From Sicily to Elizabeth Street* (Albany, N.Y.: State University of New York Press, 1984), 4–5, 8–9.

32. Ibid., pp. 5–8.

33. *Atti della Giunta per l'Inchiesta Agraria* provides the following data for most Sicilian towns: crops exported and imported, average size of land plots, types of agricultural contracts, representation of peasant landowners, presence of agricultural industries.

34. MacDonald, "Agricultural Organization, Migration and Labour Militancy."

35. John Bodnar, Roger Simon, and Michael P. Weber, *Lives of Their Own: Blacks, Italians, and Poles in Pittsburgh, 1900–1960* (Urbana, Chicago, London: University of Illinois Press, 1982), 44–48.

36. Differing aspects of this town as "representative" of western Sicily are described in Schneider and Schneider, *Culture and Political Economy*, pp. 14–16; and Gabaccia, *From Sicily to Elizabeth Street*, pp. 15–21.

37. Charlotte Gower Chapman, *Milocca, A Sicilian Village* (Cambridge, Mass.: Schenkman 1971), 60.

38. John Davis, "Town and Country," *Anthropological Quarterly* 42 (1969): 171–85; Gabaccia, *From Sicily to Elizabeth Street*, pp. 49–50.

39. Gabaccia, *From Sicily to Elizabeth Street*, pp. 45–49.

40. Anton Blok, *The Mafia of a Sicilian Village, 1860–1960* (New York: Harper Torchbooks, 1974), 47–48.

41. *Atti di Matrimoni*, Archivio Comunale, Sambuca di Sicilia.

42. Briggs, *An Italian Passage*, chap. 2.

43. Giordano, *Handwerker*, app. 1; see also Ministero di Agricoltura, Industria e Commercio, *Statistica della Società di Mutuo Soccorso* (Rome: 1873, 1878, 1885).

44. Giordano, *Handwerker*, app. 1.

45. Giovanni Schepis, *Le Consultazioni Popolari in Italia dal 1848 al 1957, Profilo Storico-Statistico* (Empoli: Ed. Caparrini, n.d.).

46. Renda, *I Fasci Siciliani*, p. 342.

47. Alfonso di Giovanna, *Inchiostro e Trazzere* (Sambuca: la Voce, 1979), 28.

48. Ibid., p. 29.

49. Schneider and Schneider, *Culture and Political Economy*, p. 185.

50. Renda, *I Fasci Siciliani, 1892–1894*, chap. 8; Roderick Aya, "The Missed Revolution: The Fate of Rural Rebels in Sicily and Southern Spain, 1840–1950," *Papers on European and Mediterranean Societies*, no. 3 (Amsterdam: Antropologisch-Sociologisch Centrum, University of Amsterdam 1975).

51. Gabaccia, "Migration and Peasant Militance," *Social Science History* 8 (Winter 1984): 67–80.

52. Most, for example, had at least one mutual benefit society by 1890.

53. MacDonald, "Agricultural Organization, Migration and Labour Militancy."
54. *Inchiesta Parlamentare*, pp. 124–25, 177–78; Sidney Sonnino, *I Contadini in Sicilia* (1925; Florence: Vallecchi, 1974), 39.
55. *Atti della Giunta*, passim; Sonnino, *I Contadini*, pp. 40–44.
56. Hobsbawm, *Primitive Rebels*, p. 6.
57. Bodnar, Simon, and Weber, *Lives of their Own*, pp. 44–48.
58. Briggs, *An Italian Passage*, pp. 5–6.
59. Direzione Generale della Statistica, *Statistica della Emigrazione Italiana* (Rome: 1881–1915).
60. Among young draftees from Sambuca, all the emigrants listed in the 1880s were artisans; during the 1890s, four out of five migrant draftees were artisans. Only after 1900 did the representation of artisans among departed draftees from Sambuca drop—to about a third of the total (*Lista della Leva*, 1880–1930, Archivio Comunale, Sambuca di Sicilia).
61. U.S. Senate, Reports of the Immigration Commission, *Immigrants in Cities*, vol. 2. (Washington: Government Printing Office, 1911).
62. For passport and *nulla osta* applications, see *Statistica della Emigrazione Italiana.*
63. For example, Virginia Yans-McLaughlin, *Family and Community, Italian Immigrants in Buffalo, 1880–1930* (Ithaca: Cornell University Press, 1977), 60–63; Josef J. Barton, *Peasants and Strangers: Italians, Rumanians and Slovaks in an American City, 1890–1950* (Cambridge, Mass.: Harvard University Press, 1975), 30–32.
64. Gabaccia, "Migration and Peasant Militance," table 2.
65. On Panepinto, see Vincenza Scarpaci, *A Portrait of the Italians in America* (New York: Charles Scribner's Sons, 1982), photo 171; on Barbato, see *Il Proletario*, 5 February 1905; on Verrò, see Pasquale M. De Ciampis, "Storia del Movimento Rivoluzionario Italiano," *La Parola del Popolo*, 9 (December 1958–January 1959): 136–63.
66. Besides De Ciampis, "Storia del Movimento Rivoluzionario," see Fort Velona, "Genesi del Movimento Socialista Democratico e della Parola del Popolo," and Nicola Mastrorilli, "Il Movimento dei Socialisti Italiani di Buffalo," both in *La Parola del Popolo* 9 (December 1958–1959); and Pozzetta, "Italian Radicals."
67. *Il Proletario*, February–May 1905.
68. See, for example, Domenico Saudino, "Ad Memoriam," *La Parola del Popolo* 9 (December 1958–January 1959).
69. Besides the articles cited in notes 66 and 67, see Pasquale M. De Ciampis, "Gli Italiani in America," *La Parola del Popolo* 26 (September–October 1976).
70. A considerable number of studies of Italian immigrants in specific American cities make no mention whatsoever of labor activities; for example, Dino Cinel, *From Italy to San Francisco* (Stanford, Calif.: Stanford University Press, 1982), as well as most of the articles collected in Robert T. Harney and J. Vincenza Scarpaci, eds., *Little Italies in North America* (Toronto: Multicultural History Society of Ontario, 1981).
71. Nelli, *Immigrants to Ethnics*, chap. 4; see also *Il Proletario*, 7 May 1905, "Da molto tempo la sezione di New Orleans giace nel più profondo stato d'apatia."
72. Nelli, *Immigrants to Ethnics*, pp. 90–91.
73. Vecoli, *"Pane e Giustizia,"* pp. 55–61.
74. U.S. Bureau of the Census, *Twelfth Census, 1900, Special Reports, Occupations* (Washington: Government Printing Office, 1904).
75. My analysis of migration from Sambuca is based on the reconstitution of the families and emigration histories of 3,000 town residents identified in town civil records (draft, marriage, birth, death, and household registration) as living in the United States at some time between 1880 and 1931.
76. See *Corriere Siciliano*, 14 March 1931, 9 May 1931, 13 February 1932; on shoemakers' strikes in Brooklyn, see *Il Proletario*, 21 May 1905 and 19 March 1905.
77. The literature on the Italian padrone is extensive; good starting places are

John Koren, "The Padrone System and the Padrone Banks," *U.S. Bureau of Labor, Special Bulletin,* no. 9 (March 1897): 119–23; and Humbert S. Nelli, "The Italian Padrone System in the United States," *Labor History* 5 (Spring 1964): 53–67.

78. Briggs, *An Italian Passage,* chap. 2.

79. Briggs, *An Italian Passage;* Cinel, *From Italy to San Francisco;* and Bodnar, Simon, and Weber, *Lives of Their Own* emphasize the movement of Italian immigrants into petty entrepreneurial and skilled trades.

80. Yans-McLaughlin, *Family and Community,* p. 118; Robert F. Harney, "Toronto's Little Italy, 1885–1945," in *Little Italies in North America,* ed. Harney and Scarpaci, pp. 52–54.

81. Francesco P. Cerase, "A Study of Italian Migrants Returning from the U.S.A.," *International Migration Review* 1 (1967): 67–74; Joseph Lopreato, "Social Stratification and Mobility," *American Sociological Review* 26 (1961): 585–96; Betty Boyd Caroli, *Italian Repatriation from the United States, 1900–1914* (Staten Island: Center for Migration Studies, 1973), 61.

82. Banfield, *The Moral Basis of a Backward Society,* p. 96; on DC support in the south, see the useful map in David I. Kertzer, *Comrades and Christians* (Cambridge: Cambridge University Press, 1980), 17.

83. While other young Italian men responded to the nationalist appeal of World War I, young men from Sambuca in the years from 1912 to 1914 went to their town halls for quite another purpose: they applied in record numbers to go to the United States. Between 70 and 80 percent of the young men born between 1893 and 1895 were abroad by the time they were called for the draft.

84. See for example, Chapman, *Milocca,* pp. 5–6.

85. Schneider and Schneider, *Culture and Political Economy,* pp. 157–58.

86. See note 60.

87. My discussion of Sambuca's artisan families and their sons and daughters is based on analysis of thirty completely reconstituted families formed by Sambuca's artisans in the 1860s and 1870s.

88. Artisans born after 1870 in Sambuca were twice as likely to have a peasant father as artisans born before 1870.

89. My study of Sambuca's returners is not yet complete; for this essay, I analyzed 244 migrants for whom I could find complete household registration files describing both family of origin and family of procreation. Forty-eight, just under 20%, were the sons of artisans; the remainder were sons of peasants.

90. Overall, 20 percent of their sons became artisans; the pattern was most pronounced among peasants returning from Louisiana.

91. Di Giovanna, *Inchiostro and Trazzere,* pp. 28–29.

92. Almost half were either returned emigrants or the sons of returned emigrants.

93. Di Giovanna, *Inchiostro and Trazzere,* pp. 28–29.

94. See, for example, Hartmut Keil, "The German Immigrant Working Class of Chicago, 1875–1890: Workers, Labor Leaders and the Labor Movement," in *American Labor and Immigration History, 1877–1920s,* ed. Dirk Hoerder (Urbana: University of Illinois Press, 1983), 156–76.

95. As it is, for example, in Eugen Weber, *Peasants into Frenchmen,* (Stanford: Stanford University Press, 1976).

Communities and Struggles

RICHARD SCHNEIROV

Free Thought and Socialism in the Czech Community in Chicago, 1875–1887

This essay originates in the problem of how to account for the militancy and socialist allegiance of Bohemian or Czech lumbershovers and other Czech workingmen in Chicago between 1877 and 1887.[1] The answer leads into a consideration of the origins of immigration from Bohemia and the relation between the formation of the ethnic working-class community of Pilsen and the local labor movement.

During Chicago's 1877 Great Upheaval the lumbershovers, according to all local accounts, were the most prominent and militant occupational group in the strike. Analysis of eighty-eight riot casualties reported in the press reveals that 42 percent lived in the Sixth Ward, which housed the Czech neighborhood of Pilsen; 22 percent of the total lived in one small precinct at the heart of Pilsen, adjacent to the lumberyards.[2] A *Chicago Tribune* reporter stoned during the upheaval by Pilsen residents called the area "a hotbed of communism . . . the worst in the city." A year after the strikes, Police Lieutenant Vesey, whose district encompassed Pilsen, told a reporter that "there is great dissatisfaction among the class of men who work in and about the lumberyards and planing mills, and nearly every one of these workingmen is a strong socialist."[3]

In the county elections of August 1877 the first socialist candidates won office under the auspices of the Workingmen's Party of the United States, later renamed the Socialistic Labor Party (SLP). The socialist political presence continued through April 1879, when an SLP mayoral candidate received 20 per cent of the vote. In three of the four elections held between 1877 and 1879 the Czech lumberyard precinct, so prominent in the 1877 strikes, contributed the highest socialist vote of any city precinct.[4]

Nine years after the 1877 affair, on the eve of the eight-hour strikes, Czech and German lumbershovers, at the urging of anarchist leader August Spies, clashed with strikebreakers at McCormick's Reaper Plant. The ensuing altercation with police left several persons dead and led directly to the convening of the fateful Haymarket meeting of 4 May 1886. In the elections that followed Haymarket, Czech workingmen again contributed to labor voting far beyond their proportion—only 2.36 percent—of the city's population.[5]

Even allowing for customary exaggeration—at its height in 1879 the Chicago SLP had only about 600 members, and thus not many Czech lumbershovers could have belonged to the party—the evidence is overwhelming that the lumbershovers and other Czech workingmen in Pilsen constituted one of the major constituencies of Chicago socialism.[6] Yet the explanations for the convergence of Bohemian nationality, lumberyard work, and socialism are far from obvious. Nineteenth-century socialism has often been associated with skilled workmen confronting industrialization—for example, German cabinetmakers and cigar makers as well as metalworkers and machinists of various nationalities. These men exercised some control over the production process and combined traditions of artisanal independence and craft pride with a propensity for political involvement.[7] By contrast, lumber work was not an occupation undergoing mechanization or division of labor; instead, it was a job involving heavy material handling associated with a pre-industrial mercantile economy. It was work that not only lacked the discipline of the machine process that Marx and Veblen thought necessary to working-class socialism but that lacked even the unifying experience of employment in a factory.[8] The uniqueness of the Czech lumbershovers' socialist proclivities is highlighted by the fact that Irish lumber vessel unloaders, coal heavers, salt laborers, and other dockworkers remained immune to socialism, despite many violent collisions with employers and police.

One may hypothesize that Czechs who undertook lumberwork were recent immigrants with Old World artisanal roots, radicalized by being forced to accept menial laboring positions. Yet the available evidence indicates that lumbershovers were agricultural laborers or rural cottagers who brought no definable skills with them to Chicago.[9] Clearly, the mainsprings of Czech lumbershover socialism must be sought in a different direction, if not in the transformation of the workplace, then in the origin of immigration in Bohemia and the formation of a Czech-American ethnic identity in the two decades following the Civil War.

Studies of immigrant groups in America have been guided by a model that focuses on the formation of ethnic identity and its persistence or disintegration in the face of pressures for assimilation into the mainstream of middle-class America.[10] Such a model deflects attention from the fact that for many immigrant groups before the so-called "new immigration" of the 1890s, the founding of new communities in America created a congenial environment for the flowering of suppressed nationalist and democratic revolutionary aspirations. For example, German immigration after the 1848 revolution fed into the radical wing of the Republican Party during the Civil War and Reconstruction. In the 1870s and 1880s, nationalism among Irish immigrants helped introduce Irish industrial workers to democratic reform currents and reinforced membership in the Knights of Labor. Thus, ethnic identity, particularly in its early stages, when class differentiation in immigrant communities was minimal, could serve as a direct path into oppositional currents in American society rather than as a force for accommodation with the dominant liberal individualism.[11]

The Czech immigration in the mid-nineteenth century and the formation of Czech-American communities exemplify this phenomenon. Yet the Czech-American experience was distinguished from that of the above groups in at least one crucial way: Czech radicalism was underpinned by an anti-religious dissent unparalleled among other European immigrants. Indeed, there is considerable evidence that the origins and formation of Czech freethought communities provide the most important context for explaining the rise of Czech socialism in Chicago beginning in the 1870s.

The religious question had been intertwined with Bohemian national history since the successful revolt led by Jan Hus in the fifteenth century against both the church and German domination. A century before Luther, Bohemia was Europe's first Protestant nation, its independence lasting until 1620, when it was forcibly re-catholicized and de-nationalized by the Jesuits and Hapsburgs. From that time forward Bohemian national traditions—political, intellectual, and cultural—were strongly anti-Catholic and anti-German.[12]

In the context of this history, nineteenth-century Czech immigration became both a political emancipation from Vienna and a religious emancipation from Rome. Yet there seems to be no clearly compelling reason that the simple anticlericalism, which by most accounts pervaded all sectors of the population in Bohemia, should have issued into free thought. As Karel D. Bicha notes, "the departure from a familiar physical and cultural environment ordinarily strengthened the ties of immigrants to their historic faith, at least in the short run." Even where religious radicalism took root in America, it was in all cases "conceived, born, nurtured, developed, and defined by the original European culture and transplanted to American in mature form."[13]

What Bicha calls the "de-catholicization of Czech immigrants" in America was predicated on the appearance in nineteenth-century Bohemia of a secular, nationalist leadership. Key members of this intelligentsia emigrated after the 1848 revolution, particularly after the upheavals of the 1860s, and provided leadership for American Czechs. Foremost among them were Ladimir Klácel, an ex-monk and well-known philosopher, Vojta Náprstek, a journalist and intellectual, and Frantisek B. Zdrůbek, an ex-seminarian. All were or became disciples of the great Czech patriot, Karel Havlíček, who imparted to them his intense hatred of the established church and his tendency toward free thought.[14]

These men were not refugees of revolution fleeing repression. They came to America willingly, even gladly. Like America's Puritan forefathers who wanted to make their settlement on the new continent a "City on a Hill," many of these leaders entertained ideas of planting a Czech colony that might be a fulfillment of the dreams of the enchained Czech nation. The nationalist middle classes of 1848 and 1849 had used America as a model not only for democracy but as an example of the success of a federal state. Among them, Havlíček idealized the United States. According to Thomas Čapek, Náprstek "pictured to himself [in his diary] an ideal Czech community in America" as early as 1847.[15] When Klácel emigrated in 1869, he wanted to organize a cooperative community in the Black Hills. In short, the men who shaped the Czech settlements in mid-nineteenth-century America wanted to transplant not their social roots but their social ideals.[16]

Czech communitarian settlements were never viable in America. Nonetheless, Czech intellectuals, despite initial difficulties, were remarkably successful in fashioning a vital free-thought culture among the newly arrived Czechs by the 1870s. Their vehicles were the benevolent societies, generally organized as part of the Czech Slavic Benevolent Society of the United States (CSPS), founded in 1854. Local lodges of the CSPS offered their members insurance for sickness, injury, and death. These functions seem to have been an extension of the voluntary benefit associations founded in nineteenth-century Czech villages. According to Josef Barton, 60 percent of the presidents of these societies in Chicago had belonged to a mutual benefit society in their native villages.[17]

Yet, local lodges also undertook to organize a broad range of cultural and political activities, a function that does not seem to have had a direct counterpart in the Bohemian village. Nor were benevolent societies copied from American workers. The first national benefit society of American workers, the Ancient Order of United Workmen, was founded in 1868. Rather, Czech benevolent societies were ethnic, working-class institutions, communal in nature, serving the same functions that the Catholic church performed for other ethnic workingmen.

The first Czech benevolent societies, however, were not dominated by free thinkers. The CSPS, according to its 1854 constitution, expressed belief in a deity. The first major benevolent society in Chicago, the Pan Slavic Slovanská Lípa, founded in 1861, attempted to unite free thinkers with Catholics and Poles with Czechs.[18] Clearly, the early forms of Czech-American ethnicity were not nearly so committed to free thought as later forms were.

In large part, the free thinkers were able to expand their influence through their control of the press. The first free-thought paper appeared among Chicago Czechs in 1867 under the name of *Pokrok* (Progress), edited by Josef Pastor, a scholarly Czech workingman. Catholics responded with the shortlasting *Katolické Noviny* (the Catholic News) edited by Father Joseph Molitor. Thus began a bitter feud within the Czech community. Though *Pokrok* continued through 1878, the free-thought cause was championed after 1875 by *Svornost,* founded by August Geringer, an immigrant to the city in 1869. To edit the paper Geringer immediately hired Zdrůbek, who only a year earlier had been a Protestant minister.[19]

Within several years these men had carried the free-thought struggle to a successful conclusion. Their triumph was confirmed in three important episodes. St. Wenceslaus, the first Czech Catholic parish in the city, had been founded in 1863 by a benevolent society. When Father Molitor was appointed, a dispute soon arose over who owned church property. A court decision that legal ownership resided in the bishop, not the parishioners, led to wholesale defections of Czech Catholics in the late 1870s, not only in St. Wenceslaus but in two other Czech parishes in the city.[20]

The second event was a series of debates held in April 1877 between Zdrůbek and Father William Čoka over the resolution that "religion destroys the moral and physical being of its faithful." Zdrůbek argued the rationalist position that faith bred blind loyalty and intellectual degeneracy. The debates were widely publicized in Czech Chicago's only daily paper, *Svornost,* and permanently fixed the battle lines between the two camps.[21]

Finally, at the very time that Catholicism was in disarray, Czechs turned en masse to benevolent societies, almost all under the leadership of the free thinkers. The first CSPS lodge in Chicago was organized in 1875. Two years later there were five lodges. In 1878 the organization of benevolent societies mushroomed, and by 1883 there were fifty-two societies led by free thinkers in Chicago, most of them benevolent societies.[22] In 1884 Zdrůbek reported that "there are very few Bohemians who would not belong to at least one benevolent, educational or social society."[23]

The new organizational strength of the free thinkers allowed them to found another counter-institution to the church, the Bohemian National Cemetery. For some time, priests had refused to bury, baptize, or marry members of free-thinkers societies. But in 1876, when Father Molitor refused to bury a Catholic woman who had not confessed at death, there was widespread outrage at the Church in the Czech community. In March 1877, Czech benevolent societies, including three Catholic societies, founded the cemetery under the leadership of Zdrůbek, Geringer, and a long-time Chicago Czech leader, Prokop Hudek.[24] Because so many Czech parishioners were nominal Catholics, preferring to remain with the church only to avail themselves of the official services of the priests, the establishment of the cemetery provided an important channel away from church rule.

By 1878 the combination of widespread anticlericalism among Czech immigrants and the energetic and skillful leadership of the free-thinking intellingentsia had ineradicably shaped the culture of a large portion of the Czech community in its most important American center, Chicago. From the 1870s through the early twentieth century all observers agreed that from 50 percent to as many as 70 percent of Chicago's Czechs belonged to the free-thinker rather than Catholic camp.[25] The bulk of these, however, were not ideological free thinkers. In 1895 the Czech suffragist Josefa Humpal Zeman, writing in *Hull House Papers,* argued that almost half "the Bohemian people [in Chicago] are simply non-church goers and call themselves 'free thinkers,' most of them having no definite philosophy and cherishing antagonism against church institutions. Of these the greater part merely imitate and repeat the sayings of the newspapers, many of which are edited by agnostics."[26]

All this suggests that through their ownership of the community's press, which in the 1870s and 1880s amounted to a monopoly, and their control of most benevolent societies and other cultural institutions the free thinkers had come to constitute the resident Czech establishment in Chicago. In their authoritative role in the community they acted as the arbiters of local culture, the bearers of national traditions, and the champions of the community's interests against Protestant zealots and rival nationalities, particularly the Germans, under whose wing Czech political activities were conducted. This is not to imply that the free-thinker establishment was an incipient capitalist class. Most accurately, it can be called an organizational elite.

Free thinkers' hegemonic position within the community was evident in the *Tribune*'s account of an 1878 demonstration celebrating the founding of Bohemian National Cemetery. "Every Bohemian society in the city" was represented at the affair, including Czech lodges of the Odd Fellows and the St. John's Benevolent Society. More than 3,000 attended the ceremony to hear an oration by Zdrůbek. Six years later another free-thinker-led demonstration included a Bohemian Catholic Turner society and two societies of Catholic foresters in addition to twenty-two CSPS lodges. There is no evidence that Czech Catholics could organize any demonstration or celebration remotely similar to these large-scale, pluralistic affairs.[27]

The free thinkers could never have assumed their leadership position had they been rigidly doctrinaire rationalists or atheists. Though free-thought Sunday schools translated the works of the American free thinker Robert Ingersoll and bestowed much of the credit for the American Revolution on Thomas Paine, Czech free thought was distinguished from other versions by its integration with the nineteenth-century renaissance of Czech national culture. Rather than a critical or revolutionary rationalism, it aspired to be a new creed, a substitute for church dogma suitable to an age of mass nationalism. Thus the free thinkers took over the annual celebrations of Jan Hus's birthday. In a play depicting the Hussite revolt, Zdrůbek personally acted out the part of the great Protestant nationalist leader.[28] Indeed, judging from the repeated calls for Czech unity in *Svornost*, Chicago's free thinkers must have been acutely conscious of their responsibility as leaders to promote conciliation and the community's general interest.

The role played by the free thinkers in the process of Czech-American ethnic identity has not gone unnoticed. But the interconnections between free thinking and socialism have not attracted much attention.[29] Yet, especially in the early phases of ethnic community building, Czech free thinkers were at least as much socialist as they were nationalist.

Both Klácel and Náprstek, the leading Czech free thinkers, were utopian socialists, followers of Charles Fourier. The new communities they hoped to build in America were realizations of cooperativist ideals as well as national ones. Klácel, in fact, penned the first exposition of socialism in the mother country in 1849, long before he emigrated. Meanwhile, the founder of Czech socialism in America, Leo J. Palda, who was also a free thinker, came to his beliefs through the reading of a tract by Klácel, as well as through his experience with the early German Social-Democratic Party. In 1870, Palda combined with three other Czech intellectuals, including the militant free thinker Josef Pastor, to edit the first Czech socialist paper in America, published by another socialist, J. B. Belohradsky. Its name, *Národní Noviny* (National Gazette), suggests the extent to which Czech socialism was linked to Czech nationalism.[30]

Národní Noviny lasted barely a year. The real triumph of socialism among Chicago Czechs was coincidental with the triumph of free thought during the 1873–1879 depression. The depression furthered this development in two important ways. The start of the depression brought widespread unemployment in the winter of 1873–1874 and in Chicago led to mass demonstrations demanding government action to provide jobs or relief for destitute workingmen. The spontaneous mobilization of thousands of workingmen encouraged German Lassallean socialists to found the Workingmen's Party of Illinois in January 1874. Though overwhelmingly German in numbers, it included three Czech sections represented in the party's inner circle by Prokop Hudek.[31]

But political socialism was only the most visible and dramatic manifestation of what may be called communal retrenchment on the part of many ethnic workingmen during the depression. Sporadic and uncertain employment and falling wages decimated the city's trade unions that had made their appearance during the boom years between 1863 and 1867, forcing many workingmen to turn to ethnic-based benevolent societies for a modicum of economic security. For example, the central bodies of Chicago's carpenters' and painters' unions went out of existence in the winter of 1873–1874, leaving only ethnic branches, including those of the Czechs, to carry on as benevolent societies. Other Czech workingmen turned to the Bohemian Workingmen's Benevolent Society or to the free thinkers' CSPS, whose first lodge in Chicago was founded in 1875, or to the Catholic Central Union, which was founded in 1876. Indeed, the latter two organizations were well suited to the needs of tramping workingmen who needed a central organization to assure continuity of benefits in the course of their travels.[32]

Workingmen's benevolent societies and ethnic forms of socialism were closely bound up with community building led by free thinkers. It may seem strange to credit free thinkers with community building in light of the divisiveness that the Zdrůbek-Molitor debates institutionalized among Chicago Czechs. The contradiction lessens, however, if one searches for this community on the neighborhood level, where more homogeneity was possible.

Such a neighborhood was Pilsen, a working-class community located on the southwest side of the city adjacent to the lumberyards. Pilsen was built on the prairie in the 1870s, following the destruction by the 1871 Chicago Fire of the older Czech neighborhood of Praha located to the east. Many Pilsen residents were recent immigrants to Chicago, attracted by the prospect of work in the rebuilding of the city and attracted to the area because it was the site of the relocation of many planing mills and other wood manufactories as well as the lumberyards. In 1876 an investigation into the neighborhood conditions of Pilsen lumbershovers revealed that "nearly all had families. They lived in one room huts, built of clapboards hastily thrown together."[33]

Census data from 1880 confirm the picture of Pilsen as a new colony of poor Czech workingmen. In the thirty-block area adjoining the lumberyards, the Fourth Precinct of the Sixth Ward, where the largest number of 1877 riot casualties had lived, 57 percent of heads of families were Bohemian-born, 23 percent German, 10.2 percent Irish, and only 3.8 percent American-born. Of those employed, 48 percent were general laborers, almost all employed in the lumberyards. Of the rest 9.4 percent were tailors, 5.5 percent carpenters, 4.9 percent planing-mill workers, 3.6 percent teamsters, and 2.6 percent saloon keepers. In short, at least two-thirds of the neighborhood's residents were common laborers or unskilled workingmen.[34]

Yet, by the mid-1880s this impoverished area was rapidly being built up. In 1884 Czech editor J. A. Oliverius "talked of the many fine buildings erected by the Bohemians and of the great change in the ward since they had settled in it so largely." Another Czech leader bragged that "the ward owed to Bohemians a large portion of its improvement, and they were heavy taxpayers. . . ."[35] That same year the Reverend E. A. Adams wrote that "a person acquainted with Bohemia in Europe, when walking around in this district feels he is in a regular Bohemian town."[36] In 1886 the *Tribune* reported that "there is not a more cleanly or better built workingmen's section in Chicago."[37]

What had happened was that poor Czech workingmen had turned in large numbers to building and loan associations. According to *Svornost,* "there are in Chicago over 35,000 Bohemians and all have a great tendency to buy real estate and to build a little

An 1883 view of the lumberyard district adjoining the South Branch of the Chicago River and the Czech community of Pilsen.
Chicago Historical Society.

house, to be able to call it their homestead."[38] This overpowering propensity to build homes would seem to accord with the observation that most immigrants from Bohemia in this period had owned their own cottages but did not hold enough land to make an adequate living and thus were forced to resort to part-time wage labor.[39]

Yet there is no reason to presume that the drive toward owning a home was equivalent to the assimilation of middle-class individualism. Building and loan associations were communal institutions with a strong class character, and not merely because of their membership. As *Svornost* argued, "our major idea in the loan associations is to help each other. Consequently, we lend the money to our members."[40] Moreover, many building and loans were organized and led by the same socialist free thinkers who had organized other Czech fraternal institutions in the 1870s. Thus, the first Pilsen building and loan association was founded in 1873 by socialist lawyer Prokop Hudek. By 1883 there were fifteen Czech building and loan associations. Before his death in 1886 Hudek claimed to have founded twelve associations in the Sixth Ward alone. J. B. Belohradsky was another socialist helping to found building associations. Between 1874 and 1883 more than 600 buildings were erected in Pilsen, in all cases subsidized by building and loan associations.[41]

Building and loan associations were Czech workers' alternatives to savings banks, most of which had failed in spring 1877. As grass-roots institutions with a pronounced democratic character they were prone to mismanagement. According to the *Tribune,* "the management of these associations has been entrusted in very many instances to persons utterly lacking in business and financial ability, unacquainted with the modes of American commercial transactions and ignorant of the English language." Nonetheless, Chicago's Czech workingmen continued to entrust their earnings to building and loan associations rather than banks, and by 1886 there were 40 of them.[42]

But, without a doubt, the central community institution in Pilsen was the fraternal order or benevolent society. Like the building associations these were in many cases closely associated with the socialists. It is likely that the influential Palda, who lived in Chicago in the mid-1870s before leaving for Cleveland, had a hand in founding the Czech Workingmen's Benevolent Society and possibly the first CSPS lodges. According to Joseph Chada, Palda "looked upon [benevolent societies] as co-operatives, useful in fighting capitalistic life insurance companies, and as necessary adjuncts of socialism, since they promoted workers' solidarity and cultural effort."[43]

From their beginning, wrote Chada, the benevolent societies "adopted programs that were more lofty than life insurance. They took over what the lipa [Pan Slavic Slovenska] had formerly propagated ethnically and culturally and became the community's prime movers of national action." For working-class leaders perhaps the most important function of the benevolent society was educational:

> Office holding became a singular honor and was vied for during every annual election. When the Czech element grew politically important enough to warrant the attention of party bosses, it was almost invariably the Czech fraternal leader who won candidacy for public office or received an appointive job. Lodge life was educative and enlightening. The meetings were workshops in parliamentary law and democratic procedure.[44]

Small wonder that the various Czech fraternal orders, including many workingmen's societies, took the initiative to found ethnic orphanages and old-age homes, singing societies, schools to propagate free thought or preserve the Czech language, and other cultural institutions. In the founding of the Bohemian National Cemetery, the most important citywide community activity of the period, representatives of twenty fraternal societies were present at the initial meeting. Of these, four were benevolent societies or Sokols (gymnastic societies) with the word "workingmen" in their names; another was the Bohemian Tailors Union. Almost half of the original sum of money donated to the cemetery came from two workingmen's benevolent societies, suggesting that in membership they were the largest of the lot.[45]

An appreciation of the unique character of Czech Pilsen—its intimate connection with free thought and socialism through community institutions—finally affords a perspective to return to the problem originally posed, the origins of Czech lumbershover militancy and socialism.

The middling peasants and rural laborers who had emigrated to Chicago's Pilsen in the 1870s had found entry work in the lumberyards and to a lesser extent in the adjoining planing mills and box factories. Their connection to the lumberyards, however, first of all must be distinguished from that of the Irish, the other ethnic group that supplied a pool of unskilled labor in Chicago. Unlike the Czechs the Irish laborers were dockworkers, who unloaded vessels. Most were hired out of saloons by vessel captains who contracted the work out to the stevedores by the job. Though Irish vessel unloaders were often unionized and commanded high wages of from $3 to $5 a day, their work was quite irregular. During the winter months, when the rivers froze, they lived off their summer earnings or turned to work in the packinghouses.[46]

Lumbershovers, on the other hand, were employed directly by lumberyard owners and worked at yard tasks ranging from unloading to sorting and piling to tallying. Their wages rarely exceeded $1.50 a day, especially during the depression. In the 1880s wages were held down by the slow but steady migration of the lumber business away from Pilsen to areas where cheaper wages prevailed. By the mid-1870s the Czechs comprised about half of all lumberyard workmen, with the rest being Poles and Germans.[47]

Two important results followed from this method of employment. First, the Czechs in the area were used to acting with the Germans and Poles but not with the Irish. This cooperation was facilitated by the fact that many immigrant Czechs spoke German as well as their national tongue. When Czechs did come into contact with the Irish, it was to underbid their labor and undermine their unions. Altogether, this produced a powerful antagonism between the two groups. Second, when work became scarce, either for economic or seasonal reasons, lumbershovers could not shift their employment like the Irish or other dock laborers without losing their jobs. Combined with subsistence wages, this limitation made their plight desperate as the depression reached its nadir in the mid-1870s.[48]

The first lumbershover strike came in June 1875 and was a short, unsuccessful affair. It was in 1876 that Czech lumbershovers established their reputation for militancy and socialism. In May a wage cut from $1.50 to $1.25 precipitated a lumbershovers' walkout. Large crowds composed predominantly of Czechs, but also including Poles and Germans, marched throughout the lumber district in an attempt to forcibly eject those men, many of them Irish, who had taken their places. Several days later, after two violent confrontations with police, the lumbershovers assembled at a large meeting called by the Workingmen's Party. They were addressed by Hudek, among others, who urged them to eschew violence in favor of organization.[49]

Not surprisingly, there was still no workplace organization among the lumbershovers in July 1877 when the Great Railroad Strike began. Nonetheless, the lumbershovers began another strike, and more importantly, played a strategic role in spreading the affair to other industries and groups of workers, including the Irish. It is likely that this newfound commitment to class solidarity reflected closer ties to the socialists. Before and during the strike the Workingmen's Party had advocated a general strike. Throughout the affair, large Czech socialist meetings were held in Pilsen and adjoining neighborhoods. One Czech socialist, Frank Norbock, was reported killed in the riots. Prokop Hudek, though doubtless opposed to the riot, spent the day bailing his countrymen out of jail.

During the riots some embittered Czech lumbershovers talked within earshot of a reporter about calling out their National Guard company, the Bohemian Sharpshooters, to defend themselves against police.[50] The militia company was in fact a community institution, an outgrowth of the Lincoln Rifles, which boasted of having been Chicago's first private military company to answer President Lincoln's call for troops in 1861. Yet, it was also a socialist-run institution, captained by ex–Civil War officer, and later SLP leader, Prokop Hudek. Threatened with the prospect of confrontation between police and workers using arms designated for a state guard unit, the National Guard's commander ordered the confiscation of the arms of the Sharpshooters that same day.[51]

Class solidarity and closer ties with the socialists were supplemented and reinforced by a community solidarity of all Pilsen Czechs—and, if casualty lists from the riot are any indication, this solidarity included Pilsen Germans and Pilsen Poles. Labor historians have not generally realized the extent to which 1877 was an uprising of urban-industrial neighborhoods. In Pilsen the community nature of the affair was dramatized in the widespread involvement of Czech women, called "Bohemian Amazons" by the press, and teenagers. At one Pilsen door and sash factory hundreds of women stoned the police. On Halsted Street, where workers and police aided by militia were engaged in a see-saw battle all morning, Czech women brought stones in their aprons to the men.

An analysis of the casualty lists compiled by the press strongly indicates the centrality of Pilsen. Of those victims whose residences could be identified, 42 percent lived in the Sixth Ward, by far the largest percentage contributed by any city ward. The community nature of Czech participation was also confirmed by J. A. Oliverius, a Republican nationalist, and the editor of the shortlived *Denní Vestník* (Daily News). In a letter to the *Tribune* Oliverius admitted that "I . . . was perhaps the only Bohemian in Chicago who opposed the powerful current of the aroused public feeling of my countrymen." Noting the "communistic feeling" that had pervaded the community since 1874, Oliverius wrote, "I don't approve of it. . . . but I cannot censure it in the same way as English papers do. A majority of the people are out of employment; what is left for the families to do?"[52]

The ties between the residents of Pilsen, the socialists, and the new free-thinker establishment were strengthened in the three years immediately following the strikes. In three of four elections held during that period the third, fourth, and fifth precincts of the Sixth Ward ranked in the top ten of the city's eighty-five precincts in socialist vote. Moreover, in each of these elections the socialists had a majority of the votes in these precincts.[53]

It is no exaggeration to say that by 1879 the SLP had emerged as the most important political representative of both class and ethnic interests of Chicago Czechs, replacing their older loyalties to the Republican Party. Czech SLP sections proliferated, reaching five in 1879, mainly in the Sixth Ward. *Svornost* editor F. B. Zdrůbek became an outspoken member of an SLP ward club. He also wrote strongly worded editorials condemning the Democrats and Republicans as "upholding the interests of the ruling classes, the capitalistic groups and their methods of oppression of all who are dependent on them." Zdrůbek predicted that Czechs "will vote as a bloc with the socialist party" that year and threatened to publish the names of those who worked against the party. Czech socialists returned the favor by endorsing *Svornost* as their official publication.[54]

The distinctiveness of Czech socialism in this period is striking in contrast to that of the Germans. The Germans took inspiration and leadership from the Social-Democratic Party in the mother country. Czech socialists could not do this, in part because of their origins and outlook, but also because Bohemia had no such party until 1878. Even after this date there was no formal connection between Czech-American socialists and Bohemian socialists until 1901.[55]

The editorials in *Svornost* reveal a dual thrust of Czech socialism in Chicago. One was "to endeavor first of all to bring about that equality and justice for all who are now being ground down by oppression under the present system."[56] This goal was defined by the SLP program of government ownership of monopolies. The other goal was to advance the interests of Czechs as an ethnic group, defined as securing jobs and political representation on public institutions such as the school board and governmental bodies such as the city council. Thus the election of blacklisted cabinetmaker and SLP leader Leo Meilbeck to the state legislature in 1878 was a source of immense pride to the local community. Meilbeck justified this trust by successfully sponsoring a bill easing the formation of building and loan associations.[57]

The SLP, however, was unable to survive the return to prosperity in the 1880s. The improvement in workers' bargaining position found an outlet in trade unionism and other nonpolitical forms of worker activity. During this period local politics came under the sway of Carter Harrison, the first mayor in Chicago's history to make a direct appeal to the city's immigrant communities and the first to attempt to incorporate the labor movement into his political machine.[58]

Harrison appealed to the Czechs through the community's socialists. In 1881 he appointed Leo Meilbeck, who had not been reelected, as assistant librarian in the city's public library. His barely veiled embrace of Czech socialists was typified in a welcoming speech he made to a national convention of Sokols held in Chicago in 1884. Harrison bragged of having discharged a police spy who had claimed that Czech socialists were about to burn down the city. He then made a special point of saying that "even if a large number of Bohemians are socialists, they have a right to be heard."[59] It is also noteworthy that Harrison's major political adviser for securing the Czech vote, lawyer Adolph Kraus, had acquired his community prestige by defending the socialist-affiliated Bohemian Sharpshooters in court.[60] Despite these gestures and the respectability that Harrison offered Czech free-thinking socialists, it was only in 1883, after Harrison had been in office four years, that a non-partisan meeting of Czech community leaders, including Zdrůbek, endorsed Harrison for reelection.[61]

It would be a mistake to view Harrison's populist politics as accomplishing the acceptance by socialist-leaning Czechs of conventional middle-class notions of social mobility. The Harrison phenomenon, in fact, was at least as much a political acknowledgment and confirmation of the deep roots that socialists had sunk in the community. There was still little class differentiation in Pilsen, and the careers of men like Kraus, Zdrůbek, and Hudek were dependent on the organizational network, fortunes, and voting power of Pilsen workingmen. The upward mobility offered by Harrison was purely political and, if anything, taught the need to play local politics rather than the Horatio Alger myth.

Clearly socialism remained a powerful current in the Czech community in the 1880s. Yet, while it remained very much an ethnic and free-thought phenomenon, it branched out into new forms and passed under new leadership. One major form, anarchism, had its origins in the extensive and savage repression endured by the Social-Democratic movement in Bohemia in the 1880s. Between 1882 and 1884 three members of this wing—Josef Boleslav Pecka, Jackub Mikolanda, and Norbert Zoula—emigrated to Chicago where, in the absence of the SLP, they formed a small group of about eighty Czech socialists. By 1883 this group had affiliated with the International Working People's Association (IWPA) and began publishing a small weekly newspaper, *Budoucnost* (Future).[62]

It is common to dwell on the distinctions between the socialists of the 1870s and the anarchists of the 1880s. Certainly the anarchists' advocacy of the violent overthrow of the state, highlighted by the Haymarket affair, was unacceptable to Czech community leaders, even including the more moderate socialists such as Zdrůbek.[63] Still, the continuity is striking. There is considerable evidence that, with the exception of the leadership, the rank and file of the two movements were substantially the same: most anarchists in 1884 were actually former socialists under new leadership.[64]

Like the socialists, the anarchists also promoted a neighborhood-based labor movement. Four of the five Czech anarchist "groups" were located in Pilsen. In 1886, Czech anarchists led the Bohemian branch of the lumbershovers' union formed that year. They also led the Czech branch of Local 21 of the Brotherhood of Carpenters and Joiners of America, which split from the national union in 1884. Both affiliated with the Central Labor Union, an anarchist-led alternative to the Trade and Labor Assembly. When the CLU held a parade on the eve of Haymarket, it included 180 Czech builders, 120 Czech bricklayers, 200 Czech bakers, and 200 members of the Bohemian Workingmen's Association, a benevolent society. Each marched separately as an ethnic labor organization.[65]

Not all socialists became anarchists. Frank Dvorak, a former leader of a Pilsen SLP ward club who had lived in America since the age of six, led many of his countrymen into the Knights of Labor. By June 1886 there were 1,657 Bohemian-born Knights in Chicago, organized in several mixed local assemblies. Dvorak was statistician of District Assembly 57, the largest D.A. in Chicago at the time.[66]

The strength of this wing of the Czech labor movement and its affinity with the constituency of the CLU-affiliated Czech unions were evident after Haymarket. The Knights and the Central Labor Union coalesced to form the United Labor Party, which participated in the fall 1886 elections. In Pilsen every precinct with a plurality or majority of Czech—born registered voters gave the ULP at least a 57 percent majority. In the 1887 city elections the ULP nominated Dvorak for Sixth Ward alderman against the wishes of the anarchists. This time Czech precincts delivered ULP majorities ranging from 65 percent to 86 percent. Czech precincts in the rest of the city were far less likely to turn out ULP majorities.[67] In short, in 1886 and 1887 Pilsen united behind moderate socialist leadership just as it had done in the late 1870s.

The ethnic impetus behind Czech socialism lasted well beyond 1887. In 1894, three Czech socialists ran for alderman on the labor ticket in three different Chicago wards. In the early twentieth century Czech socialists were a major component of Eugene V. Debs's Socialist Party. Just before World War I the Czech Federation of the Socialist Party had 1,200 members and exercised an influence in the community greatly disproportionate to its numbers.[68]

Clearly, Czech labor militancy and socialism was not simply a response to industrialization. This should not be surprising. Recent work has demonstrated that this era antedated the widespread mechanization of industry, scientific management, and the resultant homogenization of the work force.[69] Particularly for unskilled workers, class was not a spontaneous outcome of their experience in the workplace, though such experience did provide an indispensable foundation. At least partly for this reason historians have increasingly turned to the community as a necessary context for understanding various forms of class action.[70] The relationship between Pilsen and an unskilled and unorganized group like the lumbershovers must be viewed in this light.

Yet Pilsen, as we have seen, was also a unique kind of community which crystallized out of two intersecting processes. The first was the sundering of the nominal loyalty of many immigrants to the church and its transference to free-thinking socialists through a network of voluntary associations. Second, the impetus to this transformation derived from the needs of Czech workers in the depression period for economic security, solidarity, and community. The result was an ethnic community that was distinctly different from other Slavic communities and from the Irish, whose associational life centered around the church and tended to be traditionalist and hierarchical; it was also different from Protestant middle-class communities whose economic and religious life nourished liberal, individualist values. The community institutions of Pilsen, unlike either of these, were created and nurtured by Czech free thinkers and provided a congenial environment where socialism could thrive and develop in its various forms.

Notes

I would like to thank the Chicago Area Labor History Group for helpful comments during the preparation of this essay.

1. Though contemporaries normally used "Bohemian," I have generally kept to the name "Czech" in the interests of accuracy. Not all residents of Bohemia were Czech in national culture; many were culturally German. Moreover, many Czechs lived in neighboring Moravia. See Karen Johnson Freeze's essay, "Czechs," in *Harvard Encyclopedia of American Ethnic Groups*, ed. Stephan Thernstrom (Cambridge, Mass.: Harvard University Press, 1980), 261.

2. Based on newspaper lists of killed and wounded reported in the *Chicago Tribune, Chicago Times*, and *Chicago Inter Ocean*, 24 through 29 July 1877. For an analysis of the list see Richard Schneirov, "The 1877 Great Upheaval in Chicago: 'Life by Labor or Death by Fight' " (unpublished manuscript).

3. *Chicago Tribune*, 27 July 1877; 27 April 1878.

4. Election data by precinct reported in *Chicago Tribune*, 8 November 1877, 3 April 1878, 2 April 1879, and 5 November 1879.

5. On the events leading up to Haymarket see Henry David, *The History of the Haymarket Affair: A Study in the American Social-Revolutionary and Labor Movements*, rev. ed. (New York: Collier Books, 1963).

6. Membership for the SLP reported in *Investigation by a Select Committee of the House of Representatives Relative to the Causes of the General Depression in*

Labor and Business, and as to Chinese Immigration (Washington D.C.: Government Printing Office, 1879), 46th Cong., 2d Sess., 159, 160.

7. For example, see John H. M. Laslett, *Labor and the Left: A Study of Socialist and Radical Influences in the American Labor Movement, 1881–1924* (New York: Basic Books, 1970); David Montgomery, *Workers Control in America: Studies in the History of Work, Technology and Labor Struggles* (Cambridge: Cambridge University Press, 1979); Bernard H. Moss, *The Origins of the French Labor Movement: The Socialism of the Skilled Worker, 1830–1914* (Berkeley: University of California Press, 1976).

8. On Marx's views see, for example, Marx and Engels, "Manifesto of the Communist Party," in Marx-Engels *Collected Works, 1845–1848 (Moscow: Progress Publishers, 1976),* 477–519; Thorstein Veblen, *The Theory of Business Enterprise* (1902; rpt. New York: New American Library, 1963), 144–76.

9. *Chicago Tribune,* 12 August 1877.

10. See Harold J. Abramson, "Assimilation and Pluralism," and William Peterson, "Concepts of Ethnicity," both in *Harvard Encyclopedia of American Ethnic Groups,* ed. Stephan Thernstrom, pp. 150–60, 234–42.

11. On Germans see Carl Frederick Wittke, *Refugees of Revolution: The German Forty-eighters in America* (Philadelphia: University of Pennsylvania Press, 1952); see also Bruce Carlin Levine, "Free Soil, Free Labor, and Freimänner: German Chicago in the Civil War Era," in *German Workers in Industrial Chicago, 1850–1910: A Comparative Perspective,* ed. Hartmut Keil and John B. Jentz (DeKalb: Northern Illinois University, 1983), 163–82; on the Irish see Eric Foner, "Class, Ethnicity, and Radicalism in the Gilded Age: The Land League and Irish America," *Marxist Perspectives* 1 (Summer 1978): 6–55; Michael A. Gordon, "The Labor Boycott in New York City, 1880–1886," *Labor History* 16 (Spring 1975): 185–229.

12. This is based on standard histories of Bohemia and the Hussite revolt; for a convenient summary of the Hussite revolt see Charles H. George, *Revolution: European Radicals from Hus to Lenin* (Glenview, Illinois: Scott, Foresman 1962), 19–32.

13. Karel D. Bicha, "Settling Accounts with an Old Adversary: The Decatholicization of Czech Immigrants in America," *Social History–Histoire Sociale* 8 (November 1972): 45–60.

14. Thomas Čapek, *The Čechs (Bohemians) in America: A Study of Their National, Cultural, Political, Social, Economic and Religious Life* (Boston: Houghton-Mifflin, 1920), 125–36; Kenneth D. Miller, *The Czecho-Slovaks in America* (New York: George H. Doran Company, 1922), 127–28.

15. Čapek, *Čechs in America,* p. 126.

16. On Klácel and other Czech colonists see Joseph Chada, *The Czechs in the United States* (Chicago: Czechoslovak Society of Art and Sciences, 1981), 86; on the idea of America in Bohemia see Josef V. Polišenský, "America and the Beginnings of Modern Czech Political Thought," in *The Czech Renascence of the Nineteenth Century, Essays Presented to Otakar Odložilik in Honour of His Seventieth Birthday,* ed. Peter Brock and H. Gordon Skilling (Toronto: University of Toronto Press, 1970), 215–23.

17. Josef J. Barton, "Eastern and Southern Europeans," in *Ethnic Leadership in America,* ed. John Higham (Baltimore: Johns Hopkins University Press, 1978), 150–75; see also Chada, *Czechs in the United States,* 164–65; Eugene McCarthy, "The Bohemians in Chicago and Their Benevolent Societies: 1875–1946" (Master's thesis, University of Chicago, 1950), pp. 27–30.

18. Chada, *Czechs in the United States,* 137–38; idem, *The Catholic Central Union: Its Contribution to Fraternalism and America's Cosmopolitan Civilization* (Chicago: Catholic Central Union, 1952), 4, 5.

19. Čapek, *Čechs in America,* pp. 121, 127–29; names and dates for all Czech newspapers in Chicago cited in this essay from Federal Works Agency, Works Projects Administration, *Bibliography of Foreign Language Newspapers Published in Chicago* (Chicago: Chicago Public Library Omnibus Project, 1942), 7–28.

20. J. E. S. Vojan, *The Semi-Centennial Jubilee of the Bohemian National Ceme-*

tery Association in Chicago, Illinois: A Free English Version of J. J. Jelinek's Bohemian Historical Sketch (Chicago: Bohemian National Cemetery Association, 1927); Chada, *Czechs in the United States,* pp. 100, 101.

21. Chada, *Czechs in the United States,* pp. 88, 89.

22. McCarthy, "Bohemians in Chicago," p. 47; *Svornost,* 19 August 1883, from Works Progress Administration, Chicago Foreign Language Press Survey (hereafter, CFLPS), microfilm ed. (Chicago: Chicago Public Library Omnibus Project, 1943), Reel II, Part B2.

23. *Svornost,* 23 August 1884, CFLPS, Reel III, Part A.

24. Vojan, *Jubilee of Bohemian National Cemetery,* pp. 7–9; Josefa Humpal Zeman, "The Bohemian People in Chicago," in *Hull House Maps and Papers, A Presentation of Nationalities and Wages in a Congested District of Chicago by Residents of Hull-House* (New York: Thomas Y. Crowell, 1895), 124, 125.

25. For example, see *Svornost,* 27 May 1884, CFLPS; Reel III, Part A; Čapek, *Čechs in America,* p. 119.

26. Josefa Humpal Zeman, "Bohemian People in Chicago," in *Hull House Papers,* p. 124.

27. *Chicago Tribune,* 3 December 1877.

28. *Svornost,* 19 July 1883, CFLPS, Reel III, Part B3.

29. For the argument that free thinkers made a true Czech community impossible, see Karel D. Bicha, "The Community or Cooperation? The Case of the Czech-Americans," in *Studies in Ethnicity: The East European Experience in America,* ed. Charles A. Ward, Philip Shashko, Donald E. Pienkos (Boulder, Colorado: East European Monographs, 1980), 93–102; one historian who notes the close relation between free thought and socialism is Joseph Chada, *Czechs in the United States,* pp. 89–91.

30. Čapek, *Čechs in America,* pp. 137, 256; Stanley Z. Pech, *The Czech Revolution of 1848* (Chapel Hill: University of North Carolina Press, 1969), 302–3; Joseph Martinek, "One Hundred Years of the Czech Labor Movement in America," in *Panorama: A Historical Review of Czechs and Slovaks in the United States of America,* ed. Vlasta Vzaz (Cicero, Illinois: Czechoslovak National Council of America, 1970), 85.

31. *Chicago Tribune,* 12 January 1874, 26 January 1874, and 23 February 1875; Ernest Bogart and Charles Thompson, *The Industrial State, 1870–1893, vol. 4 of Centennial History of Illinois* (Springfield, Ill.: Centennial Commission, 1920), 139, 140.

32. On the demise of the carpenters and painters, see *Workingman's Advocate,* 23 November 1872 and 28 June 1873; on the Bohemian Workingman's Benevolent Society, see 11 March 1876; on the CSPS and Catholic Central Union and their relation to traveling workingmen see Chada, *The Catholic Central Union,* pp. 4–10.

33. John J. Flinn, *History of the Chicago Police* (Chicago: Police Book Fund, 1887), 158; see also McCarthy, "The Bohemians in Chicago," p. 18.

34. Statistics derived from a systematic sample taken from manuscript schedules of the U.S. Census on Population, 1880, Chicago, Sixth Ward.

35. *Chicago Tribune,* 23 March 1884.

36. *Svornost,* 27 May 1884, CFLPS, Reel III, Part A.

37. *Chicago Tribune,* 7, March 1886.

38. *Svornost,* 27 March 1883, CFLPS, Reel II, Part A2.

39. Miller, *Czecho-Slovaks in America,* p. 22, 23; Freeze, "Czechs," in *Harvard Encyclopedia of Ethnic Groups.*

40. *Svornost,* 27 March 1883, (IIA2) CFLPS, Reel II, Part A2.

41. *Chicago Tribune,* 24 February 1886, 17 May 1886; *Svornost,* 18 October 1883, (IIA2) CFLPS, Reel II, Part A2.

42. *Chicago Tribune,* 17 May 1886.

43. Josef Chada, "A Survey of Radicalism in the Bohemian-American Community" (1954 manuscript, Chicago Historical Society), p. 6.

44. Chada, *Czechs in the United States,* p. 140.

45. Ibid., pp. 147–48; Vojan, *Jubilee of the Bohemian National Cemetery*, pp. 8–12.

46. On Irish dockworkers see *Chicago Times*, 9 May 1876; *Chicago Tribune*, 1 June 1884; *Progressive Age*, 19 November 1881.

47. On Czech lumbershovers see *Chicago Times*, 9 May 1876; *Chicago Tribune*, 15 March 1881 and 29 May 1886.

48. *Chicago Times*, 9 May 1876; *Inter Ocean*, 16 May 1889.

49. *Chicago Tribune*, 14 June 1875, and 8, 9, 10 May 1876; *Chicago Times*, 9 May 1876.

50. This analysis of the Czech role in 1877 is based on accounts in the *Chicago Times, Chicago Tribune, Chicago Inter Ocean*, and *Chicago Evening Journal*, 23 through 30 July 1877; for a summary account see Richard Schneirov, "Chicago's Great Upheaval of 1877," *Chicago History* 9 (Spring 1980): 3–17.

51. On the Sharpshooters see Holdridge O. Collins *History of the Illinois National Guard* (Chicago: Black and Beach, 1884), 27; *Chicago Tribune*, 24 February 1886; Chada, *Czechs in the United States*, p. 11.

52. Letter to *Chicago Inter Ocean*, 28 July 1877.

53. See note 4 above.

54. *Svornost*, 20 February 1879, 24 March 1879, 2 April 1879, CFLPS, Reel I, Part F1, and 21 April 1879, (IF3) CFLPS, Reel I, Part F3.

55. Martinek, "One Hundred Years of the Czech Labor Movement," in *Panorama*, ed. Vzaz, pp. 85, 87.

56. *Svornost*, 21 April 1879, (IF3) CFLPS, Reel I, Part F3.

57. *Chicago Tribune*, 9 November 1878; Čapek, *Čechs in America*, p. 138; Chada, *Czechs in the United States*, p. 161.

58. On Harrison, see Claudius O. Johnson, *Carter Henry Harrison I: Political Leader* (Chicago: University of Chicago Press, 1928); see also Richard Schneirov, "The Knights of Labor in the Chicago Labor Movement and in Municipal Politics, 1877–1887," (Ph.D. diss., Northern Illinois University, 1984).

59. *Chicago Times*, 28 August 1884.

60. Adolph Kraus, *Reminiscences and Comments: The Immigrant, the Citizen, a Public Office, the Jew* (Chicago: Toby Rubovits, 1925), 34–38.

61. *Svornost*, 26 March 1883, CFLPS, Reel I, Part F1.

62. Čapek, *Čechs in America*, 140–41; Chada, "Survey of Bohemian-American Radicalism," p. 3; *Chicago Daily Mail*, 10 May 1886.

63. On the mass meeting of Czech leaders condemning the anarchists, see *Chicago Tribune*, 17 May 1886.

64. This conclusion is based on the results of a systematic study of the memberships of the SLP and IWPA made by Bruce Nelson at Northern Illinois University which he generously shared with me.

65. On the lumbershovers see *Der Vorbote*, 7 April 1886; membership in the IWPA was identified by Bruce Nelson; on the Czech carpenters see "A History of Local 54" (typescript from the archives of Local 54, United Brotherhood of Carpenters and Joiners of America, Chicago District Council, n.d.); on the demonstration see *Chicago Tribune*, 26 April 1886.

66. On Dvorak see *Chicago Tribune*, 27 February 1887; *Labor Enquirer* 2 April 1887; on the numbers of Czechs in the Knights, see Illinois Bureau of Labor Statistics, *Fourth Biennial Report of the Illinois Bureau of Labor Statistics* (Springfield: H. W. Rokker, 1886), 224–30.

67. Data on registered voters drawn from Lars P. Nelson, *Statistics Showing by Ward and Voting Precints [sic] the Original Nationality of the Voters in Chicago* (Chicago: Lars P. Nelson, 1887); voting results are from the county treasurers' race, reported in *Chicago Tribune*, 4 November 1886 and from the mayoral contest reported 6 April 1887.

68. Chada, *Czechs in the United States*, pp. 163–64; Martinek, "One Hundred Years of the Czech Labor Movement," p. 87.

69. Recent work supporting this periodization is summarized in David M. Gor-

don, Richard Edwards, and Michael Reich, *Segmented Work, Divided Workers: The Historical Transformation of Labor in the United States* (Cambridge: Cambridge University Press, 1982).

70. There have been numerous recent monographs embodying this approach to labor history, most originating in the seminal essay by Herbert Gutman, "The Workers Search for Power," in *The Gilded Age: A Reappraisal,* ed. H. Wayne Morgan (Syracuse, N.Y.: Syracuse University Press, 1968); for a survey see David Montgomery, "Gutman's Nineteenth Century America," *Labor History* 19 (Summer 1978): 416–29.

PAUL KRAUSE

Labor Republicanism and *'Za Chlebom'*: Anglo-American and Slavic Solidarity in Homestead

Homestead and Cultural Conflict

For weeks before the Homestead Lockout of 1892 began on 30 June, newspapers in nearby Pittsburgh and across the United States were predicting a deeply significant confrontation between the workers and managers of the Homestead Steel Works. The expectations for drama were fulfilled when on 6 July the locked-out steelworkers and their supporters battled 300 Pinkerton "detectives" on the banks of the Monongahela River. Three Pinkertons and nine workers were killed. Almost immediately, the lockout became part of the folklore of industrial America. Workers wrote, published, and sang songs about the conflict. And the first professional writers to consider the lockout saw it as an important juncture in American history.[1]

The fascination with Homestead continued into the twentieth century, as Homesteaders were among the most important subjects of *The Pittsburgh Survey.* But this rich interpretation of urban life enshrined Homestead in a kind of academic hall of fame, and research about the lockout came to a virtual halt. In the 1940s a scholar wrote a crisp narrative of the lockout, and the lockout also served as the backdrop for Thomas Bell's evocative novel about American Slovaks. But these undertakings owed their considerable strengths—and weaknesses—to *The Survey* and failed to offer fresh insights. Twenty years ago, the details of the lockout were recounted in a popular history sharply criticized by historian Herbert G. Gutman, who also pointed out that it was the best available account. Despite a recent renaissance of interest in Homestead, Gutman's judgment has stood the test of time.[2]

Yet recent scholarship on the lockout has illumined the thinking of the native-born and immigrant English, Welsh, and Irish steelworkers by identifying Anglo-American republicanism as an important theme in their public statements. During the lockout, these steelworkers seized upon notions such as "independence," "citizenship," and "equal rights" that they and their colleagues in the Pittsburgh district had used for decades to help define and legitimize their aspirations. But the relationship of the Homesteaders' republican rhetoric to experience at work and in politics in the years prior to the lockout has not been explored. The nature of late nineteenth-century republicanism in—and beyond—Homestead has thus remained cloudy. What did independence mean to Homesteaders? What did equal rights mean? What, in their eyes, was an American republic? One goal of this essay is to shed light on these questions.[3]

A related goal is to begin excavating the world inhabited by Homestead's first Slavic residents, most of whom were Roman Catholic Slovaks. For students of Homestead have regarded the Slavic immigrants as though they came from another galaxy instead of the northeastern provinces of the Hapsburg Empire. The result has been to leave unexplored one of the most intriguing phenomena of Homestead: the cooperation of the Slavic and Anglo-American steelworkers in the lockout.[4]

Though there are no accounts of the lockout or of life in the town authored by the first Slavic immigrants, it has been possible to retrieve important features of Homestead's Slavic community in its earliest years. The results of this investigation suggest that Anglo-Americans were not the sole proprietors of republicanism and that Slavic immigrants helped forge in Homestead a workers' version of a "modern" American republic. Indeed, it was the eclipse of this America—rooted in Anglo-American republicanism as well as in an East European counterpart—that in 1892 focused on Homestead "the breathless attention of the whole world."[5]

The essence of Homestead's republicanism was captured during the lockout by the daily press, even though it interpreted the steelworkers' actions as examples of "riot" and "disorder" rather than as expressions of an alternative way to organize society. Just a few days after the Pinkerton assault, for example, a reporter for the *New York Sun* struggled to explain why the steelworkers had placed Homestead under quasi-military rule to protect it and their jobs from any new workers hired by management. "The strikers . . . do not realize the amazing nature of their doings," the reporter concluded. "The Constitution is violated daily. . . . [yet] they seem to think that they are an orderly, law-abiding lot of American citizens simply exercising their right to defend themselves against their enemies."[6]

Exactly. Where the daily press and some of its audience saw misrule in the behavior of Homesteaders, the steelworkers saw themselves as law-abiding citizens of an embattled republican community. In it, the rights of labor, not of property, were most sacred. Defined by the Monongahela Valley's spirited labor movement of the 1870s and early 1880s, these rights included work itself and sharing in its supervision and in the determination of its value. The Homestead steelworkers, whose leaders were veterans of the labor movement, drew upon its legacy in looking to the Constitution as the guarantor of their rights. In their eyes, the lockout was an effort to take away their rights and make them "slaves."

This was the theme of the keynote address delivered by the burgess of Homestead, John McLuckie, to a mass meeting of his fellow steelworkers in June 1892. The question before all 3,800 employes of the Homestead Steel Works, McLuckie said, was to decide "if we are going to live like white men in the future." McLuckie answered by saying that while the Constitution ensured the steelworkers' rights, "including the right to live. . . . in order to live we must keep up a continuous struggle." A few days later, the lockout began. "We do not propose that Andrew Carnegie's representatives shall bulldoze us," McLuckie said. *"We are bound to Homestead by all the ties that men hold dearest and most sacred."*[7]

McLuckie's rhetoric suggests that the steelworkers of Homestead, and not only reporters and subsequent commentators, regarded the lockout as the denouement of a grand struggle. And indeed, McLuckie and his co-workers understood that the lockout arose not merely from management's desire to cut wages or, by forcing the Amalgamated Association of Iron and Steel Workers out of the Homestead Steel Works, to destroy "the most powerful independent labor organization in the world." The lockout, the steelworkers knew, signaled the end of a war for the future of America that began with Reconstruction. On the one side was "centralized capital," which counted in its ranks advocates of "the morality of improvement" and unbridled individualism. On the other side were urban and agricultural workers who, despite differences in beliefs and tactics, shared a hope for a cooperative society where right derived from the common good and the dignity of labor. The war, then, was between two ways of life—two cultures—and the Homestead Lockout was one of the final battles.[8]

To be sure, the Slavic immigrants of Homestead left no written record pointing to a desire for a "cooperative commonwealth." And beginning in the early 1880s, many Anglo-American laborers in the Pittsburgh district regarded the arrival of Slavic and other immigrants from Eastern Europe as a threat to the workers' movement. But the relationship of Slavic and Anglo-American workers in Homestead suggests that the nativist impulse did not always preclude cooperation between the two groups.[9]

In rejecting nativism, the Anglo-American steelworkers of Homestead drew upon the body of thought and experience in worker republicanism that envisioned an "amalgamation" of all laborers. This idea had animated the labor movement in the Pittsburgh district through the early 1880s and, as the movement fragmented, was carried to Homestead by steelworkers such as McLuckie, miners organized by D. R. Jones and workers in various trades who belonged to the Knights of Labor and counted Thomas W. "Old Beeswax" Taylor among their leaders. Jones and Taylor, like McLuckie, were elected burgess of Homestead. All three understood that for workers to avoid "vassalage and practical slavery," as Jones once put it, differences of "creed, color or race" had to be buried.[10]

That Jones and other labor leaders were compelled to remind workers of the need for solidarity indicates that it often remained an elusive goal. Yet Homestead workers reached the goal. Why? McLuckie explained some of the reasons in his speech to the Homestead steelworkers. When he finished speaking, another Homestead steelworker took the floor. His name was Mavierick, and he was a member of "the Pittsburgh Slavonic Order"—very likely, the First Catholic Slovak Union. No record of Mavierick's speech exists, though the daily press noted he addressed the Slavic workers in a variety of languages so that all could understand the purpose of the meeting. The purpose, other speakers had said, was to urge the workers of Homestead to stick together "whatever may occur. . . , [for] in union only was strength."[11]

The East European and Anglo-American steelworkers agreed. What were the wellsprings of this agreement?

Confronting the "Unnatural Wage System": Amalgamation

In the two decades prior to the arrival of the first East European immigrants, the dynamic of the workers' movement in the Pittsburgh district derived principally from the "second industrial revolution." With radical innovations in production and managerial techniques, the revolution threatened to displace thousands of skilled laborers who exercised, by twentieth-century standards, a remarkable degree of control in the workplace. Like the industrial revolution of the late 1700s, the second great wave of changes in both the mechanical and "domestic arrangement" of factory production was accompanied by equally radical changes in political culture. And because the second industrial revolution found its first full expression in metal making, no laborers were quicker to see the ties between factory organization and politics than the thousands of skilled iron and steelworkers who helped make Pittsburgh "the great metal manufactory of the United States."[12]

While the metalworkers of Pittsburgh began to organize in the late 1850s, their trade-union and political initiatives were galvanized by the lockout of 4,000 puddlers in 1874 and 1875. The lockout occurred as Andrew Carnegie was building the Edgar Thomson Steel Works, the world's most technically advanced metal-making facility. To many ironworkers in the Pittsburgh district, however, Carnegie's new steelworks and the decision of his colleagues to close down their mills were of the same fabric. For them Edgar Thomson and the lockout represented hard evidence that iron and steelmasters were determined to transform the expertise and power of skilled metalworkers into vestiges of a bygone era. But the puddlers' union withstood the lockout and successfully defended such "customary" rights as "a fair day's wages for a fair day's work." And in ratifying their victory over the ironmasters, the puddlers laid full claim to republicanism and the republican crusade against tyranny in the Civil War.[13]

In identifying their cause with the cause of the nation, the puddlers followed the lead of thousands of antebellum workers who had seen in the emerging industrial order a widening discrepancy between republican ideals and daily experience. And the puddlers, like their artisanal forefathers, also saw their project as the construction of a republic "in fact" and not merely in name. For the puddlers of Pittsburgh and their allies, then, the republican heritage provided what E. P. Thompson has called a "legitimising notion of right" that helped sanction and interpret workplace grievances and translate them into the language of politics.[14]

A "lockout ballad" published in the puddlers' official newspaper, the *National Labor Tribune,* captured their republican sentiments and underscored the idea that puddlers saw themselves as the guardians of "equal rights" for all laborers. Entitled "Peter Puddler and the Mill Boy," the ballad is a dialogue between the two. Peter explains to the boy that it was the ironmasters' decision to degrade labor, and not the puddlers' decision to resist, that put the boy out of work. Peter concludes his speech by explaining the most important concerns of the puddlers as the labor movement in Pittsburgh approached its greatest strength:

> The rich provide our food, you said,
> Their tyranny we should not foil,
> My little friend, our daily bread,
> We earn it dearly by our toil.
> . . . I'll strike until my latest breath,
> Against our wrongs, our rights to save,
> I'd rather see you cold in death,
> Than live to be a tyrant's slave.
> . . . Look yonder, see the banner wave—
> It is the standard of the free!
> Beneath it none shall be a slave,
> Nor will it shelter tyranny!
> We ever shall uphold our cause,
> Our rights as Sons of Liberty!
> We shall uphold our country's laws,
> And only ask equality.[15]

"Peter Puddler and the Mill Boy" was not an expression of only the puddlers' views. For the ballad reflected the thinking of all skilled workers in the Pittsburgh district who had been wrestling with the problem of how to supplant "the unnatural wages system." Puddlers, rollers, molders, cabinetmakers, printers, glassworkers—these and thousands of other craftsmen nurtured a way of life which, while tending toward a shop-floor hierarchy perpetuated by the most skilled workers, nonetheless pointed toward a social order "where the rights of men will be considered and protected before the rights of money." Schooled by a string of industrial conflicts that began prior to the Civil War, by the early 1870s skilled workers in Pittsburgh understood that their hopes for ending "wage slavery" hinged upon a solidarity that would embrace the less skilled and also cement the ties of workers in all industries.[16]

Indeed, these were the most important lessons of the lockout of 1874–1875. For the lockout exposed serious divisions between puddlers and other ironworkers. The result was that the puddlers and their colleagues decided to "amalgamate," and in the 1875–1876 period they created the Amalgamated Association of Iron and Steel Workers. As they did, thousands of other workers in the Pittsburgh district began to fashion an even wider "amalgamation" in the Knights of Labor.[17]

As the *Labor Tribune* noted, the Knights and the Amalgamated Association had a common purpose. Both arose from the sense that the wage system ignored "natural justice" by denying workers "a certain degree of comfort and measure of happiness which they should enjoy regardless of the empirical and cruel law of supply and demand." A shared desire for such comfort—what workers called a "competence"—and a shared antipathy to the "unnatural" wage system that denied this fundamental right provided the raw materials out of which industrial craftsmen such as puddlers and rollers, together with their less-skilled colleagues, began to forge the requisite solidarity for their attack against "the destructive competitive system."[18]

That the attack was aimed at a sweeping transformation of American society was clear. The *Labor Tribune*, which enjoyed the unqualified support of Knight and trade unionist, puddler and miner, thus declared:

> The work we have in hand is radical. It reaches down to the very framework of society. It involves the very principles of self-government. It will hear no compromises. The entire wage system will be wiped out. The power of capital to dictate and control will be removed. The power of labor to direct and control capital, and to reserve to itself all of its productiveness . . . will be permanently established. The revolution will be thorough. . . .[19]

Fifteen years after these words were published, the leadership of the Knights and of the Amalgamated had drifted toward accommodation, and supplanting the wage system with a "cooperative" society was no longer the goal of the labor movement in the Pittsburgh district. However, the workers of Homestead clung to a vision of society that grew from the cause of labor reform and the workplace struggles of the 1870s.[20]

One such struggle occurred in 1876 at the Edgar Thomson Works, just across the river from Homestead, when Andrew Carnegie ordered his employes to quit the Amalgamated or lose their jobs. Carnegie succeeded in ousting the union from the Edgar Thomson. But the Amalgamated returned in the early 1880s when steelworkers organized Braddock Lodge No. 97. One of its founders was a miner, a Knight of Labor, and a Greenback-Labor candidate for the state legislature who lived within sight of the mill at the time of Carnegie's initial victory over the Amalgamated. His name was John McLuckie.[21]

Defeat in the City: Retreat to Homestead

From 1876 until 1882, the labor movement in Pittsburgh groped its way toward effective political initiatives. Spurred by the great railroad "riot" of 1877, which amounted to a revolt of all workers against "organized capital," workers created an independent political voice in the Greenback-Labor Party of Allegheny County. While the party scored some unequivocal successes, it failed to overcome the traditional allegiances of most workers to the established parties. Yet in city wards and in towns such as Homestead and Braddock, where metalworkers or miners predominated, Greenback-Labor candidates such as John McLuckie and Beeswax Taylor consistently outpolled Republicans and Democrats.

These successes, the prospect of more, and the growth of the Knights of Labor and of trade unions sparked a counteroffensive by the industrialists of the Pittsburgh district. Given the intensity of their assaults, particularly in the metals industry, the workers' movement in the Pittsburgh district was remarkable more for its resilience than its weakness. Yet in 1882 the culminating expressions of both attributes left the movement badly fragmented and, insofar as it aspired to an independent politics and an alternative social order, markedly less powerful. The movement crested in the spring as trade unionists and members of the Knights, the Greenback-Labor Party, and the Irish National Land League crisscrossed the district in a flurry of organizational activity. One of their principal objects was to win support for Thomas A. Armstrong, the editor of the *Labor Tribune* who was running for governor on the Greenback-Labor ticket. Another was to maintain the ranks of striking ironworkers and miners whose organizations, struggling with internal dissension, faced a determined opposition. It was against this background that leaders of the workers' movement decided to hold a "grand labor demonstration" on June 17.[22]

The demonstration—which might be considered the first Labor Day celebration in the United States—drew 30,000 marchers and more than 100,000 observers to the streets of Pittsburgh. Workers from West Virginia and Ohio came to the city in what the Knights of Labor, the chief sponsor of the demonstration, called "a peaceable protest against the evils that exist against the many by and through the power of wealth possessed by the few." The Knights also declared that the demonstration was to support "the rights of freemen." Indeed, the participants made worker republicanism and "equal rights" the central theme of the day. As one of the hundreds of banners that workers carried proclaimed: "Are we slaves or are we freemen? Are we slaves to petty tyrants?" Other banners affirmed the key ideas around which the workers' movement in Pittsburgh had coalesced: that labor was "noble and holy" and "the source of all wealth" and that the principal desires of workers were "a fair day's wages for a fair day's work" and a "competence obtained by honest labor."[23]

In keeping with the ubiquitious assertions of labor reformers that the workers' movement was a "Grand Army of Labor" marching toward equal rights, workers paraded in five "divisions," each led by an array of "commanders" and their "aides." The "chief of staff" for the parade was Thomas Armstrong, and Beeswax Taylor rode in a carriage reserved for labor leaders. Behind them marched assemblies of the Knights, then the miners, the glassworkers, and, finally, the lodges of the Amalgamated Association. The miners were "commanded" by D. R. Jones, the president of their union.[24]

A highlight of the demonstration was provided by the Amalgamated men and Knights in the Braddock's Glee Club, whose rendition of a new song by Beeswax Taylor elicited particularly "hearty" cheers along the parade route. Entitled "Storm the Fort, Ye Knights of Labor," the song was destined to become the most popular ode of the labor movement in the 1880s. The chorus of the song declared:

> Storm the fort, ye Knights of Labor,
> God defend our cause;
> Equal rights for self and neighbor;
> Down with unjust laws.[25]

Among those dedicated to equal rights who marched with the singing steelworkers of Braddock was John McLuckie. Not far behind on horseback was steelworker John Elias Jones, who led 375 Amalgamated men employed at the Homestead Steel Works. Jones and his colleagues in the Land League and in the Amalgamated, along with Local Assembly 1785 of the Knights of Labor, had recently conducted a successful—and important—strike. The banner they carried proclaimed that in the strike, Homesteaders were Tried and Found Faithful. While the daily press reported that the banner "spoke for itself," the steelworkers of Homestead had sought to remove any doubt about the meaning of their victory. In poems and speeches, Homesteaders interpreted the strike as a republican triumph for "freedom" and "independence" over "slavery."[26]

But the victory in Homestead proved to be the last one for the labor movement in 1882. By autumn, the strikes of the miners' union and the Amalgamated ironworkers had collapsed; and the membership of the Knights in Pittsburgh was dwindling. Moreover, Armstrong's gubernatorial candidacy ended disastrously, undermined by Terrence Powderly's refusal to accept the Greenback-Labor Party's nomination for lieutenant governor. In the Amalgamated's defeat, the fissures that emerged in the lockout of 1874–1875 reappeared and signaled the beginning of the union's decade-long decline. Deeper fissures between the Amalgamated and the Knights were to appear soon, and over the course of the 1880s mine owners and manufacturers intensified their initiatives against organized labor. The workers' movement of Pittsburgh which, as Armstrong had written in the 1870s, "indicted the civilization of the nineteenth century," thus moved toward an accommodation with it.[27]

Yet thousands of workers continued to harbor doubts about "modern" American civilization and held firm in their aspirations for an alternative. In Homestead they tried to build one, and McLuckie, Taylor, and John Elias Jones were among the architects. So, too, were Slavic immigrant steelworkers. Although some Anglo-American workers protested the arrival of "pauper labor," as one parade banner had labeled Slavic immigrants, other Anglo-American workers broadened the definition of "amalgamation" to include East Europeans. Indeed, some of the Anglo-American steelworkers led down the streets of Pittsburgh by John Elias Jones had joined Slavic laborers in a "battle with Capital for *our* rights"; for Jones and his colleagues in the Land League had welcomed Slavic steelworkers as members during the Homestead Strike of 1882.[28]

From their first encounters in Homestead, then, Slavic and Anglo-American workers began to forge a solidarity that grew from Anglo-American republicanism. But the solidarity also arose from the aspirations of Slavic workers, who codified their hopes in the expression *za chlebom*. Literally, *za chlebom* means "for bread."[29] As the lockouts of 1889 and 1892 were to show, though, the Slavic steelworkers of Homestead gave the expression a wider meaning.

Republican Recruits

Slavic immigrants began arriving in Homestead just as the new steelworks opened in 1881. Among the first to work in the mill were Pavel Olšav and Juraj Terek. Like thousands of other Slovaks who came to Pittsburgh beginning in the early 1880s, Olšav and Terek grew up in the region of the Hapsburg Empire where a variety of political and demographic forces had created rapidly growing numbers of landless agricultural laborers. In search of livelihood—*za chlebom*—such workers moved from village to village, from the countryside to the urban centers of Hungary and, from Hungary to North America. Zemplín province, the birthplace of Olšav and Terek, was the principal source of Slovak emigration. And Zemplín was the home of many of the first Slovaks who came to the Pittsburgh district. Like the sixteen-year-old Olšav, Terek left home (both came from the Žalobin area) a young man, an experience common to most Slovak immigrants.[30]

Olšav and Terek soon were joined by two young women from the Žalobin region who, after crossing the Atlantic, found work as domestic servants in New York City to make sufficient money to continue on to Homestead. One of the women, Susanna Tirpaková, married Olšav shortly after her arrival. The other, Anna Tereková—probably Terek's sister—married another immigrant, Ján Špan, who was to play an important role in Homestead's Slovak community. Špan had worked in a mining town in eastern Pennsylvania prior to settling in Homestead. Precisely how these first five Slovak Homesteaders learned of the town is not known. But the one account that traces their convergence in the United States and the scattered notations of a parish priest in the 1890s suggest that the dynamic of "chain migration" that characterized Slovak immigration to all of North America also brought Slovaks to Homestead.[31]

In the ten years following the arrival of Olšav and the other pioneer Zemplínčania, the East European settlement in Homestead grew to over 1,000 persons. For Olšav and the other Slavic steelworkers life revolved around work and church. The focal point of Slavic religious activity was St. Mary's Church, organized by Irish-American Catholics in 1881. From the beginning, though, St. Mary's was not an Irish parish. Slavic Homesteaders who came to the town in the 1880s attended mass, baptized their children, and prayed for their departed in the same sanctuary and with the same priest who ministered to the Anglo-American Catholics. Only after 1891, when the first Slovak parish in the Pittsburgh district was organized in Braddock, did Homestead Slovaks venture beyond the town to fulfill their spiritual needs.[32]

While the Slavic steelworkers and their families worshipped with the families of many leading Anglo-American steelworkers, Slavic Homesteaders looked to their own for leadership. Nearly every child born to Slavic Homesteaders, for example, had Slavic godparents; and Slavs invariably served as witnesses at Slavic weddings. Members of the Slavic community, which by the late 1880s occupied the section of town nearest the steelworks, frequently turned to the same persons to serve as godparents and witnesses, and thus to ensure the spiritual and material well-being of new families and their children. Pavel and Susanna Olšav and Ján and

Anna Špan were the Homestead Slovaks most often chosen as godparents and witnesses for Slavic baptisms and weddings.[33]

Špan, the owner of a butcher shop by 1890, also was a key figure in the fraternal life of the Slavic Homesteaders. Along with Michal Mašley, a grocer, Špan organized Homestead Lodge No. 26 of the First Catholic Slovak Union, the leading fraternal benefit society of Slovak immigrants. But the Slavic laborers of Homestead turned away from their merchants and installed Olšav, who led the "brigade" of Slavic steelworkers during the lockout of 1892, as the unofficial leader of Lodge No. 26. And though Mašley was its president, Olšav represented Lodge No. 26 at its most important public appearance through 1892, receiving on its behalf the blessing of the Roman Catholic Church.[34]

In the Homestead Steel Works, Olšav and virtually every other Slavic immigrant was employed as a "laborer." This meant that the Slavic workers were responsible chiefly for loading and stocking the furnaces and converters and moving raw and finished materials. In some departments of the mill, the men worked eight-hour shifts; in others, the shift was twelve hours long. Sunday provided a respite—as did the friendly taverns located in or near the Slavic settlement. The backroom of one such establishment, owned by Vincent Waasilefski, also served as a meeting place for Slavic women who worked as domestic servants.[35]

While many aspects of the work and recreational routines of the first Slavic Homesteaders are irretrievable, the press does provide some account of how Slavic immigrants marked the Fourth of July, and how the Slovaks of Homestead sponsored a Mardi Gras ball in the "American" fashion. The immigrants' celebration of 4 July 1886 also followed "American" practice in important ways and was noteworthy enough in the view of the *National Labor Tribune* to warrant page-one coverage. The story published by the *Tribune* made no mention of participation by Slavic Homesteaders. But "the biggest jubilee over American independence ever held by representatives of a foreign dynasty" very likely brought Slavic immigrants from the Pittsburgh district to the streets of Mt. Pleasant, a mining town in the Connellsville Coke region.[36]

The highlight of the Slavic "jubilee" was a parade led by "Director General" Josef Stefanki. Leaving his headquarters, which was bedecked with the flags of his native land and of the United States, Stefanki mounted a horse to lead hundreds of Slavic immigrants dressed in military attire, a band of Anglo-American musicians, and a Slavic drill team through the streets of Mt. Pleasant. Stefanki wore the "uniform of the Revolution of 1848"; and the marchers, "armed with everything from a double-barrel shotgun to a broomstick," carried flags and banners. The banner held by immigrants at the head of the parade proclaimed in their native language: Live Forever the United States.

Many of those who marched behind the big banner were coke workers employed by coal magnate Henry Clay Frick, Andrew Carnegie's partner and the chairman of the company that owned the Homestead Steel Works. In the days before the parade, Frick and his employes agreed to end one in a long series of their bitter and typically violent disputes. The Slavic immigrants who greeted Stefanki with "tremors of admiration," then, were cheering not only "the representative of patriotic forefathers." They were cheering an "amicable" settlement of their difficulties with Frick, and the renewed opportunity to work *za chlebom.*[37]

As the celebration in Mt. Pleasant indicates, Anglo-American workers were not the sole proprietors of republican aspirations. Slavic immigrants, too, made the connection between work grievances and republicanism. Drawing on their own revolutionary heritage, which, like America's, was rooted in the abolition of compulsory labor, the Slavic-Americans who marched in Mt. Pleasant declared an allegiance to American independence—an independence that allowed them to pursue their livelihood. In Homestead, Anglo-American workers made similar declarations. And in the Homestead lockouts of 1889 and 1892, the joint initiatives of Anglo-American and Slavic immigrants pointed to how deeply shared such an understanding of independence could be. It was an understanding which neither Frick nor Carnegie could countenance.

The Lockout of 1889

In nearly all respects, the Homestead Lockout of 1889 was a "dress rehearsal" for the lockout of 1892. Both disputes arose on the one hand out of management's desire to reduce labor costs and solidify control of the production process by removing workers' organizations from the mill. On the other hand, the disputes reflected the determination of Anglo- and Slavic-American steelworkers and their families to preserve what they construed as their fundamental rights in a "modern" America where work and cooperation, and not competition and the accumulation of wealth, reigned supreme. At stake for the Anglo-Americans were the fading legacies of labor republicanism, equal rights and workers' control. For Slavic immigrants, the initiatives of Andrew Carnegie and his associates threatened the fulfillment of aspirations embedded in the colloquialism, *za chlebom.* But as the cooperative undertakings of Homesteaders suggest, the language of East European and Anglo-American could lend itself to ready translation.[38]

By the spring of 1889, the owners and workers of the Homestead Steel Works understood that a decisive confrontation was close at hand. For Homestead was the last stronghold of unionism in the steel mills of the Pittsburgh district. Andrew Carnegie had ousted the Knights of Labor from the Edgar Thomson in 1888, and indications were that the Amalgamated's effort to organize a new Bessemer mill in Duquesne would not succeed. Carnegie celebrated his victory in Braddock by giving the workers a library, which he called a monument to his "partnership" with them. In his dedication speech, Carnegie said he wanted to erect a library for his employes in Homestead, too. "I am only too anxious to do for them what I have done for you," Carnegie told the Edgar Thomson workers. "[But] our men there [in Homestead] are not our partners. They are not interested in us. . . . I know that for the success of [the] Homestead works, regarded from the point of view of the capital invested. . . . the present system at Homestead must be changed."[39]

The Homestead workers interpreted Carnegie's speech as a thinly disguised threat. Their leaders embarked on campaigns to boost the official membership of the Amalgamated—which counted in its seven Homestead lodges about one-third of the 2,500 men employed at the works—and to cement the ties of the skilled and less-skilled, many of whom were Slavic immigrants. John McLuckie, Hugh O'Donnell, and other leaders of the steelworkers understood that "King Carnegie" had "his gun loaded for them," as one labor newspaper put it, and that a successful defense of their rights depended on tight-knit organization. "All or most of you have read the speech of Mr. Carnegie to the workmen of Braddock. . . ." one steelworker told his colleagues in "a timely appeal" to join the Amalgamated. "Now the question is, 'Are you still willing to act as the tools for others—to sell your rights as free men and to remain slaves?' "[40]

The legacy of the pre-1882 workers' movement was nearly as telling in a resolution voted by all the steelworkers when they responded to Carnegie's proposal "to change the present system at Homestead." For Carnegie had told the workers that unless they accepted wage cuts, a sliding scale with a reduced base used to determine piece rates for the skilled men, and a contract that recognized individuals and not unions, their jobs would be declared vacant and management would seek new hands. In the eyes of devoted trade unionists such as McLuckie and John Elias Jones, agreeing to Carnegie's ultimatum would violate the basic tenets of labor reform that they had brought to Homestead. The right to "a fair day's wages," the right to organize, the right to an ill-defined but "equitable" portion of the profits created by their labor—all these claims were threatened by Carnegie's proposal. Signing it, the steelworkers of Homestead thus avowed, "would be giving up everything that is dear to the heart of every true workingman. . . ." Even the *Labor Tribune*, grown cautious as the insurgent spirit of the Pittsburgh workers' movement had retreated to Homestead, concluded that the dispute pitted "those who earn bread by the sweat of their brow" against "those who tend toward plutocracy."[41]

Indeed, the right to "earn bread," and the less-skilled workers' own sense of what constituted a "fair" wage, were two key factors that drew together the entire Homestead community under the leadership of the skilled Amalgamated men. Taking advantage of the Amalgamated's easing of membership requirements, which allowed the least skilled steelworkers to join, the Amalgamated lodges in Homestead enlisted 1,500 workers in the weeks immediately preceding the lockout. The Knights of Labor also began an organizational drive aimed at the machinists in the mill, and leading steelworkers made certain that Slavic laborers were included in the planning for a possible work stoppage. Experience in Braddock had taught that Carnegie, despite his famous declaration against hiring new workers during a strike or lockout, indeed was willing to hire such men and to protect them with Pinkertons. When the Homestead steelworkers decided to reject Carnegie's proposal, then, the crucial problem for them was how to prevent new workers from starting operations in the mill.[42]

Thus, the steelworkers of Homestead took the town into their possession and sealed it off. Directed by an advisory committee of men chosen from each Amalgamated lodge in Homestead, armed steelworkers guarded all approaches to the town. The workers allowed no one to enter unless proof was furnished that he was not a "black sheep." Calm prevailed from July 1, when management closed down the works, until July 10. That morning, 100 Pinkertons arrived in Pittsburgh. While management did not dispatch them to Homestead, it did send a train carrying thirty-one workers—some of them Slavic immigrants—under the escort of the county sheriff.[43]

Nearly 2,000 Homesteaders greeted the train as it pulled into town, forming a barrier between it and the steelworks. Most of the workers on board fled into the nearby woods, but the sheriff tried to lead several of his charges into the mill. The crowd made way for the sheriff, though it barred the workers who tried to follow. Together with the employment agent who had hired and accompanied the men to Homestead, three were forced to "run the gauntlet." Marched into town, the agent and the three "black sheep" were assaulted physically and verbally by men, women, and young boys who formed the mile-long column. The agent, his face "almost unrecognizable from the blows he received," had the roughest going. And at the end of the gauntlet, four women gave him "a tongue lashing he will always remember." Of the employment agent, one woman asked: *"What does he mean by coming here trying to take the bread out of our mouths?"* To Homesteaders, the meaning was clear enough. The daily press interpreted their response as "misrule."

Two days later, the sheriff returned to Homestead with 125 men he had deputized and an order barring the workers from congregating on property owned by Carnegie. Disembarking from a railroad car, the authorities were greeted by an even larger crowd than the one that had assembled on July 10. This time, Homesteaders would not allow the sheriff to move.

For twenty minutes the crowd and the deputies faced each other in silence. "It was a crucial point," one reporter observed. "An angry murmur ran through the crowd and broke into a sullen roar." Some women "urged the men to defend their homes"; others "threatened what their intentions were if the deputies would attempt to go through the gates." Just as the crowd verged on assaulting the deputies, one of them broke ranks. The deputy tore off his badge and coat and threw his revolver to the ground, saying he was going home. To the cheers of the crowd, the other deputies followed suit. By late afternoon, all but one of the deputies had boarded return trains to Pittsburgh. "The strikers treated the officers very kindly after they saw they had won a victory, and paid some of their fares home," one newspaper reported. "Many of the strikers gave them the coats off their backs in exchange for their uniforms." The lone deputy who refused to leave was physically assaulted. One of the assailants very likely was the woman seen by the Reverend John Bullion, the priest at St. Mary's Church, smashing her umbrella over a man's head.[44]

With the departure of the sheriff and the deputies, Homestead was left in an uneasy quiet. O'Donnell, at the suggestion of the sheriff, agreed to negotiate with management on the condition that it make no effort to open the mill for two days. But the workers remained on guard, for the press continued to report that the Pinkertons and more new workers were on their way. Meanwhile, the advisory committee appointed a group of workers to conduct substantive negotiations. The result was a complicated three-year agreement that recognized the Amalgamated as the representative of all workers—including the less-skilled—and guaranteed reinstatement. The contract gave Carnegie a good deal of satisfaction, too, for the steelworkers consented to a sliding scale whose overall effect substantially cut labor costs by reducing the base that determined the salaries of roughly 1,600 skilled laborers. The base used to calculate the wages of other skilled workers remained unchanged, as did the wages of most of the less-skilled.[45]

Though some of the skilled workers who faced wage cuts as large as 30 percent were irritated, they put aside their objections when the steelworkers met to ratify the agreement. "It looks like a cold deal," one of the skilled men said, "but we're all in the same boat, and the minority must be sacrificed to the majority." To be sure, the majority was delighted with the agreement, as it had preserved the right of the skilled and less-skilled to work, maintained "fair" wages for most of the workers, and left intact the power exercised by Amalgamated men in directing work operations on the mill floor. To celebrate, cheering women and children joined the workers on the streets of the town amid fireworks and cannon fire.

Not everyone in Homestead joined the festivities on 14 July, however. For just as the workers' representatives were putting the finishing touches on the agreement, John Elko—a Carpatho-Rusyn or Slovak steelworker assigned to patrol a strategically important rail approach—was killed. Elko had jumped onto a passing train to determine if it were carrying Pinkertons or new workers. With Elko's wife and five-month-old daughter looking on, his legs became entangled in the wheels. Elko's colleagues carried his body back to town. "The scene of his rudely amputated foot in his shoe lying on the board on which he was carried home is a horrible spectacle hundreds will never forget," observed one reporter. "His late associates are anxious to test their appreciation of him."

They did. The seven Homestead lodges of the Amalgamated immediately raised $200 for Elko's family and promised to support them as long as they remained in Homestead. Indeed, Elko's funeral became a solemn occasion for the whole town. Nearly 2,000 steelworkers attended. The Anglo-American steelworkers, observed one reporter, saw Elko *"in the light of a patriot who falls at his post. . . . Although a Hungarian, he had imbibed American principles, and was one of the foremost in the late strike."*[46]

1892: Toward the Limits of Labor Republicanism

Slavic- and Anglo-American steelworkers pushed their cooperative efforts a step further during the Lockout of 1892, as the Slavic workers organized their own lodge of the Amalgamated Association. Again, they joined Anglo-American steelworkers in sealing off Homestead to defend their shared rights. And again, the women of Homestead were active in the defense of the town. Indeed, the women's assault on the Pinkertons as they ran the gauntlet summed up a quarter-century's struggle in the Pittsburgh district for an American republic where the rights of workers would not be sacrificed to the needs of industrialists. For as the Slavic- and Anglo-American women attacked, they shouted: "We are the people!"[47]

Of course, the declaration of the women was not a conscious allusion to the labor republicanism of the 1870s. And there are no references to the republican tradition in the few instances when the press recorded the words of Slavic immigrants in July 1892. Yet for both Slavic and Anglo-American Homesteaders, the confrontation on 6 July was between the legacy of republican justice and a new morality which valued, in the language of Thomas Armstrong, "money over men." For the right to earn "a fair day's wages for a fair day's work" and to achieve a competence remained the principal material desire of Anglo-American Homesteaders into the 1890s. And the Slovak expression that summed up the impetus for Slavic immigration—*za chlebom*—pointed to similar desires for modest material comfort and a modicum of "independence."[48]

That Pavel Olšav, Peter Fares, Joseph Sotak, and other Slavic Homesteaders joined their Anglo-American colleagues on the front line of the town's defense on 6 July was not, therefore, in the least remarkable. And when Sotak jumped to the aid of an Anglo-American steelworker wounded in the gunfight with the Pinkertons, Sotak was reaffirming a solidarity that Homesteaders took for granted. So, too, was Fares, who carried a loaf of bread to his position and who, like Sotak, was killed by the Pinkertons. Fares was shaking the loaf at the Pinkertons when he was shot. "You cannot take this from our mouths," were his last words. With these sentiments, Peter Puddler would have agreed.

In the days that followed, Homesteaders reaffirmed the solidarity of Anglo- and Slavic-Americans steelworkers as well as the declaration shouted by the women who attacked the Pinkertons. Thousands of Homesteaders, "the people," turned out to bury Fares and the other steelworkers who died. And the steelworkers' advisory

Pinkerton "detectives" running the gauntlet in Homestead after their 6 July 1892 surrender to the townspeople.
From Myron R. Stowell, *"Fort Frick," or The Siege of Homestead* (Pittsburgh: Pittsburgh Printing Company, 1893).

committee issued a statement which, in calling Carnegie's policies "subversive of the fundamental principles of American liberty" and "unconstitutional, anarchic and revolutionary," equated the republican rights of workers to their jobs with the rights of all Americans. "We"—the workers—"are the people," the women had shouted, and a republic must protect the people's rights: this was the meaning of the advisory committee's statement, too.

In asserting that theirs was "the cause of American liberty," however, the steelworkers formally extended the meaning of republicanism in a new direction, for the advisory committee declared that the general public and the employes of the Homestead Steel Works shared with its owners "equitable rights and interests in the . . . mill." *Iron Age,* the trade journal of metal manufacturers, was quick to point out that such an idea smacked of "socialism." And indeed, *Iron Age* had hit upon a truth: the steelworkers of Homestead understood that labor republicanism no longer could hold off "organized capital." Something new was required—something beyond a republic—to ensure the rights of working people.

Yet this was, after all, 1892—the year which marked the triumph of corporate America. But the triumph was not complete. No jury would convict the Homestead steelworkers charged with riot, conspiracy, treason, and murder. And while the lockout placed "the employers in the saddle" and Homestead became a place where, "If you want to talk. . . , you must talk to yourself," many workers in the town considered themselves "socialists" in the early 1900s and voted for Eugene Debs in large numbers. Indeed, from the "Hunkie" steel strike of 1919 and the unionizing efforts of the early 1940s to the recent closings of the steelmills in the Monongahela Valley, the Homestead Lockout has stood for the struggle of steelworkers and their families for "their American rights." In this regard, the words of the steelworkers' advisory committee of 1892 take on a contemporary meaning:

> The most evident characteristic of our time and country is the phenomenon of industrial centralization, which is putting the control of each of our great national industries into the hands of one or a few men, and giving these men an enormous and despotic power over the lives and the fortunes of their employes and subordinates—the great mass of the people; [it is] a power which eviscerates our national Constitution and our common law, and . . . which, though expressed . . . as the right of employers to manage their business to suit themselves, is coming to mean in effect nothing less than the right to manage the country to suit themselves.[49]

Notes

I thank Dirk Hoerder, Marjorie Scheer, and Mark Stolarik for their helpful readings of earlier drafts of this essay.

1. Philip S. Foner, *American Labor Songs of the Nineteenth Century* (Urbana: University of Illinois Press, 1975), 243–45, has the texts of some of the workers' songs. The best of the many secondary accounts of the lockout is Joseph Frazier Wall, *Andrew Carnegie* (New York: Oxford University Press, 1970), 537–82.

2. *The Pittsburgh Survey* was published in *Charities and the Commons* beginning in January 1909, and then in a six-volume series that included John A. Fitch, *The Steel Workers* (New York: Russell Sage Foundation, 1910), and Margaret F. Byington, *Homestead: The Households of a Mill Town* (New York: Russell Sage Foundation, 1910). J. Bernard Hogg, "The Homestead Strike of 1892" (Ph.D. diss., University of Chicago, 1943), is the single scholarly account of the dispute. Arthur G. Burgoyne, *The Homestead Strike of 1892* (Pittsburgh: University of Pittsburgh Press, 1979 [1893]), and Myron R. Stowell, *"Fort Frick," or The Siege of Homestead* (Pittsburgh: Pittsburgh Printing Co., 1893), are contemporary narratives. Leon Woolf, *Lockout: The Story of the Homestead Strike of 1892* (New York: Harper and Row, 1965), was reviewed by Herbert Gutman in *Pennsylvania Magazine of History and Biography* 90 (1966): 273–76. Byington's study and Bell's novel, *Out of This Furnace* (New York: Little, Brown, 1941), were republished in the 1970s.

3. On the ties of Anglo-American steelworkers to republicanism, see Linda Schneider, "The Citizen Striker: Workers' Ideology in the Homestead Strike of 1892," *Labor History* 25 (1982): 47–66, and idem, "American Nationality and Workers' Consciousness in Industrial Conflict, 1870–1920: Three Case Studies" (Ph.D. diss., Columbia University, 1975), pp. 253–342. By saying that workers "used" republicanism, I do not mean that there is a simplistic relationship between public discourse and "action" or, indeed, that discourse and action are distinct. On the contrary, they cannot be understood in isolation. This idea is usually overlooked by those students of republicanism who see it as an "ideology" that has motivated only the politically powerful.

4. Though the work of Fitch and Byington retains importance, it helped codify the condescension that pervades the literature on Slavic Americans. Steven R. Cohen's "Steelworkers Rethink the Homestead Strike of 1892" (*Pennsylvania History* 48 [1981]: 155–77) is the latest example of scholarship written in a vein which, while ignoring Slavic workers, also charges that they "neither understood nor much cared for" the world that Anglo-Americans sought to protect. Such thinking also informs the work of Thomas Bell, himself the son of Slovak immigrants drawn to the mills of Homestead and Braddock. See *Out of This Furnace*, pt. 1.

Throughout this essay, I use the word, "Slavic" to describe those peoples who are ethnic Slavs. Ukrainians, Poles, Slovaks, and Carpatho-Rusyns are among such peoples. I have included native-born and immigrant Irish, Welsh, and English steelworkers and their families in the category of "Anglo-American."

5. *Pittsburgh Post*, 27 June 1892. Among the recent work informed by the idea that building an alternative to industrial capitalism was a possibility in the late 1800s is James Holt, "Trade Unionism in the British and U.S. Steel Industries, 1880–1914: A Comparative Study," *Labor History* 18 (1977): 5–35.

6. *New York Sun*, 10 and 11 July 1892.

7. *Pittsburgh Post*, 20 June 1892; *National Labor Tribune* (hereafter, *NLT*), 25 June 1892; and *World*, 3 July 1892. For a discussion of "the social ethic of the 'white man' " that found expression in the speech and writing of nineteenth-century steelworkers, see Mary Ellen Freifeld, "The Emergence of the American Working Classes: The Roots of Division, 1865–1885" (Ph.D. diss., New York University, 1980), pp. 514–27. The office of burgess was equivalent to that of mayor.

8. David Brody, *Steelworkers in America: The Nonunion Era* (New York: Harper and Row, 1969), 51–56, has the best conspectus on why Carnegie and his associates wanted to crush the Amalgamated. Among the contemporary accounts of this desire, see *Pittsburgh Post*, 7 and 8 June 1892, which provides the description of the Amalgamated cited in the text. While still powerful, by 1892 the Amalgamated was on the brink of collapse, and both workers and managers understood that. For a fine discussion, see Shelton Stromquist, "Working Class Organization and Industrial Change in Pittsburgh, 1860–1890: Some Themes" (seminar paper, University of Pittsburgh, 1973), pp. 25–48. On the morality of improvement, see Raymond Williams, *The Country and the City* (New York: Oxford University Press, 1973), 60–67; on culture as "a way of life," see his *Marxism and Literature* (New York: Oxford

University Press, 1977), 11–20. Francis G. Couvares, "Work, Leisure, and Reform in Pittsburgh: The Transformation of an Urban Culture, 1860–1920" (Ph.D. diss., University of Michigan, 1980), pp. 1–103, offers a splendid overview of workers' culture. Many historians have lost sight of the shared origins and goals of the insurgent movements of American agricultural and urban laborers in the Gilded Age. Chester McArthur Destler, *American Radicalism, 1865–1901* (New London, Conn.: Connecticut College, 1946), chaps. 1 and 4, warrants a second look.

9. While some Homestead steelworkers did join the Junior Order of American Mechanics, for example, many more rejected the brand of nativist republicanism that found expression in it and in similar fraternal orders. See *Homestead Local News* (herafter, *HLN*), 12 and 19 September 1891, and 23 January and 12 March 1892. For a discussion of nativism in the 1880s, see John Higham, *Strangers in the Land: Patterns of American Nativism, 1860–1925* (New York: Atheneum, 1971), chap. 3.

10. Jones's statement, made in reference to miners of European ancestry, is in *NLT*, 16 August 1879. Taylor, who was a Chartist in England in the late 1830s, was one of the most famous labor leaders in the United States in the late 1870s and early 1880s. History has not been particularly kind to his memory, however.

11. *Pittsburgh Post*, 20 and 25 June 1892; and *NLT*, 25 June 1892. The First Catholic Slovak Union was a fraternal benefit society of Slavic immigrants, the overwhelming majority of whom were Slovaks.

12. The phrase "domestic arrangement" is borrowed from Charles Babbage, *On the Economy of Machinery and Manufactures* (New York: Augutus M. Kelley, 1963 [1835]). The description of Pittsburgh is from Ralph Keeler and Harry Fenn, "The Taking of Pittsburgh," *Every Saturday*, 18 March 1871, pp. 262–63.

13. The main issue in the lockout was the ironmasters' desire to reduce the base of the "sliding scale" agreement with the puddlers' union, called the Sons of Vulcan. The scale set puddlers' piece rates by linking them to the selling price, or "card rate," of bar iron. The base of the scale determined the ratio between the piece and card rates. The puddlers interpreted the proposed reduction of the base as an effort to reduce the *value* of their labor. As the puddlers held that only they could determine the value of their labor, they saw the lockout as an assault against their understanding not only of wages, but of fundamental justice. I have used the word "customary" in the sense that informs Eric Hobsbawm's "Custom, Wages and Work-Load in the Nineteenth Century," in his *Labouring Men: Studies in the History of Labour* (London: Weidenfeld and Niolson, 1965), 344–70.

The success of the puddling process, which transformed pig iron into malleable metal, depended on the skills acquired by puddlers through years of experience. Steelmaking facilities such as the Edgar Thomson Works used Bessemer converters and, later, open hearth furnaces, to make the transformation.

14. Sean Wilentz, *Chants Democratic: New York City and the Rise of the American Working Class, 1788–1850* (New York: Oxford University Press, 1984), esp. 237; E. P. Thompson, *The Making of the English Working Class* (New York: Vintage Books, 1966), 68; and Herbert G. Gutman, "Protestantism and the American Labor Movement: The Christian Spirit in the Gilded Age," in his *Work, Culture and Society in Industrializing America* (New York: Vintage Books, 1977), 87. One theme of Wilentz's fine study is that the republican tradition "bifurcated' in the antebellum years, with artisans fashioning an oppositional tradition and entrepreneurs building one that legitimized industrial capitalism. While republicanism in antebellum Pittsburgh awaits its historian, my study of the postwar years confirms the proposition that the tradition did divide.

15. *NLT*, 17 April 1875. For a discussion of the "equal rights" persuasion, see Alan Dawley, *Class and Community: The Industrial Revolution in Lynn* (Cambridge, Mass.: Harvard University Press, 1976), 1–10. Note, however, that Dawley's work is informed by the largely unsubstantiated idea that the tradition of equal rights, as it emerged from the Civil War, served as an obstacle to worker "radicalism."

16. *Vulcan Record*, 1874, p. 16; *NLT*, 15 January 1876. For a discussion of con-

flict and cooperation between the skilled and less skilled, see John William Bennett, "Iron Workers in Woods Run and Johnstown: The Union Era, 1865–1895" (Ph.D. diss., University of Pittsburgh, 1977), chap. 3. For an alternative interpretation, see Freifeld, "Emergence of the American Working Classes," pp. 440–47. On the leadership exercised by skilled workers in nineteenth-century workers' movements, see Bryan D. Palmer, "Most Uncommon Common Men: Craft and Culture in Historical Perspective," *Labour/Le Travailleur* 1 (1976): 5–31.

17. *NLT*, March 6, 1875; Stromquist, "Working Class Organization," pp. 28–29; and Bennett, "Iron Workers," pp. 58–59. For an overview of the ironworkers' unions and the drive to amalgamate, see Fitch, *Steel Workers*, chap. 8. While the Knights of Labor owed their initial burst of organizational activity in the Pittsburgh district to the Monongahela miners, the first assembly in the city was organized by ironworkers in 1873.

18. *NLT*, 13 March and 19 June 1875, and 8 January 1876; Dawley, *Class and Community*, p. 151; and J. A. H. Murray, ed., *The Oxford English Dictionary*, vol. 2 (Oxford: Clarendon Press, 1933), 718–19. In criticizing the wealthy and in staking out a claim to "a sufficiency of means for living comfortably"—means that typically included the ownership of a small house—American workers made a distinction between private property for use and private property for accumulation. This distinction has been overlooked by most Western political theorists since the time of Locke, for one of his greatest apparent achievements was to remove the natural limits on individual appropriation. Informing the idea of a competence, however, was the notion that there is no right to unlimited appropriation. Here, then, should end the tiresome debate over the belief of American workers in the sanctity of private property. Marx, who did distinguish between property for use and property for accumulation, certainly would not begrudge workers their aspirations for achieving a competence.

19. *NLT*, 28 August 1875. Similar rhetoric can be found in virtually every editorial published by the *NLT* through 1877. As the puddlers' union repeatedly expressed support for the *NLT*, its editorials serve as an excellent reflection of the puddlers' thinking. The paper also was the official organ of the Knights of Labor and of other labor organizations in the Pittsburgh district. The best published sketch on the *NLT* is in John D. French, " 'Reaping the Whirlwind': The Origins of the Allegheny County Greenback Labor Party in 1877," *Western Pennsylvania Historical Magazine* 64 (1981): 97–119.

20. "Cooperation" meant different things to different groups during the Gilded Age. But from the mid-1860s until the early 1880s, when the labor reformers of Pittsburgh spoke or wrote of a cooperative society, they usually meant a society in which the workers would own the means of production. The framework most helpful in understanding cooperation and other paths to an American "countersystem" has been offered by Sean Wilentz, "Artisan Republican Festivals and the Rise of Class Conflict in New York City, 1788–1837," in *Working-Class America: Essays on Labor, Community, and American Society*, ed. Michael H. Frisch and Daniel J. Walkowitz (Urbana: University of Illinois Press, 1983), 64. Wilentz, drawing on the work of William H. Sewell, Jr., suggests that social scientists abandon the search for a class consciousness that fits neatly into the received categories of Marxist analysis. The outstanding theoretical basis for such a view is Thomas E. Wartenberg, "Marx, Class Consciousness, and Social Transformation," *Praxis International* 2 (1982): 52–69.

21. *NLT*, 28 October 1876; *HLN*, 1 March 1890; and Jonathan Garlock, comp., *Guide to the Local Assemblies of the Knights of Labor* (Westport, Conn.: Greenwood Press, 1982), 407.

22. On the threat seen in the labor movement following the disturbances of 1877, see Pennsylvania General Assembly, *Report of the Committee Appointed to Investigate the Railroad Riots in July, 1877* (Harrisburg: Lane S. Hart, state printer, 1878), 18, 37, and 38. On the Land League in Pittsburgh, see Victor A. Walsh, " 'A Fanatic Heart': The Cause of Irish-American Nationalism in Pittsburgh During the

Gilded Age," *Journal of Social History* 15 (1982): 187–204. For an overview that is more sensitive to the league's critique of American capitalism, see Eric Foner, "Class, Ethnicity, and Radicalism in the Gilded Age: The Land League and Irish America," in his *Politics and Ideology in the Age of the Civil War* (New York: Oxford University Press, 1980), 150–200.

23. My account of the parade is based on *NLT,* 29 April, 20 and 27 May, and 10 and 24 June 1882; *Irish World and American Industrial Liberator,* 1 July 1882; *Pittsburgh Post,* 17 and 19 June 1882; *Pittsburgh Evening Telegraph,* 17 June 1882; *Pittsburgh Commercial Gazette,* 19 June 1882; *Homestead Times* (hereafter, *HT*) 10 and 17 June and 1 July 1882; and Stromquist, "Working Class Organization," pp. 17–24.

24. D. R. Jones moved to Homestead in 1885. He was elected burgess of the town in 1886 and 1887.

25. *NLT,* 27 May 1882, has the original version of "Storm the Fort." The reference to "unjust laws" in the chorus is to Pennsylvania's anti-conspiracy statute, which was used by industrialists to prosecute unions and their supporters. Such prosecutions reached a peak just prior to the parade, as D. R. Jones and members of the miners' union, Homestead steelworkers, and the *NLT* all faced court action. With revisions suggesting the changing experience of workers, "Storm the Fort" was republished many times. For other versions, see Foner, *American Labor Songs,* p. 154; and Dawley, *Class and Community,* pp. 3 and 193.

26. *NLT,* 7 January, 11 and 18 February, 4 March, and 6 May 1882; *HT,* 2 February 1882; *Pittsburgh Evening Telegraph,* 2 March 1882; and *Pittsburgh Post,* 6 March 1882. The strike at Homestead in 1882 involved the same issues of control that were at stake in 1876 at the Edgar Thomson Works in Braddock.

27. Correspondence between Powderly, the grand master workman of the Knights, and R. D. Layton, his chief acolyte in Pittsburgh, suggests that Powderly turned down the nomination both because of his personal rivalry with Armstrong and because he feared the loss by the Greenback-Labor Party would wound the Knights and threaten his supremacy in the order.

28. D. R. Jones, who left his work for the miners' union to become a lawyer, remained an advocate of workers' rights after his election to the Pennsylvania legislature in 1888. However, Jones's allegiances to the goals of the workers' movement of the 1870s and early 1880s were not so strong as those of Taylor and McLuckie. Taylor was elected burgess of Homestead in 1888. McLuckie served as burgess in 1890 and 1892. John Elias Jones, like several other steelworkers, served on the town council. A Welshman, he was financial secretary of the Land League in Homestead.

The quotation on the cooperation of Anglo-American and Slavic steelworkers during the Homestead Strike of 1882 is from a letter written by steelworker John J. O'Donnell, the president of the Land League in Homestead, to *Irish World,* 29 July 1882; italics added. O'Donnell wrote that his colleagues included both Anglo- and Slavic-Americans. On the appeal of the Land League to East European immigrants, see Foner, "Class, Ethnicity, and Radicalism."

29. I have used the Slovak variant *"za chlebom"* for an expression common to all Slavic emigrants. In Slovak, the idiom *"ist' za chlebom"* means to seek livelihood or employment. See Victor R. Greene, *The Slavic Community on Strike: Immigrant Labor in Pennsylvania Anthracite* (Notre Dame, Ind.: University of Notre Dame Press, 1968), 28 and 221, for a different interpretation. Also see Sylvia June Alexander, "The Immigrant Church and Community: The Formation of Pittsburgh's Slovak Religious Institutions, 1880–1914" (Ph.D. diss., University of Minnesota, 1980), chap. 1.

30. *HT,* 13, 20, and 27 August 1881, 11 March, 2 April, 26 August, and 14 and 28 October 1882, 17 March 1883, and 1 March 1884; Jozef A. Kushner, *Slováci Katolíci Pittsburghského Biskupstva* [Slovak Catholics of the Pittsburgh Diocese] (Passaic, N.J.: Slovenský Katolícky Sokol, 1946), 49 and 54–61; St. Mary Magdalene Church, Homestead, *Register of Baptism, 1881–90,* pp. 1 and 8; *Homestead Tax Assessments, 1883,* in Board of Assessment and Revision of Taxes, Allegheny County, Pa.,

Real Property and Assessment Books: Homestead and Mifflin Township, Pa.; First Catholic Slovak Union (hereafter, FCSU), Lodge 26, "Membership List," p. 322, Immigration History Research Center, St. Paul, Minn., which was kind enough to locate the membership list; June Granatir Alexander, "Staying Together: Chain Migration and Patterns of Slovak Settlement in Pittsburgh Prior to World War I," *Journal of American Ethnic History* 1 (1981): 59–61; and idem, "Immigrant Church," pp. 31–32; and Marian Mark Stolarik, "Immigration and Urbanization: The Slovak Experience, 1870–1918" (Ph.D., diss., University of Minnesota, 1974), chap. 1. I thank Charles Blocksidge and Louis Caputo, Jr., for granting access to the assessment books, and Rev. Bernard Costello, pastor of St. Mary's Church, for permission to use records at the church.

31. Kushner, *Slováci Katolíci*, pp. 49, 56, and 101; St. Michael's Roman Catholic Church, Braddock, Pa., *Register of Death, 1891–1952*, pp. 3–4, 28, and 29. I thank the Reverend Edward Kunco for allowing me to use the records on deposit at St. Michael's Church, Braddock. The difficulty in determining the origins of Slavic and indeed of most Homesteaders is exacerbated by the destruction of the manuscript census of 1890.

32. A handful of Galician Jews, Magyars, and Italians, as well as a larger number of German-Americans, also lived in Homestead prior to the Lockout of 1892. While the overwhelming majority of the Slavic immigrants were Roman Catholic Slovaks, some East Europeans were Carpatho-Rusyns who adhered to the Byzantine Rite Catholic Church. And smaller numbers of Protestant Slovaks and Roman Catholic Poles also lived in the town. However, the Slavic settlement in Homestead constituted a unified community into the early 1890s, as its members worked and worshipped together, lived in the same neighborhoods, and joined the same fraternal benefit societies.

33. Kushner, *Slováci Katolíci*, pp. 56–57; St. Michael's Church, Munhall, *75th Anniversary* (Pittsburgh: n.p., 1972), 1; and FCSU, Lodge 26, "Membership List," pp. 320–22. This paragraph also is based on an examination of the parish records at St. Mary's in Homestead and St. Michael's in Braddock. St. Michael's Church in Munhall—which adjoined Homestead and actually was the site of the Homestead Steel Works—was organized by Homestead Slovaks in 1897. Thanks go to the Reverend Richard Zula for providing me with a copy of the parish history.

34. M. P. Schooley and J. R. Schooley, comps., *Directory of Homestead* (Homestead: The Local News, 1890), 130 and 172, and Schooley and Schooley, comps., *Directory of Homestead* (Homestead: The Local News, 1892), 114, 148; *Braddock Tribune*, 17 September 1892; Burgoyne, *Homestead Strike*, p. 192; Stowell, *Fort Frick*, p. 250; Kushner, *Slováci Katolíci*, p. 57; FCSU, Lodge No. 26, "Membership List," pp. 320–22; and *Homestead Tax Assessments, 1890, Ward 2*.

35. Schooley and Schooley, *Directory of Homestead, 1892*, p. 182; *HT*, 1 April and 18 November 1882, 4 and 14 February 1884, 21 March 1885, 26 April 1890, and 2 May 1891; St. Mary's Church, *Register of Baptism, 1881–90*, p. 59; and Evelyn Patterson, interview with the author, 11 October 1981. Mrs. Patterson, the great-granddaughter of one of the steelworkers shot in the confrontation with the Pinkertons in 1892, is a librarian at the Carnegie Free Library in Homestead. The best sources on the occupations of Slavic steelworkers in Homestead are U.S. House of Representatives, Committee on the Judiciary, *Investigation of the Employment of Pinkerton Detectives in Connection with the Labor Troubles at Homestead, Pa.*, (Washington: Government Printing Office, 1893), 52d Congress, 2d Session, 1892–93, Report 2447, 5–18; and Allegheny County, *Real Property and Assessment Books: Homestead and Mifflin Township.*

36. *Národnie noviny*, 4 February 1890; also quoted in Stolarik, "Immigration and Urbanization," p. 51; and *Mount Pleasant Journal*, reprinted in *NLT*, 10 July 1886. Stolarik concludes that Slovaks often celebrated the Fourth of July and that the festivities typically were held in honor of a Slovak national hero. On the comingling of Old and New World "traditions" in the thought and behavior of Slavic immigrants, see John Bodnar's rich essay, "Immigration and Modernization: The Case of

Slavic Peasants in America," in *American Working-Class Culture: Explorations in American Labor and Social History*, ed. Milton Cantor (Westport, Conn.: Greenwood Press, 1979), 333–60.

While I have no hard evidence directly linking the communities of Slavic coke workers in the Connellsville region to those in the Pittsburgh district, the press noted during the Lockout of 1892 that some Slavic workers employed at the Homestead Steel Works formerly worked in the coke region.

37. *NLT*, 6 February and 3 and 10 July 1886; and miscellaneous clippings and letters in Max Schamberg Papers, personal collection of Jane Berkey, Pittsburgh. Schamberg, the Austro-Hungarian consul in Pittsburgh during the 1880s, helped settle a number of the violent labor disputes involving Frick and the Slavic workers he employed. I thank Berkey for allowing me to use the Schamberg papers.

The legacy of the Revolution of 1848, which resulted in the formal abolition of serfdom in the Hapsburg Empire, is largely unexplored in literature dealing with Slavic-Americans.

38. Hogg, "Homestead Strike," chap. 3, was first to suggest that the lockout of 1889 was a dress rehearsal for the lockout of 1892.

39. Andrew Carnegie, *Dedication of the Carnegie Library at the Edgar Thomson Steel Rail Works, Braddock: Address to Workingmen*, (Pittsburgh: n.p., n.d., c. 1889), 13, 15. Carnegie's 1888 victory at the Edgar Thomson decimated the Knights of Labor in Pittsburgh. Earlier in the decade Carnegie had succeeded in removing the Amalgamated from the mill.

40. *NLT*, 3, 13, 20, and 27 April 15 June and 20 July 1889; and *Commoner*, 27 April 1889.

41. *NLT*, 25 May, 15 June, and 1 July 1889; *Iron Age*, 23 May and 27 June 1889; *American Manufacturer*, 24 May and 21 June 1889; *Pittsburgh Chronicle-Telegraph*, 18, 20, and 23 May, 20 and 21 June, and 15 July 1889; *Pittsburgh Post*, 15 July 1889; and Amalgamated Association, *Proceedings of the Fifteenth Annual Convention of the National Lodge* (Pittsburgh: n.p., 1890), 2961–77. Until 1888, when Carnegie introduced a sliding scale at the Edgar Thomson Works, wages for skilled workers in the steel industry were determined by a contractual scale built on a fixed base that set piece rates in accord with the selling price of iron, markedly more expensive than steel. Contracts typically lasted a year, when the base would be renegotiated. As the yearly scales were so pegged to iron, Carnegie and other steelmasters wanted an arrangement that reflected both the capital outlays for the new technologies of steel and the prices in the steel market. While ironworkers in the Pittsburgh district had fought to keep their sliding scale, steelworkers claimed that because Carnegie's sliding scales drastically reduced the base that set the ratio between piece rates and market price, the scales would transfer an inequitable portion of the profits to the owners.

42. *Commoner*, 28 April 1888, and 6 July 1889; *Pittsburgh Post*, 1, 3, 14, and 15 July 1889; *Pittsburgh Times*, 1 July 1889; *Iron Age*, 2 April 1888; *NLT*, 28 April 1888; Jesse S. Robinson, *The Amalgamated Association of Iron, Steel and Tin Workers* (Baltimore: Johns Hopkins Press, 1920), 43; Andrew Carnegie, "An Employer's View of the Labor Question" and "Results of the Labor Struggle," *Forum* 1 (1886): 114–25 and 538–51; and Wall, *Carnegie*, pp. 522–27.

43. The details in this and in succeeding paragraphs are drawn primarily from *Tribune*, 13 July 1889; *Pittsburgh Post*, 11, 12, 15, and 15 July, 1889; *Herald*, 13 July 1889; *Pittsburgh Chronicle-Telegraph*, 11 and 12 July 1889; *Pittsburgh Press*, 12–14 July 1889; *Pittsburgh Times*, 12 July 1889 (italics added); *Pittsburgh Commercial-Gazette*, 12 and 13 July 1889; and Amalgamated Association, *Proceedings, 1890*, pp. 2962–64. "Black sheep" was the term of disapprobration used by metalworkers in the nineteenth century to describe laborers hired during strikes and lockouts.

44. The daily press was particularly interested in the behavior of Homestead women during the lockout of 1889—and again in 1892, when they played a more prominent role in violence directed at the Pinkertons.

45. In all likelihood, Carnegie could have defeated the Amalgamated at Home-

stead in 1889. But under pressure to fill back orders in a bullish market, and feeling the pressure of competitors who had reached agreements with the union, management decided that the advantages of continued operations with some reduction in labor costs outweighed a protracted struggle. When the steel market was glutted in 1892, company officials decided that such a struggle was not too costly.

46. *Pittsburgh Post* and *Pittsburgh Times*, 16 July 1889 (italics added); St. Mary's Church, *Register of Baptism, 1881–90*, p. 76; and Albert Elko, interview with the author, 20 June 1983. The death of John Elko provided the immediate impetus for organizing the First Hungarian Slovak Sick Benefit Society of St. Michael the Archangel, as it was founded five days after his burial. The society was the precursor of Lodge No. 26 of the FCSU.

47. The details in this and in succeeding paragraphs are taken primarily from *Pittsburgh Post*, 21–23, 26, and 28 June and 4 July 1892; *Tribune*, 7 July 1892; *World*, 7 and 8 July 1892; *Sun*, 7 and 8 July and 7 August 1892; *Herald*, 8 July 1892; *Pittsburgh Commercial-Gazette*, 6 June and 7 and 9 July 1892; *Iron Age*, 28 July 1892; Stowell, *Fort Frick*, pp. 43–44 and 250; U.S. House, *Labor Troubles at Homestead*, p. 12; St. Michael's Church, Braddock, *Register of Death, 1891–1952*, pp. 3–4; and Burgoyne, *Homestead Strike*, pp. 93, 192. That Slavic immigrant steelworkers created their own labor organization and then joined the Amalgamated violates the received wisdom regarding the first generation of Slavic immigrants as well as the centerpiece of the canonical literature on the Amalgamated: that it was the prototype for an "aristocracy of labor."

48. The Slovak expression, *ist' za chlebom*, carries with its literal meaning decided connotations of "independence." *Na svojom chlebe*, for example, means to be on one's own; *byt' na vlastnom chlebe* means to be on one's own or to be one's own boss. Furthermore, *za chlebom* implied that the search for livelihood was a quest that required sacrifice. (I thank Professor John Krynski of Duke University for calling my attention to this point.) While the expression did not directly equate the quest with a religious or spiritual venture, a translation of *za chlebom* that pins its meaning on "looking for money" is decidedly limited. Unfortunately, such a translation informs most of the literature on Slavic immigrants.

See page 10 of Schooley and Schooley's *Directory of Homestead* (Homestead: The Local News, 1891) for an example of the continuing importance of achieving a competence in Homestead. On the conjuncture of the aspirations of East Europeans and American "republicans," see Rowland Berthoff, "Peasants and Artisans, Puritans and Republicans: Personal Liberty and Communal Equality in American History," *Journal of American History* 69 (1982): 579–98. Note, however, that in these shared aspirations, Berthoff sees an "ideological consensus" on the virtues of private enterprise and acquisitiveness. Such a view overlooks the findings of David Montgomery and Herbert G. Gutman, among others. See Bodnar, "Immigration and Modernization," pp. 336–37, for a convincing argument that Slavic immigrants repudiated acquisitiveness.

49. Byington, *Households of a Mill Town*, p. 175; Fitch, *Steel Workers*, chaps. 16 and 18, esp. pp. 216, 232, and 235, and the comments of an unidentified steelworker, Ch-11, 20 January 1908, in Fitch's unpublished research notes; Michael Nash, "Conflict and Accommodation: Some Aspects of the Political Behavior of America's Coal Miners and Steel Workers, 1890–1920" (Ph.D. diss., State University of New York—Binghamton, 1975), pp. 139–45. In 1941, the steelworkers' local in Homestead erected a monument near the mill and dedicated it to the "memory of the Iron and Steel Workers who were killed in Homestead, Pa., on July 6, 1892, while striking against the Carnegie Steel Company in defense of their American rights." That 1892 marked the consolidation of the corporate state is based primarily on the fact that in 1892 the most sustained challenge to corporate America in the nineteenth century—the farmers' revolt—was turned back. I am indebted to Charles Hill, the grandson of John Fitch, for the use of his research notes.

GARY R. MORMINO AND
GEORGE E. POZZETTA

Spanish Anarchism in Tampa, Florida, 1886–1931

A century ago, revolutionaries driven by a messianic faith threatened to paralyze world governments through apocalyptic acts of terror. Motivated by anarchist dreams of brotherhood and nihilist rejection of authority, terrorists' propaganda by deed outraged the public, terrified the ruling classes, and canonized a handful of dreamers.

Tampa, Florida, seemed an unlikely setting for such a libretto. City leaders waged a fifty-year campaign to combat real and imagined threats to the establishment by radicals in general, anarchists in particular, and most especially *los lectores,* the readers of the cigar factories, who, it was suggested, fomented subversive thoughts from their tribunes. Tampa, with its scores of cigar factories created a unique industrial and social setting. When the Board of Trade lobbied for cigar factories in late 1885, it had not bargained on the importation of radical ideologies along with Spanish and Cuban emigrants. This essay will examine the origins, development, and nature of Spanish anarchism in Tampa, Florida, in the period from 1886 to 1931, a study not of radical violence—of which there was little—but of group dynamics and organization—of which there was much.[1] This is offered as a small installment on the larger agenda of work remaining to be done on the diaspora of anarchism from Spain to the Americas.

Old World

To understand Hispanic radicalism, and its diffusion abroad, one must appreciate the contours of Spanish history. Emigration has played a fundamental role in Spanish society for five hundred years. The major points of origin for Tampa's Spaniards were the northwestern provinces of Asturias and Galicia, which have justly been called the nursery of Spanish emigrants.[2] "The Asturians do not leave Spain because of money," a proverb says "but for the sheer adventure of it."[3] However, a protracted class struggle, a repressive Spanish government, and a bankrupt economy—not quixotic lust for adventure—motivated several thousand Asturianos and Gallegos to go to Tampa.

Asturias and Galicia shared an important role in the history of Iberia. Galicia's climate is moist, but its granite-strewn soil is unyielding. An observer described Galicia in 1581 as a barren region, where the coarse rye bread seemed unfit for human consumption.[4] Landholding patterns aggravated the plight of the *campesinos* (peasants). The disentailment of church lands beginning in the later eighteenth century, which in France had satisified the land-hungry, only increased the misery of the lower classes. Unlike southern Spain, dominated by the *latifundia,* northern Spain was characterized by hopelessly small family plots. In part because of the primitive roads and isolation, in part because of the burdensome laws of tenancy, much of northwestern Spain was governed by the antiquated system of *foros* (hereditary quitrents). Peasants, pressed by the landowner, exercised little control over their own lives, since lawyers, bankers, and priests generally ruled the small villages. In the later nineteenth century the church, having lost its lands and agrarian roots, shifted attention to other domains and in the process lost its most fervent supporters, the agrarian masses. "Pray to God and the saints," suggested a Spanish proverb, "but put fertilizer on the crops." To many, the church, in its defense of the established order, symbolized the inequities of Spain.[5]

Declining agricultural prices, the result of a worldwide glut in the late nineteenth century, cruelly coincided with a spiraling birthrate. Between 1768 and 1900, Spain's population doubled to 8.6 million persons. Moreover, the population density of northern Spain figured among the highest in Europe.[6] Spaniards reacted to the social and economic upheaval through a variety of responses. Between the 1880s and 1920, 820,000 Spaniards—peasants, artisans, and professionals—emigrated to the Americas. At home, numerous others embraced the doctrines of anarchism. And, of course, emigrants and ideology accompanied each other.

In Spain, anarchism possessed a passionate fascination with *los miserables*—landless laborers, tenant farmers, peasants, and failing artisans who felt the sting of class hatred and saw the chasm between rich and poor more sharply than anyone. "Where law is an open fraud, public life a chimera, and politics the personification of corruption," noted a Spanish observer, "the organization of 'No Law!' is a logical and natural answer. . . ."[7] Temma Kaplan has argued that anarchism also appealed to small-scale producers and independent peasants.[8]

A logical outgrowth of nineteenth-century Spanish social and economic conditions, the anarchist movement quickly moved from the cafes and doctrinal stage into action, capturing the imagination of the rural and urban proletariat. Anarchist doctrines had circulated in Spain from the 1840s, thanks largely to the efforts of disciples of Pierre-Joseph Proudhon, Ramon de la Sagra, and Francisco Pi y Margall. Yet it was not until 1868, following the First International and the liberal revolution that led to the overthrow of Queen Isabela II, that ideas and activists from Russia, France, and Italy came to Spain.[9]

Michael Bakunin's writings enjoyed an immediate and long-lasting influence in Spain. His philosophy, drawn from millenarian Christianity, the Enlightment, and Proudhon, emphasized at its core the inherent good of humankind and the repressive nature of institutions and hierarchies. Whereas Rousseau argued the perfectibility of life through the proper balance of institutions, Bakunin insisted on removing the political yoke of the state.[10]

Bakunin and Marx passionately disagreed over the means and ends of the revolution. Marx's admiration for the disciplined and centralized German proletariat differed from Bakunin's mistrust of institutionalized classes and his faith in the precapitalist masses of Russia, Spain, and Italy. He believed in the spontaneity of the rural masses and an atavistic desire to restore community as the basic unit of social life. The legacy of the Spanish labor movement stands as a testimonial to the loggerhead between Marx and Bakunin: socialism vs. anarchism, institutions vs. spontaneity, political action vs. propaganda by deed, authority vs. freedom.[11]

Bakunin's message especially electrified the dispossessed Spanish rural classes, because it offered the promise of communal control of a world long dominated by reactionary clergy, corrupt bureaucrats, and the dreaded Guardia. Bakunin's appeal to direct action also found a receptive audience among a people who venerated the social bandit and envisioned future blows for freedom.[12]

In 1881, five years after Bakunin's death, anarchists organized the *Federacíon de Trabajadores de la Región Española.* The movement, soon declared illegal, spread to the countryside and industrial cities. In the largely rural provinces of Asturias and Galicia the countryside convulsed with rent strikes, cattle maiming, assassinations and arson. The Spanish establishment trembled, for threats came not only from mass peasant uprisings but, perhaps even more chilling, from the solitary terrorist.[13]

Bakunin's greatest legacy lay in the convincing strength of his propaganda by deed. In the quarter-century following his death, anarchism leaped from the salons of Madrid to the front page. Manifestos soon flooded the countryside, pronouncing Peace to Men, War to Institution.

Although terrorism was never more than a minority doctrine—running counter to other anarchist sentiments such as self-improvement and rationalist education—apocalyptic and infectious acts of violence, designed to remove symbols of social and political order, riveted Spain between 1890 and 1912. In 1912, for example, Spain's Premier José Canalejas y Mendes died at the hands of Manuel Padrinas, a Spanish anarchist who had lived in Tampa, Florida.[14] Ironically, propaganda by deed, designed to stir up the laboring masses, resulted only in splintering the anarchist movement and increasing local police repression.

Yet, not all Spaniards hoisted placards of bread and revolution and struggled at home. Responding to the turmoil and flux of the 1880s and 1890s, thousands traveled a different path of social change, emigration. Some went to search out an American dream; others resolved to remake America into their anarchist dream.

Emigration

Students of Spanish anarchism have largely devoted their energies to examining the exceptionally long lasting and important influence this ideology has had on the development of peninsular Spain. Consequently, little attention has been given to the diffusion of Spanish anarchism to the various parts of the colonial empire. Yet the fact remains that developments in both spheres were related. Indeed, the connective tissues joining the motherland and its outposts acquired a durability and strength that allowed them to survive until well into the twentieth century.

Cuba was the pearl of the Spanish colonial world, and as such it served as a lodestar for both disaffected radicals and conservative elites. The end of the Ten Years War in 1878 brought peace, but also social turmoil. Spain encouraged and subsidized immigration to Cuba in the 1880s, precisely at the moment the island's factories and cities were flooded with emancipated slaves and rural migrants.[15] For Spain, it was hoped, immigration would serve as a social safety valve and at the same time increase the loyalist population abroad. But the full spectrum of political ideologies present in Spain re-formed in Cuba, and the doctrines of anarchism occupied a conspicuous place in this ferment.[16]

An important early influence in the spread of anarchist ideas was Roig San Martín, the island's noted anarchist activist.[17] San Martín had worked in his early career as a *lector* in the tobacco industry and had received his "training" at the hands of militant cigar workers. By the early 1880s San Martín had participated in the founding of a variety of worker's groups, and in 1887 he began publishing the island's first anarcho-syndicalist newspaper, *El Productor.*[18] Roig San Martín's leadership was also important in the formation of the Circle of Workers (1885). This organization attempted to provide a foundation for a broadly based workers' movement. Its reform agenda included evening schools for workers, day care centers, an orphanage, and other social welfare insitutions for the working class. In the years surrounding the turn of the century, the island witnessed a remarkable growth of anarchist groups in small towns, particularly in Havana and Santa Clara provinces.[19]

Although records are scanty, it appears that the greatest number of Spanish anarchists in Cuba were Catalans, who were much influenced by the worker's movement in Barcelona. Publications from Barcelona were widespread, and many carried over into the settlements of Spaniards who ultimately made the transition from Cuba to Florida.[20]

The work of Spanish anarchists in Cuba can be most clearly seen in labor organization and in the independence movement. In the years before the outbreak of Cuba's successful war for independence (1895), anarchists played important roles in the early labor movement. This was particularly true in the case of the cigar makers, artisans who occupied something of a vanguard position in the struggle to organize Cuban workers. The increased radicalization of the cigar work force was seen in a steadily upward spiral of strike activity beginning to take place after 1880.[21] So disruptive did labor militance become that an increasing number of cigar factory owners (particularly those in Havana, the center of Cuba's cigar industry) sought locations away from the island. Ironically, as radicals achieved greater success and greater disruption of the industry, the colonial government adopted increasingly stringent measures against them, thus pressuring many to leave the island. Large numbers of these men then found their way to such expatriate centers of Spanish-Cuban cigar manufacturing as Key West, Tampa, and New York, some of which had been founded largely to escape the radicals' influence and which had been populated by political exiles and radicals from the Ten Years War (1868–1878).[22]

On a wider level, the 1892 Congreso Obrero in Havana proved to be an important step in the developing relationship between the workers' movement in Cuba and anarchism. Guided by the principles of "revolutionary socialism," the Congress proclaimed a vigorous proletarian ideology, urging among other things the adoption of the general strike and declaring unequivocally that *"los obreros formamos una sola clase."*[23] For years, however, the pursuit of working-class goals often found itself at loggerheads with the continuing struggle for independence that periodically disrupted the island. To understand the curious mixture of worker militancy, radical ideology, and patriotic fervor requires an understanding of the cigar-making outposts that were founded by Spaniards based in Cuba.

Perhaps the most remarkable of these was begun by a gifted businessman, Vicente Martínez Ybor. Born in Valencia in 1818, Martínez Ybor came to Cuba in 1832 to avoid compulsory military service. There, he had a meteoric rise in the cigar industry, ascending from apprentice to broker to manufacturer. Displaying a deft touch and entrepreneurial instinct, he helped modernize a primitive tobacco economy. He seized what was upon his arrival essentially a cottage industry, organizing the farmers of the lush Vuelta Abajo region and later erecting factories in Havana. Martínez Ybor rationalized the industry, creating new markets, concentrating wealth, and expanding operations to meet a virtually insatiable world appetite for hand-rolled Cuban cigars.[24]

The gathering storm of Cuban independence nearly swept Martínez Ybor into its vortex. His less-than-secretive support for the separatists stemmed principally from economic motivation: with a free Cuba he could escape burdensome Spanish taxes. But he also displayed throughout his career a genuine sympathy for the Cuban cause. In 1868 the Ten Years War forced Martínez Ybor into an exile that took him to Key West, Florida, a Cuban sanctuary as Spanish authorities enforced draconian measures in Havana. By 1870, more than a thousand Cubans had obtained asylum in Key West, and in 1873 Cubans claimed a majority of the island's population. Cigar making accompanied Cubans to the island, whose notorious humidity was suitable for the brittle tobacco leaf. Key West blossomed into the leading manufacturing city of Florida; in 1873 annual output totaled 25,000,000 cigars.[25]

Martínez Ybor may have sparkled as the brightest luminary among *patrones de tabaqueros,* but a number of like-minded countrymen rivaled him in stature. Born in the post-Napoleonic era and sensing the diminution of opportunities in the peninsula, Spaniards such as Ignacio Haya, Enrique Pendás, and Peregrino Rey followed and perfected the example set by Martínez Ybor. Intensely patriotic, fiercely conscious of their dependence upon a Cuban workforce, these *patrones* favored Spaniards for the upper echelon positions in the industry, thus stimulating emigration from Iberia and Cuba.[26] While the businesses of Ignacio Haya and Martínez Ybor flourished during the early 1880s, the owners disapproved of the nascent labor movement, which contained anarchist elements and which threatened their control of the industry. Thus, a search began for a new cigar capital.

In 1884 Gavino Gutiérrez, an able Spanish engineer, had visited Tampa, Florida, and informed Martínez Ybor about its humid climate, outstanding transportation facilities, and bright prospects for investment. Assurance of labor peace and police protection punctuated the discussions; the Tampa Board of Trade agreed to sell Martínez Ybor land on which to create a separate company town northeast of Tampa.[27] Ybor City was born in the spirit of Pullman, Illinois, and the southern mill towns. An industrial community plotted by Gutiérrez, financed by Martínez Ybor and Haya, and vitalized by Cuban and Spanish workers, began to show signs of life in the spring of 1886.

The emergent Spanish community manifested a vitality and cohesiveness that helped create an ethnic *paella* unique for the South. Quite naturally, it was shaped in its initial years by the Spanish population pool existing in Cuba and, to a lesser extent, in Key West. The great majority of Tampa's Spaniards had spent time in Cuba working in the cigar trade centered in Havana. Generally, they had followed a pattern of migration characterized by the flow of skilled labor and mercantile activity and long periods of sojourner status. Indeed, many Spaniards "commuted" between Spain and the Americas for extended periods of time, maintaining separate households on both sides of the Atlantic. Many came to the Americas with designs of accumulating enough money to purchase land and eventually return to the *patria chica* (Old World villages).[28]

Asturian and Galician villages such as Ferrera de los Gavitos, Pintueles, Las Villas, Cándamo, Moutas, and Infiesto sent steady streams of Spaniards to Cuba and later to Florida. Spaniards, in patterns similar to those of Italians, left the Old World in chain migrations, assisted by a complex and well-organized network of kinfolk, compatriots, and agents. Typical was the career of Fermín Souto. "I was born in the little village of Ferrol de Galicia in June of 1858," Souto told an interviewer in 1935. "My father was a stone cutter . . . my mother was born and raised in the country. I am, therefore, a plebian. My parents were poor people, and in those days a poor man could only look forward to a very meager education. On October 30, 1870, a friend took me to Havana, Cuba."[29] A half-century later, María Ordieres followed the example of Souto. "I was born and raised in Cándamo, Asturias," explained Ordieres. "My father heard that in Tampa, Florida, the cigar industry was in need of workers. So in 1923 he left for Tampa. By brother and I followed since we were the oldest and could work."[30]

Life in Tampa's Latin Community

The size of the "Latin" (a local term, meaning Spaniards, Cubans, and Italians) community grew rapidly after 1890. The Spanish population, though small during the first decade and a half, exercised a powerful influence. In 1890, the U.S. Census, a notoriously poor indicator of the true count of immigrants, registered 233 Spaniards and 1,313 Cubans in Tampa. By 1900, almost a thousand Spaniards had gathered there, as well as 3,533 Cubans and 1,315 Italians. In 1910, Tampa's Latin community boasted 2,337 Spanish-born residents, 3,859 Cubans, and 2,519 Italians.[31] Held together by a vibrant Latin culture, infused with a set of distinctive work rhythms, and pulsating with a heightened political consciousness, Ybor City offered its Spanish *compãneros* contrasting values and alternatives: solidarity buffered by individualism, a comfortable life-style set off by strident demands for reform and revolution, an elite work force challenged at every point by a Cuban proletariat.

Boosters may have advertised Ybor City as a planned industrial community, but the enclave's first decade reflected the rawness of a mining camp and the dangers of a frontier presidio.[32] Small, inexpensive, wooden-framed houses soon clustered alongside brick factories, testimonials to the business sagacity of Haya and Martínez Ybor. Realizing the profits to be reaped in Florida real estate and the necessity of domesticating the male work force by bringing workers' families to Tampa, businessmen created the Ybor City Land Improvement Company. The corporation shrewdly sold inexpensive houses to workers and induced foreign and domestic cigar factories to relocate in Ybor City.

Customs did not easily surrender to new economies. Cubans, buffeted by escalating tensions in the homeland, proved reluctant homeowners. Their peripatetic life-style, which permitted—and at times forced—them to move from factory to factory, from Tampa to Key West to Havana, militated against property accumulation.

Spaniards maintained a very distinctive demographic profile. Persistently high ratios of males to females characterized the Spanish presence. The boardinghouse served as an important institution for single Spanish men, serving also as a hothouse for radical politics. In 1900, fully one-third of Tampa's Spaniards lived in boardinghouses, a percentage unchanged a decade later. In 1910, census takers discovered 810 Spanish boarders, as compared to only 352 Cubans and 45 Italians. Whereas Martínez Ybor and Ignacio Haya moved freely and comfortably within Tampa's Anglo establishment, few rank-and-file Spaniards could even be understood beyond the confines of their ethnic enclave: Fewer than 19 percent spoke English in 1910.[33] Clustered in their boardinghouses and insulated in their factories, Spaniards turned inward for support; and the result was an imaginative and resourceful outpouring of organizational energies.

Traditions of immigrant mutual aid run deep in the history of American cities. Immigrants, in order to protect themselves from a real or imagined hostile world, and to reinforce their Old World value systems, created cooperative institutions. In Ybor City, voluntary associations played roles far beyond that of the usual burial societies and folk fairs.

To understand the powerful sway exercised by ethnic institutions, one must realize the milieu from which these societies emerged. Ybor City was an instant town and, moreover, a community emerging from Tampa, which prior to 1880 numbered fewer than a thousand persons. Consequently, there existed few institutions to minister to the immigrants and, given the southern penchant toward self-help and conservatism, little likelihood of future assistance from the Anglo culture.

In July 1887, Guillermo Machado, a Spanish physician, founded La Igual, a milestone in Ybor City health care. Scores of cooperative medical programs evolved, based on the concept of "The Equal," offering cigar makers and families cradle-to-grave protection. Tampa's medical fraternity railed against Ybor City's "socialist doctors," threatening to bar them from medical practice, a feat they later accomplished.[34]

The organization of the Centro Español in 1891 and Centro Asturiano in 1902 set new standards for ethnic participation. Modeled after Havana's powerful namesakes, the Centro Español and Centro Asturiano embarked on campaigns to facilitate programs of mutual relief and promote a vibrant cultural life. Most remarkably, the institutions housed a diverse collection of personalities: cigar manufacturers and workers, anarchists and nationalists, Asturians and Galicians. The organizations set the course for the future, allowing second-generation sons born in Cuba and Tampa to become members, a practice not observed at the Havana *centros*.[35]

Tampa's Spanish insitutions embarked on a building frenzy to offer their membership modern and inexpensive health care. In 1904, Centro Español constructed a $90,000 hospital for members and their families, an institution far superior to any public facility in Tampa. Asturians completed Sanatorio Covadonga in 1905, a modern hospital with rooms for sixty patients and a pharmacy. While members of the Tampa medical establishment branded these facilities as socialistic, few denied their efficacy.[36]

Anarchist Clubs

Spanish anarchists arriving in Tampa after the years of initial settlement found a community that possessed a wide spectrum of radical ideologies. The proliferation of speaking clubs or debating societies that developed in the city revealed most clearly the diverse nature of Tampa's radical community. By 1900 they flourished in all sections of Ybor City and West Tampa, a separate settlement clustered around cigar factories located across the Hillsborough River.

Although records are very scanty, it appears that anarchist groups were the most numerous. This was almost certainly true of the years prior to 1898, when expatriate Cuban anarchist groups in support of independence swelled the numbers. Yet, throughout the period under review, those groups organized and attended by Spaniards formed the majority.[37]

Most of these groups were small entities organized for the purpose of self-education and debate. Most had a secretary, who was responsible for maintaining correspondence with like-minded individuals elsewhere and for supplying a small club library (usually composed of inexpensive pamphlets and anarchist newspapers). More often than not, meetings were held in the homes of members, although some of the larger groups were able to rent meeting space in the union hall or the ethnic club buildings. The immigrant press in Tampa is filled with announcements of anarchist group meetings throughout the years before World War I.[38]

Not all organizations were small, restrictive clubs attracting limited clienteles. The celebrated Spanish anarchist Pedro Esteve, for example, guided the fortunes of Antorcha, a cultural center open to freethinkers of all nationalities. Antorcha offered free classes on many subjects, musical recitals, literary gatherings, and a gymnasium for exercise and sport. When not engaged in activities of the mind, members could take fencing lessons under the tutelage of a young Italian socialist named Arturo Massolo. Radicals infused Tampa with a vibrant Spanish-language theatre. In 1918, *El Internacionale* announced that *Aurora,* "a socialist drama of the first order," would be performed at the Centro Asturiano.[39] English, Spanish, and Italian blended freely in Antorcha, but Spanish was generally recognized as the official language.

Though hardly typical of Spanish anarchists in Tampa, Pedro Esteve moved through a career in the cigar city in a way that sheds light on the social and cultural conditions present. Esteve was born in Barcelona in 1866, where he played an important role in the developing Catalan anarchist movement.[40] He worked with the principal anarchist newspaper of Barcelona, *El Productor,* and there learned the trade that would be his working career. Toward the end of the nineteenth century he emigrated to Brooklyn, where he became active in the publication of *El Despertar.* Soon thereafter, he moved to Paterson, New Jersey, a well-known center of anarchist activity. Both locations contained large numbers of anarchists of differing ethnic backgrounds, but Italians and Spaniards predominated.[41] Shortly after the turn of the century, Spanish anarchists in Tampa invited Esteve to come southward and take up residence in the cigar city. With funds collected from various groups, supporters supplied Esteve with his own printing shop, La Políglota (The Multi-Lingual), and a residence.[42]

Esteve played a leadership role in the development of anarchist thought in Tampa. He established free evening schools for workers and made books available to a growing cadre of followers. Publicly, he appeared frequently in the major immigrant clubs of the city, debating socialists and radicals. When socialist or anarchist luminaries visited Tampa, a public debate with Esteve invariably was the capstone of their stay. Among others, he crossed verbal swords and broke bread with Emma Goldman, Elizabeth Gurley Flynn, the Italian anarchist Luigi Galleani, and Italian socialists Giuseppe Bertelli and Arturo Caroti.[43]

Esteve was also active in the workers' movement of Tampa, constantly exhorting cigar workers to organize in order to resist capitalist oppression. His press received union contracts for printing (for many years he printed the union newspaper, *El Internacional*). He continued to write articles for various anarchist journals, including *La Questione Sociale* of Paterson, New Jersey, and *El Despertar* of New York.[44] In 1911, a close friend, the Italian anarchist Alfonso Coniglio, collected and published a series of Esteve's essays under the title of *La Legge* (The Law). Earlier Esteve had written *Memoria,* a tract on the 1893 International Anarchist Conference held in Chicago.[45]

Esteve was not alone in the publishing field. Some of the larger groups printed newspapers, the most noted prior to 1900 being *El Esclavo,* which began in 1894. Most of these journals were very short-lived, existing only on the subscriptions and donations of a small membership. Their fugitive careers can be traced by scattered handfuls of surviving issues and frequent notices of anarchist activities contained in more permanent presses found in large urban centers. Anarchist newspapers printed in New York City and Paterson, for example, carried columns that occasionally reported on events in Tampa.[46] These short bylines are often the only surviving evidence of personalities and events existing in the anarchist culture of places like Tampa.

Anarchist groups tried to meet the social and cultural needs of their members, as well as provide for their political education. To accomplish these goals, they collected small monthly dues, from ten to twenty-five cents per member. A portion of these funds went toward the purchase of volumes for club libraries. Whether it was a single shelf of books in a member's home or a collection numbering into the hundreds, each group supplied some access to literary material.[47] The collections typically featured a wide assortment of reading items, ranging from simple spelling and grammar texts to Spanish-language editions of the great radical masters. The works of Michael Bakunin, Karl Marx, Peter Kropotkin, and Enrico Malatesta were to be found on nearly all shelves. Most volumes in these holdings were small, inexpensive pamphlets offering polemical essays on various topics or excerpts from larger studies. Some were printed in Tampa (usually at Esteve's La Políglota) and featured the writings of local literati. More numerous, however, were the publications contained in several educational series sponsored by leftist cooperatives. Most popular in Tampa were three series: *Biblioteca Socialista-Anarchia, Biblioteca Popolare Educativa,* and *Libreria Sociológica,* distributed from several northeastern locations.[48]

Spanish residents also had access to anarchist ideologies through other channels. The various unions representing cigar workers all subsidized newspapers that invariably carried excerpts from leftist tracts and not infrequently featured extensive debates between socialists and anarchists. Printed in Spanish and distributed widely throughout Tampa, these journals provided important sources of information for the wider community. Among the labor papers that followed these practices (in order of appearance) were *La Federacion, El Federal, Boletín Obrero,* and *El Internacional.*[49]

The popularity of anarchist clubs and readings profoundly influenced the position of the Catholic church in the immigrant community. To outside observers, the church, enlisting the aid of Jesuit, Franciscan, and Scalabrinian missions, might logically have figured to become the key institution to broker among Spanish, Cuban, and Italian immigrants. But the church, vilified in the Old World and rejected in the New, contributed little to Ybor City's social world. Anarchists continued to attack religion as vehemently in Florida as they had in Spain, and the condemnations struck responsive chords in each of Ybor City's immigrant groups. Cubans despised the church because of its support for Spanish colonialism; Spanish radicals never forgave the church for ignoring the common people; Sicilians remembered indolent, wealthy priests amidst a starving peasantry. The Catholic church, thundered Nestor Carbonell, a supporter of Cuban independence, "stands as the enemy of scientific truth, justice, and liberty." Jesuit father W.J. Tyrell confessed to his superiors in a 1911 report that not 3 percent of Ybor City's population came to church and, more to the point, that community members "have no respect for religion or priest."[50]

Cuba

The impassioned battle over Cuba set the terms for debate in Ybor City from 1886 through 1898. The cause of Cuba Libre alienated Spaniards even more from other members of the Latin work force and deeply divided *peninsulares* between anarchist critics of the colonial policy and fervent nationalists.

Cubans dominated the Ybor City work force. For the city's 1,313 Cubans in 1890, a figure which nearly tripled during the following decade, the struggle for revolution transcended all other issues. Cubans in Ybor City defined themselves as exiles, whose sharpened sense of class consciousness and political awareness infused the cigar industry with their ethos.[51]

In Tampa, the appearance of José Martí in 1891 electrified the Cuban community. But Martí did not singlehandedly forge the tools of revolution; rather, he found in Tampa the resources necessary to temper a movement. If Martí embodied the movement, the proletariat of Ybor City was its soul. The most tangible result of Martí's visit was the creation of the Cuban Revolutionary Party, organized in 1892. "El Día de la Patria" became the theme song of Ybor City: one day's salary for the homeland. Spanish agents shadowed Martí's movements and came perilously close to poisoning the Apostle of Cuban Liberty.

Caught in a vicious crossfire between defenders of empire and torchbearers of revolution were the Spanish anarchists. Some Cuban radicals perceived anarchism as a Trojan horse, designed to confuse the protagonists over the immediate aim of the war. Martí worked assiduously to enlist the support of anarchists to the side of the independence movement. In this effort he was remarkably successful, particularly after the 1892 Congreso Obrero, which contained a heavy anarchist element. Martí was careful, for example, to praise effusively the actions of the anarchist leaders who had expressed sympathies for the revolution.[52]

Support for the Cuban revolution posed several ideological and personal problems for Spanish anarchists. Indeed, not all rallied to the cause of Cuban independence, as some were pulled more strongly by nationalist feelings. Yet, many believed, as Pedro Esteve claimed, "it is good to love *'la patria'* but it is better to love liberty and justice."[53] Martí and the Cuban anarchist Carlos Baliño were able to win over what was probably a majority of Spanish anarchists in Tampa to the revolutionary cause. Baliño in particular argued that it would be absurd to endorse individual liberty and oppose collective liberty. For his part, Martí readily pledged guarantees of freedom to anarchists in the new republic to come.[54]

The sinking of the U.S.S. *Maine* in Februry 1898 ominously redefined the presence of Spaniards; whereas natives earlier suspected them of un-American traits, they now existed as dangerous enemy aliens, to be feared. Furthermore, the fact that 50,000 American soldiers were destined to disembark from Tampa seriously brought into focus the Spanish problem, a potential fifth column. "Dark scowls lurk upon the faces of American men as Spanish is heard spoken," observed a correspondent from the *New York Times Illustrated Magazine.* In a preemptive strike, the army seized control of Centro Español in April 1898, commandeering the building until August. Scores of Spaniards fled Tampa.[55] For the Cuban community, the era of exile ended; emigrés became immigrants. Cubans shifted the struggle for social justice from Havana to Tampa, as a new era of labor militancy dawned.

Beleaguered by the crises of the 1890s, bewildered by the non-English "ghettoes" in their backyard, and befuddled by an inability to control the aliens, Tampans lashed out at Latins in a series of confrontations. The war and concomitant events in the 1890s encapsulated the three value clusters most nervously contemplated by nativists: fears of Catholicism, alien hordes, and foreign radicalism.[56] The last-named quality was the one natives most feared. The sinister image of the Spanish anarchist threatened parts of

Tampa for nearly fifty years. Bred in the villages of Asturias and Galicia, incubated in the meeting halls of Havana and Key West, and fought over in the factories of Ybor City and West Tampa, anarchism and radicalism set the terms of debate for labor relations between 1886 and 1931.

Labor

"The cigar industry is to this city what the iron industry is to Pittsburgh," rejoiced the *Tampa Morning Tribune* in 1896.[57] Fully aware of the fragility of a one-industry town, city fathers resolved to protect the factory owners at all cost. "Tampa can afford to lose cigarmakers," editorialized the paper, "Tampa cannot afford to lose cigar factories."[58] The city's economic fortunes rose and fell with the public's demand for and the industry's supply of hand-rolled, premium cigars. By 1895, the city had attracted 130 cigar factories, which accounted for 75 percent of the city's payroll. Nearly 10,000 first- and second-generation immigrants labored in the city's cigar factories by 1910.[59] Cigars had made Tampa the most important industrial city in Florida; city leaders resolved to keep it that way but were troubled by the dynamics of an industry they did not understand.

Tampa's cigar industry was characterized by skilled workers possessing a special work ethos. Dominated by a pre-modern craft mentality with a complement of artisan work styles and outlooks, it created an industrial environment governed by the rhythms of the individual. There existed within factories a clear occupational hierarchy, organized along ethnic lines during the early decades. The first major division existed between salaried and piecework employees. The former category included foremen, managers, skilled clerical staff, salesmen, and accountants, most of whom were Spaniards. The salaried staff also included *selectores* (selectors of tobacco), positions dominated also by Spaniards. They also commanded most of the higher-paying positions of the next hierarchy, which included banders, packers, and box makers. The coveted position of *chavatero* (knife sharpener) was always held by an Asturian or Gallego. Cubans, and later Italians, filled the most plentiful positions, such as bunchers, rollers, and strippers, although cigar making offered potentially high-paying wages for skilled workers.

Cigar makers maintained distinctive work styles. They exercised, above all, a fierce independence, coming and going as they pleased, taking extended coffee breaks, and pocketing free cigars when they left. While Ybor City was a one-industry town, it was

The working conditions and worker morale of the Tampa cigar factories are reflected in this workday photograph. Before the 1931 strike, *un lector* would have been likely to be present in the room, seated above the workers. Special Collections, University of South Florida, Tampa.

not a one company town. Numerous small enterprises proliferated, allowing for diversity within the ranks of owners and making control more difficult.

No institution dramatized Ybor City's *ambiente* more than *la lectura,* the practice of reading in the cigar factories. Reading to the assembled workers from a raised platform (*tribuna*) had begun in Cuba during the late nineteenth century, and the custom followed to Tampa. Prototypes of *los lectores* could be found in the Spanish villages, where the *obreros conscientes*—local, self-educated activists for education and other workers' rights—served as teachers, propagandists, and apostles of the oral tradition. *El lector* articulated the pre-modern aspects of the cigar industry.

Selection of readers followed a strict procedure. Each candidate (always male—although large numbers of women worked in the industry—and always Cuban or Spanish, except for one Italian) auditioned in front of workers, demonstrating clarity of voice, conviction, and dramatic talents. For their stentorian efforts, readers collected a princely salary from donations by the workers. "You know when we read in the factory, we were employed by the cigarmakers, not the owners," recollected Wilfredo Rodríguez, the last Tampa *lector* still alive, stressing the salient feature of the job, the readers' independence.[60]

Readings reflected the proletarian themes of the class struggle. "We had four daily shifts (*turnos*)," explained Abelardo Gutiérrez Díaz, a Spanish-born *lector.* "One was used to read national news stories. Another was devoted to international political developments. The third concerned itself entirely with news from the proletarian press. And lastly the novel."[61] Favorite novelists included Emile Zola, Victor Hugo, Miguel de Cervantes, Alexander Dumas, Armando Palacio Valdes, Benito Pérez-Galdós, Vicente Blasco-Ibáñez, and Pedro Mata. The philosophical works of Gorky, Marx, Malatesta, Kropotkin, Bakunin, and Tolstoy appeared frequently, as well as contemporary papers such as *Tierra y Libertad,* an anarchist paper published in Barcelona, *El Despertar, Cultura Proletaria,* and the *Daily Worker.* "These were partisan newspapers," a retired *lector* recalled. "Some were anarchist and communist publications. All were read."[62]

Factory owners and city officials frequently blamed readers for the industry's labor problems. "They [the manufacturers] say we became too radical, reading the news from labor organizations and political groups," explained Honorato Henry Domínguez, a former *lector.* "We read those things, it is true," he confessed. But, he added, "we read only what the cigarmakers wanted us to read."[63] The reader served as disseminator, not originator of the class-conscious literature. "The reader enlightened the worker," reminisced Emmanuele LaRosa, born in 1891 and a veteran strike leader.[64] This was certainly true in the case of young men who turned to anarchism. Esteve's friend Alfonso Coniglio amplified the reader's image: "But it was at La Rosa Español that I first heard a reader. It was a small factory but we had our own reader. Oh, I cannot tell you how important they were, how much they taught us. Especially an illiterate like me. To them we owe particularly our sense of the class struggle."[65]

A crazy-quilt pattern of radical ideologies, ethnic rivalries, establishment terror, and truculent strikes characterized labor relations in Tampa in the years between 1886 and 1931. "People date their lives from various strikes in Tampa," recalled one native.[66] Still today, Latins relate their family histories to the yardstick of the great strikes of 1901, 1910, 1920, and 1931.

From the beginning, labor problems plagued Ybor City, ironic in view of the fact that Martínez Ybor came to Tampa to avoid such quarrels. In January 1887, the first major labor disturbance wracked Ybor City. Led by Ramón Rubiera, a fiery Cuban labor organizer, the strike began over the hiring of a foreman at the Martínez Ybor factory. Rubiera's Cuban Federation of Trade Unions urged the hiring of Santo Benites, a Cuban, to blunt Spanish control of an industry dominated by Cuban workers. The Spanish-dominated Knights of Labor union called for a strike, demanding the removal of Benites. Following his dismissal, the Cuban Federation counterstruck, precipitating several acts of violence that resulted in the death of a Cuban cigar maker and the injuring of four others. Throughout the trouble, Tampa papers reported polemical debates between anarchist and socialist factions within the labor movement.[67]

Native Tampans reacted to the new wave of labor and ethnic turbulence with measured tones. The Tampa Board of Trade, at a special meeting, pledged full police powers to protect property, and a vigilance committee organized and circulated petitions at the factories. Authorities identified the alleged troublemakers and warned them to leave Tampa within twelve hours or suffer the consequences. The *Tribune* supported such action, predicting that the aggressive posture "will no doubt have a most salutary effect upon any other . . . citizens of anarchist tendencies who still may be lurking in our midst."[68]

Ultimately, the organizers of the strike and seventy-five workers left Tampa under police escort. Although Martínez Ybor later allowed the deported workers to return, an irreparable breach between owners and workers, Cubans and Spaniards, police and radicals had been opened. The first May Day parade in Ybor City added an interesting footnote to the episode. According to Cuban historian José Rivero Muñiz, "the greater part of the demonstrators were Spanish anarchists. . . . "[69]

Shortly after the 1887 skirmishes, union organizers visited Ybor City and expressed pessimism over the future promise of union success.[70] Little did they realize that Ybor City would soon become a labor stronghold, a battleground for union factions. As late as the 1930s, Tampa—on the basis of its cigar factories—reported the highest percentage of union workers of any southern city. Between 1887 and 1894 alone, twenty-three strikes occurred, revealing the volatile nature of cigar work and especially cigar workers.[71]

Anarchists performed an instrumental role in shaping the character of the Ybor City labor movement. A variety of aggravating circumstances, from brittle tobacco or tepid drinking water to ethnic slurs or contract violations could empty a factory with the simple command *"¡Para las calles!"* (To the streets!) This tactic infuriated the business community, who charged Latins with being fickle pawns of outside agitators. In reality, cigar makers grasped at an opportunity to control their lives and assert their independence. Given the individualized factory structure within Ybor City, control—for an hour or day—was easily realized. Keeping power meant something else.

The anarcho-syndicalist model, with its strong emphasis on education, local control, and nonpolitical direct action, found advocates among the Spanish work force. Ybor City offered an ideal environment in which to test anarcho-syndicalist methods, such as sabotage, obstruction, and the general strike. Just as anarchism appealed to the village-oriented peasants in Spain, so too did syndicalism promise a reservoir of strength at the factory level.

Tampans feared their once peaceful town now resembled Paris or the Haymarket. The *Tribune* explained that Latins "when subjected to the devilish influences of even one unprincipled socialist, communist, or anarchist . . . are transformed into little less than madmen, and there is no peace, no order, until the cause is removed."[72] In 1892, officials acted swiftly to remove such cancerous influences upon the body politic. A vigilance committee, composed of 100 of the city's rulers, including past and future mayors, hung a banner across Ybor City's Bijou Theatre. The manifesto, written in Spanish and signed by Herman Glogowski, Tampa's Jewish immigrant mayor, read:

> TAMPA VIGILANCE COMMITTEE . . .
> hereby give warning to all—
> Cubans, Spaniards, and all others—
> that lawlessness in Ybor City
> must cease.[73]

Tenaciously, the Spanish radicals clung together and persisted. In April 1893 the *Tribune* hinted that within Ybor City, "there is in full blast to-day a club of Nihilists numbering more than a 100 members with sympathizers on the outside. . . . " Rumors circulated that the nihilist cell featured pictures of August Spies (the hero of Haymarket) and his *compañeros.*[74]

La Huelga de Pesa, the Weight Strike of 1899, marked an important watershed in Ybor City's labor relations. Cigar makers, the majority of them still unorganized in 1899, met stiffening resistance to their growing independence. The introduction of weight scales in the Martínez Ybor factory symbolized a new day in the industry. Ostensibly, the scales were designed to weigh an allotted amount of tobacco, but in reality, principles were at stake: power and custom. To weigh the tobacco affronted a Spaniard's dignity. Many of the pioneer *patrones* were dead; and a new era had arrived in Ybor City, personified by Yankee efficiency and corporate rationality.[75]

Management enforced a lockout at the factories in June 1899; and by July, 4,000 workers were shut out. Thousands returned to Cuba. "A complaint so trivial as to be almost ludicrous has caused the wholesale paralysis of industry," railed the *Tribune.* The establishment paper warned its readers, "Tampa is afflicted with one of the most dangerous and obnoxious classes of people just now that ever has been tolerated by any civilized community. It is the professional agitator. . . . These people are regular anarchists. . . . "[76]

The resolution to the Huelga de Pesa came with surprising swiftness. In August, management conceded to the workers' every demand. The Weight Strike was significant in two other ways: first, it was the only major strike won by workers; second, it led to the formation of an important union, La Sociedad de Torcedores de Tampa, commonly called La Resistencia (for its call to resist capital).

The real victory in 1899 came not on the picket lines but in corporate boardrooms. In September 1899, industry journals announced the creation of the Cigar Trust, succeeded two years later by the American Tobacco Company.

In retrospect, the wildcat strikes, work stoppages, and impassioned marches set the stage for Tampa's first great labor struggle of the twentieth century. La Resistencia called workers "to resist the exploitation of labor by capital" and aimed to organize all workers into one central union. In 1901, La Resistencia attempted to establish a closed shop in Tampa, a policy opposed by the powerful amalgamate, the American Cigar Company. A protracted, tumultuous four-month strike ensued, marked by mass evictions, violence and suffering.[77]

La Resistencia succeeded in organizing Ybor City's first panethnic union, claiming a membership of 1,558 Cubans, 550 Spaniards, and 310 Italians in November 1900. Leaders organized a decentralized union that attracted artisans other than cigar makers, such as Ybor City bakers, waiters, and carpenters. A newspaper, *La Federación,* articulated the society's goals.[78]

Ethnic tensions and labor jurisdiction issues immediately threatened the stability of La Resistencia. Cuban workers in the Ybor and Manrara factories withdrew from the union in February 1900 and organized a rival union, La Liga Obrera de Tampa, patterned after La Liga de Trabajadores Cubanos de Habana. In March 1900, another schism threatened the enclave's labor unity. Selectors Local 440, an international local organized specifically for Spanish-speaking workers, precipitated a strike when officials at La Rosa Española factory refused to recognize two unions, La Resistencia and the International. The competing unions refused to budge and declared war on factory owners who recognized the rival.

The impasse climaxed in July 1901 when La Resistencia called for a general strike. Only a handful of factories staffed by International workers remained open as Ybor City fell silent, save for the *cocinas económicas* (soup kitchens operated by the union) and demonstrations. Meanwhile, Tampa's business elite grew impatient over the mounting losses caused by cigar makers without pay. The *Tribune* editorialized that perhaps a show of force—specifically, soup kitchen shutdowns, arrests of strikers on charges of vagrancy, and vigilante raids—would expedite matters. Thus inspired, a citizens committee composed of business leaders abducted thirteen strike and union leaders on the evening of 5 August 1901. Hired thugs shanghaied the Latins to Honduras and warned them never to set foot in Tampa again. Since the deportees included the president and treasurer of the union, strike funds conveniently froze.

Landlords subsequently agreed to evict striking tenants. Even the most famous cigar maker, Samuel Gompers, refused his aid, claiming La Resistencia failed to conform to American trade union means and goals. As a coup de grace, manufacturers appealed to cigar workers in Key West and Cuba to come to Tampa. The federal government assisted the boat lift, facilitating transportation and quelling riots in Key West and Cuba. By late November 1901, the strike had been broken; and La Resistencia died in 1902.[79]

The decade between 1901 and 1910 witnessed economic prosperity in the cigar industry, accompanied by large numbers of Latin immigrants and the expansion of Ybor City. In 1910, the Cigar Makers International Union (CMIU) had grown to 6,000 members and claimed representation in the city's largest factories. Cigar workers protested that owners precipitated the general strike of 1910 as a means of testing their open shop demands and squelching growing union strength. The first direct confrontation began in June 1910 when manufacturers affiliated with the Clear Havana Cigar Manufacturers Association (commonly called The Trust) dismissed selectors belonging to International Local 493. Grievances accumulated and by August 1910, 12,000 cigarmakers were out of work. A *Tribune* reporter covered a mass union meeting where allied craftsmen joined the 5,000 demonstrators. "It was a demonstration such as has reared its head within the gates of old Barcelona, that hot-bed of Latin civic disturbance. . . . "[80]

As economic dislocations resulting from the strike shattered the area economy, Tampans reacted with customary anger. In reaction to the alleged influence of so-called socialist and anarchist agitators, businessmen formed the reliable citizens' committee. The killing of an American bookkeeper employed at the Bustillo and Díaz Company electrified the city. Authorities arrested two Italians on suspicion of complicity, but before they could be brought to trial, a mob seized them and lynched both. Soon thereafter, the Balbotín Brothers' factory was burned by arsonists, and the *Tribune* building narrowly missed the same fate. The leaders of the strike, including Spaniard José de la Campa, were arrested for "inciting a riot and being accessories [to murder]. . . . "[81]

Cigar factories reopened in October 1910, protected by citizens' armed patrols. Arbitrary arrests, illegal searches, random physical beatings—all flagrant violations of civil rights—characterized thc actions of these groups. The patrols raided the Labor Temple in Ybor City, as well as the offices of *El Internacional,* destroying the presses, intimidating its staff, and arresting its editor. Again large numbers of strikebreakers arrived in Tampa, with at least tacit complicity of immigration officials. Tampa's second general strike in a decade came to an unhappy end for cigar makers.[82]

Unlike La Resistencia, the International Union did not disappear following its defeat in 1911. Instead, it remained and slowly rebuilt its strength. On the eve of World War One, the radical movements of America in general and Ybor City in particular crested. The war, with its unrestrained impulses for 100 percent Americanization, the Espionage and Sedition Acts, and the Red Scare that accompanied it, retarded the leftist movements.[83]

One might suspect that Ybor City radicals, with their tumultuous history of social and economic unrest, would have been victimized by the war and its excesses. Careful readings of the *Tampa Morning Tribune* and the *Tampa Daily News* revealed no such repression. Yet a scanning of the Spanish-language press and interviews with survivors convey a different story, one of harassment and conflict. Fortunately, the Federal Bureau of Investigation's opening of previously closed files now allows a more comprehensive appraisal of the war years. Documents compiled by the Special Bureau of Investigation indicate an unmistakable pattern of government espionage, establishment violence, local and federal paranoia over the Ybor City problem. Literally hundreds of pages of testimonials and reports substantiate a vigorous policy of federal and local interventionism.[84]

In November 1919, Bureau of Investigation agent A.V. French reported to his Washington superiors:

> I can state that the Italian-Spanish colonies of West Tampa and Ybor City, Florida are the most advanced toward the 'Social Revolution.' I could say that they have established here a Soviet on a small scale. They do what they like and if they wouldn't be a little frightened by the action taken by the U.S. Government in the north against the Reds, I would have the impression of being in Russia.[85]

A letter from a prominent Tampa family decried "an intolerable and unbearable situation . . . there is a bunch of anarchists, IWW's and Radical Socialists.[86]

Agents reported generally unsuccessful efforts to infiltrate the radical infrastructure, especially the Spanish-language papers. Undercover spies posed as Red Cross Employment Bureau officials to obtain desired information. A vast network of agencies and individuals, including Tampa City Hall, the Spanish consul, the police department, the American Legion, and local newspapers, supplied torrents of information to the Bureau of Investigation.

The institution of the reader was under special attack. A March 1919 dispatch indicated that "every reader in the factories in Tampa was reading Bolsheviki literature." The agent lamented the problem of translating the extensive Spanish materials.[87] Dossiers catalogued alleged radicals. José Millares, for example, was "a reader and a socialist"; Augustin Sanchez an "admitted anarchist and reader"; and Abelardo Hernandez a "reader at Cuesta Rey," "a Spaniard," and a "radical."[88]

If the readers agitated the Latin work force, the solitary terrorist threatened the very foundation of law and order. In 1920, a young Latin brazenly boasted to a disguised agent that he had "in his viens the same blood of Brescia [*sic*]." Gaetano Bresci, an Italian anarchist from Paterson, New Jersey, had assassinated King Umberto of Italy in 1900.[85] In 1913, the Mexican consul warned that anarchists in Tampa plotted to kill President Victoriano Huerta of Mexico, then involved in a test of wills with the United States. Agents quickly arrested and deported Manuel Salina, a Cuban who was editor of *El Obrero Indústrial,* and Maximiliano Clay, an Asturian anarchist who worked as a reader. Salinas and Clay had allegedly been friends with Manuel Padrinas, the assassin of the Spanish Prime Minister in November 1912.[90]

The government's vigilance in Tampa's radical community became part of a self-fulfilling prophecy. Considered part of a worldwide conspiracy, Ybor City served, in the government's view, as a cell for radical plotting, a network connected to other nefarious communities, such as Paterson, Barre, and Everett. For the radicals, the point was not to be part of a conspiratorial cabal but to help sustain the existence of a radical network of ideas and communication, of which Ybor City gave and received.

The deportations, seizures, and intimidations seriously weakened the Ybor City anarchist and radical community. The 1920–1921 strike revealed the toll the Red Scare had taken. Radicals had surrendered their leadership role to traditional union leaders, who fought for closed shops. By the 1920s, the radical edge of the Ybor City labor movement dulled. The labor wars of attrition had taken their toll, as had the vigilante police tactics of the establishment. The last great strike occurred in 1931, appropriately over the presence of the reader. The workers lost.[91] Radicalism had once pervaded the workers' movement; by the 1920s it was reduced to a faded subculture. The Spanish influence was also blunted by demographics. In the 1890s, most Spaniards were young, single males; but by the 1920s, domestic life had subdued the rebellious core. Finally, and certainly most ironically, the successes of capitalism convinced many Latins that while Tampa might never become a worker's utopia, the rewards to be won at the cigar bench or grocery store were more realistic than a dream of a classless society. While anarchism was an ideology born of Old World scarcity, Ybor City was rooted in New World abundance.

To unravel the Spanish anarchist strand from the weave of the Ybor City fabric is difficult. The same is true of the role played by these individuals in the wider phenomenon of Spanish immigration. Time has not been kind to these men and women. Today, their activities have largely been forgotten, and it is difficult to find anyone willing or able to share memories and records documenting their past. In part this may be true because the causes they championed so often failed. Yet, as with leftists elsewhere, to overlook their presence would be a mistake. Though small in number, they were a significant part of the Spanish diaspora, a movement of peoples that is only now beginning to receive the attention it deserves.

Though absent from the Tampa scene now, the anarchists did force the dominant institutions of society to react to their presence. In the process, the institutions themselves—and the social values that underlay them—were changed. To look, therefore, at only the end product, without reference to the anarchist experience, is to miss an important formative aspect of this community's history.

Notes

The authors wish to express their appreciation to Professor James Amelang for his insightful comments on this essay. Gary Mormino thanks the University of South Florida, College of Social and Behavioral Sciences, for a Research Enhancement Grant, 1984.

1. A rich body of literature exists detailing the phenomenon of Spanish anarchism. Readers desiring an overview of the topic might consult the following: Gerald Brenan, *The Spanish Labyrinth: An Account of the Social and Political Background of the Civil War* (Cambridge: Cambridge University Press, 1964); Murray Bookchin, *The Spanish Anarchists: The Heroic Years 1886–1936* (New York: Free Life Editions, 1977); Robert Kerr, *Red Years/Black Years: A Political History of Spanish Anarchism, 1911–37* (Philadelpha: Institute for the Study of Human Issues, 1978); Temma Kaplan, *Anarchists of Andalusia* (Princeton, N.J.: Princeton University Press, 1978); Joan Connelly Ullman, *La Semana Trágica. Estudio sobre las causas socieoeconomicas del anticlericalismo en España* (Barcelona: Ediciones Sintesis, 1972); Eric J. Hobsbawm, *Primitive Rebels: Studies in Archaic Forms of Social Movements in the Nineteenth Century* (New York: W. W. Norton, 1959). Several studies examine the impact of anarchism in Argentina, but relatively little has been done on the dispersion of Spanish anarchism out of Spain.

2. R. A. Gómez, "Spanish Immigrants to the United States," *Americas* 19 (July 1962): 59–77; Salvador de Madariaga, *Spain: A Modern History*, 2d ed. (New York: Praeger, 1958), 136.

3. Julio Cuevas, interview with authors, 29 July 1983, Tampa, Florida.

4. Fernand Braudel, *The Mediterranean and the Mediterranean World in the Age of Philip II*, 2 vols. (New York: Harper & Row, 1972), 1:588.

5. Enrique Alvarez Suarez, *Asturias* (n.p.: Maten Artes Graficas, 1924), 92–104; Richard Herr, *Spain*, Modern Nations in Historical Perspective Series (Englewood Cliffs, N.J.: Prentice Hall, 1971), 115–22; Brenan, *The Spanish Labyrinth*, p. 93; Kerr, *Red Years/Black Years*, p. 10; Madariaga, *Spain*, pp. 135–39; Raymond Carr, *Spain, 1808–1939* (Oxford: Clarendon Press, 1966).

6. Ann M. Pescatello, *Power and Pawn: The Female in Iberian Societies and Cultures* (Westport, Conn.: Greenwood Press, 1976), 30; Madariaga, *Spain*, p. 133.

7. G. H. B. Ward, *The Truth about Spain* (London: Cassell and Co., 1911), 136.

8. Kaplan, *Anarchists of Andalusia*.

9. Ibid, p. 133; James Joll, *The Anarchists* (Cambridge, Mass.: Harvard University Press, 1980), 207; Pescatello, *Power and Pawn*, pp. 23–24; George Woodcock, *Anarchism: A History of Libertarian Ideas and Movements* (New York: New American Library, 1962), 356–57.

10. Richard B. Saltman, *The Social and Political Thought of Michael Bakunin* (Westport, Conn.: Greenwood Press, 1983); Madariaga, *Spain*, p. 146; Joll, *The Anarchist*, pp. 72–73; Fernando Savater, *Para la Anarquía* (Barcelona: Tusquets Editor, 1977), 119–28.

11. Savater, *Para la Anarquía*.

12. Bookchin, *The Spanish Anarchists*, pp. 89–109.

13. Madariaga, *Spain*, p. 151; Brenan, *The Spanish Labyrinth*, p. 94.

14. Joll, *The Anarchist*, 3, pp. 117–274; Herr, *Spain*, pp. 128–29; *Tampa Daily Times*, 12 November 1912, p.1; *Tampa Morning Tribune*, 14 Nov. 1912, p. 1; Rafael

Nuñez Florencio, *El Terrorismo Anarquista, 1888–1909* (Madrid: Siglo Veintiuno, 1983).

15. Duvon C. Corbett, "Immigration in Cuba," *Hispanic American Historical Review* 22 (May 1942): 302–8; Louis A. Pérez, *Cuba between Empires, 1878–1902* (Pittsburgh: University of Pittsburgh Press, 1983), 4–38.

16. Instituto de Historia del Movimiento Comunista y de la Revolución Socialista de Cuba, *El Movimiento Obrero Cubano, Documentos y Artículos, 1865–1925* (Havana: Instituto Cubano del Libro, 1963), 17–26; Ramiro Guerra y Sánchez et al., *Historia de la Nación Cubana*, "Antecedentes del Movimiento Obrero," (Havana: Editorial Historia de la Nación Cubana, 1952), 247–54.

17. Guerra y Sánchez, "Antecedentes," p. 266.

18. Ariel Hidalgo, *Orígenes del Movimiento Obrero y del Pensamiento Socialista en Cuba* (Havana: Instituto Cubano del Libro, 1976), 101–2.

19. José Rivero Muñiz, "El Tabaquero en la Historia de Cuba," *Islas* 5 (June 1963): 300–302; *El Movimiento Obrero durante la Primera Intervención* (Santa Clara, Cuba: Universidad Central de Las Villas, 1961), 211.

20. John Dumoulin, "El Movimiento Obrero en Cruces, 1902–1925: Corrientes Ideologicas y Formas de Organizacion de la Industria Azucarera," *Islas* 62 (January–April 1979): 83–122.

21. Paul Estrade, "Las Huelgas de 1890 en Cuba," *Revista de la Biblioteca Nacional de José Martí* 21 (January–April, 1979): 27–51.

22. Gaspar Gallo, "El Tabaquero en el Trayectoria Revolucionaria de Cuba," *Rivista bimestre cubana* 22 (1936): 108.

23. Dumoulin, "El Movimento Obrero," p. 96; Gaspar Jorgé García Gallo, *Biographía del Tabaco Habano* (Santa Clara, Cuba: Universidad Central de Las Villas, 1959), 139.

24. Glenn Westfall, "Don Vicente Martínez Ybor, the Man and His Empire: Development of the Clear Havana Industry in Cuba and Florida in the Nineteenth Century" (Ph.D. diss., University of Florida, 1977), pp. 10–11, 16–21.

25. Ibid, pp. 30–45; Gerald E. Poyo, "Key West and the Cuban Ten Years War," *Florida Historical Quarterly* 57 (January 1979): 289–308.

26. *Tampa Morning Tribune*, 10 April 1895, p. 1; 17 April 1895, p. 1; 17 November 1896, p.1; 11 May 1906, p.1; 12 November 1915, p.7; 10 January 1909, p. 1; 17 March 1926, p. 1.

27. Emilio Del Rio, *Yo Fuí Uno de Los Fundadores de Ybor City* (Tampa: n.p., 1950), 9–11; José Rivero Muñiz, *Los Cubanos en Tampa*, trans. H. Beltram as *The Ybor City Story: 1885–1954* (Tampa: n.p., 1976), 6–14; Durward Long, "The Historical Beginnings of Ybor City," *Florida Historical Quarterly* 59 (July 1971): 31–44.

28. Gómez, "Spanish Immigrants to the U.S.," pp. 59–77; Carr, *Spain*, pp. 10–11; *Gran Enciclopedia Asturiana*, s.v. "Emigracione," 17 vols. (Gijón: S. A. Vitoria, 1981): 7:78.

29. Fermín Suoto, interview, Federal Writers' Project volume, P. K. Yonge Library of Florida History, University of Florida (Tampa, c. 1936), 3–5.

30. María Ordieres, interview, Federal Writers' Project volume, University of Florida, p. 1.

31. U.S., Bureau of the Census, *Compendium of the Eleventh Census: 1890*, table 20, (Washington: Government Printing Office, 1892), 672–73; *Twelfth Census of the United States: 1900, Population*, vol. 2, table 27 (Washington: Government Printing Office, 1902), 214; *Thirteenth Census of the United States: 1910, Population*, vol. 2, table 2, (Washington: Government Printing Office, 1912), 330.

32. *Tampa Guardian*, 9 and 30 June 1886 and 27 October 1886; *Tampa Weekly Times*, 16 April 1886; *Tampa Journal*, 12 January 1888 and 2 January 1890, p. 5; Tampa City Council, Minutes, 26 March 1888, Minutes Book 2; "Early Days in Ybor City, as Narrated by Fernando Lemos," Federal Writers' Project volume, University of Florida, p. 56.

33. U.S. Congress. Senate, *Reports of the Immigration Commission, Immigrants in Industries*, 61st Cong., 2d sess., 1910, pt. 14, "Cigar and Tobacco Manufactur-

ing," tables 162, 163, and 191, and p. 234; *Twelfth Census, 1900,* Manuscript Census Schedules; *Thirteenth Census, 1910,* Manuscript Census Schedules; Karen Weltz, "Boarders in Tampa, 1900 and 1910" (Unpublished manuscript, University of South Florida).

34. Loy Glenn Westfall, "Immigrants in Society," *Americas* (July–August 1982): 43; José Avellanal Papers, Special Collections, University of South Florida.

35. El Centro Asturiano en Tampa Inauguración del Edificio Social 15 de Mayo de 1914 (commemorative program, Tampa, n.p.); Durward Long, "An Immigrant Cooperative Medicine Program in the South, 1887–1963," *Journal of Southern History* 31 (November 1965): 417–34; Federal Writers' Project, "Ybor City, Tampa's Latin Colony."

36. Salatha Bagley, "The Latin Clubs of Tampa, Florida" (Master's thesis, Duke Univesity, 1948); *Tampa Tribune,* 8 June 1965, p. 3B.

37. This estimate is based upon a close reading of the surviving leftist press available for Tampa, citations from the English-language press, and oral interviews. Specific references will follow as more precise details are documented.

38. *El Internacional,* 9 March, 30 July, and 27 August 1915, 8 December 1911, 4 August 1905; Sirio Bruno Coniglio, interview with George Pozzetta, Clearwater, 2 May 1976. The interview is in the Oral History Collection, University of Florida, Gainesville.

39. Angelo Massari, *The Wonderful Life of Angelo Massari,* trans. Arthur Massolo (New York: Exposition Press, 1965), 107; *El Internacional,* 1 March 1918, p.4.

40. Diego Abad de Santillan (pseud., Sinesio Garcia Delgado), *Contribución a la História del Movimiento Obrero Español. Desde Sus Origines hasta 1905* (Puebla, Mexico: 1962), 188, 283, 392–93.

41. Ibid., 292–293; José Alvarez Junco, *La Ideologia Política del Anarquismo Español (1868–1910),* (Madrid: Siglo Veintiuno de Espana, 1976), claims (p. 632) that *El Productor* ceased publication in 1893.

42. Angelo Massari, *The Wonderful World of Angelo Massari,* p. 107.

43. *El Internacional,* 17 November 1905; *La Federación,* 16 February, 2 and 9 March 1900; *La Parola dei Socialisti,* Chicago, 14 and 21 May and 2 July 1910; Emma Goldman, *Living My Life,* 2 vols., (New York: Dover Publications, 1970), 1:150. Elizabeth Gurley Flynn, *The Rebel Girl: An Autobiography, My First Life (1906–1926),* rev. ed. (New York: International Publishers, 1976), 62, 184.

44. *La Cronaca Sovversiva,* Barre, Vt., 21 November 1903; New York *Il Martello,* New York, 8 April 1922; *La Questione Sóciale,* Paterson, N.J., 4 July 1906.

45. Another collection of Esteve's writings is contained in the pamphlet *Reformismo, Dictadura, Federalismo* (New York: n.p., 1922). This pamphlet, a copy of which is contained in the Biblioteca Publica Arus, Barcelona, contains articles published in *Cultura Obrera.* Professor Ullman has kindly made a copy of Esteve's 1893 *Memoria* available to us. The Immigration History Research Center, University of Minnesota, Minneapolis, holds a copy of Esteve's *La Legge.*

46. *La Cronaca Sovversiva,* Barre, Vt., 19 September 1903 and 17 November 1917; *El Despartar,* New York, 10 September 1901; *Il Diretto,* New York, 15 February 1919. Consult also Ramon Sempau, *Los Victimarios: Notas Relativas al Proceso de Monjuic,* prologue by Emilio Junoy (Barcelona: Garcia y Manent, 1900), 343. Professor James Amelang kindly made this reference available.

47. *L'Aurora,* Tampa, 17 and 31 May 1912; *La Voce della Colonia,* Tampa, 10 and 17 June 1911.

48. This assessment is based upon an examination of club holdings in Tampa, including the libraries of the principal Spanish ethnic organizations (Centro Español and Centro Asturiano). Italian groups in the city followed similar patterns. See George E. Pozzetta, "An Immigrant Library: The Tampa Italian Club," *Ex Libris* 1 (1978): 10–12.

49. Copies of these newspapers are available on microfilm at the P. K. Yonge Library of Florida History, University of Florida, Gainesville. The largest holdings are for *El Internacional,* which has a run extending from 1904 to 1946.

50. Archdiocese of Saint Augustine, Florida, "Financial Statement, Ybor City Mission," Tampa, 1911; Nestor Leonelo Carbonell, "El Catolicismo Romano," *Patria,* 5 Febuary 1898, p.2; Julio Caro Baroja, *Introducción a una História Contemporánea del Anticlericalismo Español* (Madrid: Ediciones Istmo, 1980).

51. Louis A. Pérez, "Cubans in Tampa: From Exiles to Immigrants, 1892–1901," *Florida Historical Quarterly* 57 (October 1978): 129–40.

52. Frank Fernández, "Los Anarquistas Cubanos (1865–1898)," *Guangara Libertaria* 5, no. 17 (1984): 4–5; José Martí, *Obras Completas,* vol. 1 (Havana: Editorial Nacional de Cuba, 1963–1966); Louis A. Pérez, *Cuba between Empires.*

53. *Patria,* 7 November 1892, cited in Fernández, "Los Anarquistas Cubanos," p. 7. Authorities had expelled Esteve from Spain after he denounced the government for turning Cuba into "a mere hacienda."

54. Fernández, "Los Anarquistas Cubanos," p. 7. More information on the career of Baliño is contained in *Carlos Baliño, Documentos y Artículos* (Havana: Departamento de Orientación Revolucionaria del Comite Central del Partido Comunista Cubano, 1976); "Our Havana," *Tampa Tribune,* 25 May 1894, p. 1; *Patria,* 6 May 1896, p. 2.

55. A. Rouse, "Tampa Camp Scenes Described," *New York Times Illustrated Magazine,* 15 May 1898, p. 10; Federal Writers' Project, "Ybor City Historical Data," p. 401; Tampa City Council Meeting, Tampa, Minutes, 2 April 1898; "Tampa's Dynamite Fiend," *Starry Flag Weekly,* 18 June 1898, Special Collections, University of South Florida Library.

56. John Higham, *Strangers in the Land: Patterns of American Nativism, 1860–1925* (New Brunswick, N.J.: Rutgers University Press, 1955).

57. *Tampa Morning Tribune,* 30 July 1896.

58. *Tampa Morning Tribune,* 30 July 1899.

59. *Tampa Morning Tribune,* 18 December 1911; Roland Rerrick, *Memoirs of Florida,* 2 vols. (Atlanta: Southern Historical Association, 1902), 2:22; *Immigrants in Industries,* p. 87.

60. Wilfredo Rodríguez, interview with authors, Tampa, 1 April 1982.

61. Louis A. Pérez, "Reminiscences of a *Lector:* Cuban Cigar Workers in Tampa," *Florida Historical Quarterly* 53 (April 1975): 445–46.

62. Ibid.

63. *Tampa Tribune,* 12 September 1977.

64. Emmanuele LaRosa, interview with authors, Tampa, 30 July 1983.

65. José Yglesias, *The Truth about Them* (New York: World Publisher, 1971), 207.

66. José Yglesias, quoted in Studs Terkel's *Hard Times* (New York: Avon Books, 1970), 133.

67. *Tampa Tribune,* 24 and 26 January 1887, and 12 March 1887; Gerald Eugene Poyo, "Cuban Emigré Communities in the United States and the Independence of Their Homeland, 1852–1895" (Ph.D. diss., University of Florida, 1983), pp. 224–25.

68. Poyo, "Cuban Emigré Communities"; Tampa Board of Trade, Minutes, 8 March 1887, Ledger 1, p. 41.

69. Rivero Muñiz, *Los Cubanos en Tampa,* p. 42.

70. *Cigar Makers' Official Journal* 14 (January–November 1889).

71. Durward Long, "Labor Relations in the Tampa Cigar Industry, 1885–1911," *Labor History* 12 (Fall 1971): 551.

72. *Tampa Tribune,* 8 September 1892. See also *Tampa Daily Tribune,* 7 May 1891; and *Tampa Tribune,* 12 and 28 August 1891.

73. *Tampa Tribune,* 2, 6, 7, and 8 September 1892.

74. *Tampa Tribune,* 18 April 1893.

75. Gary R. Mormino, "Tampa and the New Urban South: The Weight Strike of 1899," *Florida Historical Quarterly* 60 (January 1982): 337–56.

76. *Tampa Morning Tribune,* 11 July 1899.

77. Durward Long, "La Resistencia: Tampa's Immigrant Labor Union," *Labor History* 6 (Fall 1965): 193–214.

78. *Tampa Morning Tribune,* 1 and 10 November 1900.

79. Long, "La Resistencia"; George Pozzetta, "Alerta Tabaqueros! Tampa's Striking Cigar Workers," *Tampa Bay History* 3 (Fall–Winter 1981): 19–29.

80. *Tampa Morning Tribune,* 12 August 1910; George Pozzetta, "Italians and the Tampa General Strike of 1910," in *Pane e Lavoro: The Italian American Working Class,* ed. George Pozzetta (Toronto: Multi-Cultural History, 1980), 29–47.

81. Pozzetta, "Italians and the Tampa General Strike," in *Pane e Lavaro,* ed. Pozzetta.

82. This information is from Spanish- and English-language newspapers of 1910.

83. James Weinstein, *The Decline of Socialism in America, 1912–1925* (New York: Vintage Books, 1967).

84. Investigative Case Files of the Bureau of Investigation, 1908–1922, National Archives (hereafter, ICFBI).

85. A. V. French to Bureau of Investigation, 21 November 1919, ICFBI, Old German Files, #362112.

86. M. E. Gillett and Son to Bureau of Investigation, 15 November 1919, ICBFI, Old German Files, #631112. The former served as Tampa Mayor during the 1890s.

87. Byrd Douglas to Bureau of Investigation, 9 August 1919, ICBFI, Old German Files, #362112.

88. Byrd Douglas to Bureau of Investigation, 2 and 5 August 1919, ICBFI, Old German Files, #362112.

89. Unnamed agent to Bureau of Investigation, 27 January 1920, ICBFI, Old German Files, #362112.

90. Justice Department Report on Anarchists, 3 March 1913, ICBFI, Justice Department, #5606.

91. Robert P. Ingalls, "Radicals and Vigilantes: The 1931 Strike of Tampa Cigarworkers," in *Southern Workers and Their Unions,* 1880–1975, ed. Gary Fink and Merl Reed (Westport, Conn.: Greenwood Press, 1981), 44–57.

MICHAEL G. KARNI

Finnish Immigrant Leftists in America: The Golden Years, 1900–1918

I'm going to America;
Everyone is on his way.
The American shores are
Sanded with gold, they say.

I'll embark from Hankoniemi,
On a small boat and go;
'Cause Finland can't support
The children of her poor.[1]

Many immigrants from Finland optimistically sang this song as they left the homeland for the New World. Any place, they reasoned, would provide better opportunities than life as a tenant farmer or a simple hired farmhand in a land beset as late as Finland in the 1890s by crippling famine. But there certainly was no gold sanding America's shores. A generation later, approximately one-fourth of the Finns living in the United States espoused radical philosophies and were singing a different song. Here is one dismal verse that greeted midsummer celebrants in Minnesota:

You dropped into the pits of darkness,
into the black resisting bowels
of Butte and Pittsburgh,
into the red entrails of Cuyuna;
the tunnels of Houghton swallowed you down,
and the taste of copper burned your mouth.
O children of labor,
rising like red ghosts out of Mesaba
coated with iron
Did you dream of Tuonela
in the bowels of Keewatin?
Or of the Pyhätunturi as you coughed up your lungs
in the carbon pits of Wyoming?[2]

In other words, the harsh conditions many Finns left in Finland were simply replaced by harsh conditions in the United States. The

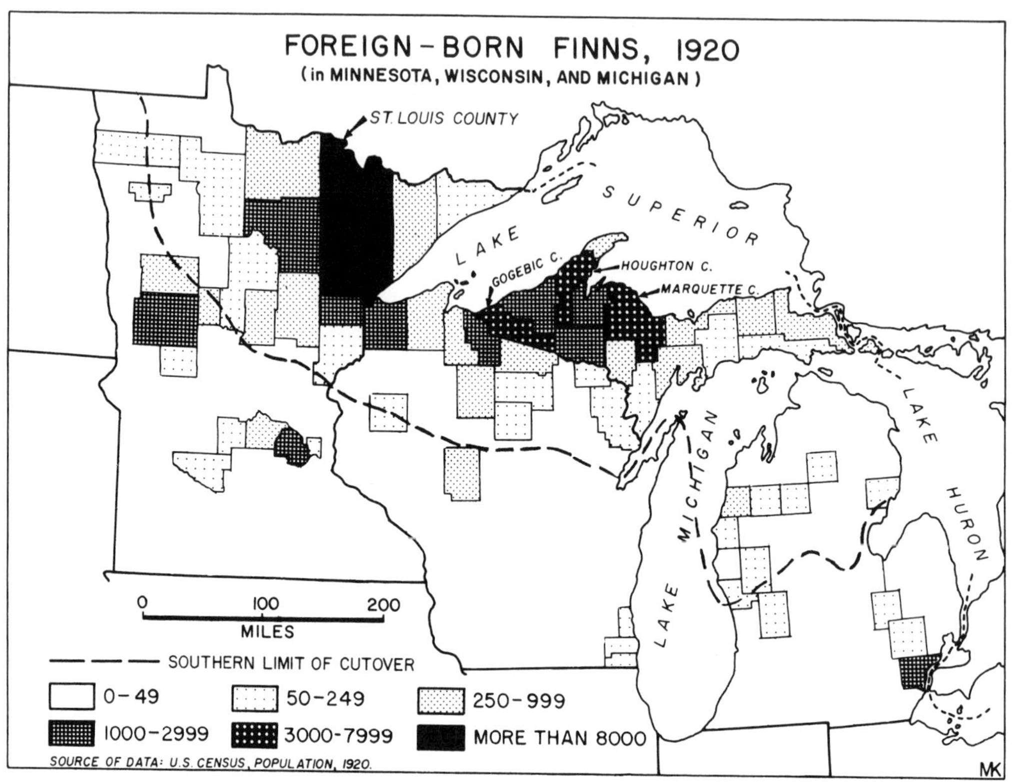

Foreign-Born Finns, in Minnesota, Wisconsin, and Michigan, 1920.

only difference was the agent of exploitation. In Finland the emigrants—mostly landless peasants and sharecroppers—had been regarded as little more than chattel by landowners who treated them only with the thought of wringing as much labor from them at as little cost as possible. Upon arrival in America, the laborers found conditions were different, but the exploitation was similar. Companies wanted labor in basic extractive industries, again at minimal cost. The result for at least one-fourth (perhaps even one-third) of Finnish immigrants to the United States was, with the urging of exiled radicals among them, a turn leftward to socialism and industrial unionism.

During the first twenty years of the present century, when over 200,000 Finnish immigrants arrived on these shores, the nervous optimism of many was replaced by grim resolve. Coming to regions in America—places such as the Upper Peninsula of Michigan with its copper and iron mines and the Mesabi range of northern

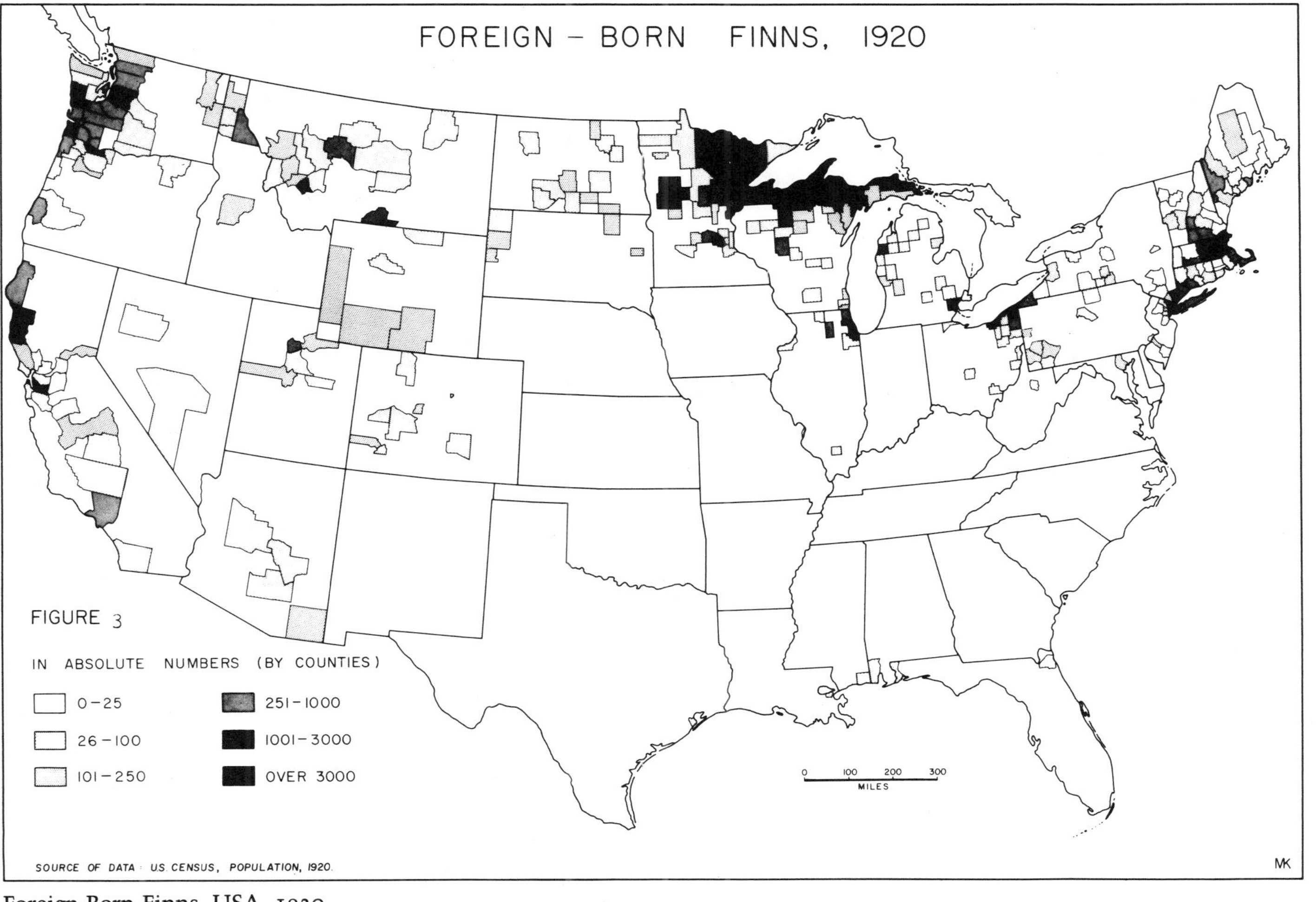

Foreign-Born Finns, USA, 1920.

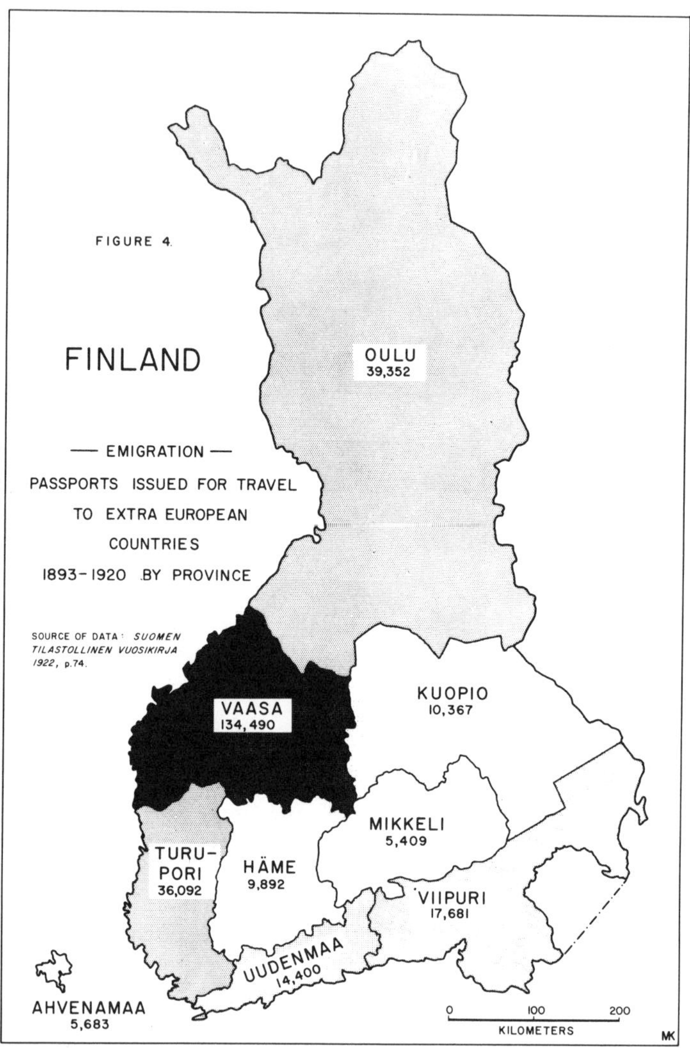

Emigration from Finland, 1893–1920, by province, *Suomen Tilastollinen Vuosikirja 1922*, p. 74.

Minnesota with its iron ore—where all they could sell an employer was youthful strength, they learned there were two ways to cope. One, and perhaps easiest and wisest, was to give in and work hard despite the exploitation of an abundance of foreign-born workers by companies who needed only brute strength to dig iron, copper, silver, lead, or gold, or to spend the winter in lice-infested lumber camps on the northern frontier. The other was to fight back. During the first two decades of the twentieth century, Finnish immigrants organized more than 270 socialist locals scattered throughout the United States. The members of these locals built meeting halls, started newspapers, performed locally written "proletarian" plays in dozens of Finnish playhouses, agitated, educated themselves (and the public), went on strike, and thought they saw a new day aborning after the successful Russian Revolution.

What follows is an attempt to show how socialism and, later, the precepts of the Industrial Workers of the World (IWW), gained impetus among Finnish immigrants and what the consequences were. However, it is first necessary to describe the land the immigrants left and the forces at work there as the century turned. The essay moves on to show that the exploitative environment the Finns experienced in the mines made a turn to radicalism one logical consequence, despite the fact that the Finnish-American obsession with communism during the 1920s and 1930s was essentially a youthful revolt that ended in near disaster.

Conditions in the Fatherland

Scholars in Finland have traced the economic and political conditions in Finland among the poor rural classes from the earliest recorded periods of Finnish history into the twentieth century.[3] But John I. Kolehmainen and George W. Hill have rendered the best impressionistic portrait of the squeeze the growing landless classes were in. They quote an immigrant ballad that tells the tenants' problem:

O tenant unfortunate
  who cannot die, yet cannot live,
Your fields, however fertile,
  no grain or bread do give!
The green meadows, too, near the village,
  your master seizes as his pillage.[4]

As late as the turn of the century, Kolehmainen continues, "no general law had been enacted to safeguard the interests of the tenants. . . ." As late as 1912, 56,616 of Finland's tenants "were spending 596,260 'horse days' and 1,788,408 'foot days' on the holdings of their landlords, at the same time paying cash rentals amounting to nearly two million marks."[5] In addition, landlords raised rents arbitrarily, refused to compensate for the privilege of renewing leases, and failed to honor the leases when it pleased them.

Conditions were even worse for the landless cottagers, dayworkers, and hired hands who constituted 43 percent (207,000 persons) of the rural population in 1901. When not provided with rooms by their employers, they often lived in dreary huts scattered in the most barren places:

A tiny log dwelling, a cheerless cottage;
A low hut beside the hill.
Supper waits on the table:
Black bread, a piece of fish,
Potatoes in a gnarled wooden bowl,
Salt water, a pitcher of watered milk,
These were the delicacies.[6]

But in most cases, dayworkers were homeless and thus dependent on their employer for bed, food, and even clothing. Hours were so long during harvest seasons, for an average daily pay of from two to two and one-half marks (women even less), that one farmhand remarked jokingly: "In the evening as I went to sleep, I threw my trousers over the rafters; they were still swinging when I was awakened in the morning."[7] Pay was cut to about one mark per day during the winter months.

One way to ease these problems was to emigrate. Between the 1860s and 1920s, over 300,000 Finns left Finland for the United States. The first group came as recruits to work the copper diggings of northern Michigan during the American Civil War. These recruits were from a small Finnish community in northern Norway where they had been engaged in Norwegian mining when the copper recruiters found them.[8]

After this start emigration grew, from a trickle during the 1870s, 1880s, and 1890s to a torrent in the first two decades of the twentieth century. The early arrivals can be placed into two classes. A small but steady stream of religious separatists called Laestadians (after their leader Lars Levi Laestadius) came seeking land on which to farm and practice their pietistic form of Lutheranism. They shunned American industry except as a last resort, for they believed the noblest work a man could do was till the soil.[9]

Most of the early emigrants were young people from the rural communes of northern and western Finland. Displaced by famine in the 1860s and 1890s and by changes in farming methods that reduced the need for landless workers, these young Finns headed to places in Massachusetts, New York, Ohio, Michigan, and Minnesota, where they knew other Finns lived and worked. They eagerly took jobs in quarries and canneries, on the docks, and in the mines and lumber camps, hoping to become prosperous and return to Finland.

By the turn of the century, a full-blown movement for political independence from Russia was under way. Tremendous gains were made in improving education and literacy. Industrialism was advancing, and the Finnish Diet—long little more than a rubber-stamp institution—was vigorously seeking broader, more autonomous powers. Also labor unions and socialist politics had made their appearance.[10] To leave the fatherland during such critical and exciting times, the clergy, intellectuals, and upper classes told the emigrants, was both unpatriotic and immoral. But pinched by their restrictive economic conditions and anxious to be independent and economically self-sufficient, many of the young emigrants sang mockingly as their steamers left Hankoniemi pier: "No land, no fatherland."

While economic factors—the need to find work and the desire to own land—must be cited as the main reasons for Finnish emigration, another reason is particularly important. From the 1890s until Finnish independence from Russia in 1917, relations with Russia, traditionally cordial, took a turn for the worse. Under the feared Nikolai Bobrikov, Governor General for Finland from 1898 until 1904 (when he was assassinated by a Finnish student), a tyrannical policy of Russification was under way. The main irritant in this policy was a new system of conscription which would no longer allow Finnish soldiers to serve in Finland under Finnish officers—a tradition observed since 1809, when Finland had become a grand duchy of Russia. Added to the conscription issue were political troubles caused by the slow but obvious disintegration of czarist Russia and the rise of leftist politics in Finland. Censorship and political repression were used to blunt the rising independence movement and the concurrent rise of social democracy. Ardent nationalists and socialists went into exile in the years preceding the General Strike of 1905. Many of these exiles found their way to Finnish enclaves in the United States, where they quickly took a leading role in immigrant associational life.[11]

Conditions in the United States

Most of the immigrants were young, most were male, over 93 percent had come from rural backgrounds, most could read, and most had less than $20 in their pockets upon arrival. And they were optimistic about their futures. If expectations were still high after the trip to the eastern seaboard, they plummeted when the emigrants reached their destinations inland. Irene Paull perhaps spoke for many when she said:

> I was small when I came along with thousands to the land of the free at the turn of the century, my mother holding me up to see the Statue of Liberty! We rode the train with others going to the North Country, and I looked out the window and saw what I would never forget—the red Mesabi! Everything was red—the roads, the water in the ditches, the miners' clothes, the big open pits, the sidewalks, the skin of the people. The red ore seemed to penetrate, to drive into everything. I came to know it stood for US Steel, who claimed our lives, our thoughts, our allegiance. Father worked in the red mine; my mother would cry when she tried to wash the red dirt from his clothes and body. The neighbors around us spoke a strange language—my mother would wash the clothes and cry for Finland.[12]

Instead of paradise, the Finns were quickly mired in almost unimaginable squalor. Mining locations (as groups of company-owned houses were euphemistically called) with names such as Negaunee, Ishpeming, Keewatin, Aurora, and Biwabik may have sounded romantic because of their Indian origins. But to the thousands of immigrants who lived in them, they were something else. The tarred paper shacks, log huts, and cheap company barracks have been compared to slums and immigrant ghettos of large cities—dirty and overcrowded.[13] About the only difference was that miners on the Mesabi were forced to keep hogs, chickens, and cows to provide them with food in the wilderness of the early mining regions. The problem of overcrowding was made worse by the fact that married immigrants who had houses took in single boarders. One man who grew up in Soudan, Minnesota, remembers his mother's boarders. When he grew tired in the evening, he said, he would take any available bed. At midnight, when the shift changed, he would be forced to move to make way for the bed's owner. He would then find one that was recently emptied by a miner going to work at midnight. "But at least I didn't ever have to sleep in a cold bed," he said.[14] Added to the problem of poor housing were the problems of high rent, food, and fuel, especially in northern Minnesota where transportation and the extremely cold weather made the costs of living quite high.

Working conditions were worse. Immigrants from all over Europe labored under deplorable conditions for low pay and nonexistent chances for promotion. Officials of the Oliver Iron Mining Company, the Mesabi's largest employer, stated matter-of-factly that they discriminated against the foreign-born when deciding worker promotions: "We move men along faster than in other companies, but we don't push any but the American-born on to the [steam] shovels or other machines."[15] Immigrants from southern and eastern Europe, therefore, were forced to drudge as manual laborers while advancement went to the few native-born workers, to Cornishmen (who were often mine developers because of the mining experience they had gained in their native Cornwall), and to Scandinavians. (Finns were not regarded as Scandinavians but as Russians.) During 1905 and 1906, the death rate for Mesabi workers was about eight per thousand employed. Between 1905 and 1909, 277 workers were killed in St. Louis County, Minnesota, alone.[16] Previous attempts to earn redress through strikes had resulted in the gunshot deaths of five Finnish miners between 1888 and 1905.[17]

Reaction to Life in America

In reaction to their own disappointment in America, the Finns banded together in associations designed both to educate themselves to America's ways and to remake America through collective action into the paradise they had crossed the ocean to find. Finnish organizations proliferated and flourished: there were church groups, temperance societies, workingmen's associations, and cooperatives of all kinds (including mortuaries, boardinghouses, and even threshing cooperatives), gymnastic societies, fraternal orders, glee clubs, and mixed choruses, debating societies, drama groups, reading circles, and publishing associations. Every group, from the local temperance chapter to the socialist local, had women's guilds and youth leagues to serve as auxiliaries to the larger bodies—which in turn belonged to state, regional, and national federations. All of the organizations conducted their business in the ubiquitous "Finn Halls" that still dot the towns and countryside of Finnish enclaves in the region. And all groups sponsored publishing networks for nationwide communication.

Organized church and temperance activities were the first to develop in the 1880s and 1890s. But the late 1890s also saw the development of worker's clubs designed for the members' self-education and mutual aid. Often based on models such as the Knights of Labor, Finnish workers' associations soon appeared in all Finnish communities from coast to coast. Until 1906 none of these associations showed any official involvement in union activity or any adherence to socialism. But the organizations did present, to the experienced organizer, a ready-made network of potential unionists or socialists.

During the early evening of 31 July 1906, a small parade, led by a man carrying a red flag, wound its way through the downtown streets of Hibbing, Minnesota, in the heart of the Mesabi iron mining region. All but one of the marchers were Finnish immigrants who had gathered from as far away as Seattle and Philadelphia as delegates to a conference to found a national federation of Finnish-immigrant socialist clubs. The conference was to begin the next morning and was scheduled to be in session a week. The non-Finn in the parade was Teofilla Petriella, an organizer from the Western Federation of Miners (WFM) who had worked with good success among Finnish miners in the copper district just to the east of the Mesabi in northern Michigan. He was in Hibbing making preparations for a WFM organizing drive set for the winter and spring of 1906–1907, and he was determined to exploit rising Finnish sentiment for socialism to the benefit of his union.[18]

The 1906 Hibbing meeting was, in fact, the culmination of a five-year effort by Finnish-immigrant socialist leaders to convert a kind of unexpressed, raw socialist spirit they perceived among Finnish workers into a political organization that could join the radical effort to change American politics and to win concessions for American workers. It was named Suomalainen Sosialistijärjestö (SSJ). Most of these Apostles of Socialism, as the agitators were called, were exiled leftists from Finland who were virtually tireless in their efforts to convert their fellow immigrants to socialism. For example, one of the best know Apostles, Martin Hendrickson, went on a nine-month speaking tour in which he made 190 speeches in 122 Finnish communities in 28 states to about 45,000 Finns. In that nine months he traveled over 13,000 miles and converted 5,000 Finns to the cause.[19]

The success Hendrickson and his fellow Apostles had was aided by more than just the deplorable working conditions outlined. They were aided by a spirit of anticlericalism that had been spreading widely among the Finnish lower classes for three decades before the turn of the century. Anticlericalism was largely a reaction to an impersonal state church that extended its official authority deeply into the private lives of all Finns. The reaction among the lower classes took two basic forms: pietism and apathy. The pietistic movements that swept the country were intended to purify and simplify the church and make it more responsive to human needs. By the turn of the century, the pietists had been successful to a remarkable degree in transforming the state church into a folk church. But for large numbers of peasants (and intellectuals), the answer was simply to turn one's back on the church. Many Finns left their homeland glad to be free of its restrictions and bureaucracy. It seems that the socialists such as Hendrickson were quite successful in directing young immigrants' anticlerical feelings toward socialism, especially in industrial areas such as northern

Minnesota where just the ordinary problems of life and work were indeed difficult. Socialism appealed, in theory at least, because it offered immediate, material remedies.[20]

One young convert to socialism later wrote about how seriously he and his fellow socialists took the concept of collective action and worker solidarity as the key to making themselves equal to the test of changing the American system. Their dedication extended into every sphere and every moment of their lives. In reference to his life in a cooperative boardinghouse in a Minnesota mining town, Kusti Siirtolainen said:

> In the cooperatively organized boarding house liquor was forbidden. Coffee was considered harmful. In its stead many drank milk or hot water with cream and sugar. Very few used tobacco. In addition to gymnastics, wrestling and other forms of athletics, we took care of our health by taking hot and cold baths, by dieting and denying ourselves various foods. For several years I didn't eat meat or white bread; I didn't drink coffee, nor liquor; I didn't smoke. The results of this religious-like communal life were so good that very few, even today, realize its great social significance. From the saloons we turned to the reading rooms in which we read all kinds of literature but especially sociological and economic explanations of life.[21]

John Wiita, perhaps the most highly placed Finnish immigrant among American communists in the 1920s and 1930s, has recounted his early experiences in Minnesota similarly. After arriving from Finland in 1906, he held a variety of jobs on the Duluth docks and on the Mesabi range. He carried on as most young, single immigrants did—carousing, drinking, fighting, and traveling wherever there were rumors of work. But in 1908 he became one of the organizers of a *poikatalo,* or men's boarding house, a cooperative in Duluth. Soon, he discovered Työväen Opisto (Work People's College), located in an industrial suburb of Duluth, and the Socialist Party. He quickly moved up in the administration of the college, became an editor for *Työmies* (The Workingman), located just across the bay in Superior, Wisconsin; imposed self-exile on himself during World War I by slipping across the border into Canada; and eventually became one of the most prominent leftists in North America. Of his conversion to socialism from a conservative religious sect in the early years of the century, Wiita says:

> I know that my joining the membership activities of the Finnish Socialist Branch in Superior [Wisconsin], lifted my cultural level, and aroused my eagerness to study and understand social and political questions. I well

remember such high points as when Eugene V. Debs, socialist candidate for president of the United States came to Superior, in 1908 on his famous 'Red Special' train, and when 'Big Bill' Haywood—Western Federation of Miners and later IWW leader—spoke at the Superior Opera. These and other somewhat similar occasions lifted our spirits and strengthened our belief in the cause of the working people.[22]

When one considers all the factors at work influencing Finnish workers toward socialism and radical labor—the unfulfilled expectations in America, the deplorable working conditions, the youthful anticlericalism of the workers, the presence of skilled and dedicated socialist agitators—it is not surprising that the organizers of the Finnish Socialist Federation (SSJ) chose Hibbing as the location of the founding convention. All these conditions were present in northeastern Minnesota in 1906, perhaps more so than in any other place where Finns lived and worked.

If the police missed the significance of the Hibbing parade and street rally of 31 July they were given a second chance to learn on 5 August. On that day several hundred Socialists and sympathizers, led by the Hibbing and Chisholm Socialist clubs' bands playing the "Marseillaise" and "The Worker's March," paraded out of town to the public picnic grounds. Cheering vigorously, they heard the well-known agitators Kaapo Murros, Alex Halonen, Martin Hendrickson and Vilho Boman give long speeches, blistering capitalists and clerics. This time the police were listening more carefully, with the aid of interpreters. The picnickers noted with amusement that the bushes of the park seemed to be full of Finnish conservatives "clucking with alarm" at the goings-on.[23]

Thus, the Finnish Socialists had generated a tension in northern Minnesota. After the founding convention concluded its business, the delegates returned home to implement their newly framed resolutions, one of which was to support strong "class-conscious unions" such as the WFM and IWW.[24]

The following summer, the WFM was making headway with its organizing efforts among Mesabi miners when it was undercut by a spontaneous strike of Duluth dockworkers. The WFM plan had been to organize at least 50 percent of all workers before demands were made to the companies, but it was forced to act early. In mid-July, forced too soon by the dockworkers' example, the WFM asked the Oliver for an eight-hour day, an end to the system of bribes and bonuses, a minimum wage of $2.50 per day for open pit workers, and $3.00 a day for underground workers. The Oliver refused and fired 300 union members. On 20 July 1907, the first great strike on the Mesabi began.

American Response to Finnish Radicalism

The strike lasted two months and it was marred by violence on both sides. The Oliver spent $250,000 for "special deputies" and strikebreakers to help it win. The company was able to import approximately 1,300 Montenegrans and Croatians from eastern port cities to break the strike.[25] Finnish socialists were quite visible during its process. The front page of the 27 July 1907 issue of Hibbing's *Mesaba Ore* noted that during a strike demonstration "fully ninety per cent of those in line were Finlanders—fiery followers of the Red Flag. . . . The remainder of the motley crowd was made up of Austrians [in reality, South Slavs from the Hapsburg Empire], Italians, and Montenegros [*sic*]—not one American appearing in line."[26] In the same issue the *Ore* called the leaders of the WFM "a band of murderers, cut-throats, leeches and grafters whose motto is ruin, rapine, bloodshed, and destruction." Petriella was called "a festering, putrid ulcer on the body politic" who "has found a large following in a class of Finnlanders [*sic*] . . ." who "in their own turn have long sought the opportunity to make trouble."[27]

The *Minneapolis Journal* noted that "the largest number of Mesabi workers came from Finland, in the frozen north, a land where Russia's oppression has bred a hatred of government and a rampant form of socialism. . . . No more dangerous fusing of raw material could be devised it seems. It is just as though the big corporation that brought them to the Range had assembled the ingredients of dynamite, to be mixed and await the percussion cap."[28]

Mining companies after the strike created a blacklist, designed to deny Finns reemployment. At the time the strike occurred, about 18 percent of the Oliver's work force consisted of Finns. After the strike, the proportion was only 8 percent. In actual numbers, this means that 1,200 Finnish men were denied employment by the largest ore mining company in Minnesota. In 1963 an Oliver historian said that the 1907 strike not only created a blacklist but also gave birth to an espionage network to suppress organized labor—a system which hired spies from all the major ethnic groups in northern Minnesota to report men who talked unionism or who read leftist Finnish, South Slavic, or Italian newspapers.[29]

How the Finns were perceived by their employers after the 1907 strike can be learned from the *Reports of the U.S. Commission on Immigration* published about two years after the strike. While the Finns' abilities to withstand the brutal working conditions were praised by every superintendent interviewed, each superintendent also saw a serious flaw in Finnish attitudes:

All the races employed on the Vermilion Range are good laborers. . . . The mines are all underground properties and require steady hard labor in their operation. Slovenians and Finns do the common heavy work. . . . As to the efficiency and progress, adaptability, and other such qualities, all of the races are good. . . . There is one exception, though, and that is the case of the Finns. These people are good laborers but trouble breeders.

This superintendent, of course, went on to say that he refused to hire any Finn who had the reputation of being a socialist or wore the Socialists' red button. It was his desire, he said, to weed out this element from among the Finns. Another superintendent said, "The Finns are good workers when they want to work, but they are not to be depended on." Still another said, "For hard, physical work, the Finns are preferred, but they are a troublesome lot, and among the younger men are many who are anarchists." And, finally, a superintendent from the Mesabi: "Among the old Finns are many good, steady men, but the younger set, and especially those who have received little education, are troublesome and agitators of the worst type."[30]

A few months after the strike ended, the federal government took notice of the Finns. On 4 January 1908, a district attorney in St. Paul refused to grant citizenship papers to a group of sixteen Finns, one of them an alleged socialist by the name of John Swan from the city of Eveleth. Second papers were witheld on the grounds that "being a Finn he [Mr. Swan] is a Mongolian and not a 'white person' " within United States law. The case, however, was thrown out of district court in Duluth on 17 January by Judge W. A. Cant, who said that though perhaps the Finns had been "Mongols" in the remote past, "their blood has so been tempered by the Teutonic and other races that they are now among the whitest people in Europe."[31] Needless to say, the racist language used by the legal establishment based on an erroneous nineteenth-century attempt to trace the origin of the Finnish language to its source, became a lasting source of irritation to the Finns in Minnesota.[32]

The strike had damaged the Finnish reputation severely. Finnish strikers were reviled by nearly every social group—including the conservative Finns, who formed an anti-socialist league to win back the confidence of the employers.[33] Cut off from the major source of employment in the area, the former strikers had to find a means of survival. One alternative was to move to the land and take a homestead. That many did so is borne out by the number of strongly Finnish communities that surround both the Mesabi and Vermilion iron ranges. The strike of 1907 and the reaction that followed it were significant influences on Finnish rural settlement. Alango Township (from the Finnish *alanko,* or lowland) north of the city of Virginia is instructive. Between 1900 and 1910 its population grew from zero inhabitants to 335. In 1915, 77 of 81 farmers in Alango were Finns. By 1920 some 50 percent of all Finns lived on farms. The state with the largest number—4703—was Minnesota.[34]

Despite the reaction to Finnish involvement in the strike of 1907, Finnish socialism grew. By 1909, when the second national conference of the Finnish Socialist Federation was held, membership had climbed from about 2,500 in 1906 to 5,100 members in 162 locals.[35] The delegates to the 1909 meeting, however, mindful of the accusations of anarchy and atheism hurled at them during the strike, made public a series of resolutions disavowing anarchism and affirming their belief in parliamentary, not revolutionary, socialism. And they stressed that religion was regarded by the Federation as a personal matter. Allegations of atheism were therefore unfounded.

By 1912 the Federation had grown to 217 locals with a total membership of 13,677.[36] That same year the Federation published four newspapers—three general papers and one for women: *Työmies* (The Workingman)—located in Hancock, Michigan, until it was driven out during the copper strike of 1913–1914—is the oldest leftist newspaper in the United States, having been founded in 1903.[37] *Raivaaja* (The Pioneer) is also still published in Fitchburg, Massachusetts as a liberal newspaper. *Toveri* (Comrade) and *Toveritar* (Female Comrade) began in Astoria, Oregon. *Toveritar* was moved to Superior in the early 1930s when *Toveri*'s equipment was shipped to Soviet Karelia to provide a voice for Finns recently moved from America to the Republic of Work. *Toveritar* is still published, as *Naisten Viiri* (Women's Banner), once each week in the pages of *Työmies-Eteenpain.*[38] A left-wing socialist newspaper was begun in Duluth in 1914 by those who eventually espoused the IWW. First called *Sosialisti,* its name was changed to *Teollisuustyölainen* (Industrial Worker) one year later. In the early 1920s, its name was changed again, this time to *Industrialisti* (the Industrialist)—and so it remained until 1975, when publication ceased. These papers reached a total of over 25,000 readers at the time of the Russian revolution.[39]

Growth of the Finnish Socialist Federation

The growth of the Federation and related enterprises continued until late 1914, when it was stopped by a split in socialist ranks. Peak membership before the split reached 17,000 members in 273 locals.[40]

Contemporaneous to this growth and militancy was another institutional development that would play a significant role in the fortunes of the Finnish socialists—the creation of Työväen Opisto (Work People's College) in Smithville, near Duluth, Minnesota. By slowly taking control of publicly available stock in a Finnish theological seminary, socialists soon discovered they could dictate the school's direction. Needless to say, they quickly dropped religion from the curriculum and added subjects more to their liking. At the annual meeting of the board on 6 and 7 June 1907, the constitution was changed to make the school a "worker's college"; and a socialist became secretary of the board. Work People's College attracted seventy students during the second term of 1907. The only prerequisite for entrance was that a student must have "labored for his class." On 21 June 1908, the board unceremoniously directed that all "religion books" be disposed of, for lack of space. And before stock certificates reflecting the new name could be printed, the treasurer merely crossed out the words "Suomalainen Kansan" (Finnish National) and wrote the word "Työväen" (Work People's) above the word "Opisto" (or College) on the old certificates.[41]

As would be expected, all subjects pertaining to the church were replaced by English, Finnish, history, economics, political science, geography, evolution, and the history of socialism. Bookkeeping and other business subjects formed the core of the "practical" courses offered by the school. Enrollment increased steadily in subsequent years, reaching a high of 150 students in 1914. After World War I began in Europe and dried up emigration for the duration, enrollments fell by half and leveled off at that point until the mid-1920s.

Perhaps the most significant development in the early years of Work People's College was the hiring of Leo Laukki in September of 1907. Laukki had just entered the United States after a career that had seen him go from a proletarian childhood to Russian Officer's School, service as a lieutenant in the Russian army, participation in the Finnish General Strike of 1905 and the Viapuri garrison mutiny of 1906, as well as experience in radical journalism in Finland. After his arrival in America, he became the flamboyant leader and chief theoretician of the IWW Finns. By the fall of 1908, Laukki had been appointed director of the college, a position from which he could and did exert a powerful influence on the politics of the central district of the Finnish Socialist Federation. It was under Laukki's leadership that Work People's College reached its zenith in 1913–1914, when over 150 students were taught by eight teachers on a two-building campus overlooking Lake Superior and Duluth Harbor.[42]

After Laukki in 1907, another teacher with impressive credentials was added to the faculty. He was Yrjö Sirola, who by the time he had reached America in 1911 as a political exile, had a long history of involvement in radical causes. He had taken a leading role in the General Strike and thereafter became a leader of the left wing in the Finnish Social Democratic Party. He was to leave America in 1913 to return to Finland to work for independence and revolution. Ultimately, he would be deeply involved in the Civil War and become a leader of the Finnish Communist Party in exile in Russia, with Otto V. Kuusinen, and a member of the inner circle of the Comintern. He would also later look back on his flirtation with the IWW and the concepts of industrial unionism as a phase in his personal evolution to revolutionary communism.[43]

At the 1912 national convention of the SSJ, Laukki and Sirola openly espoused industrial unionism and brought down on themselves harsh criticism from more moderate delegates, led by the eastern division within the Federation. The moderates alleged that the college's curriculum in practice ignored the Socialist Party program and instead was geared to teaching sabotage. After one such charge, leveled specifically at articles written by Laukki in 1911 and printed in *Työmies*, Laukki clarified his philosophy. He acknowledged that there was a deep ideological split in the Federation (SSJ) that basically pitted the Eastern District against the Midwestern. But he denied that he was antiparliamentarian, that he believed in fanaticism, or that he advocated sabotage. He went on to say, however, that he did believe the socialistic revolution, if it were ever to come, needed more than a political base; it also needed an economic one. The workers needed economic power, which could be obtained only by taking over industry through an industry-wide union.[44]

Laukki's disavowal of sabotage and syndicalism mollified the moderates. The Federation was not split, and the implied consensus of the moderates was that since Work People's College was supported with $11,000 per year from the Federation's locals, the teachers at the college ought to conform to the wishes of the majority of Federation members. Laukki and Sirola returned to the college and continued to teach as before.

The Copper Strike of 1913–1914 and the Emergence of the IWW

On the horizon was the Copper Strike of 1913–1914, an event that made more Finnish socialists think in terms of direct action as an effective alternative to the ballot box. Northern Michigan mining companies employed 14,300 miners, the majority of whom were Finns. The WFM had been active among them since at least 1904. And despite the loss of the WFM-led Mesabi strike of 1907, the Finns had not yet lost faith in the union. The leaders of the union decided in 1913 that it was strong enough to make demands on the copper companies for shorter hours and higher pay. Such demands were made in June. The eighteen companies in the area refused to negotiate and hired "special deputies." Also, after the strike began, on 23 June, the Michigan State Militia was called to protect life and property. The strike, which lasted 265 days, was ultimately unsuccessful. But it was punctuated by several important events for the Finnish radicals, who took a leading role in it. First the *Työmies,* located in Hancock, took an active stand on behalf of the strikers and as a result wore out its welcome in northern Michigan. Since Hancock was the home of Suomi College, seminary and college of the Suomi Synod and headquarters of the largest Lutheran body among Finns in North America, the conservative Finns were very active in forming citizens' alliance groups and anti-socialist leagues.[45] *Työmies* published daily strike bulletins in both English and Finnish and saw its circulation climb up to 16,000 by December. Friction between the paper and the conservatives rose to such a point by Christmas that the conservatives made sufficient allegations to the authorities as to prompt the police to arrest the *Työmies* office staff for sedition.[46] The case never came to trial and the staff was released. It was obvious, however, that *Työmies* would find life difficult in Hancock after the strike. Shortly, a special stockholders' meeting was held, and plans were made to move the paper to the more congenial atmosphere of Superior, Wisconsin.[47]

The second important event for the Finns was the tragic Italian Hall panic of Christmas Eve in Calumet.[48] That night a party was held for over 100 strikers' children. At the height of the festivities, someone allegedly yelled Fire! At the same time, the Calumet fire siren began to wail. A panic ensued as women and children rushed down a stairway to the main exit. Unfortunately, the doors openend inward; and before they could be opened, the panic-stricken people had piled up against them. The few minutes that followed left some eighty people dead, including abouty sixty children, more than half of them Finnish.[49] The grief-stricken strikers were quick to blame the local Citizens' Alliance and local law enforcement authorities. Rumors also circulated to the effect that members of both groups planned the tragedy and had actually held the doors closed to prevent people from getting out. The mystery was never resolved, but it sent a shock wave through the radical community that served only to tighten the resolve of workers to fight the companies harder. When the companies offered to defray the funeral expenses of the victims, the offer was scornfully refused. Within a week, thousands of people gathered in Calumet to witness the mass funeral.

The Finnish radical press exploded in rage. Dozens of articles were written castigating the copper barons and the butchers of the Citizens' Alliance. *Raivaaja* perhaps best conveyed the horror and enormity of the tragedy in its monthly periodical *Säkeniä* (Sparks), whose cover picture showed a number of mutilated bodies in the morgue. Other photographs in the issue showed the victims' mass grave with many of the coffins so small as to look like miniatures, all of them ready to be lowered into the frozen hardscrabble of northern Michigan.[50]

The failure of the strike forced a careful reexamination by the Finns of the Western Federation of Miners. Union leaders were accused of incompetence and arrogance. The Finns complained bitterly that they had not been trusted with a large enough role in planning and executing the strike. Laukki and the radicals countered that the WFM was no longer the class-struggle union it had been in the early years of the century; in fact, it was coming to resemble a typical organization of labor professionals and elitists.[51]

It was amidst such events as these and in such an emotion-charged atmosphere that the Central District Delegate Convention of the Finnish Socialist Federation was convened in Duluth on 21 Febuary 1914. The Copper Strike was still in progress, thousands of Finns still mourned the victims of the Christmas Eve panic, and *Työmies* was under fire from both the conservative Finns and the Michigan authorities. What emerged after several days of heated debate at this convention was a split Federation. Laukki and his followers openly castigated their conservative comrades and established a newspaper, called *Sosialisti,* in which to print their beliefs. That the convention was heated is evident too in the fact that 441 pages of minutes were printed. Laukki was able to persuade the majority of locals in Duluth, Superior, and Minnesota's Iron Range to forsake the Socialist Party and break away.[52]

Thus the evolution from the original founding convention in Hibbing in 1906 was complete. It had taken nine years and had left the Finnish Socialist Federation wrecked, at least in the Central District. What had begun as a parliamentary socialist organization moved leftward to anarchosyndicalism. But this was no cause for alarm to the readers of *Sosialisti* and the followers of Laukki. As

1916 dawned, the radicals actually had much to be optimistic about. The parliamentary fights with the moderates were a thing of the past. Everybody in Duluth and on the Mesabi was like-minded now on the issue of unionism. Also, the radicals had their ideologies nicely reconciled, a healthy newspaper in which to articulate and broadcast them, a worker's college in which to teach them, and an industrial arena in which to test them.

In fact, the industrial arena lay only sixty-five miles north of *Sosialisti*'s office and the campus of Work People's College. The Mesabi Iron Range had been quiet for eight long years, but the Finns still remembered 1907 and the blacklist. The IWW Finns at the head of the lakes had to wait only a few months for a chance to try a more militant brand of unionism against U.S. Steel's special deputies.

On 25 June 1916, Joe Greeni, an Italian miner in Biwabik, opened his pay envelope and found that he had been paid at a lower contract rate than he had expected. In disgust, he walked off the job. To his surprise, he was followed by the whole shift.

The 1916 Mesabi Range Strike

Thus, the second, and last, great strike on the Mesabi began.[53] This time, Slavic, Italian, and Finnish miners who had little intercultural contact, lived in separate neighborhoods, maintained their national languages and religions—in short, a group of people who were often used against each other as strikebreakers—were out together. They quickly spread the word of the spontaneous walkout westward, down the length of the Mesabi. Shortly, the Mesabi was all but shut down by angry workers. The strike had started spontaneously and threatened to die quickly if help did not arrive. An appeal was sent to Big Bill Haywood in Chicago, and the IWW responded immediately.

Within a few days, Carlo Tresca, Sam Scarlett, Frank Little, Joseph Schmidt, Joseph Ettor, and, in a few weeks, Elizabeth Gurley Flynn[54] were on the range, organizing the strikers and preparing demands. Their oratory rang through the Finn Halls as they sought support for the strike and simultaneously tried to educate the workers about their rights as employees and citizens.

A long list of demands was drawn up, with contracts, hours, and pay issues being the most significant. The miners wanted the contract system for underground mining eliminated because it was abused by both upper and lower echelons of management. They demanded an eight-hour day for the whole range and that it be "portal to portal" in nature. They further demanded $2.75 per day for open pit miners and $3.00 to $3.50 per day for underground work, the higher sum being for "wet conditions." To help prevent credit purchasing, they also requested pay periods twice each month instead of only once.

The Oliver responded by hiring over 1,000 special deputies to keep the mines open. The company position was that the strike was to be ignored and the miners were to be either persuaded or coerced into returning to work. The pool of unskilled immigrant labor, however, had dried up since the onset of World War I, and steel orders had risen significantly because of European war needs. The special deputies overstepped their legal authority and openly harassed picketers. As a direct result, three people were killed. John Alar, a Slovenian miner from Virginia, Minnesota, was shot by a mine guard on 23 June, an act which unified the workers and prompted a 3,000-man parade to the cemetery for his funeral. Carlo Tresca was the funeral speaker, and he administered an oath of vengeance when he said, "We will take a tooth for a tooth, an eye for an eye, or a life for a life."

Elizabeth Gurley Flynn appeared after 4 July and spent the rest of the summer in northern Minnesota, traveling the Mesabi's 100-mile length regularly, speaking time and again at the Virginia Finnish Socialist Opera House and winning friends among the workers. At the height of the strike, about 10,000 miners were out; but as hard as they tried, they could not wait out the companies. The strikers were further hampered by the jailing of the national IWW leaders, Tresca, Scarlett, and Schmidt, who were accused of instigating two deaths in Biwabik. (The real cause of these deaths was a raid of a Croatian home by special deputies looking for a suspected "Blind Pig" there. One deputy and an innocent bystander were killed.) In September the strikers voted to go back to work, defeated. Surprisingly, however, a 10 percent pay raise was instituted later in the fall, probably because wartime demands for steel had forced a raise in production.[55]

Sosialisti and Laukki's group worked feverishly in support of the strike. Organizers were sent to the range to work in conjunction with the locals to swell picket lines and recruit new union members. Demonstrations were organized in Duluth and the Mesabi Range cities for raising funds; and *Sosialisti* moved to new heights of stinging rhetoric. On the day IWW officials presented the widowed Mrs. Alar with a benefits check, for example, *Sosialisti* ran a photograph of the event and devoted half of the front page to coverage of John Alar's funeral. The photograph is indeed touching. It shows a black-shawled and kerchiefed Eastern European woman in Old World dress surrounded by three small children and with an infant in her arms. Elizabeth Gurley Flynn stands behind as Joseph Ettor presents the check to the uncomprehending Mrs. Alar. *Sosialisti* captioned the photograph as follows:

> . . . look at this photograph! Look! Look long and ponder! Then cut it from the page and put it on the wall of your home. And continue to look at it and ponder. It speaks—do you hear? Do you understand? It speaks. It says many things. It tells of the wage slave's patience and of the history of struggle. It speaks of history of the slave's martyrdom. It speaks of how Capitalism's gunmen murder workers like dogs, when the workers dare ask for a bit more bread for themselves. . . . See how it speaks! It commands us to fight. . . . It urges us to join the One Big Union and strike Capitalism down. . . . [56]

This language represents *Sosialisti*'s uncompromising stand on the strike. The paper also regularly published the names of Finnish "scabs," a practice that ended in a lawsuit against the paper a few months after the strike.

The fact that the Mesabi strikers actually voted to go back to work and the pay raises granted during the fall after the strike were interpreted as a limited victory for the strikers. The miners and the IWW resolved to fight U.S. Steel early in 1917 with a more organized front and finally bring the giant corporation to its knees. To that end, Elizabeth Gurley Flynn made several trips to the range during the fall and winter of 1916–1917 to keep strike sentiment alive, and the IWW locals in the timber industry struck the Virginia–Rainy Lake Company's giant sawmill in Viginia and its logging camps between the Mesabi Range and the Canadian border in late December—at the height of the cutting season.[57] The strike failed within a month, but it served its tactical purpose of reminding workers in the area that there would be a showdown in the spring.

Through the efforts of Elizabeth Gurley Flynn, a compromise was reached to release Tresca, Scarlett, and Schmidt from jail. In early December the three IWW leaders were free in a trade-off—their release in return for lengthy jail sentences for three of the Coatians whose home had been raided by special deputies. The only person victimized by that illicit search who did not serve time in jail was the pregnant wife of a Croatian named Masonovich.[58]

World War I and the Demise of the IWW

Hopes for a crippling strike on the Mesabi, raised by the partial success of 1916, were nursed throughout the early months of 1917. As it turned out, however, 1917 was not a safe year for radicals of any stripe. April brought America's entry into World War I, and, as a bonus, a Federal crackdown on "Reds" and a wave of official Red-baiting by patriots. Finnish IWW members fared badly on the Mesabi and in Duluth. Incidents of harassment and persecution were numerous. In one case, members of the Eveleth unit of the National Guard, freshly returned from Mexico, where they had participated in the war against Pancho Villa, took it upon themselves to march the three miles to Virginia's Finnish Socialist Opera House, the IWW headquarters on the east end of the Mesabi, and tear down the red flag and replace it with the Stars and Stripes. The same thing happened at Worker's Hall in Hibbing. Finns in the Duluth-Superior area were arrested throughout the spring months for organizing demonstrations against the draft, for being "criminal syndicalists," and for disseminating IWW literature. On 30 August seventeen Finns from the area were arrested as "slackers" for not registering for the draft.[59]

Although there is some confusion about how the Finnish leftists came to the conclusion, they thought that since they were technically citizens of Russia and therefore guests in the United States, it was unnecessary for them to register for the draft. When some were arrested for failure to register, others took to the woods, and still others escaped into Canada. In Minnesota folklore today there are many stories told of Finns hiding in the wilderness near Winton (the last location with civilization in it in the United States just a few miles through the wilderness from remote western Ontario), and of a group of Finns hiding on an island in Birch Lake near the town of Babbitt.[60]

Among those who went to Canada were newspapermen Elis Sulkanen and Onni Saari and the rapidly rising John Wiita. Wiita said in an interview that he calmly sneaked into Canada a few miles from the border crossing near Grand Marais, Minnesota, on the main route from Minnesota to Fort William and Port Arthur (known today as Thunder Bay), Ontario. He said he lived for a few months in rural Ontario with Elis Sulkanen and then went to work making railroad ties. He actually stayed in Canada several years working for Finnish leftist papers. But, he said, during the war years, people in his position received no harassment from Canadian officials because of the lack of manpower. Men were needed to fill the places of those fighting in Europe. As soon as the war was over, the official attitude changed rapidly.[61]

A severe blow was dealt to Finnish IWW fortunes in April 1918, when five prominent Finnish leaders from the Duluth area—Leo Laukki, Fred Jaakola, Charles Johnson, William Tanner and Frank

Westerlund—were indicted by Judge Kenesaw Mountain Landis with the Chicago 166. These five Finnish leaders, with the national leadership of the IWW, were charged with crimes varying from opposition to the war to attempting to overthrow the government. All were convicted and given severe sentences and fines. While free on bail, pending appeal, Leo Laukki fled to Russia, where he died in the 1930s after working as a newspaper correspondent in Tashkent.[62] His departure, though it did not kill the Finnish IWW movement, dealt it a blow from which it never fully recovered.

The results of the federal crackdown and Laukki's departure, however, were not readily apparent. The circulation of *Teollisuustyölainen,* the name to which *Sosialisti* had been changed, actually increased during the war years. After only four short months as *Teollisuustyölainen,* the name was changed to *Industrialisti;* and the journal was able to claim a circulation of about 10,000 daily in 1920. But the paper was hurt in 1920, when it was found guilty of "disseminating syndicalism and its teachings." The editorial staff was jailed until bail of $8,000 per person could be raised, and the paper suffered a severe financial drain over the next three years as the case was appealed.[63]

The World War I years represent perhaps the lowest point in the fortunes of the Finnish radicals in the western Great Lakes region. Their once-flourishing Finnish Socialist Federation had been violently split by the emerging left wing. Now the once-powerful *Työmies* was languishing in Superior, reviled as a "yellow rag." *Sosialisti-Teollisuustyölainen-Industrialisti* was beset by harassment and persecution. And the enrollments at Work People's College had dropped considerably. Both the federal government and the Finns' own hot tempers had taken their toll on the radical movement. Added to these problems was the Minnesota Public Safety Commission, an extralegal investigative bureau established by the Minnesota state legislature during World War I to look into "unpatriotic groups" such as Germans and Finns. The commission was able to arouse a strong sense of patriotism in conservative Finns, who then doubled their harassment of radicals in their midst.[64]

Solidarity had been replaced by factionalism; and optimism had given way to, at best, a bitter resolve to hang on in the face of what seemed terrible odds. It was indeed a turbulent, disappointing period, not only in the Great Lakes region but for radicals all over the world. Although the Bolshevik Revolution and the Civil War in Finland would lead to a new unity among Finns of the upper Midwest, the Golden Age of Finnish radicalism had ended; and only hope and time carried the radical spirit through the years of limbo after its end.

Notes

1. Folksong, translated by Helen Kruth, 1973, "Finnish Immigration to America," in *70th Anniversary Souvenir Journal, 1903–1973* (Superior, Wis.: Työmies Society).

2. Irene Paull, "America Sings to the Sons of Suomi," Walter Harju Collection, Immigration History Research Center (hereafter, IHRC), University of Minnesota.

3. See particularly Eino Jutikkala's *Suomen Talonpojan Historia* (Helsinki: Werner Söderström Osakeyhtiö, 1958), especially the section titled "Torpparikysymys," (the tenant question), 370–80; and Eino Jutikkala, ed., *Suomen talous- ja sosiaalihistorian kehityslinjoja* (Porvoo, Finland: Werner Söderström Osakeyhtiö, 1969).

4. John I. Kolehmainen and George W. Hill, *Haven in the Woods: The Story of Finns in Wisconsin* (Madison: State Historical Society of Wisconsin, 1951), 14.

5. Ibid.; "horse days" and "foot days" refer to the "in-kind" portion of the rental agreement whereby the tenant was compelled to spend so many days per year working his draft animals in his landlord's fields and so many days working himself.

6. Ibid., p. 16.

7. Ibid.

8. Arnold Alanen, "The Norwegian Connection: The Background in Norway for Early Finnish Emigration to the American Midwest," *Finnish Americana* 6 (1983–1984): 23–24.

9. Matti Kaups, "*Suuri Läänsi*—Or the Finnish Discovery of America" (Ph.D. diss., University of Minnesota, 1966), p. 89; see also Marvin Lamppa, "Embers of Revival: Laestadian Schisms in Northern Minnesota, 1900–1940," in *Finnish Diaspora*, vol. 2, ed. Michael G. Karni (Toronto: Multicultural History Society of Ontario, 1981), 193–213; and Uras Saarnivaara, *Amerikan laestadiolaisuuden eli Apostolisluterilaisuuden historia* (Ironwood, Michigan: National Publishing Co., 1947).

10. For information on this period in Finnish history, see Eino Jutikkala and Kauko Pirinen, *A History of Finland* (New York: Praeger Publishers, 1974); and W. R. Mead, *Finland* (New York: Fredrick A. Praeger, 1968). The best works in English on modern Finnish political and labor history are John H. Hodgson, *Communism in Finland* (Princeton, N.J.: Princeton University Press, 1967); Carl Erik Knoellinger, *Labor in Finland* (Cambridge, Mass.: Harvard University Press, 1960); and Pekka Kalevi Hamalainen, *In Time of Storm: Civil War and the Ethnolinguistic Issue in Finland* (Albany: State University of New York Press, 1979).

11. For a good treatment in English of this period, see William R. Copeland, *The Uneasy Alliance: Collaboration between the Finnish Opposition and the Russian Underground* (Helsinki: Suomen Tiedeakatamia, 1973).

12. Paull, "America Sings to the Sons of Suomi."

13. Neill Betten, "The Origins of Ethnic Radicalism in Northern Minnesota," *International Migration Review* 4 (Spring 1970): 52. For more details on the events leading to the strike of 1907, the strike itself, and the consequences of it for Finns in Minnesota, see Michael G. Karni, "The Founding of the Finnish Socialist Federation and the Strike of 1907," in *For the Common Good: Finnish Immigrants and the Radical Response to Industrial America*, ed. Michael G. Karni and Douglas Ollila (Superior, Wisconsin: Työmies Society, 1977), 65–87.

14. Sever Karni, interview with author, Cook, Minnesota, 19 April 1972. The memories of Sever Karni, my father, were among the first sources available to me when I began serious study of the Finnish immigrant experience in this country.

15. Betten, "Origins of Ethnic Radicalism in Northern Minnesota," p. 51.

16. Hyman Berman, "Education for Work and Labor Solidarity: The Immigrant

Miners and Radicalism on the Mesabi Iron Range" (Unpublished manuscript, University of Minnesota, 1964), p. 6.

17. For accounts of early strikes on the Mesabi, see Edward Marolt, "The Development of Labor Unionism in the Iron Mining Industry of the Virginia-Eveleth District" (Master's thesis, University of Minnesota, 1969), pp. 19–49; John Sirjamaki, "Three Iron Range Communities: A Study in Development" (Ph.D. diss., Yale University, 1940); and Berman, "Education for Work and Labor Solidarity. . ."

18. *Pöytäkirja, Amerikan Suomalaisten Sosialistiosastojen Edustajakouksesta, Hibbingissa, Minn., Elokuun 1–7 p. [1 to 7 August] 1906* (Hancock, Michigan: Työmies Society, 1907), p. 1; Michael G. Karni, "Yhteishyvä- or, For the Common Good: Finnish Radicalism in the Western Great Lakes Region, 1900–1940" (Ph.D. diss., University of Minnesota, 1975), pp. 115–17.

19. Martin Hendrickson, *Muistelmia Kymmenvuotisesta Raivaustyöstäni* (Fitchburg, Mass.: Raivaaja Publishing Co., 1909), 106–7.

20. A. William Hoglund, "Breaking with Religious Tradition: Finnish Immigrant Workers and the Chuch, 1890–1915," in *For the Common Good,* ed. Karni and Ollila, pp. 23–64; Douglas Ollila, "The Formative Period of the Finnish Evangelical Lutheran Church in America or Suomi Synod" (Ph.D. diss., Boston Unversity, 1963), pp. 10–48, 264–316.

21. Kusti Siirtolainen [pseud.], Life History (unpublished), quoted in Walfrid Jokinen, "The Finns in America: A Sociological Analysis" (Ph.D. diss., Louisiana State University, 1955), pp. 150–51.

22. John Wiita, unpublished autobiography, folder 12, IHRC, University of Minnesota, pp. 9–10.

23. *Pöytäkirja,* Hibbing, 1907, pp. 140–41.

24. Ibid., p. 176.

25. *Report of the Immigration Commission,* vol. 18, *Immigrants in Industries: Iron Ore Mining* (Washington Government Printing Office, 1911), 229–300.

26. *Mesaba Ore,* 27 July 1907, p. 1.

27. Ibid., p. 2.

28. *Minneapolis Journal,* 28 July 1907, p. 1.

29. A good account of Oliver Iron Mining Company's blacklist and spy system is given in Frank L. Palmer, *Spies in Steel* (Denver: Labor Press, 1928). Hyman Berman offers verification of Palmer's book in "Education for Work and Labor Solidarity," p. 41, nn. 63, 42. Further verification of Palmer's book appeared in "Steel Company Spies," an article written by one-time National Labor Relations Board arbitrator James M. Shields in *North Country Anvil* 3 (December–January, 1972–1973).

30. *Immigration Commission Reports,* pp. 340–41.

31. Hans R. Wasastjerna, ed., *History of the Finns in Minnesota* (New York Mills, Minn.: Parta Printer, 1957), 477; *Duluth Evening Herald,* 22 January 1908, p. 1.

32. As late as 1957, the issue of "Mongolianism" still bothered many Finns. In that year, the Knights and Ladies of Kaleva, a middle-class fraternal group, commissioned an amateur anthropologist to write a book "scientifically" disproving, once and for all, the theory that Finns are Asians. See S. C. Olin, *Finlandia: The Racial Composition, the Language and a Brief History of the Finnish People* (Hancock, Mich.: Finnish Publishing Co., 1957).

33. See, for example, *Pöytäkirja, Ponsikomitea, Eveleth Citizens' Committee,* 19 February 1908; Ollila, "The Formative Period," p. 305; see also Kaarlo Salovaara, Eveleth, Minnesota, to J. J. Hoikka, Crystal Falls, Michigan, 17 August 1907, Finnish American Historical Archives, Suomi College, Hancock, Michigan.

34. *Fourteenth Census of the United States, Vol. V, Agriculture,* 319; *Vol. II, General Reports,* pp. 768, 958, 1961; Wasastjerna, ed., *History of the Finns in Minnesota,* p. 565.

35. *Pöytäkirja, Kolmannen Amerikan Suomalaisen Sosialistijärjestön Edustajakokouksesta* (Fitchburg: Raivaaja Publishing Co., 1909), 16–17.

36. *Pöytäkirja, Kolmannen Suomalaisen Sosialistijärjestön Edustjakokouksesta,*

Duluth, Minn., Kesak. 1–5, 7–10, 1912 (Hancock, Mich.: Työmies Publishing Co., 1912), 53–54.

37. It is still published under the name *Työmies-Eteenpäin* in Superior, Wisconsin.

38. In 1978, *Naisten Viiri* stopped publication as an independent newspaper and merged with *Työmies-Eteenpain,* in which it appears as a section.

39. Karni, *"Yhteishyvä,"* p. 91.

40. *Yhdysvaltain Suomalaisen Sosialistijärjestön Edustjakokouksen Pöytäkirja, 1914* (Astoria, Ore.: Toveri Publishing Co., 1915), p. 34.

41. For information on Work People's College, see *Pöytäkirja Työväen Opiston Johtakunta,* April 1904–May 1911 (original copy on file at Turku University, Institute of General History; microfilm at IHRC, University of Minnesota); Työväen Opisto Collection, IHRC; *Work People's College Bulletin* (1 December 1923), p. 1; Douglas Ollila, "The Work People's College: Immigrant Education for Adjustment and Solidarity," in *For the Common Good,* ed. Karni and Ollila, pp. 87–94; and Michael G. Karni, "Work People's College: Source of Comradeship and Common Education" (Paper read at Society for the Advancement of Scandinavian Studies Convention, Nashville, Tennessee, 1 May 1982).

42. Karni, "Yhteishyvä," pp. 156–57.

43. Hodgson, *Communism in Finland,* pp. 16–19.

44. *Pöytäkirja,* 1912, pp. 255–58.

45. For good discussions of this strike, see Arthur E. Puotinen, *Finnish Radicals and Religion in Midwestern Mining Towns* (New York: Arno Press, 1977), 226–89; Carl Ross, *The Finn Factor in American Labor, Culture and Society* (New York Mills, Minn.: Parta Printers, 1977), 119–38.

46. *Työmies,* 19 December 1913, p. 1.

47. The proceedings of this meeting are published as *Työmies Kustannusyhtion Ylimääräisen Yhtiokokouksen Pöytäkirja* (Superior, Wisconsin: Työmies Publishing Co., 1914).

48. The Italian Hall panic seems to live permanently in the folklore of the Finnish ethnic group, even into the third generation. See Arthur E. Puotinen, "Copper Country Finns and the Strike of 1913–1914," in *The Finnish Experience in the Western Great Lakes Region: New Perspectives,* ed. Michael G. Karni, Douglas Ollila, and Matti Kaups (Vammala, Finland: Institute for Migration, 1975), 143–56; and the accompanying response by Raymond A. Wargelin. Puotinen quotes a song written by Woody Guthrie called "The Italian Hall Massacre," rerecorded by Arlo Guthrie in 1970. It tells the story of the "massacre" in graphic detail.

49. The number of victims varies with each source consulted.

50. *Sakeniä,* February 1914.

51. Karni, *"Yhteishyvä,"* pp. 167–68.

52. Ibid., pp. 171–75.

53. For details of the 1916 Mesabi Strike, see Douglas Ollila, "Ethnic Radicalism and the 1916 Mesabi Strike," *Range History* (December 1978), pp. 1–10; Michael G. Karni, "Elizabeth Gurley Flynn and the Mesabi Strike of 1916," *Range History* (Winter 1981), pp. 1–6; and Berman, "Education for Work and Labor Solidarity."

54. Karni, "Elizabeth Gurley Flynn and the Mesabi Strike of 1916," p. 2.

55. Ibid., pp. 5–6; Ollila, "Ethnic Radicalism and the 1916 Mesabi Strike," p. 10.

56. *Sosialisti,* 28 June 1916, p. 1; translation by Douglas Ollila.

57. John E. Haynes, "Revolt of the Timber Beasts: The IWW Lumber Strike in Minnesota," *Minnesota History* 42 (1971): 163–64.

58. Karni, "Elizabeth Gurley Flynn and the Mesabi Strike of 1916," p. 3.

59. These instances are picked almost at random only to suggest the pressures on radical Finns during World War I. See *Eveleth News,* 16 August 1917, 30 August 1917; *Työmies,* 11 April 1917 and 11 May 1917.

60. See Anthony Pleva to John Lind, Minnesota Public Safety Commission, 29 August 1917, Minnesota Historical Society; Marvin Lamppa, interview with author, 16 August 1981, Embarrass, Minnesota.

61. John Wiita, unpublished autobiography, folder 3, IHRC, pp. 1–3.

62. Michael G. Karni, "John Wiita: Finnish-American Revolutionary," *Range History* (December 1978), p. 8.

63. Karni, "*Yhteishyvä*," pp. 191–93.

64. See Public Safety Commission papers, Minnesota Historical Society, St. Paul, Minnesota; Douglas Ollila, "Defects in the Melting Pot: Finnish American Response to the Loyalty Issue, 1917, 1920," *Turun Historiallinen Arkisto* 31 (1976): 397–413.

Work, Organization, and Strikes

JAMES R. BARRETT

Unity and Fragmentation: Class, Race, and Ethnicity on Chicago's South Side, 1900–1922

Working-class fragmentation—the failure of workers to identify with one another across ethnic, racial, sexual, and skill lines and to act collectively on the basis of class interests—is often assumed in the historiography of early twentieth-century America. American workers probably *were* more heterogeneous during this era than at any other time in the nation's history. Employers in many basic industries reorganized production methods and in the process restructured labor markets, drawing their workers from a much wider social and geographic spectrum than they had in the nineteenth century. While an earlier generation of "old immigrant" and native-born men remained dominant in most skilled occupations, the "new immigrants"—largely unskilled farmers and farm laborers from southern and southeastern Europe—were rapidly displacing them from the ranks of common laborers and machine tenders. The number of women entering the manufacturing labor force actually leveled off after the turn of the century, but the overall proportion of women in the wage-earning population continued to increase. Finally, Blacks secured positions in many manufacturing industries for the first time during World War I as a result of war production and the shortage of immigrant labor. Racial diversity grew, considerably complicating the process of class formation.[1] While the uniqueness of the American working-class experience has often been exaggerated, it is difficult to imagine a more complex population than the one that experienced the birth of the new corporate political economy at the beginning of this century.

Nowhere was such diversity greater than in Chicago's Union Stock Yards and the surrounding slaughtering and meat-packing plants. When Immigration Commission investigators studied the industry in 1908 and 1909, they found more than forty nationalities represented. The work force was demographically diverse not only in terms of ethnicity but also in terms of race, age, gender, and work experience. Mixed in with older, skilled Irish and German butchers were thousands of young Eastern European peasants and laborers only recently arrived from the forests and farms, as well as from urban areas, of the Austro-Hungarian and Russian empires. While men did most of the industry's heavy work, they were joined by a growing stream of young, single women and later, during World War I, by housewives and mothers. Thousands of Black migrants from the South arrived during the war, making the industry one of the most important employers of Black labor in U.S. manufacturing. Packed into the crowded neighborhoods of Chicago's vast industrial South Side, these workers seem to exemplify the divisions within the American working class during this era.

Yet a study of these butcher workmen demonstrates that the existence of diversity did not lead inevitably to fragmentation. How did workers from such diverse backgrounds interact with one another, as they undoubtedly did in many circumstances? Is it possible to distinguish factors that contributed to class cohesion from those that led to fragmentation? This case study reminds us just how complicated social relations among American workers were and are. It considers several approaches to the problem of class fragmentation in light of what happened in the Chicago Stock Yards during the early years of this century and concludes with some observations about what the case study can tell us concerning the interplay of class, race, and ethnicity.

Conceptions of Working-Class Fragmentation and American Labor History

Several labor historians have analyzed the problem of fragmentation similarly. Herbert Gutman has argued that the continual influx of "preindustrial" migrants into American society meant that various groups—native-born artisans, earlier immigrants, and the new immigrants of the early twentieth century—experienced the wrenching process of adjustment to life and work in industrial society at different times and paces. No single generation saw "the making of the American working class." Indeed, Gutman seems to suggest that continual migration contributed to a process of disintegration, an *unmaking,* throughout the late nineteenth and early twentieth centuries.[2]

Others have discussed the same problem in generational terms. David Montgomery suggests that there were two generations of industrial workers in the United States by the turn of the century, the first consisting of native-born workers and members of older immigrant groups (particularly Germans, Irish, and British) and the second composed largely of eastern and southeastern European immigrants augmented later by Black migrants from the South. By the late nineteenth century, many of the more "mature" workers from the earlier generation had lived in industrial towns and cities most of their lives. They had, to use Hobsbawm's phrase, learned "the rules of the game," creating subcultures built on strong social, economic, and cultural institutions that supported them daily and in times of stress. They governed themselves at work and often in the community as well through a moral code emphasizing solidarity, mutualism, and craft if not class pride. Often these subcultures were supported by ethnic and religious organizations that took on class characteristics because of the occupational makeup of the communities and their problems.[3] The dominant milieu in many parts of Chicago's South Side, for example, was a traditional Irish-American Catholicism fused with militant craft unionism.

By the turn of the century, however, such subcultures were increasingly undermined by the introduction of mass production work and the massive influx of new immigrant groups. While new production methods rendered craft organization much less effective, the creation of new ethnic communities, populated by workers who shared neither the industrial nor the social and cultural experiences of the earlier generation, threatened the prospects for solidarity among American workers.[4]

In the steel industry, the primary division between the first generation of skilled Irish and British steelworkers and the second of Slavic common laborers was fundamentally psychological. While the earlier group was firmly rooted in the mills and the towns that grew up around them, many of the new immigrants viewed their stay in the industry as a temporary situation. They bore their troubles, hoping to return home and resume their old way of life on the land. Separated by a generation of work and trade union experience as well as by profound cultural differences, the two groups had little in common and found it difficult to identify with one another on the basis of class interests.[5]

Labor economists have explained class fragmentation by focusing on the divisive effects of segmented and hierarchical labor market structures. They argue that employers accentuated or arbitrarily created status distinctions among workers by providing a wide range of wage rates and benefits and by making employment for some workers more secure than for others. The consequent stratification of the working class on the basis of differences in status, wages, and benefits inhibited class organization and action. Where these objective differences in work situations overlapped with significant racial, ethnic, and sexual divisions—as was so often the case in American industry—their divisive effects were enhanced.[6]

Like the Marxist theory of a labor aristocracy,[7] labor market segmentation theory attempts to explain the role of the more privileged strata of the working class. These workers, the theory maintains, were incorporated into the developing structure of monopoly capitalism through higher wages, greater employment security, and various welfare schemes. In this respect, radical labor market theory is the economic counterpart to the argument that the labor movement was ideologically integrated into corporate society during the early twentieth century under the auspices of a pervasive "corporate liberalism." Enlightened corporate leaders insured a relatively high standard of living and labor reform legislation for the AFL's constituency in exchange for stable industrial relations and conservative labor politics.[8]

Gabriel Kolko's formulation of this fragmentation theme comes closest to putting labor historians out of business entirely. Drawing on evidence of strong ethnic subcultures, figures on reemigration and wage differentials, and other data, Kolko pictures the working-class community as a "splintered society," unable to unite around common grievances and goals. This failure and the frustration and despair it bred have been reflected, he argues, in unusually high rates of crime, emotional problems, alcoholism, and other forms of social deviance. Their failure to develop class consciousness and a social democratic labor movement has rendered twentieth-century American workers "lumpen people in a lumpen society."[9] While not always drawing such dire conclusions regarding the social worth of contemporary American workers, many historians and other scholars share Kolko's view of early twentieth-century American workers as a highly fragmented social group.[10]

Both the New Left historians of corporate liberalism and the radical labor economists relate their analyses of class fragmentation to specific characteristics of monopoly capitalism. On the one hand, the strong market position of the largest firms in each industry allowed them to buy off many of the skilled, organized male workers, most of whom came from native-born or older immigrant backgrounds. On the other, the expansion of labor markets through immigration and internal migration not only kept the lid on labor costs, it also discouraged the growth of class consciousness by increasing the diversity of the working-class population.

The Case of Chicago's Packinghouse Workers

The packinghouse workers make an excellent case study of the unmaking, or perhaps the remaking, of the American working class during the early twentieth century. Both the strong market position of the "Big Five" packers and the sophistication of their huge corporate bureaucracies made them prime candidates for corporate liberalism.[11] The situation of the butcher workmen themselves and their behavior over time demonstrate both the obvious potential for fragmentation among such a group of workers and considerable success under certain conditions in uniting on the basis of class interests.

The packers were pioneers in work organization and technology. Extensive division of labor and a primitive sort of assembly (or, in this case, disassembly) line had emerged in hog slaughtering by the mid-nineteenth century, but the complete conversion of the industry to mass production methods awaited the perfection of the refrigerated railroad car and the emergence of a national market for dressed meat in the late 1870s. As late as 1880 the job of slaughtering and cutting up a steer was still often done by one man, the "all-round butcher." During the next two decades, the big packers reorganized this process, gradually introducing more and more division of labor, as they consolidated their hold over the national market and expanded overseas. By the turn of the century, the same function was executed in assembly-line fashion by a gang of 330 men, each person doing the same minute manipulation a thousand times during a full workday. The same extreme division of labor was applied to canning, sausage making, and by-product departments throughout the plants. This dramatic reorganization of work seriously undermined the power and control of the skilled butcher and greatly increased production speed.[12]

The new production methods also allowed the packers to reorganize the labor market. By the early twentieth century the industry relied on what labor economists term a dual labor market. About one-third of the work force was spread out over a hierarchical job structure ranging from the common labor ranks up to the few highly skilled jobs left in the industry. The other two-thirds of the butcher workmen were considered common labor. In practice, this meant that they were paid a standard wage rate which fluctuated with economic conditions and unemployment in the industry. It also meant that many of them were essentially casual laborers, hired for a week, a day, or even a few hours at a time. Chicago had, in fact, a very large casual labor market in which immigrant packinghouse workers were but one component. The existence of this large, heterogeneous, floating population might be expected to inhibit the development of class solidarity among common laborers and between them and the more skilled butcher workmen to whom they posed a threat.[13]

Table 1 Nationality of Employees in the Slaughtering and Meat-packing Industry of Chicago, 1909
(N = 15,489)

	Proportion
Native-born	
White	18.9%
Black	3.0
Foreign-born	
Bohemian and Slovak[a]	10.0
German	10.4
Irish	7.5
Lithuanian	12.0
Polish	27.7
Russian	2.9
Other[b]	7.6
TOTAL	100.0%

SOURCE: Calculated from U.S. Immigration Commission, *Reports*, vol. 13, *Immigrants in Industry, Part 2: Slaughtering and Meat Packing*, (Washington, D.C.: Government Printing Office, 1911), 204.
[a]Includes a small proportion of "Austrian."
[b]Includes workers from 32 different nationality groups.

The creation of a large market for common labor resulted in a constant social recomposition of the industry's labor force from the 1880s through the early 1920s. Bohemians, Poles, Lithuanians, and other Eastern Europeans increasingly displaced the original generation of skilled Irish and German butchers, so that by 1909 Slavic groups represented more than 50 percent of the labor force in Chicago (see Table 1). Like Brody's Slavic steelworkers, most of these butcher workmen had come into the country since the turn of the century. Blacks entered the industry as strikebreakers during an 1894 strike, and there were about 500 of them in the stockyards ten years later. By the time of the First World War, when thousands of Black migrants poured into the plants, many of the Slavic immigrants had still been in the country less than ten years. In the early 1920s, when Mexican migrants began arriving, Blacks already made up about a third of the labor force in the city's two largest plants. Generally, skill levels overlapped with racial and ethnic differences. Recent immigrants and Blacks settled into the common labor ranks, while the shrinking group of older immigrants clung to the more skilled jobs. Finally, throughout the early twentieth century, women comprised an increasingly large proportion of the industry's work force. By 1920 13 percent of the packinghouse employees were women. Their wage rates and employment security were even worse than those for male common laborers.[14]

Employers tried to turn such diversity to their advantage. Studying the industry as it was in 1904, John R. Commons found that the large firms intentionally mixed nationalities in the various departments of their plants, hoping that language and cultural differences would keep the workers divided. An employment agent at Swift explained how the strategy worked:

> Last week we employed Slovaks. We change about among various nationalities and languages. It prevents them from getting together. We have the thing systematized. We have a luncheon each week of the employment managers of the large firms of the Chicago district. There we discuss our problems and exchange information.[15]

Newer ethnic groups entering the Yards often came first as strikebreakers. This and the fact that some foremen and strawbosses practiced favoritism toward those of their own nationality only heightened the danger of interethnic and interracial conflict.[16]

Meat packing, then, was a model of the dual labor market that radical economists have described as characteristic of early monopoly capitalism. It is difficult to fully appreciate the problem of class formation and fragmentation, however, by focusing exclusively on the workplace and labor market as labor economists and historians of mass production work have done.[17] Here the emphasis of labor historians on the cultural diversity of the laboring population and the generational quality of class formation becomes crucial. In the case of Chicago's packinghouse workers and among American workers more generally, some of the most significant factors affecting class formation were cultural and community-based.

The diversity of the labor market was not only reflected in but also reinforced by separate racial and ethnic communities, each of them with its own social structure and cultural institutions. Most of the remaining Irish and German butchers lived either in Bridgeport and Canaryville, just east of Union Stock Yards, or in one of the outlying neighborhoods of the South Side. The more recent Slavic immigrants clustered in ethnic enclaves in Packingtown, the area immediately south and west of the Yards. Black workers were isolated in the Black Belt, a deteriorating ghetto more than a mile east of the Yards. These three communities were separated from one another by various man-made barriers—elevated lines, railroad tracks, factories, and the Union Stock Yards themselves (see the map of the neighborhoods).[18]

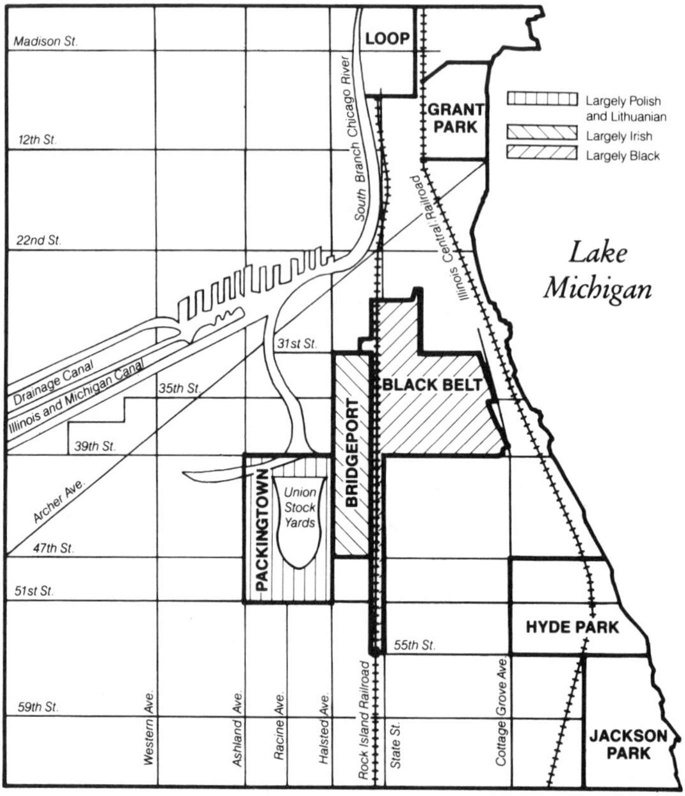

Three Working-Class Communities on Chicago's South Side, 1920. An earlier version of this map appeared in the *Journal of Social History* (1984).

Behind these physical barriers lay more important social and cultural ones. Each community spawned its own leaders as well as religious, fraternal, and political groups, all organized along ethnic or racial lines. Polish workers attended Polish parishes, socialized with one another in the Polish Falcons or other fraternal groups, drank together in Polish neighborhood bars, married within their own ethnic group, and sent their children to Polish Catholic schools. Lithuanians, Bohemians, and other immigrant communities all had comparable networks. Blacks went about a similar process of institution building over in the Black Belt, where the Urban League, the YMCA, and local churches were particularly active in helping migrants settle into jobs and housing during the era of the great World War I migration.

The creation of such subcultures was, of course, a natural and healthy response of migrant peoples seeking to adjust to the rigors of life in a large industrial city and at the same time nurture traditions and values that were distinctively their own. But it is also true that the ethnic and racial identification reflected in the creation of such communities could be, and sometimes was, used not only by employers but also by ethnic leaders within the communities to divide workers and maintain their own power.

Community-based barriers to class formation were most dramatically demonstrated in the July 1919 race riot that rocked the city's South Side, claiming the lives of twenty-three Blacks and fifteen whites, including several packinghouse workers. While white butcher workmen had little to do with the attacks on Blacks, the riot ended any prospect of creating an interracial labor movement in the Yards for more than a generation.[19] In both workplace and community, it seems, Chicago's packinghouse workers were divided from one another.

Having documented these very real divisions, however, we are faced with a paradox: Between 1900 and 1904, in the midst of a very heavy influx of recent Slavic immigrants and young women, and once again in the First World War, during the great migration of Blacks from the South, packinghouse workers achieved considerable unity.

In the early twentieth century, unionization spread quickly from the older generation of butcher workmen, particularly the Irish, who had a long tradition of union organization and solidarity, to the Slavic immigrants. The new immigrants not only flooded into the union but also built the kind of strong shop-floor organizations that labor historians have generally associated with more "mature" industrial workers. They restricted output and engaged in wildcat strikes, adapting these and other tactics to mass production work and challenging management's prerogatives in the workplace. Young women workers—often viewed as a particularly docile group—organized, struck, and fought for their rights within the union as well as in the plants.[20]

During the war years the new immigrants provided the main source of union strength and worked to integrate Black migrants into the movement. Shop-floor organization emerged once again, this time with a small but solid core of Black activists sharing rank-and-file leadership with Slavic immigrants and German and Irish veterans. An organizing drive swept through the neighborhoods of the city's South Side, galvanizing workers from a wide range of backgrounds into an effective movement that significantly improved conditions in the plants.[21] In the industry's two major

Strike in Packingtown on Chicago's South Side, August 1904. Chicago Historical Society.

strikes (1904 and 1921–1922) immigrant communities remained solidly behind the workers' movement.

In both of these periods the butcher workmen overcame labor market segmentation and significant social and cultural barriers. Yet both of these movements eventually disintegrated. How can we explain their impressive unity in the face of such striking diversity and still account for their ultimate fragmentation by the early 1920s?

The Sources of Cohesion and Fragmentation

Several factors help to explain the paradox: (1) the degree of social contact in the plants and community among various groups of workers; (2) the structure and strategies of the packinghouse unions themselves; (3) the attitude of community leaders and institutions toward working-class organization; and (4) the general political and economic context and the balance of class forces within which the organization took place.

The broad shape of work and community life suggests that the butcher workmen were deeply divided, but when we go beyond the aggregate statistics to analyze the sort of microscopic units most significant in socialization—work group, tenement house, saloon, union local—we find more interaction among diverse groups than the broader patterns would suggest.

The apparent ethnic and skill stratification in the plants, for example, is somewhat deceptive. As a result of the packers' hiring policies, work groups in packing were quite mixed, ethnically, racially, and in terms of skill. The ethnic breakdown for a 255-man cattle-killing gang at the turn of the century in Table 2 certainly understates the importance of the Slavic immigrants who poured into the industry in the following two decades, but it suggests the diversity in the labor force.

By 1917 the same gang was apt to include many Polish, Lithuanian, and other "new immigrant" common laborers, as well as Black migrants, and a residue of skilled butchers from the ranks of the native-born and the older immigrant groups. The most highly skilled Irish splitter worked with Polish and Black laborers at his side. While the pace was often grueling, killing gangs and other work groups spent part of the day standing around talking, waiting for the next batch of animals to arrive. Even among the newest ethnic groups, there were significant numbers of English-speaking people who provided links between the generations of butcher workmen. This allowed for an informal process of acculturation that facilitated unionization in both periods.[22]

This ethnic pluralism in many of the packinghouse work gangs contrasts sharply with the situation in the steel industry, where ethnic and racial segregation by department minimized interethnic social contact on the job. Significantly, relations in steel between "new" and "old" immigrants and between skilled and unskilled

Table 2 Ethnic Diversity in a Chicago Cattle-killing Gang, 1900
(N = 225)

German	98	English	6	Welsh	2
American	50	French	3	Swedish	1
Irish	29	Dutch	2	Norwegian	1
Polish	13	Canadian	2	Swiss	1
Bohemian	13	Russian	2	Finnish	1
				Italian	1

SOURCE: Charles J. Bushnell, "Some Social Aspects of the Chicago Stock Yards, I," *American Journal of Sociology* 7 (1901), 168.

were notoriously bad. In contrast to packing, labor organization in the steel industry remained weak up until the 1919 strike, and even during this strike steelworkers remained divided, with the new immigrants providing the bulk of the strikers.[23]

In packing, the same work process and labor market that seemed to divide workers from one another also created serious shared grievances that offered a basis for unity. Irregular working hours, frequent lay-offs, pressure for intense speed, and arbitrary foremen were all problems shared by the most skilled knife man and the common laborer. Because of widespread division of labor in the industry, it was fairly easy for common laborers to fill in on more skilled jobs. Thus, the army of laborers gathered outside the Stock Yards gates each morning looking for work represented a very real threat to the wages and conditions of the skilled men.

Saloons in the vicinity of the Stock Yards were another point of social contact among the myriad groups comprising the labor force. While many neighborhood saloons were ethnically segregated, those bordering the Yards and the packing plants were quite mixed, tending to draw workers from particular departments in a plant regardless of skill or ethnicity. Many of the men who owned and tended bar in these saloons were Irish butchers who had retired or been blacklisted for labor activity during the late nineteenth century. It is doubtful that these establishments were racially integrated, but they clearly provided a common ground for the "mature" generation of butcher workmen and the Slavic common laborers. Here, in fact, much of the early organizing went on, while the settlement house served a similar function for the ethnically diverse group of young women workers in the industry.[24]

Turning from workplace to community, we find more common ground. Urban and ethnic historians have noted recently that the popular conception of the "immigrant ghetto" is misleading, since most immigrant neighborhoods were quite heterogeneous, providing frequent contact among a number of ethnic groups.[25] The apparent ethnic residential segregation in Packingtown is a case in point. While ethnic groups certainly clustered, most blocks were mixed, frequently containing two or three and sometimes as many as four or five different ethnic groups. More importantly, individual tenement buildings were also ethnically mixed. Over half of the multifamily Packingtown dwellings in 1905 housed at least two different ethnic groups. Poor ventilation and overcrowding meant that families sat together on front porches and children played in streets and alleys. The social ecology of the community, then, also suggests considerable opportunity for interethnic contact.[26]

Historians have generally viewed the acculturation of immigrant workers as a top-down process and an instrument of social control employed by personnel managers, evening school teachers, and settlement house workers.[27] Such efforts represented an element in the immigrant worker's process of adjustment, but their influence has probably been exaggerated. Formal "Americanization"—through citizenship classes and government naturalization procedures, for example—proceeded very slowly in these communities. For 1908–1909, the University of Chicago Settlement's Citizenship School reported a total enrollment of 112, a tiny fraction of the community's foreign-born. The packers, like most employers, took little interest in Americanization until the war years, when they did sponsor classes and patriotic pageants. In these cases there were larger numbers of workers involved, if only because they were captive audiences at the affairs, which were generally held during work hours. But even the packers' own study of literacy and naturalization conducted during the war found that less than two-thirds of foreign-born women in the plants could speak English. Three-fourths of male immigrant employees were not citizens, and 43 percent of them had not even filed their first papers in the naturalization process, despite the fact that they had been living in the country an average of fifteen years.[28]

Yet such figures do not necessarily mean that immigrant workers failed to come to terms with their new lives. There were alternative conceptions of Americanism to those of management, but historians have largely ignored them. Acculturation of newcomers from diverse backgrounds took place informally at work and in neighborhoods, as well as through the efforts of working-class institutions.[29] In packing, there was an informal but conscious push by union militants to assimilate new groups into the broader working-class community and the labor movement, an effort that might be termed "Americanization from the bottom up."

In a world organized largely along nationality lines, the union was a rare institution because it brought the immigrant into contact with those from other ethnic backgrounds on the basis of shared class interests. Commissioner of Labor Ethelbert Stewart, who studied the problem among Chicago packinghouse workers in 1904, argued that the union represented "the first, and for a time the only, point at which he [the immigrant] touches any influences outside of his clan." Settlement house reformer Mary McDowell agreed. "The labor union has been the only institution that has brought the immigrant in touch with English-speaking men for a common purpose and in preparation for self-government."[30]

If foremen emphasized punctuality, diligence at work, and respect for private property in their Americanization programs and company papers, the union had its own message, which stressed standing up with fellow workers for one's rights and expressing one's opinions freely. An immigrant's introduction to the workings of the American political and economic system frequently came through conversations with fellow workers, discussion and debate at union meetings, and labor movement publications.[31]

In the 1900–1904 period, the Irish were the "Americanizers," and they made their bridges to the new immigrant communities in a number of ways. The use of interpreters at local union meetings encouraged participation by even the most recent immigrants. Hog Butchers' Local 116 provided spontaneous translations into five different languages; the more ethnically diverse sheep butchers required seven. Local 116 found an organizing gold mine in their vice-president, Frank Klawikowski, who spoke several Eastern European languages as well as English. Multilingual union leaflets and newspapers were printed in both periods of organization. The *Butcher Workman* carried columns in Lithuanian and Spanish during the World War I years, as well as in Polish, Bohemian, German, and English. The Stockyards Labor Council, which directed the wartime organizing campaign, appointed Polish, Lithuanian, and Black organizers and collaborated with the Women's Trade Union League on special educational programs for immigrants. In both periods newcomers were quickly integrated into the leadership at both the official local union level as officers and business agents and at the unofficial shop-floor level as committeemen and shop stewards.[32]

Antanas Kaztauskis, a Lithuanian laborer on the cattle-killing floor, described his experience with the union in 1904:

> It has given me more time to read and speak and enjoy life like an American. . . . It is combining all the nationalities. The night I joined the Cattle Butchers' Union I was led into the room by a negro member. With me were Bohemians, Germans and Poles, and Mike Donnelly, the President is an Irishman. . . . We swore to be loyal to our union above everything else except the country, the city and the State . . . to do our best to understand the history of the labor movement, and to do all we could to help it on. . . . I help the movement by being an interpreter for the other Lithuanians who come in. That is why I have learned to speak and write good English. The others do not need me long. . . . they are quickly becoming Americans.[33]

The structure of the union itself could facilitate or obstruct this process of acculturation. In the 1900 to 1904 era, organizers steadfastly refused appeals from some ethnic leaders to organize on a nationality basis, opting instead for departmental locals. All the workers in the city's cattle-killing gangs, for example, were members of the same Amalgamated Meat Cutters and Butcher Workmen's local, regardless of skill or nationality.[34] This arrangement maximized contact and solidarity across ethnic lines and provided the institutional context for the Americanization process. Each local union became an instrument of education, reflecting the values of the labor movement and the broader working class community and imparting these to the immigrants.

In contrast, the complicated organizational structure during World War I actually reinforced existing divisions by creating separate locals based on skill, nationality, and race. The full explanation for this tragic decision remains obscure, but some of the pressure for racially segregated locals came from leaders within the Black community who feared that the voice of the Black minority would be muted in an interracial mass local. These organizational divisions were aggravated by factional leadership conflicts that drew immigrant laborers, Blacks, and native-born whites into opposing camps. The residential, social, and organizational segregation of Black workers in particular deprived them of the informal social contacts and conscious program of assimilation that had drawn Polish and other new immigrant groups into the movement. Black and white union militants made valiant efforts to bridge this gap, while the packers manipulated it to their advantage.[35]

The existence of separate racial and ethnic communities could lead to either unity or fragmentation, depending upon the role played by important community leaders and institutions. In the case of Packingtown, strong ethnic identity and organization facilitated class mobilization. In both of the industry's major strikes, community leaders and ethnic religious, fraternal, and business organizations supported the workers morally and financially, while large crowds comprising all segments of the population turned out to attack scabs. In the 1904 strike, the overwhelming majority of strikebreakers had to be recruited from other neighborhoods and even other cities because of the pressure for community solidarity in Packingtown. Scabs could neither drink nor cash their checks in neighborhood saloons. Polish and Lithuanian newlyweds turned over wedding gifts to the union's strike fund, while priests in all but one of the community's ethnic parishes urged their flocks to remain loyal to the union.[36]

The community's response during the 1921 strike was comparable. The White Eagle Dairy distributed free milk, while a Lithuanian bakery provided hundreds of loaves of bread. Newspapers reflecting a broad range of opinion covered strike activities sympathetically, while both clerical and free-thought fraternal groups offered support. Catholic parishes, fraternal organizations, and small businessmen were particularly supportive in the Polish community, the real backbone of resistance in both strikes. In Packingtown the welfare of the community was seen as linked to that of the union.[37]

The role of community in the Black Belt was quite different. Like the recent Slavic immigrants, most Black packinghouse workers were relative newcomers to urban industrial society; and they faced a difficult process of adjustment. In the case of the white immigrants, unions played an important role in this process and greatly influenced the immigrants' views. In the case of the Black migrants, however, this formative experience was shaped by individuals and institutions whose interests were tied to those of the packers. While some race leaders clearly identified with the union, the Chicago Urban League, the Wabash Avenue YMCA, several Black churches, and other community institutions depended directly on the packers for financial support and urged Black butcher workmen to be loyal to their employers. Certainly the packers took an instrumental view of this relationship. Their contributions to the Urban League, for example, rose sharply during union organizing drives and strikes but fell away after the packers had destroyed labor organization in the industry. More generally, packinghouse employment provided the community's most important source of income. By 1920 the packers employed over half of the Black manufacturing workers in the city. At a time when white employers and craft unions excluded Blacks from many occupations, the packers offered well-paying jobs and critical financial support for Black community institutions.[38]

The packers developed personnel programs tailored to the needs of the Black migrants. "Efficiency clubs," for example, sponsored choral groups, picnics, and a very successful sports program. As a result, the clubs were popular among the migrants, many of whom were searching for social contacts.[39]

The packers supplemented this community strategy with one aimed at creating racial friction within the plants. They victimized Black and white union activists and favored non-union Blacks in hiring and advancement. Considerable evidence suggests that the packers also employed small groups of anti-union Blacks to harass union workers in the weeks preceding the 1919 race riot.

Austin "Heavy" Williams, for example, quickly became a straw boss on the cattle-killing beds at Wilson's and also served as a recruiter for the Wilson Efficiency Club, which met at the Wabash Avenue YMCA. In both capacities Williams counseled new Black workers against becoming involved in the union. While Williams himself was never accused of violence against union men, several Black workers under his influence were. Some carried knives and guns to work, and one of them badly wounded a Black union activist with a heavy pritching stick normally used to move cattle carcasses. Many of the wildcat strikes and other disturbances that broke out in the plants during the weeks before the 1919 race riot involved this small group of anti-union Blacks and similar groups at other packinghouses.[40]

Racial conflict, then, was not simply the inevitable, if tragic, outcome of labor market competition. The packers exploited racial divisions through their selectively paternalistic policies. Their efforts paid off in the 1921–1922 strike when most black workers stayed at their jobs and helped to defeat the union.

Finally, the general political and economic climate and the balance of class forces in Chicago directly influenced the limited success and the ultimate failure of the butcher workmen to overcome their divisions. Union strength was greatest during the economic boom just after the turn of the century and during the severe labor shortage of the war years. It was weakest in the high unemployment of the 1904 recession and the postwar depression. The butcher workmen's organization was particularly vulnerable in such downturns because of the large proportion of unskilled in the industry.

More importantly, union strength in both periods grew within the context of strong social movements. Chicago's working class was highly organized and militant during the early years of this century. Nearly every union in Chicago was a constituent of the powerful Chicago Federation of Labor; and by 1903 these unions had organized more than half of the city's entire labor force, including many unskilled immigrants and more than 35,000 women. During the First World War, journalist Ray Stannard Baker found the city's labor movement "more closely organized, more self-conscious, more advanced in its views" than any other in the country. The progressive wing of the city's labor federation created, staffed, and partly financed the early wartime organizing in the Yards. In 1919 the Federation launched an independent labor party in which packinghouse workers played a prominent role. But labor strength was more than a matter of organizers and money. During the 1904 strike, the packinghouse teamsters went out in sympathy with the butcher workmen, and workers from other neighborhoods helped with picketing. A woman or man working in the Yards during the early twentieth century was surrounded by a labor ethos that bolstered the worker's own efforts.[41]

Likewise, the fragmentation of the Stock Yards movement was part of a general collapse of the labor movement in Chicago and indeed throughout the country. Most of the strikes that engulfed the nation in 1904 and 1921–1922, like those of the butcher workmen in these years, were defensive actions in which workers fought to save their unions. Conditions in Chicago were particularly grim in the years following the First World War. The cumulative effects of economic depression, political factionalism in the labor movement, and the strengthening of nativism and racism among the more Americanized skilled workers caused the virtual disintegration of a movement that had been quite strong during the war.[42]

When class solidarity has emerged in the United States, it has often been crushed by government intervention. Certainly state power hobbled efforts to sustain an interethnic, interracial class movement in the Chicago stockyards. During the early stages of the 1904 strike, police showed restraint and even fraternized with strikers. But as the struggle dragged on, the packers brought their influence to bear on city authorities. Once it became clear that the police, and not the union or crowd, controlled the streets around the Yards, strikebreakers poured in, and the strike was lost.[43]

In keeping with the national pattern during the war and the early 1920s, government action was resolute and decisive at both the federal and local levels. Government arbitration offered the packers a degree of flexibility in the tight wartime labor market and saddled union officials with the responsibility of disciplining their members. The packers took this opportunity to develop an alternative to independent labor organization by erecting an elaborate welfare system and an employee representation plan. But the packers' version of the American Plan included a stick as well as a carrot. Federal arbitration ended precisely when the union was weakest, and the packers declared war with a large wage cut. When workers resisted, local government power was thrown decisively on the side of management. A sweeping injunction outlawed virtually all picketing, and hundreds of mounted policemen invaded the immigrant neighborhoods surrounding the plants. The strike was crushed, ending labor organizations in the industry until the late 1930s.[44]

The Study of Working-Class Formation and Fragmentation

The story of Chicago's packinghouse workers suggests that the problem of working-class fragmentation in the early twentieth century remains a matter for investigation rather than assumption. On one level, the situation provides substance for economic and cultural theories of fragmentation. The labor force was divided through hierarchical job structures that reinforced racial and ethnic divisions. On Chicago's South Side, the varied work experiences of skilled Irish butchers, recent Slavic immigrants, and Black migrants were also reinforced by the physical and social distance separating these groups. Not surprisingly, many of the packers' personnel policies were designed to accentuate these barriers.

But this study also suggests that such divisions can easily be overdrawn. The butcher workmen were clearly divided between primary and secondary labor markets, but in opposition to this tendency toward fragmentation there were countervailing pressures inherent in the changing character of manufacturing in these years. Much larger plants with finely integrated production systems could link the fates of very large, socially diverse groups of workers who might otherwise have had little in common with one another.[45] In packing, a significant intensification of work and the downward pressure on wages caused by casual hiring methods and the army of unemployed at the Yards gate provided a rationale for more skilled, Americanized butcher workmen to reach out to the unskilled Black and Slavic newcomers. In a peculiar way, the hiring practices of the packers and the structure of work in the industry actually facilitated this effort. Rather than dividing the various social groups that composed the labor force, mixed work gangs brought them together, presented them with shared grievances, and offered the opportunity to begin an informal process of socialization.

The effects of social and cultural division are also complex and require further study. In the community, as in the workplace, there were numerous points of contact among white immigrant workers and between them and native-born whites. The existence of strong racial and ethnic subcultures, for example, was not necessarily an impediment to class formation. As Greene has shown for Slavic coalminers and Brody for immigrant steelworkers, the cohesion of such communities often facilitated organization and mobilization in strikes.[46] This was clearly the case with the new immigrants in packing during both union periods.

In addition to analyzing the position of important community leaders and institutions on the question of interethnic and interracial working class solidarity, we must also consider the influence of both employers and the broader working-class movement in the process of integrating newcomers into the industrial workplace and community. The packers and the unions contended for the loyalty of the new immigrants and the Black migrants. Considering the diversity of the labor force, the unions were remarkably successful at integrating the immigrants in both periods of organization. Although the Black community was divided over the issue of unionization, the labor movement was generally less successful among the Black migrants. Here paternalistic personnel practices, continuing discrimination in the labor market, racially segregated neighborhoods, and a lingering suspicion of the "white man's union" combined to keep most Black butcher workmen in the packers' camp. Because of the diversity of the working-class population in the United States, a careful analysis of the conditions under which various minorities "settled in" is essential to understanding the problem of class formation and fragmentation.

Here the Chicago case study draws attention to the social, economic, and political context—the situation within which class formation took place. In both periods of union strength, cohesion and organization along class lines developed as part of a general upsurge supported by a militant, well-organized labor movement and by mobilized ethnic working-class communities. Fragmentation and decline came within the context of economic depression, unemployment, and government and employer attacks on the metropolitan and national labor movements. Under such pressures, the racial, ethnic, and skill "fault lines" in the broader working-class community contributed to the disintegration of the class movement. But such diversity is not sufficient in and of itself to explain the relative weakness of class identity.

The Chicago case study demonstrates that there are important questions that must be probed before conventional assumptions concerning class formation and fragmentation in the highly diverse American population are accepted. How common were relations across skill, ethnic, and racial lines, and what form did they take? How did these relations affect class organization and conflict? What is the most realistic way to conceptualize the connection between class and ethnic consciousness in light of the fact that some groups exhibited both simultaneously? Such questions can lead to a better understanding of the remaking of the American working class in the early years of the corporate political economy.

Notes

For comments on earlier versions of this essay, the author wishes to acknowledge the efforts of David Brody, John Bodnar, Steven Vincent, and Anthony LaVopa. Thanks are also due to Jenni Barrett for her work on the map. An earlier version of this essay appeared in the *Journal of Social History* 18 (1984), 37–56. The author and editor express their appreciation to the journal for the right to reprint the material here.

1. Philip Taylor, *The Distant Magnet: European Emigration to the U.S.A.* (New York: Harper and Row, Harper Torchbook Edition, 1972), 48–65; David Montgomery, *Workers' Control in America: Studies in Work, Technology, and Labor Struggles* (New York and London: Cambridge University Press, 1979), 34–37; Daniel Nelson, *Managers and Workers: Origins of the New Factory System in the United States, 1880–1920* (Madison: University of Wisconsin Press, 1975), 81–85, 145–47; David Brody, *Workers in Industrial America: Essays in the Twentieth Century Struggle* (New York: Oxford University Press, 1980), 14–21.

2. Herbert Gutman, *Work, Culture, and Society in Industrializing America: Essays in Working Class and Social History* (New York: Alfred Knopf, 1976), chap. 1.

3. David Montgomery, "Gutman's Nineteenth Century America," *Labor History* 19 (1978): 416–29; idem, *Workers' Control in America*, pp. 9–31; Richard J. Oestreicher, "Solidarity and Fragmentation: Working People and Class Consciousness in Detroit, 1877–1895" (Ph.D. diss., Michigan State University, 1979), pp. 122–32, chap. 5. See also E. J. Hobsbawm, "Custom, Wages, and Workload in the Nineteenth Century," in *Labouring Men: Studies in the History of Labour* (London: Weidenfeld and Nicolson, 1964), 344–70.

4. Oestreicher, "Solidarity and Fragmentation," chap. 8; John Bodnar, *Immigration and Industrialization: Ethnicity in an American Mill Town* (Pittsburgh: University of Pittsburgh Press, 1977), chaps. 1 and 2; David Brody, *Steelworkers in America, the Nonunion Era* (New York: Harper and Row, Harper Torch Book Edition, 1969).

5. The argument summarized here is David Brody's in *Steelworkers in America.* On reemigration of the "new immigrants" of the early twentieth century as a group, see J. D. Gould, "European Inter-Continental Emigration, The Road Home: Return Migration from the U.S.A.," *Journal of European Economic History* 9 (1980): 41–112; Frank Thistelthwaite, "European Migration Overseas in the Nineteenth and Twentieth Centuries," in *Population Movements in Modern European History*, ed. Herbert Moller (New York: Macmillan, 1964), 73–91. See also, "A Century of Immigration," *Monthly Labor Review* 18 (1924): 1–19.

6. Richard Edwards, *Contested Terrain: The Transformation of the Workplace in the Twentieth Century* (New York: Basic Books, 1977), especially chaps. 9 and 10; David M. Gordon, Richard C. Edwards, and Michael Reich, *Segmented Work, Divided Workers: The Historical Transformation of Labor in the United States* (London and New York: Cambridge University Press, 1982); idem, eds. *Labor Market Segmentation* (Lexington, Mass.: D. C. Heath, 1975); Andrew Friedman, *Industry and Labour: Class Struggle at Work and Monopoly Capitalism* (London: Macmillan, 1978); Jill Rubery, "Structured Labour Markets, Worker Organization, and Low Pay," *Cambridge Journal of Economics* 2 (1978): 17–36.

7. On the concept of a labor aristocracy, see Frederick Engels, "Preface to the English Edition," *The Condition of the Working Class in England* (London: Panther Books, 1969), 29–35; E. J. Hobsbawm, "The Labor Aristocracy in Nineteenth Century Britain," in *Labouring Men*, pp. 272–315. For critical evaluations of the theory, see John Field, "British Historians and the Concept of a Labor Aristocracy," *Radical History Review* 19 (1979): 61–85; and the conference papers abstracted in *Bulletin of the Society for the Study of Labour History* 40 (1980): 6–11.

8. James Weinstein, "The IWW and American Socialism," *Socialist Revolution* 1 (1970): 3–42; idem, *The Corporate Ideal in the Liberal State* (Boston: Beacon Press, 1968); Ronald Radosh, "The Corporate Ideology of American Labor Leaders from Gompers to Hillman," *Studies on the Left* 6 (1966): 66–68; idem, "Labor and the American Economy: The 1922 Railroad Shop Crafts Strike and the 'B & O Plan'," in *Building the Organizational Society: Essays on Associational Activities*, ed. Jerry Israel (New York: Free Press, 1972), 73–87; Gabriel Kolko, *Main Currents in Modern American History* (New York: Harper and Row, 1977), 80–83, 176–77.

9. Kolko, *Main Currents in Modern American History,* chap. 3. (The quotation is on p. 99.)

10. For a sociologist's view of the problem, see Gerald Rosenblum, *Immigrant Workers and American Labor Radicalism* (New York: Basic Books, 1968).

11. The "Big Five" included Swift, Armour, Hammond, Morris, and Schwarzchild and Sulzberger (later, Wilson and Company).

12. John R. Commons, "Labor Conditions in Slaughtering and Meat Packing," in *Labor and Trade Union Problems,* ed. John R. Commons (Boston: Ginn and Company, 1905), 223–28; Ethelbert Stewart, "Productivity in Meat Packing," *Monthly Labor Review* 18 (1924): 14–21; U.S. Bureau of Corporations, *Report on the Beef Industry* (Washington, D.C.: Government Printing Office, 1905), 17. On the growth of a national market for dressed meat and the structure of the big packing corporations, see Alfred Chandler, "The Origins of Big Business in American Industry," *Business History Review* 33 (1959): 1–31; and Mary Yeager, *Competition and Regulation: The Development of Oligopoly in the Meat Packing Industry* (Greenwich, Conn.: JAI Press, 1981); and on the early technology in the industry, Siegfried Giedion, *Mechanization Takes Command: A Contribution to Anonymous History* (New York: W. W. Norton, 1948), 93–96, 213–40, and the illustrations on 89, 97, and 217. For a full analysis of the transformation of work referred to here, see James R. Barrett, "Immigrant Workers in Early Mass Production Industry: Work Rationalization and Job Control Conflicts in Chicago's Packing Houses, 1900–1904," in *German Workers in Industrial Chicago, 1850–1910: A Comparative Perspective,* ed. Hartmut Keil and John B. Jentz (DeKalb, Illinois: Northern Illinois University Press, 1983), 104–24.

13. Commons, "Labor Conditions in Slaughtering and Meat Packing," pp. 243, 245–46; U.S. Bureau of Corporations, *Report on the Beef Industry,* pp. 17–18. See also U.S. Department of Labor, *Bulletin Number 252* (Washington, D.C.: Government Printing Office, 1919). For discussions of the casual labor problem in Chicago, see Carlton Parker, *The Casual Laborer* (New York: Harcourt, Brace, and Howe, 1920), chap. 2; Grace Abbott, "The Chicago Employment Agency and the Immigrant Worker," *American Journal of Sociology* 14 (1908): 289–305; and Alice Solenberger, *One Thousand Homeless Men: A Study of Original Records* (New York: Russell Sage Foundation, 1919), 7–8.

14. U.S. Bureau of Labor Statistics, *Report Number 56* (Washington, D.C.: Government Printing Office, 1905), 3; U.S. Immigration Commission, *Reports, XIII, Immigrants in Industry, Part 11, Slaughtering and Meat Packing* (Washington, D.C.: Government Printing Office, 1911), 199–201; Alma Herbst, *The Negro in the Slaughtering and Meat Packing Industry in Chicago* (Boston: Houghton Mifflin and Co., 1933), xxii; Paul S. Taylor, *Mexican Labor in the United States: Chicago and the Calumet Region* (Berkeley: University of California Press, 1930), 37–40, 50–51, 74, 153; Sophonisba Breckinridge and Edith Abbott, "Women in Industry: The Chicago Stockyards," *Journal of Political Economy* 19 (1911): 632–54; *Fourteenth U.S. Census, 1920, Manufactures* (Washington, D.C.: Government Printing Office, 1923), 364.

15. John R. Commons, Introduction to Elizabeth Brandeis and Don D. Lescohier, *History of Labor in the United States, 1896–1932,* vol. 3 (New York, 1935; reprint, New York: Augustus M. Kelley, 1966), xxv.

16. Herbst, *The Negro in the Slaughtering and Meat Packing Industry,* pp. 16–17; Ethelbert Stewart, "The Influence of Trade Unions on Immigrants," U.S. Bureau of Labor Statistics, *Bulletin Number 56* (1905), reprinted in *The Making of America, Labor,* ed. Robert M. LaFollette (Chicago, 1906; reprint, New York: Arno Press, 1969), 228; Sterling Spero and Abram L. Harris, *The Black Worker* (1931; reprint, New York: Atheneum, 1968), 264.

17. Harry Braverman, *Labor and Monopoly Capital: The Degradation of Work in the Twentieth Century* (New York: Monthly Review Press, 1974); Daniel Nelson, *Managers and Workers;* Edwards, *Contested Terrain;* Gordon, Edwards, and Reich, *Segmented Work, Divided Workers.* Each of these works, however, has influenced my own approach considerably.

18. On Packingtown, Bridgeport, and Canaryville, see James R. Barrett, "Work and Community in 'The Jungle' " (Ph.D. diss., University of Pittsburgh, 1981), chap. 3 and pp. 326–28, 348–52. The best social and economic profile of the Black Belt in this era is Allen Spear, *Black Chicago: The Making of a Negro Ghetto* (Chicago: University of Chicago Press, 1967), 129–200.

19. For a thorough, scholarly analysis of the riot and the social problems from which it sprang, see William M. Tuttle, *Race Riot: Chicago in the Red Summer of 1919* (New York: Atheneum, 1970). Tuttle, however, argues for a causal link between the growth of class consciousness and organization on the one hand and the growth of white racism on the other. In my own view, this relationship was far more complex than Tuttle's formulation suggests. See Barrett, "Work and Community in 'The Jungle,' " pp. 318–58.

20. On unionization in this era, see David Brody, *The Butcher Workmen: A Study in Unionization* (Cambridge, Mass.: Harvard University Press, 1963), chap. 2; Commons, "Labor Conditions in Slaughtering and Meat Packing," pp. 243–45; and Barrett, "Work and Community in 'The Jungle,' " chap. 4. On shop floor organization and conflict, see Barrett, "Immigrant Workers in Early Mass Production Industry," pp. 110–16. Leslie Woodcock Tentler, in *Wage Earning Women: Industrial Work and Family in the United States* (New York: Oxford University Press, 1979) argues for the docility of women workers in this era.

21. Brody, *The Butcher Workmen*, chap. 4; Barrett, "Work and Community in 'The Jungle,' " pp. 306–8, 316–25.

22. For the ethnic and skill composition of work gangs, see the Commons article cited in note 12 and Carl Thompson, "Labor in the Packing Industry," *Journal of Political Economy* 15 (1906): 88–108. For figures on English speakers among the new immigrants, see U.S. Immigration Commission, *Reports, XIII, Immigrants in Industry, Part 11*, p. 260; and for unionization as a process of acculturation, Barrett, "Work and Community in 'The Jungle,' " chap. 4.

23. Bodnar, *Immigrants and Industrialization*, pp. 35–50; Brody, *Steelworkers in America*, pp. 120–21, 246–47, 260–61.

24. Dominic Pacyga, "Villages of Packinghouses and Steel Mills: The Polish Worker on Chicago's South Side, 1880–1921" (Ph.D. diss., University of Illinois, Chicago, 1981), pp. 189–91; Thompson, "Labor in the Packing Industry," pp. 107–8; "Prohibition Survey of the Stockyards Community," 1926, Mary McDowell Papers, Folder No. 7, Chicago Historical Society; Perry Duis, "The Saloon and the Public City: Chicago and Boston, 1880–1920" (Ph.D. diss., University of Chicago, 1975), pp. 639, 645–46; Charles J. Bushnell, "Some Social Aspects of the Chicago Stock Yards," pt. 2, *American Journal of Sociology* 3 (1901): map number five. See also, John M. Kingsdale, "The 'Poor Man's Club': Social Functions of the Urban Working Class Saloon," *American Quarterly* 25 (1973): 472–89.

25. Thomas Philpott, *The Slum and the Ghetto* (New York: Oxford University Press, 1978), 67, 72, 141; Kathleen N. Conzen, "Immigrants, Immigrant Neighborhoods, and Ethnic Identity: Historical Issues," *Journal of American History* 66 (1979): 603–15.

26. These observations are based on Edith Abbott and Sophonisba Breckinridge, "Housing Conditions in Chicago, III: Back of the Yards," *American Journal of Sociology* 16 (1911): 435–68 and on a computer-assisted analysis of a unique 1905 manuscript census of the community. For a full description of this data base, see Barrett, "Work and Community in 'The Jungle,' " Appendix B.

27. Edward G. Hartman, *The Movement to Americanize the Immigrant* (New York: Columbia University Press, 1948). For the efforts of managers and middle-class reformers to use Americanization programs as a means of social control, see Gerd Korman, "Americanization at the Factory Gate," *Industrial and Labor Relations Review* 18 (1965): 396–419; Nelson, *Managers and Workers*, pp. 144–45; Brody, *Steelworkers in America*, pp. 189–197; Stephen Meyer, "Adapting the Immigrant to the Line: Americanization in the Ford Factory, 1914–1921," *Journal of Social History* 14 (1980): 67–82. The most subtle treatment of this theme remains

Herbert Gutman's "Work, Culture, and Society in Industrializing America, 1815–1919" in his collection of essays under the same title.

28. *Chicago Record Herald*, 10 October 1909; "Citizenship School in 1908–1909 School Year", and "Community Study, 1918," Mary McDowell Papers, Folders 11 and 20, Chicago Historical Society. On the packers' Americanization programs, see *National Provisioner* 63 (25 September 1920): 18–19, 25–26, 42–43; *Swift Arrow* 1 (12 May 1922), 5; Records of the Mediation and Conciliation Service, Record Group 280, Case 33/864, Box 44, pp. 632–82, National Archives and Records Service, Suitland, Maryland.

29. For brief, perceptive comments on informal socialization of immigrants at work, see Montgomery, *Workers' Control in America*, pp. 42–43; and for a treatment that considers the efforts of both management and unions to Americanize Slavic immigrants, see Neil Betten, "Polish-American Steelworkers: Americanization through Industry and Labor," *Polish American Studies* 33 (1976): 31–42.

30. Stewart, "The Influence of Trade Unions on Immigrants," p. 226. McDowell is quoted in Howard Wilson, *Mary McDowell, Neighbor* (Chicago: University of Chicago Press, 1928), 99.

31. Stewart, "The Influence of Trade Unions on Immigrants," pp. 231–33.

32. Ibid., pp. 229–31; *Amalgamated Meat Cutters and Butcher Workmen Official Journal*, July 1901, May 1902, November 1902, and March 1903; Olive Anderson, "Chicago League Organizing Stockyards Women Workers," *Life and Labor* 7 (April 1918): 84. I derived the following breakdown for 25 floor committeemen for whom I was able to determine race and ethnicity in the period 1918–1919: Polish—9, Black—5, Bohemian—3, German—3, Irish—3, and Lithuanian—2.

33. Antanas Kaztauskis, "From Lithuania to the Chicago Stockyards—An Autobiography," *Independent* 57 (4 August 1904): 248.

34. Theodore Glocker, *The Government of American Trade Unions* (Baltimore, Md.: Johns Hopkins University Press, 1913), 19–20, 28; Commons, "Labor Conditions in Slaughtering and Meat Packing," p. 233.

35. For evidence of Black support for segregated locals, see the testimony of William Z. Foster, Secretary of the Stockyards Labor Council, before the Chicago Commission on Race Relations in the Commission's *The Negro in Chicago* (Chicago: University of Chicago Press, 1922), 428–29; William Z. Foster, *American Trade Unionism* (New York: International Publishers, 1947): 22–23; Alma Herbst, *The Negro in the Slaughtering and Meat Packing Industry*, pp. 30–31. On factionalism in the World War I movement, see Barrett, "Work and Community in 'The Jungle,'" pp. 318–67.

36. *Chicago Tribune*, 20, 24, 26, 29, and 30 July, and 5 and 8 August 1904.

37. *Dziennik Ziednoczenia*, 4 and 15 February 1922; *Dziennik Chicagoski*, 1, 3, 5, 7, 9, 10, 11, 12, and 23 January, and 4 and 10 February 1922. See also Dominic Pacyga, "Crisis and Community: Back of the Yards, 1921," *Chicago History* 6 (1977): 167–77. (Translated articles and editorials from the Polish newspapers are available in the Chicago Foreign Language Press Survey, which is on microfilm at the Chicago Historical Society.)

38. Spear, *Black Chicago*, pp. 169–74; Tuttle, *Race Riot*, pp. 99–100, 140, 147–148, 151; Arvarh Strickland, *History of the Chicago Urban League* (Urbana: University of Illinois Press, 1966), 38, 44–45, 48–49, 74; Walter A. Fogel, *The Negro in the Meat Industry* (Philadelphia: University of Pennsylvania Press, 1970), 29; Chicago Commission on Race Relations, *The Negro in Chicago*, p. 147. See also James R. Grossman, "A Dream Deferred: Black Migration to Chicago, 1916–1921" (Ph.D. diss., University of California, Berkeley, 1982), pp. 269–77.

39. Chicago Commission on Race Relations, *The Negro in Chicago*, pp. 147–48; Tuttle, *Race Riot*, p. 151; Grossman, "A Dream Deferred," pp. 272–274.

40. See the testimony of Robert Bedford, William Bremer, Gus Grabe, Frank Custer, Austin "Heavy" Williams, Jack Johnstone, Joseph Hodges, and Louis Mihora before Judge Joseph Alschuler in the Records of the Federal Mediation and Conciliation Service, RG 280, Case 33/864, Boxes 42 and 46, at the National Archives and

Record Service, Suitland, Maryland. See also Grossman, "A Dream Deferred," chap. 5.

41. Steve Sapolsky, "Class Conscious Belligerents: The Teamsters and the Class Struggle in Chicago, 1901–1905" (unpublished manuscript, University of Pittsburgh, 1974); Glocker, *The Government of American Trade Unions*, p. 24; Montgomery, *Workers' Control in America*, pp. 57–58; Foster, *American Trade Unionism*, pp. 19–22. The quotation, from Ray Stannard Baker, is in Tuttle, *Race Riot*, p. 141.

42. Montgomery, *Workers' Control in America*, pp. 20, 97. For an analysis of the general decline of the labor movement in these years, see David Montgomery, "New Tendencies in Europe and the United States, 1916–1922," in *Work, Community and Power: The Experience of Labor in Europe and America, 1900–1925*, ed. James E. Cronin and Carmen Siriani (Philadelphia: Temple University Press, 1983), 95–97; and for the relationship between this broader context and the disintegration of the movement in the Stockyards, Barrett, "Work and Community in 'The Jungle,'" pp. 318–76.

43. Howard B. Meyer, "The Policing of Labor Disputes in Chicago: A Study" (Ph.D. diss., University of Chicago, 1929), chap. 9; *Chicago Tribune*, 14 August 1904.

44. Pacyga, "Crisis and Community," pp. 166–77; Benjamin Stolberg, "The Stockyards Strike," *Nation* 141 (25 January 1922), 90–92; *Dziennik Chicagoski*, 8 and 9 December 1921. The combination of court injunctions and massive police force was employed to crush strikes in industries and communities throughout the country during 1921 and 1922. See Montgomery, *Workers' Control in America*, 160; Edwin Witte, *The Government in Labor Disputes* (New York and London: McGraw-Hill, 1932).

45. Gordon, Edwards, and Reich, *Segmented Work, Divided Workers*, chap. 4.

46. Victor Greene, *The Slavic Community on Strike* (South Bend, Ind.: Notre Dame University Press, 1968); Brody, *Steelworkers in America*; David Brody, *Labor in Crisis: The Steel Strike of 1919* (Philadelphia: J. B. Lippincott Co., 1965).

MAXINE SCHWARTZ SELLER

The Uprising of the Twenty Thousand: Sex, Class, and Ethnicity in the Shirtwaist Makers' Strike of 1909

On 22 November 1909 thousands of shirtwaist makers crowded into Cooper Union in New York City to consider a general strike in the trade. This was an unusual strike meeting because the potential strikers were women, most of them Jewish immigrants, and because they were very young, some only thirteen or fourteen years old. "I think [Samuel] Gompers must have been astounded to stand up on that platform and look into that audience," said Leon Stein, historian emeritus of the International Ladies Garment Workers' Union. "He was accustomed to seeing railroad workers, muscle, miners with muscle, teamsters who knew how to throw horses around, and he looked out into this audience and when he began to talk he said, "My dear *children,* do you know what you are going to do now?"[1]

Despite their youth, the shirtwaist makers assembled at Cooper Union were not "children," and before the evening was over they knew exactly what they were going to do. Although most had never been to a union meeting before, they knew that several of the largest factories in their industry were already on strike and that workers had already been beaten and arrested on the picket line. Before the formal speeches began, the young women waiting in Cooper Union discussed the possibility of a general strike among themselves. The *Jewish Daily Forward* recorded fragments of their conversation. "What if a general strike is decided upon? Who knows how many will join in it? Who can tell how long it may last?" They were nervous and apprehensive,. but they were also desperate for change. "When will there be another chance to improve the conditions? Are we to suffer forever?"[2]

After the meeting was called to order, the shirtwaist makers listened for two hours as an apparently endless stream of officials, including Gompers, talked to them in general terms, stressing solidarity while advising caution and deliberation. Because of the speakers, or perhaps in spite of them, the young workers made their decision. When one of their number, Clara Lemlich, interrupted the formal program to move that a general strike be called immediately, they rose in a body, cheering, stamping their feet, and shouting their approval. When the chairman asked if they would pledge loyalty to the strike with the traditional Jewish oath, thousands of right arms shot up and thousands of voices responded in Yiddish, "If I turn traitor to the cause I now pledge, may this hand wither from the arm I now raise." By the next evening over twenty thousand shirtwaist makers had walked away from their jobs. Although thirty thousand eventually participated, the strike became known as the "uprising of the twenty thousand."[3]

In the Progressive Era, the uprising of the twenty thousand, the largest women's strike in American history, captured the imagination of journalists, clergy, intellectuals, and reformers. With unions struggling toward respectability, it was the first major step toward the organization of the growing garment industry. It was an immigrant women's strike, at a time when immigrants were despised as strikebreakers and women were considered unorganizable. When it ended, on 15 February 1910, after thirteen weeks of bitter struggle, it was hailed, with as much optimism as accuracy, as a victory for labor and for women.

This study will review the origins, development, and results of the strike. It will explore the interaction of sex, ethnicity, and social class among the strikers, their supporters, and their opponents. Finally, it will argue that the "girls' strike" was part of a tradition of labor activism among immigrant women often overlooked in its own time as well as today.

The Shirtwaist Trade: Workers and Working Conditions

Between 1890 and 1910 there was a sharp increase in the number and proportion of women in the American labor force, much of it due to the influx of southern and eastern Europeans. By 1900 three-quarters of the women employed in factories were immigrants or their daughters.[4] At the time of the shirtwaist strike, the garment trades were the largest and richest industrial employers of women, the fifth largest industry in the nation, and notorious for fostering "that infamous Sweating System, the lingering traces of which the shirtwaist makers strike attempted to wipe out."[5]

The manufacture of shirtwaists (women's blouses) began in New York City in the early 1890s. While many older types of garment manufacture were done at home, shirtwaists were made in factories,

This photograph from the December 1909 *Independent* shows the shirtwaist makers on the picket line. Foreign-born and poor, they honored their cause by picketing in their holiday best, including, for those who could afford it, the broad-brimmed decorated hats that replaced the immigrant kerchiefs as symbols of Americanization and respectability. *Independent,* 23 December 1909, p. 1418.

or shops, as they were called, where workers could gather, communicate, and, potentially, organize. By 1909 more than 600 shops in the city employed more than 30,000 workers. Most of the work was done in shops with 20 to 50 workers; but a few dozen large firms, employing several hundred each, dominated the industry.[6]

Between 80 and 85 percent of the workers were women. Slightly more than half (including virtually all the men) were Russian Jews;

35 percent were Italians, 7 percent were mainstream Americans, a few were black, and the remainder, also few, were from at least ten other European backgrounds. The shirtwaist makers were mainly single, most of them under twenty. They worked to help support their families, a task for which the wages of one male breadwinner, especially an immigrant, were usually inadequate. In the case of the many Jewish women who immigrated alone, the wages made it nearly impossible to maintain themselves.

While most middle-class American women expected to be supported by a father or a husband, immigrant women were accustomed to producing as well as consuming the family income. Paid work outside the home was common among South Italian women, usually under the protection of male relatives, as social mores dictated. East European Jewish women kept shops, peddled, and earned money in many other ways, supporting families that sometimes included husbands who devoted all their time to religious study. Though they might have looked forward to leaving the work force after marriage, neither Italian nor Jewish young women considered work itself unusual or oppressive.[7]

Working conditions in the shirtwaist factories, however, were oppressive. A normal workweek was fifty-six hours, but rush seasons meant long hours of overtime at no extra pay, and slack seasons meant waiting hours before being sent home with no work and no pay. Workers, who were paid by the piece—and therefore often forced themselves to work at a pace that was destructive of their health—received their money in tiny, easily lost tickets, redeemable for cash at a later time.[8]

The work force was stratified by age, ethnicity, and sex. Those experienced operators—some 50 to 60 percent of the workforce—who sewed garments together, pressed them, or made buttonholes, trimmings, or other specialized parts earned $7 to $12 a week, with native-born Americans occupying the higher-paid jobs. "Learners," the youngest girls and newest immigrants, made up about a third of the work force and earned $3 or $4 a week for such tasks as basting or removing threads. Men held the most skilled positions, earning $15 to $23 a week as cutters or pattern or sample makers. Moreover, employers often used the men as subcontractors, giving each a set fee for the production of a quantity of merchandise. The actual work was done by three to eight so-called learners (some of them skilled workers desperate for employment) recruited by the subcontractor and paid as little as possible to maximize his profit.[9]

Employers charged the workers for needles, electricity, and machine parts, at rates that gave them a 20 to 25 percent profit.

Workers were charged twenty-five cents for a locker to hold a hat "often not worth a quarter"; they also were made to pay for the boxes they used as chairs.[10] If they spoiled a piece of cloth, they were fined several times its value. The workers complained of constant harassment, "of forewomen following a girl if she left the room hurrying her back again . . . of frequent 'mistakes' in pay envelopes hard and embarrassing to rectify; of a system of registration on the time clock that stole more than 20 minutes from the lunch hour; of the office clock . . . put back an hour so that they should not know that they are working overtime."[11]

Despite these conditions, little progress was made in unionization before the general strike of 1909. In 1901 the newly organized Ladies Waist Makers Union of Greater New York became Local 12 of the one-year-old International Ladies Garment Workers' Union (ILGWU). The leaders of Local 12, Russian Jewish men, were better at rhetoric than organization. "Murder! The exploiters, the bloodsuckers, the manufacturers. . . . Pay your dues. . . . Down with the capitalists! Hurrah!" proclaimed their circulars, probably frightening the workers more than the employers. Whatever the reasons, its membership was down to six in 1905, when it reorganized as Local 25. By the fall of 1909, Local 25 had only 100 members and four dollars in its treasury.[12]

Organization was difficult because the work force was scattered among many small shops, because most aspects of the trade were easily learned and because a steady influx of immigrant labor in need of immediate work was always on hand to replace workers. Organization was further impeded by jurisdictional disputes between the ILGWU and the Industrial Workers of the World (IWW) and by the panic and depression of 1907 and 1908. Yet another impediment was the fact that unionization of immigrant industries was not a priority for the largely skilled, native-born members of the American Federation of Labor, which ignored Italian garment workers, expressed hostility to the socialist-oriented United Hebrew Trades (which organized Jewish workers in New York City) and, in order to protect jobs, favored restriction of immigation from southern and eastern Europe and from Asia.[13]

Ethnic divisions impeded early efforts to organize, as did the female composition of the work force. The Jewish male union leaders considered Italian women workers "slow" and "stupid" and therefore did not reach out to them.[14] Common wisdom held that women workers (regardless of ethnicity) were unorganizable because they were by nature unaggressive, or because, anticipating marriage, they lacked permanent commitment to their jobs or because, supported by fathers or husbands, they worked only for "pin money."[15]

Although the shirtwaist makers did not work for pin money, there were real conflicts between union membership and traditional sex roles. Single as well as married women had domestic responsibilities that, added to a long workday, left little time for union activities. Some believed that "nice" girls did not join unions or, as a young artificial flower maker put it, "I got a fellow. Vy should I join?"[16] Traditional South Italian women could not attend meetings at night without a male member of the family, a cultural factor that helps to account for the overwhelming preponderance of Jewish women at the historic Cooper Union meeting. Because of their low salaries, women of all ethnic groups were discouraged by high dues; and the men's-club atmosphere of meetings, often held at late hours in saloons, was also discouraging. Even in predominantly women's trades, such as the shirtwaist industry, male unionists often ignored women or actively discouraged their participation.[17] Tension between male unionists and the female shirtwaist makers was aggravated by the fact that the former might be subcontractors for whom the latter worked.

"Can women alone strike, and strike successfully?" asked the *Outlook* in December of 1909, referring to the uprising of the shirtwaist makers.[18] The answer should have been clear. Women in the United States had a long tradition of labor activism.[19] Women's strikes were frequent in the nineteenth century, and the Knights of Labor had women organizers (several of them Irish immigrants) in both mixed and women's locals. By 1900, organized women were an important component of the bookbinding, textile, and hat and cap trades, among many others.[20] For their part, many immigrant women had experienced religious, political, and economic oppression in their homelands and had sacrificed much to come to the United Sates; they demanded that America live up to its promise of justice and a better life.

Immigrant women, married as well as single, were a greater proportion of the work force than native-born American women. They also developed a history of activism. Bohemian women in the New York cigar-making trade, Swedish women in the Chicago garment industries, and Polish "spool girls" in the textile mills of Chicopee, Massachusetts, showed that immigrant women could organize and strike on their own behalf, often more militantly than their male counterparts.[21]

Despite cultural and sex role barriers, "given a chance, women were devoted and successful union members," wrote labor historian Alice Kessler-Harris.[22] They were often denied this chance, however, because of opposition on two fronts—from the union itself and from the employer. Many male unionists were apprehensive about the increasing number of women workers, fearing for their own jobs, or were reluctant to devote resources to the organization of "temporary" workers. Statements from Gompers and other high-ranking AFL officials at the turn of the century indicate that they favored organization of women currently in the labor market in order to protect men's wages. Their ultimate goal, however, was to provide a "family" wage for men, so that all women could be sent home, in the interests of motherhood, the family, and civilization.[23]

The "Uprising"

Employers were not ambivalent. They saw women, especially immigrant women, as a reserve labor force whose main value was cheapness. Manufacturers in the highly competitive shirtwaist trade made every effort to thwart unionization. They deliberately seated Yiddish-speaking women next to women who spoke only Italian to prevent communication and fostered ethnic discord by spreading false rumors about one group and attributing them to the other.[24] Employers also formed tightly controlled "employees associations" and, when all else failed, fired union sympathizers.

Not surprisingly, the union itself was the issue that touched off the strike of 1909. The year 1909 brought prosperity back to the garment industry. It also brought new activism into New York's labor movement, as former IWW members and immigrants influenced by revolutionary movements in Europe entered the locals. Critical of the cautious "pennywise business" ways of experienced ILGWU and AFL officials, who stressed building membership and treasuries and discouraged strikes, the newcomers wanted action.[25]

In 1908 the Triangle Waist Factory had organized a company union, the Triangle Employees Benevolent Association, "to prevent this irresponsible union [Local 25] from gaining the upper hand."[26] In September 1909 a dispute over the distribution of the Association's funds caused many workers to question its good faith and turn to Local 25. Although they met with Local 25 and the United Hebrew Trades behind locked doors and drawn shades, the company discovered their identities and dismissed them, claiming a lull in the trade. When the company advertised for more help the next day, Local 25 called a strike. A strike broke out independently at the Leiserson Company, so that by October workers from two of the largest shops were walking the picket line.

The Triangle Company hired prostitutes and pimps to harass the strikers, while Leiserson surrounded its shop with professional thugs, called "gorillas." Twelve to twenty strikers were beaten up in a single day; their assailants went unpunished. The strikers, however, were regularly arrested and fined up to ten dollars—ironically, for assault.[27] According to Helen Marot, an observer from the Women's Trade Union League, it was a women's strike from the beginning. "The men strikers were intimidated and lost heart, but the women carried on the picketing, suffering arrest and abuse from the police and the guards employed by the manufacturers. At the end of the third week they appealed to the Women's Trade Union League (WTUL) to protect them, if they could, from false arrest."[28]

The WTUL was an association of trade union and middle-class women (the latter known as "allies") organized in 1904 to promote the welfare of working women through unionization, legislation, and education, with emphasis in 1909 on unionization.[29] Seeing that the strikers were being treated unfairly, the League intervened in their support. On 4 November, Mary Dreier, the wealthy and socially prominent president of the New York branch of the WTUL, was arrested on the picket line—where she had been attacked by a scab—and charged with assault. "There was consternation when the sergeant learned that the prisoner was not a working girl, a striker, but a cultured and wealthy woman." The sergeant ordered Miss Dreier's release and apologized.[30]

Involvement of the New York WTUL brought the strikers respectability and publicity. With the exception of the labor press, newspapers had heretofore ignored the strike. Dreier's arrest, however, made excellent copy. In the weeks that followed, the press aroused public sympathy by writing not only about the society women arrested in the garment district but also about the economic plight of the "girls" and their treatment on the picket line and in the police courts.

In late October, Local 25's executive committee (six of whose fifteen members were women) convinced the membership that the time was right for a general strike in the trade and appealed to the ILGWU for assistance. Although the local now had a thousand new members, the overwhelming majority of the workers were still unorganized. Experienced trade unionists, including John Dyche, secretary treasurer of the ILGWU, warned that the history of general strikes in unorganized trades was the history of failure. Nevertheless, on 18 November Local 25 flooded the garment district with brochures in Yiddish, Italian, and English, inviting the shirtwaist workers to a meeting at Cooper Union on 22 November to learn "what was going on in the trade" and "when the general strike will be called."[31]

The skeptical leaders of the ILGWU and the hopeful officials of Local 25 expected neither the crowd that appeared at Cooper Union on 22 November, its enthusiastic approval of the general strike, nor the mass walkout on 23 November. Years later Pauline Newman, then a young striker from the Triangle Company, described the feelings of the strikers: "Thousands upon thousands left the factories from every side, all of them walking down toward Union Square. It was November, the cold winter was just around the corner, we had no fur coats to keep warm. . . . I can see the young people, mostly women, walking down and not caring what might happen. The spirit, I think, the spirit of a conqueror led them on. They didn't know what was in store for them, didn't really think of the hunger, cold, loneliness, and what could happen to them. They just didn't care on that particular day; that was *their* day."[32]

There was doubt as well as euphoria, as suggested by Natralya Urosova's account of her experience on 23 November: "I did not know how many workers in my shop had taken that oath at the meeting. I could not tell how many would go on strike in our factory. . . . when we came back the next morning to the factory, though, no one went to the dressing-room. We all sat at the machines with our hats and coats beside us, ready to leave. . . . And there was whispering and talking softly all around the room. . . . 'Shall we wait like this?' 'There is a general strike.' 'Who will get up first?' 'It would be better to be the last to get up, and then the company might remember it of you afterward, and do well for you.' But I told them . . . 'what difference does it make which one is first and which one is last?' Well, so we stayed whispering, and no one knowing what the other would do, not making up our minds for two hours. Then I started to get up. . . . And just at the same minute all—we all got up together, in one second. No one after the other; no one before. And when I saw it—that time—oh it excites me so yet. I can hardly talk about it. So we all stood up, and walked out together. And already out on the sidewalk the police stood with the clubs."[33]

Many of the young strikers went out because of loyalty to one another. Although the main cause was economic—"we'd rather starve quick than starve slow"[34]—young women who earned little struck in support of younger women who earned less. A fifteen-year-old explained this to a reporter: "My boss he says, 'what's the matter with you? . . . You make ten dollars a week. You ain't got no kick.' I says, 'If I ain't got no kick for myself I got one for them girls you ain't paying but three or four dollars. . . . Look at Sadie here. Say, it is to cry to see that girl." Thirteen-year-old Sadie supported herself and a crippled grandfather on $3.50 a week.[35]

From the beginning the strikers focused with remarkable intensity and unanimity on the goal of the closed, or union, shop. While one commentator attributed their sudden devotion to the union to an almost religious conversion, the strikers explained their position rationally. "How long . . . do you think we could keep what the employer says he will give us without the union? Just as soon as the busy season is over it would be the same as before."[36] Fewer than 3 percent had joined the union before the strike; 85 percent had joined by mid-December.[37]

Theresa Malkiel, a socialist supporter of the strike, wrote a fictionalized but authentic diary of the uprising in which she recorded the comments of some of the new union members. "It's a good thing, this strike is; it makes you feel like a real grown up person," said one. "The bosses have always been that proud—something better than us. . . . we ought to be glad that we went out on strike—it teaches us self respect," said another.[38]

The union demanded a 52-hour week with no more than two hours of overtime on any day; notice of slack work in advance, or promptly on arrival in the morning; a uniform scale of prices in each shop negotiated by workers and management; abolition of the ticket and the subcontracting systems and charges for equipment; and, most important, the union shop. Male union officials negotiated with the newly formed employers' association, which represented mainly the larger shops. Virtually every other aspect of the strike was carried out by the women alone. If they had the occasional help of outsiders, these were also usually women.

"The girls took upon themselves the duty of picketing," wrote Marot, "believing that the men would be more severely handled. . . . it is the spirit of martyrdom that sends young girls . . . often insufficiently clad and fed, to patrol the streets in midwinter with the temperature low and with snow on the ground. . . . After two or three hours of such exposure, often ill from cold, they returned to headquarters, which were held for the majority in rooms dark and unheated, to await further orders. It takes uncommon courage to endure such physical exposure, but these striking girls underwent as well the nervous strain of imminent arrest, the harsh treatment of the police insults, threats and even actual assaults from the rough men who stood around the factory doors."[39]

Middle-class sympathizers, including many members of the WTUL, stressed the sufferings of the strikers and their youth, inexperience, and vulnerability to rally support not only for trade unions but also for protective legislation for women workers. The evidence indicates, however, that the strikers were not always passive victims. Despite a code of "ladylike" conduct issued by the union, strikers sometimes gave, as well as received, blows and insults.[40]

Though most of the strikers were new to the labor movement, leaders like Clara Lemlich were already experienced organizers and strikers. While the press portrayed Lemlich as a Joan of Arc who arose from nowhere on 22 November to make her famous motion for a general strike, she was already well known on the East Side as a labor activist. Steeped in Russian revolutionary songs and literature before her immigration, she was a founder of Local 25, a member of its executive committee, and an experienced striker. As the leader of the Leiserson picketers, she was arrested seventeen times, on which occasions six of her ribs were broken.

Although peaceful picketing was legal in New York,[41] 723 women were arrested and 19 sentenced to the workhouse during the first month of the strike; an average of $2,500 bail was required each day.[42] The hostility of the police, who arrested strikers on little or no provocation and ignored the most blatant assaults by scabs or hired guards, was matched by the anti-labor bias of the judges. "You have no right to picket; you have no right to be on Washington place. Every time you go down there you will get what is coming to you and I shall not interfere," a judge said to a striker who had been assaulted.[43] "You are on strike against God and Nature, whose firm law is that man shall earn his bread in the sweat of his brow," said another.[44]

Although police brutality against Jews and other immigrants was not unknown in New York,[45] the treatment of the shirtwaist makers reflected their sex more than their ethnicity. As historian Meredith Tax points out, the authorities tried to break the strikers' spirits by classifying them as prostitutes. They knew that the factory worker surviving on a few dollars a week valued the thin line that separated her from the prostitute, perhaps an acquaintance who, weary of the factory, hoped (usually in vain) to ease the struggle for bread by abandoning respectability.[46]

The police and the employers called the strikers whores, "as if the way to stop them from rebelling as workers was to put them back in their places as sexual objects."[47] Seventeen-year-old Yetta Ruth told of the sexual harassment she experienced at the station house: "The officers treated me in such a manner that a girl is ashamed to talk about it. . . . The policeman asked me with how many men I was living. . . . One policeman showed me a torn pair of pants and asked me to mend them. . . . One man went to some place and winking to me, said, 'Come along, Yetta!' "[48]

The strikers bore financial as well as physical and psychological burdens. Few had savings to fall back on, and strike benefits for the entire thirteen weeks averaged less than $2 for each striker. Many women refused any, so that married men could have more. According to Marot, complaints of hardship came "almost without exception" from the men, while it was occasionally discovered that "a girl was having one meal a day and even at times none at all."[49]

In every shop, natural leaders arose as needed. Only a few of their names were recorded. Esther Lobetkin, a recent arrival from Russia, worked twenty-four hours a day—"a sandwich at midnight and a casual hour of rest kept her on her feet." Arrested again and again, she would shout from the patrol wagon, "Do not lose courage. We'll win yet." Bessie Switski and her sister fought hired "guerillas" in front of their shop day after day until their employer was finally forced to come to terms.[50]

Organizing and fund-raising were as demanding as picketing. At the age of sixteen Pauline Newman toured upstate New York, raising as much as $6,000 for the strike funds. "I had never been out of town in my entire life and didn't even have a suitcase," she remembered many years later.[51]

Solidarity and Feminism: A Women's Strike

Carefully orchestrated demonstrations gained attention and public support. On 3 December 10,000 strikers marched to City Hall to protest the illegal and brutal actions of the police. On 5 December 8,000 strikers gathered for a political demonstration in the Hippodrome under the auspices of prominent suffragist Alva Belmont (her marriage to millionaire O. T. P. Belmont interestingly no obstacle to her politics) and the Political Equality Association. Speakers included Belmont, Dr. Anna Shaw, and other suffragists; Dr. William Maxwell, superintendent of the city's schools; Leonora O'Reilly of the WTUL, and socialist spokeswoman Rose Pastor Stokes. Although tensions had already surfaced between the minority of strikers who wanted to return—or who already had gone back to work (mainly Americans and Italians)—and the majority who were still out (mainly Jews), Malkiel's diary described the Hippodrome meeting as a unifying event.

The last public event was in Carnegie Hall on 2 January 1910. While a broad spectrum of political and religious leaders spoke about the rights of working people, 350 strikers sat on the platform, each wearing a sign reading ARRESTED. On the front row were 20 who had spent time in prison; their placards said WORKHOUSE. Banners throughout the hall proclaimed that "The workhouse is no answer to a demand for justice" and "Peaceful picketing is the right of every worker."[52]

In December, representatives of the employers' association and union spokesmen Morris Hillquit and John Mitchell negotiated a tentative settlement. The employers agreed to most of the strikers' economic demands but refused to discuss the union shop. On 27 December the strikers met to vote on the proposed settlement. "Girls with sore throats and broken noses; girls with wet, torn shoes and girls without hats or coats. . . . Their vote was wanted and they came. Tired, half starved, and almost dropping from weakness, they stood up on the tables, clung to the banisters, steadied themselves on window sills and hung onto the balcony railings. . . . they tried not to miss a single word uttered from the platform." They voted to hold out for the union shop.[53]

In an age that applauded (or deplored) women's increasing participation in the economic and political life of the nation, public attention—often orchestrated by the feminists of the WTUL—focused upon the uprising as a *women's* strike. Marot attributed the "unyielding and uncompromising temper" of the strikers to their sex. Drawing on stereotypical arguments used by others to show why women were unorganizable, she claimed women made the best strikers because of their less permanent attitude toward their trade and their lighter financial burdens. To this she added their "genius for sacrifice," and their "ability to sustain, over prolonged periods, response to emotional appeals. . . ."[54] More astutely, labor journalist Alice Henry attributed the activist women's capacity for hard work and self-sacrifice to sex role socialization. "They have brought with them into their public work the habit of self-sacrifice and that over-conscientiousness in detail which their foremothers acquired during countless generations when obedience, self-immolation, and self-obliteration were considered women's chief duties."[55] The historical development of a women's subculture in which women shared experiences such as work, recreation, and childbirth and childcare, may have promoted solidarity and the willingness of strikers to sacrifice for one another.

There was at least some feminist consciousness among the strikers. Malkiel's *Diary* noted that strikers saw male officials as resistant to women's leadership: "they're afraid that us women will outdo them when we get down to do things in a business-like way."[56] Malkiel challenged the double standard; women were held as responsible as men for misdeeds, "but when we want to have our say we ain't as good as they are."[57] Many of the strikers were favorably impressed by their middle-class suffragist supporters and influenced by their feminist ideas, although a firm self-consciousness about their own pioneering role as women labor activists remained.

Despite the ongoing controversy about restriction of immigration from southern and eastern Europe, or perhaps because of it, most observers sympathetic to the strike did not stress the strikers' ethnicity, which was heavily Jewish. Of a total of 30,000 strikers, approximately 21,000 were Jewish women, 2,000 were Italian women, 1,000 were American women, and 6,000 were men, almost all of them Jewish.[58] Jewish women were clearly overrepresented in relation to their proportion in the industry's work force, while Italian women were underrepresented.

Participation by Jewish women is not surprising. Although traditional east European Jewish culture reserved the more prestigious roles of religious study and community leadership for men, women had important economic responsibilities and were therefore permitted, indeed expected, to go about their business without male escort. Accustomed at an early age to moving freely and assertively in the markets or factories of Russia and the United States, many Jewish women saw themselves as strong and independent. Free from the male obligation to study religious law, some acquired secular education in Hebrew, Yiddish, or Russian schools in Europe or in U.S. night schools. A few had political experience as socialists, trade unionists, Zionists, or political revolutionists before immigration, and many more were influenced by these movements.[59] In New York, Jewish women organized a successful city-wide strike against the kosher meat "trust" in 1902,[60] demonstrated successfully against curricular innovations they feared would dilute their children's education,[61] and as early as 1904 were taking landlords to court for housing abuses. Thus the Jewish shirtwaist maker had female role models for activism in her community, perhaps in her own family.

In the Yiddish-speaking Jewish community of New York, where a broadly based "progressive" working-class culture flourished, class and ethnic solidarity coincided to provide widespread support for the strikers, "our wonderful fervent girls."[62] A secularized messianism contributed to the fervor of the strikers and their supporters, who demanded a just social order in the "golden land." Unlike Gompers, most east European immigrant Jews did not see socialism and trade unionism as contradictory, so these elements united in support of the strike. The nominally socialist *Forward,* which was widely read by Yiddish-speaking Jews of all political persuasions, provided news and editorial support and raised money for the strikers; and Yiddish theaters, their actors unionized, opened their halls for union meetings and fund-raising. Community support crossed class lines to include Americanized notables such as settlement worker Lillian Wald and Rabbi Steven S. Wise.

Like their Jewish counterparts (though perhaps to a lesser extent), South Italian women had a tradition of European activism. During the 1890s, tens of thousands belonged to agricultural unions and participated in strikes and protest marches alongside the men in their families. By 1908 the female membership of the Italian Textile Federation about equalled that of the men, and women had begun to assume leadership roles.[63]

Italian women's relatively low participation in the shirtwaist strike can be attributed to the union's failure to lay groundwork for their organization, the shortage of Italian organizers during the strike, and the family situation of the young workers. In New York, the shirtwaist makers did not work in family groups and therefore could not strike as they had done in agrarian Italy. Unlike their Jewish counterparts, young, single Italian women rarely immigrated alone unless they came to join their fiancés. Most of the Italian shirtwaist makers lived with their parents, immigrants who were often less skilled and even poorer than their Jewish counterparts. In these circumstances, traditional subordination of the individual to the interests of family made it difficult for an Italian daughter, who might earn more than her father, to support the strike.

Salvatore Ninfo, a socialist cloak maker, opened a special strike office for Italian workers under AFL auspices. Arturo Caroti, a former IWW official recruited by the WTUL, tried to educate or, all else failing, buy off Italian fathers; but their daughters continued to cross the picket line. Although *L'Araldo Italiano* printed a statement by Ninfo that 1,000 Italians were standing shoulder to shoulder with the Jewish strikers, the Italian press and community provided inconsistent support. Fragmentation within the Italian labor movement affected the strike, as IWW leaders, denouncing Ninfo and the AFL, tried to recruit the shirtwaist makers for the

IWW.[64] Despite these handicaps, some Italian women were loyal strikers, including a fifteen-year-old who was sentenced to the workhouse. The prominence of Italian women in subsequent garment strikes in New York (where several thousand, led by the IWW, protested a "protocol" settlement in 1911) and Boston, as well as in the famous textile strikes in Lawrence, Massachusetts, and Paterson, New Jersey, demonstrated that Italian women were both organizable and militant.[65]

Participation of native-born American women was broad but short-lived; most returned to work within a few weeks. According to Marot, they were motivated by sympathy for the immigrants rather than by class consciousness or the desire for a union and were alienated by "the daily, almost hourly tutelage" of the ideologically oriented "Russian" (Jewish) union officials. Marot concludes, however, that "their sense of superiority . . . had received a severe shock; they could never again be quite so confident that they did not in the nature of things belong to the labor group."[66]

Employers tried to keep their few Black workers from joining the strike and to recruit Black scabs. Though there were Black union members, their numbers were few; and Blacks complained of union neglect. Ethnic priorities conflicted with class and sex solidarity in the Black community, where industrial jobs were scarce. "Why should Negro working girls pull white working girls' chestnuts out of the fire?" editorialized the *New York*, a Black weekly that helped employers recruit strikebreakers.[67] Some favored using the strike to help Black workers enter the trade, while others placed class solidarity above the pressing need for employment. The Cosmopolitan Club, (middle-class, racially integrated, and "progressive") urged "women of colour to refrain from acting as strikebreakers in the shirtwaist making concerns of New York because we regard their action as antagonistic to the best interests of labor." Labor, in turn, was asked to "exercise a proper concern" for Black workers.[68]

Intellectuals and clergy wrote letters, articles, and sermons in support of the strike. Most help came, however, from three overlapping constituencies: ethnic communities, workers, and women. Each was more effective when reinforced by one or both of the others, as in the Jewish community where ethnic, class, and sex interests generally coincided, and of course, less effective when they did not.

Working-class support came from the unions, the Socialist Party, the labor press, and private individuals. Aided by the WTUL, shirtwaist makers in Philadelphia went on sympathy strike, motivated perhaps by ethnic and sexual, as well as class, solidarity. The ILGWU, the teamsters, and other unions sent money; but the amounts were usually small. "If only the union men in the city would give 50 cents each it would mean over $175,000—or, in other words, victory for the girls,"[69] wrote Malkiel. The artificial flower makers of New York, a tiny union consisting, like the shirtwaist makers, mainly of young Jewish women, however, sent $100, their entire treasury. (Here again ethnic, class, and gender interests coincided.) The Socialist Party demonstrated for the strikers, but Socialist Party women were their most active supporters, playing a major role, with the WTUL, in organizing the strikers, speaking in their behalf, protecting the pickets, and enlisting others in the cause.[70] The *New York Call* and the *New York Journal* issued special editions to benefit the strike. The IWW, active in later strikes involving immigrant women, played a minor role, although Mother Jones, one of its founders, came to New York to speak. Individual working people gave financial and moral support. "My opinion is the shirt makers are right," wrote a garment worker in an immigrant class at the Civic Service Home in Boston; "I, too, am working by waists on a power machine which is sucking up my strength. . . . It is impossible to stay in such conditions."[71]

The strongest support came from women, foreign- and American-born, from every part of the political, economic, and social spectrum. Rose Pastor Stokes, the ghetto socialist who had married an American millionaire, stayed among the strikers, helping in many ways. Josephine Sykes Morgenthau, the wife of Henry Morgenthau, Sr., and Helen Taft, daughter of the president, gave time, money, and publicity. College women contributed money, as did Alva Belmont, former wife of William Vanderbilt; Anne Morgan, daughter of financier J. P. Morgan; and other members of what was popularly known as the Mink Brigade, although their well-publicized donations were small compared to their means, the need, and the contributions, in pennies, of the strikers themselves.[72]

The most important single source of support from women was the ubiquitous WTUL. League members organized the shops and strike halls, marched with the pickets, testified for them in court, secured volunteer legal services, furnished $29,000 bail, managed newspaper publicity, participated in arbitration, arranged parades and demonstrations, raised funds, and paid strike benefits. Their trade unionist members (many of them socialists)—Leonora O'Reilly and Rose Schneiderman are two examples—worked effectively with the strikers, whose class and ethnic backgrounds they often shared, while wealthy allies such as Mary Dreier provided publicity, respectability and access to the resources of the socially prominent.[73]

The strike that had inspired such unity in its early weeks lost coherence as the winter wore on. The refusal of the strikers to abandon their demand for the union shop alienated AFL leaders and many middle-class sympathizers, although the WTUL stood with the strikers to the end. Class and ideological differences disrupted the formerly united ranks of women supporters. After the Carnegie Hall meeting, Anne Morgan issued a press statement that socialists were taking advantage of "these poor girls . . . to teach them fanatical doctrines."[74] Eva McDonald Valesh, an associate of Gompers and former managing editor of the *American Federationist,* publicly attacked both the socialists and the WTUL, which she denounced as a socialist front, on the same grounds.[75] Scabbing also weakened the unity of the strike, as did the fact that smaller shops, having settled with the union, were producing goods for larger firms who therefore had no reason to make concessions. By the end of January some of the largest shops had settled without recognizing the union. On 15 February 1910, with 1,100 workers and thirteen shops still out, the union declared the strike officially over.

The strike had cost $100,000, a fabulous sum at that time, and had produced mixed results. According to a 1910 investigation, 356 of 450 shops had signed up with the union by the time the strike ended, although often the agreements did not meet all the union demands. Nineteen manufacturers, including some of the largest, did not accept the union shop. The vast majority, including most who rejected the union shop, abolished the subcontracting system and accepted the 52-hour week and the two-hour daily limit on overtime. The workers were less successful in getting extra pay for overtime. Nor, given the nature of the trade, was work distributed evenly through the year. Wages were now set by a committee in each shop, so that at the time of the investigation "generalization was impossible as to whether there had been . . . any considerable improvement in the average wage throughout the trade."[76]

Impact and Aftermath

The "uprising of the 20,000" demonstrated the capacity for cooperation—and conflict—among the various progressive reformers. Suffragists used the strike to help enlist immigrant and working-class women, including strikers Clara Lemlich and Pauline Newman, in their cause, although class and ethnic differences made the alliance an uneasy one.[77] The public spotlight on the wages and working conditions of the shirtwaist makers fed the growing movement for protective legislation for women workers. This was ironic because the shirtwaist makers had fought for self-governing unions, not paternalistic legislation, and because in the 1920s, focus on protective legislation—as opposed to the then newly introduced Equal Rights Amendment—helped undermine the unity of the women's movement.[78]

Although its history reveals the tensions between the socialists, the IWW, and the AFL, the strike was clearly beneficial to the cause of trade unionism. It initiated mass action in the garment industry in New York (and elsewhere), inspiring the general strike of 60,000 men and women cloak makers in 1911. Although union membership declined after the strike was over, it organized the shirtwaist makers and was a factor in the successful rise of the ILGWU, which by 1914 was the third largest union in the AFL. The strike also enhanced the reputation of the WTUL with working women, with the AFL (at least temporarily), and with the federal government, which by 1919 had appointed at least thirty-eight WTUL members to government positions.[79]

The strike did not mark a turning point in the history of women in the AFL, however. Even though in 1913 the AFL employed women organizers and raised funds to organize women, only one out of every thirty-four females organized in 1920, in contrast to one out of every nine male workers.[80] As before the strike, observers attributed the scarcity of unionized women to their domestic responsibilities, their concentration in unskilled occupations, and their belief that work was temporary. In fact, and also as before the strike, a major cause was lack of effort to organize them. In the 1920s the WTUL concentrated increasingly on education and protective legislation rather than unionization. More significantly, neither the leaders nor the rank and file of the AFL made serious efforts. When constituent unions refused to admit women, the AFL, arguing local autonomy, did not press them; nor did it encourage separate women's locals. Techniques for organizing women developed earlier by the WTUL were not used; and when women were organized, they were not given responsible posts or trained to direct their own locals. Union contracts in the garment industry, which the shirtwaist makers and other immigrant women had been instrumental in winning, institutionalized their segregation into lower-paid jobs.[81] The problem of women's status in organized labor remains unresolved; as late as 1979 there was not one woman on the executive council of the AFL-CIO.[82]

Although most of the nation's women remained unorganized, the impact of young Jewish union women, including the shirtwaist makers, on the developing garment industry and the ILGWU was great. "With most, the strike has been their initiation into trade unionism," wrote Alice Henry in 1915; and their determination had forced the AFL leaders to take a more active stand.[83]

The activism of individual Jewish women from the garment industries continued long after the shirtwaist makers strike and took many forms. Rose Schneiderman, an organizer for the WTUL during the strike, remained a labor organizer and suffragist, was the first woman to run for the United States Senate (on the Labor ticket in 1920), and served on the Labor Advisory Board of President Roosevelt's National Recovery Administration. Theresa Malkiel continued to work for the interests of women, especially immigrant women, within the Socialist Party. Pauline Newman devoted her life to organizing for the ILGWU. The more radical Clara Lemlich moved from suffrage back to Marxism, community organizing, and educational and political work.[84]

Within Local 25, militant Jewish women spearheaded an effort between 1919 and 1923 to get rid of a leadership they regarded as "too practical" and "conservative" and fought, with little success, for increased class consciousness and democratization of the ILGWU.[85] At the same time, they launched a successful effort to make the union more than "a mere question of bundles, to give it a soul," by establishing an education department and a recreation center, Unity House. Under the leadership of Fannia Cohn and Julia Poyntz, educational, cultural, and recreational programs were introduced in other locals of the ILGWU, where their users as well as their organizers were mainly immigrant Jewish women.[86] "When I was asked to join the union, I felt I had to join it, but now I feel I would give up my life for an organization that will educate its members," wrote one, suggesting the importance of this innovation.[87] In the Socialist Party as well as the AFL, Jewish, Finnish, German, and other immigrant women have made distinctive contributions in the years after the shirtwaist strike.[88] Italian, Hungarian, and Slavic women participated in the Standard Steel Car strike at Hammond, Indiana, in 1910,[89] and reporters and labor organizers noted the importance of women in the great multiethnic strike in Lawrence, Massachusetts, in 1912. Like the Jewish women who insisted their union have a soul, the women of Lawrence marched for "bread and roses, too."[90]

Nor was immigrant labor activism limited to women of European background. Mexican-born Sara Estele Ramírez was a labor organizer at the turn of the century. In the 1930s, Chicanas helped organize the ILGWU in Texas and played leading roles in pecan shellers' strikes in San Antonio and in cannery and agricultural strikes in California's San Joaquin Valley.[91]

Opposed by male co-workers as well as by employers, separated by barriers of ethnicity and class from potential female supporters, and burdened by the multiple responsibilities of homemaking in a new environment, immigrant women did not find it easy to enter the American labor movement. Organization was most successful in sex-segregated industries, such as the shirtwaist trade, where women did not usually compete directly with men for the same jobs and men were therefore less resistant to women in the work force. Organization of immigrant women was also facilitated when women organizers were used, as was the policy of the WTUL in the shirtwaist strike and the IWW in the strike at Lawrence.

As the history of the shirtwaist makers' strike suggests, women were more likely to become engaged in the labor movement if their ethnic backgrounds supported such activism and if they were not heavily burdened with domestic responsibilities. Generalizations about women's activism based on ethnicity must be approached with caution, however, because even within a single ethnic group, women were divided by social class, religious and political belief, age, education, family situation, region or province, and whether they were rural or urban. Women who had participated in or been influenced by upheavals in the homeland—the German revolution of 1848; the Mexican revolution of the early twentieth century; continuing battles for the independence of Ireland, Poland, and other suppressed nationalities; or the civil war between Reds and Whites in Finland after the Russian Revolution—or women whose parents had passed these traditions down to them were more likely to become activists in the United States. The militance of Mary Septak and other Slavic women, for example, can be linked to their background in eastern Europe, where peasant women often assumed conspicuous roles in social protests to protect the men, who were more subject to reprisals.[92]

Experience with injustice in the United States, particularly following upon injustice in their homelands, often turned women toward activism. They frequently identified the perpetrators of injustice in the United States with their old oppressors: Slavic women in Pennsylvania called the constables who came to evict them "Cossacks," and Theresa Malkiel compared the shirtwaist maker's treatment by anti-labor judges and policemen in New York to the tyranny of czarist Russia.[93]

"Everything I do—wash, iron, cook, clean, sew. . . ." A textile worker in the Lehigh Valley in the 1920s described her daily routine. "Get up at 4:30, feed the chickens, make the breakfast, get ready the lunches, and it is time to start to work. Six o'clock come home, make eats for children, washing at nighttime, and make clothes for children."[94] Such women had little time for union meetings. Not surprisingly, then, married women were more likely to participate, often heroically, in short-term labor activities such as strikes than in long-term organizational work or the day-to-day responsibilities of running a union.

Many of the married women who became involved in labor activities did so for the sake of their children. Recognizing this, a Finnish women's newspaper sponsored by the IWW recruited women by addressing their maternal concern: "We think of our children's fate. . . . Capitalism crushes even young workers' lives and uses the best youths of the land like cattle in their bloody sports."[95] Jessie Lopez de la Cruz, daughter of Mexican-American immigrants, describes how she and other Mexican-American migrant laborers turned to unionism: "I had a little girl who died. . . . only five months old. The cause was the way we were living. . . . flies . . . no place to refrigerate the milk. . . . It was like that for all of us. . . . hunger, malnutrition, no money to pay the doctors. When the union came, this was one of the things we fought against."[96]

Although immigrant women were more likely to be occasional strikers than full-time organizers, significant numbers devoted their entire lives to the labor movement. Unlike their male counterparts, most immigrant women were forced to choose between full-time, long-term commitment to the labor movement and traditional family life, a choice especially painful for women whose ethnic cultures often valued motherhood even more highly than American culture. Mother Jones did not begin her career as an organizer until after her husband and children died in a yellow fever epidemic. Rose Schneiderman and Pauline Newman remained single, as did most other professional labor activists. On the life created by these choices, Newman wrote, "While my life . . . is *very interesting*—it is at the same time a very lonely life. . . . Always alone. It is dreadful."[97]

Doubly invisible as immigrants and women, immigrant women have received insufficient recognition for their contributions to the labor movement. The shirtwaist makers' strike of 1909, however, did receive recognition—because the women who struck were so young and because the strike took place in New York City, where the media exposed the brutality of the employers and police to a "progressive-minded" public. The shirtwaist strike demonstrated that the most "unorganizable" workers—young, often unskilled, foreign "girls"—could be organized. The shirtwaist strikers defied traditional middle-class American stereotypes of women as dependent, fragile, and unable to understand economic or political issues. Like many less celebrated but equally heroic immigrant women, they left a twofold legacy, militance against injustice and commitment to one another.

Notes

1. Interview with Leon Stein, recording, "In America, They Say Work Is No Shame," program no. 4, *The Golden Cradle: Immigrant Women in the United States,* produced by Deborah George and Louise Cleveland (Washington, D,C.: Soundscape, 1983). Available from National Public Radio, P.O. Box 818, Niles, Michigan 49120. Voice emphasis by Stein.

2. Quoted in Meredith Tax, *The Rising of the Women: Feminist Solidarity and Class Conflict, 1880–1917* (New York: Monthly Review Press, 1980), 1–2. Chap. 8 of this book is the best recent account of the strike.

3. See Louis Levine (pseud. Louis Lorwin), *The Women's Garment Workers: A History of the International Ladies Garment Workers* (New York: B. W. Huebach, 1924), a comprehensive standard history of the ILGWU which includes an authoritative chapter on the shirtwaist makers' strike. See also Paula Scheier, "Clara Lemlich Shavelson: 50 Years in Labor's Front Line," *Jewish Life* (November 1954): 7–11.

4. William H. Chafe, *The American Woman: Her Changing Social, Economic, and Political Roles, 1920–1970* (New York: Oxford University Press, 1972), 54–55; Niles Carpenter, *Immigrants and Their Children,* Census Monographs 7 (Washington: Government Printing Office, 1927), 290. For a general history of immigrant women in the United States, see Maxine Schwartz Seller, *Immigrant Women* (Philadelphia: Temple University Press, 1981).

5. Philip Davis, "The Shirtwaist Makers' Strike," *Chautauquan* 59 (June 1910): 101.

6. Levine, *The Women's Garment Workers,* pp. 145–46.

7. For specific information on working women in Italy, including statistics by province, see Emiliana P. Noether, "The Silent Half: *Le Contadine del Sud* before the First World War," in *The Italian Immigrant Woman in North America,* ed. Betty Boyd Caroli, Robert F. Harney, and Lydio Tomasi (Toronto: Multicultural History Society of Ontario, 1978), 3–12. This anthology is one of the best single sources on Italian immigrant women in the United States. See also Jean Scarpaci, *La Contadina: The Plaything of the Middle Class Woman Historian* (Toronto: Multicultural History Society of Ontario, 1978).

On life and work of Jewish women in eastern Europe, see Mark Zborowski and Elizabeth Herzog, *Life Is with People: The Culture of the Shtetl* (New York: Schocken, 1969). On Jewish women in the United States, see Charlotte Baum, Paula Hyman, and Sonya Michel, *The Jewish Woman in America* (New York: Dial Press, 1975); and Jacob Rader Marcus, *The American Jewish Woman, 1645–1980;* and idem, *The American Jewish Woman: A Documentary History* (both New York: Ktav Publishing House, 1981).

8. *Outlook,* 11 December 1909, p. 799.

9. Levine, *The Women's Garment Workers,* pp. 146–47. See also Woods Hutchinson, M.D., "The Hygienic Aspects of the Shirtwaist Strike," *Survey* 23 (22 January 1910): 545.

10. Levine, *The Women's Garment Workers,* p. 147.

11. Constance Leupp, "The Shirtwaist Makers' Strike," *Survey* 23 (18 December 1909): 384.

12. Levine, *The Women's Garment Workers*, pp. 148–49.
13. Philip S. Foner, *The Policies and Practices of the American Federation of Labor, 1900–1909*, vol. 3 of *History of the Labor Movement in the United States* (New York: International Publishers, 1964), 256–65.
14. Edward Fenton, *Immigrants and Unions, A Case Study: Italians and American Labor, 1870–1920* (Cambridge, Mass.: Harvard University Press, 1957), 483–85.
15. Examples of early thought on the difficulty of organizing women are Alice L. Woodbridge, "Women's Labor," *American Federationist* 1, no. 66 (June 1894); John R. Commons, "Women in Unions," *American Federationist* 13 (June 1906): 382–84; Lillian Wald, "Organization amongst Working Women," *Annals of the American Academy of Political and Social Science* 27 (1906): 638–45.
16. Mary Van Kleeck, "Artificial Flower Makers," *Survey* (1913), reprinted in *America's Working Women: A Documentary History, 1600 to the Present*, ed. Rosalyn Baxandall, Linda Gordon, and Susan Reverby (New York: Vintage Books, 1976), 174.
17. John Andrews and W. D. P. Bliss, *History of Women in Trade Unions: Woman and Child Wage-Earners in the United States*, vol. 10 (Washington: Government Printing Office, 1911), 144–45; Alice Henry, *The Trade Union Woman* (New York: D. Appleton and Co. 1915), 153.
18. *Outlook*, 11 December 1909, p. 799.
19. Two excellent recent histories of women workers in the United States, with material on immigrant women, are Alice Kessler-Harris, *Out to Work: A History of Wage-Earning Women in the United States* (New York: Oxford University Press, 1982); and Barbara Mayer Wertheimer, *We Were There: The Story of Working Women in America* (New York: Pantheon Books, 1977). See also Andrews and Bliss, *History of Women in Trade Unions*; and Philip Foner, *Women and the American Labor Movement*, 2 vols. (New York: Free Press, 1980).
20. Andrews and Bliss, *History of Women in Trade Unions*, pp. 135–52.
21. Alice Kessler-Harris, "Where Are the Organized Women Workers?" in *Women's America: Refocusing the Past*, ed. Linda K. Kerber and Jane De Hart Mathews (New York: Oxford University Press, 1982), 227; and Andrews and Bliss, *History of Women in Trade Unions*, pp. 93–94.
22. Kessler-Harris, "Where Are the Organized Women Workers?" in *Women's America*, ed. Kerber and Mathews, p. 227.
23. Ibid., pp. 225–38; Foner, *The Industrial Workers of the World, 1905–1917*, vol. 4 of *History of the Labor Movement in the United States*, vol. 4, pp. 219–33.
24. Leupp, "The Shirtwaist Makers' Strike," p. 384; Tax, *The Rising of the Women*, p. 212.
25. Levine, *The Women's Garment Workers*, p. 143.
26. James J. Kenneally, *Women and American Trade Unions* (Montreal: Eden Press Women's Publications, 1981), 61.
27. *Outlook*, 11 December 1909, p. 800.
28. Helen Marot, "A Woman's Strike—An Appreciation of the Shirtwaist Makers of New York," *Proceedings of the Academy of Political Science in the City of New York* 1 (1910): 120.
29. On the early history of the WTUL and its troubled relations with the AFL, see Tax, *The Rising of the Women*, pp. 93–124; and Kenneally, *Women and American Trade Unions*, pp. 47–60.
30. William Mailly, "The Working Girls' Strike," *Independent* 67 (23 December 1909): 1417.
31. Levine, *The Women's Garment Workers*, p. 153.
32. Pauline Newman at the New York State School of Industrial and Labor Relations, Cornell University, taped talk, March 1975, as quoted in Wertheimer, *We Were There*, p. 301.
33. Sue Ainslie Clark and Edith Wyatt, "Working Girls' Budgets: The Shirtwaist Makers and Their Strike," *McClure's Magazine* 36 (November 1910): 81, as quoted in Tax, *The Rising of the Women*, pp. 216–17.
34. Leupp, "The Shirtwaist Makers' Strike," p. 383.

35. Sarah Comstock, "The Uprising of the Girls: Some Circumstances of the Strike of Over Thirty Thousand Garment Makers," *Collier's* 44 (25 December 1909): 14.
36. Marot, "A Woman's Strike," p. 124; see also Ida M. Tarbell, "The Shirt-Waist Strikers," *American Federationist* (March 1910): 209.
37. *Outlook*, 11 December 1909, p. 800.
38. Theresa Malkiel, *Diary of a Shirtwaist Striker* (New York: Cooperative Press, 1910), 5, 9.
39. Marot, "A Woman's Strike," p. 126.
40. Ibid., p. 127; Comstock, "The Uprising of the Girls," pp. 15–16.
41. Leupp, "The Shirtwaist Makers' Strike," p. 385.
42. Levine, *The Women's Garment Workers*, p. 159.
43. Leupp, "The Shirtwaist Makers' Strike," p. 385.
44. Levine, *The Women's Garment Workers*, pp. 158–59.
45. Moses Rischin, *The Promised City: New York's Jews, 1870-1914* (Cambridge, Mass.: Harvard University Press, 1977), 192. See also Maxine Seller, *To Seek America: A History of Ethnic Communities in the United States* (Englewood, N.J.: Jerome Ozer), 116–17.
46. Tax, *The Rising of the Women*, p. 220.
47. Ibid.
48. *New York Call*, 4 December 1909, as quoted in Tax, *The Rising of the Women*, pp. 220–21.
49. Marot, "A Woman's Strike," p. 126.
50. Levine, *The Women's Garment Workers*, p. 157.
51. Pauline Newman, in Wertheimer, *We Were There*, pp. 304–5.
52. Levine, *The Women's Garment Workers*, p. 164.
53. Malkiel, *Diary*, pp. 55–56.
54. Marot, "A Woman's Strike," p. 124.
55. Henry, *The Trade Union Woman*, p. 158.
56. Malkiel, *Diary*, p. 47.
57. Ibid., p. 15.
58. Andrews and Bliss, *History of Women in Trade Unions*, p. 222.
59. Baum, Hyman, and Michel, *The Jewish Woman in America*, pp. 74–89.
60. Paula Hyman, "Immigrant Women and Consumer Protest: The New York City Kosher Meat Boycott of 1902," *American Jewish History* 70 (1980): 91–105.
61. Diane Ravitch, *The Great School Wars, New York City, 1805–1973: A History of the Public Schools as Battlefield of Social Change* (New York: Basic Books, 1974), 224–25.
62. Irving Howe, *World of Our Fathers* (New York: Harcourt Brace Jovanovich, 1976), 300. Howe's book describes this subculture.
63. Emiliana Noether, "The Silent Half," and Claire LaVigna, "Women in the Canadian and Italian Trade Union Movements at the Turn of the Century: A Comparison," both in *The Italian Immigrant Woman*, ed. Caroli, Harvey, and Tomasi; see esp. pp. 7, 33, and 37.
64. Fenton, *Immigrants and Unions*, pp. 479–91.
65. Levine, *The Women's Garment Workers*, p. 226; Wertheimer, *We Were There*, pp. 353–68; Foner, *The Industrial Workers of the World*, p. 323.
66. Marot, "A Woman's Strike," p. 123.
67. Tax, *The Rising of the Women*, p. 224.
68. "Woman's Sphere," *New York Call*, 4 January 1910, as quoted in Tax, *The Rising of the Women*, p. 225.
69. Malkiel, *Diary*, p. 51.
70. Henry, *The Trade Union Woman*, p. 96.
71. Davis, "The Shirtwaist Makers' Strike," p. 103.
72. Malkiel, *Diary*, pp. 24, 41.
73. For material on WTUL leaders, see Keneally, *Women and American Trade Unions*, pp. 51–52; and Wertheimer, *We Were There*, pp. 267–292.

74. Tax, *The Rising of the Women*, p. 231.
75. Ibid., pp. 231–34; also Keneally, *Women and American Trade Unions*, pp. 66–67.
76. Study conducted by the New York School of Philanthropy, spring 1910, reported in *Survey* 25 (1 October 1910): 7–8.
77. Tax, *The Rising of the Women*, pp. 170–79.
78. On the complex relationship between the movement for protective legislation, trade unionism, and the Equal Rights Amendment, see Chafe, *The American Woman*, pp. 112–32; and Kessler-Harris, *Out to Work*, pp. 180–214.
79. Helen Marot, *American Labor Unions* (New York: Henry Holt & Co., 1914), 75; and Fannia Cohen, "Uprising of the Dressmakers," *American Federationist* 36 (November 1929): 1327.
80. Chafe, *The American Woman*, p. 70.
81. See Theresa Wolfson, *The Woman Worker and Trade Unions* (New York: International Publishers, 1926); Ann Washington Craton, "Working the Women Workers," *Nation* 124 (23 March 1927): 311–13; Katherine Fisher, "Women Workers and the American Federation of Labor," *New Republic* 27 (3 August 1924): 265–67; Keneally, *Women and American Trade Unions*, pp. 40–145; Chafe, *The American Woman*, pp. 66–81; and Baum, Hyman, and Michel, *The Jewish Woman*, pp. 146–48.
82. Marcus, *The American Jewish Woman, 1645–1980*, p. 110.
83. Henry, *The Trade Union Woman*, p. 135.
84. Baum, Hyman, and Michel, *The Jewish Woman*, pp. 152–58. See also Rose Schneiderman and Lucy Goldthwaite, *All for One* (Middlebury, Vt.: Paul S. Eriksson, 1967). On Malkiel, see Sally M. Miller, "From Sweatshop Worker to Labor Leader: Theresa Malkiel, a Case Study," *American Jewish History* 68 (December 1978), 189–205; and idem, "Other Socialists: Native-born and Immigrant Women in the Socialist Party of America, 1901–1917," *Labor History* 24, no. 1 (Winter 1983): 84–102. On Pauline Newman and Fannia Cohn, as well as Rose Pesotta, see Alice Kessler-Harris, "Organizing the Unorganizable: Three Jewish Women and Their Union" *Labor History* 17, no. 1 (Winter 1976): 5–23, an excellent account of the problems of women organizers.
85. Levine, *The Women's Garment Workers*, pp. 353–55; Wolfson, *The Woman Worker*, p. 169.
86. Levine, *The Women's Garment Workers*, pp. 493–99; Wolfson, *The Woman Worker*, pp. 198–201.
87. Levine, *The Women's Garment Workers*, p. 495.
88. Wolfson, *The Woman Worker*, pp. 192–207; Miller, "Other Socialists."
89. Foner, *Industrial Workers of the World*, p. 297.
90. Tax, *The Rising of the Women*, pp. 241–75.
91. George M. Green, "The ILGWU in Texas, 1930–1970, *Journal of Mexican-American History* 1 (Spring 1971): 144–69; Kenneth Walker, "The Pecan Shellers of San Antonio and Mechanization," *Southwest History Quarterly* 69 (July 1965): 44–58; Alfredo Mirande and Evangelina Enriquez, eds. *La Chicana: The Mexican-American Woman* (Chicago: University of Chicago Press, 1979), 229–32.
92. Novak, *The Guns of Lattimer: The True Story of a Massacre and Trial* (New York: Basic Books, 1978), 174.
93. Malkiel, *Diary*, p. 14.
94. Caroline Manning, *The Immigrant Woman and Her Job*, United States Department of Labor Women's Bureau Bulletin No. 14 (Washington, D.C.: Government Printing Office, 1930), 60.
95. Robert E. Park, *The Immigrant Press and Its Control* (New York: Harper and Brothers, 1929), 244–45.
96. Ellen Cantarow, *Moving the Mountain: Women Working for Social Change* (Old Westbury, N.Y.: Feminist Press and McGraw-Hill, 1980), 118.
97. Wertheimer, *We Were There*, p. 289.

STEVE FRASER

Landslayt and *Paesani:* Ethnic Conflict and Cooperation in the Amalgamated Clothing Workers of America

In the fall of 1910, thousands of Chicago garment workers marched the city's streets in a strike against Hart, Schaffner and Marx, the largest manufacturer of men's clothing in America. It was a protracted, bitter battle stretching on into the punishing Chicago winter. Like the rising of the 20,000 in New York City the previous year, the great Hart, Schaffner and Marx (HSM) strike marked a turning point in the effort to organize immigrant industrial workers. Not only did it materially improve conditions for thousands of garment employees, but it forced the flagship of the industry to recognize and bargain with its employees. Moreover, because of the singular significance of the company, the strike gave birth a few years later to the Amalgamated Clothing Workers of America (ACWA), a quasi-industrial union which, together with the International Ladies Garment Workers Union, finally put an end to the demoralizing cycle of rebellion and abortive organization that had characterized the needle trades since well before the turn of the century. The ACWA endured, and it did so as a polyglot organization that managed to overcome those centrifugal forces of ethnic particularism that threatened to tear the new union apart.

If ethnic cooperation proved to be one secret of the ACWA's success, it was by no means easily accomplished. Signs of trouble appeared even as the movement was born. Indeed, at the very height of the HSM strike a committee of Italian workers, probably affiliated with the Industrial Workers of the World, issued "A Call for Action," denouncing the pending arbitration agreement with the company, which had been worked out by the mainly Jewish leadership of the strike. "Don't hesitate, Don't mediate, Don't arbitrate, Don't wait," it cried, urging the workers to continue their strike and not be "whipped back to work under an arbitration agreement."[1]

It would be misleading to suggest that the source of this rank-

and-file opposition had entirely to do with ethnic antagonism between Italians and Jews. In fact, the very presence, however shadowy, of the IWW immediately suggests that the dispute was at least equally political in nature. But as the history of the ACWA unfolded, it became increasingly difficult to distinguish clearly between political, cultural, and organizational differences. All these sources of tension—and even outright animosity—tended to carry with them an ethnic charge. That being the case, it was especially worrisome whenever *landslayt* and *paesani* (immigrant brethren from the villages of Eastern Europe and southern Italy, respectively) found themselves at odds, because they comprised the two critical ethnic groups without whose cooperation there could be no ACWA.

Ethno-Occupations

Workers in the men's clothing industry represented a remarkably diverse array of ethnic groups: native-born, old, and new immigrants. "Hebrews" were the largest such nationality group, followed by Italians, Poles, Bohemians, Lithuanians, Slovaks, and Russians. Jews and Italians predominated in almost every major market, including New York, Rochester, Boston, Philadelphia, Cincinnati, and Toronto. For the industry as a whole, Jews accounted for somewhat less than 40 percent, and Italians slightly more than 30 percent, of the work force, although by the mid-twenties those proportions were steadily shifting in favor of the Italians. Clearly, if only from the standpoint of their sheer numerical weight, serious trouble between Italian and Jewish workers had to be avoided or resolved at all cost.[2]

More importantly, Jews and Italians clustered in distinct occupational niches in the industry that lent their joint organization strategic importance. Jews could be found working at almost every level of the industry's job structure, but they tended to dominate the most skilled trades—cutter, off-presser, pocket-maker, etc.—working in smaller shops or for contractors. It was an appropriate setting for those many Jewish garment workers who shared the ambition to become contractors and petty manufacturers in their own right. Moreover, a sizable proportion of Jewish workers were immigrants from the tailoring centers of Byleorussia-Lithuania where handicraft production still survived, albeit precariously, and so they came equipped with skills still prized by manufacturers in the New World.[3]

Male immigrants from southern Italy, however, tended to congregate in larger factories or "inside shops" (larger factories in which all production operations from cutting to finishing were carried out on the premises) associated with the centralized, captal-intensive sector of the industry. In fact, the high tide of Italian immigration coincided with the renewed growth of the inside shop in the period before the war. Often assuming their stay in America would be temporary, they were far less likely to cultivate entrepreneurial aspirations, and moreover they lacked the dense network of ethnic ties that drew so many Jewish and other east European immigrants into the shops of petty manufacturers and contractors.

Some Italians arrived with tailoring skills mastered in the old country and established custom tailoring shops or took up positions in American factories as skilled tailors, pocketmakers, sleeve sewers, pressers, and even, on occasion, designers. Most, however, learned the tailoring trade in the United States. They operated sewing machines and performed a wide range of semiskilled jobs. They dominated certain such trades, so that, for example, Italians comprised 50 percent of the bushelmen in New York City. The development of the "section system" in large inside factories made it "possible for a Sicilian peasant that knows nothing at all about tailoring to learn any special operation in a short time."[4]

While Italian men thus populated the industry's most modern sector, as semiskilled operatives, Italian women could be found toiling in the medieval gloom of the tenement workshop apartments that comprised the industry's thriving, pre-modern sector. Often supplanting Jewish women, who tended to leave the industry after marriage, married Italian women especially became the industry's chief source of homeworkers. Homework was a form of family economy in which young and old participated, although most homeworkers were older women, almost all unable to read English and only slightly more likely to speak it. Families were often recruited by *paesani* living in neighboring tenements. Younger, unmarried Italian women did enter the factory but continued to perform traditional jobs as fellers and finishers in sections segregated from the male labor force, ususally under the supervision of an Italian foreman, and in factories close to Italian neighborhoods.[5]

Any serious plan to permanently unionize the industry could not hope to succeed unless it incorporated these two dominant ethno-occupational groups. This was especially true given the intensely competitive circumstances under which business was carried on, an internecine contest that focused mainly on the costs and conditions of labor. Smaller manufacturers were forever seeking to underbid the "Giants of Broadway," using ingenious means, both legal and extralegal, for reducing labor costs, while the industry's elite manufacturers responded, in part, by farming out less-skilled work to contractors and homeworkers. This meant that because of their separate occupational locations in the industry's segmented structure, Italians and Jews could be pitted against one another, even if unintentionally, and that at the very least so long as one group remained unorganized, unionism everywhere was imperiled.[6]

As a matter of fact, until the ACWA came along, the AFL's affiliate in the field, the United Garment Workers, more or less ignored both Italians and Jews as well as the rest of the industry's immigrant work force. Consisting largely of a native (and nativist) skilled elite as well as workers in overall factories in the trans-Appalachian border states, the UGW was hardly a factor to be reckoned with in the big urban clothing markets. Moreover, it was not only prejudiced against immigrants but tainted with corruption and entirely docile, relying on the sale of the union label both to protect the few shops it managed to organize and more important to swell the union's treasury. The union's quarterly journal, the *Garment Worker,* inveighed against the deskilling of the tailoring trade, especially as it flooded subdivisions of the industry with unskilled immigrants. The UGW leadership in New York found the Jews "a very unsatisfactory lot. Their attitude toward this country is antagonistic, they are irreligious and radical."[7]

The HSM strike thus represented in every sense a new departure even though it was officially conducted under the auspices of the UGW. In fact, the UGW leadership made several efforts to terminate the strike on terms amounting to almost total capitulation and were only prevented from doing so by the solidarity of the immigrant strikers and the emergence of a new local leadership. That leadership—Sidney Hillman, Sam Levin, Frank Rosenblum, Bessie Abramovitz—while heavily Jewish, also included Italian militants like Anunzio Marimpietri. Together they were determined to build a new union, one that would be militant, industrial in scope, and ethnically integrated.[8]

Cultural Legacies

This vision of ethnic solidarity was inspiring, but neither its moral force nor its obvious practical value could magically dissolve the obstacles standing in its way. In particular, Jewish and Italian garment workers were separated by cultural background, organizational rivalries, and by political ideology. It is useful to briefly review each of these obstacles to Jewish-Italian collaboration be-

The defeat of the powerful Hart, Schaffner & Marx company at the hands of the Amalgamated Clothing Workers of America is announced in huge headlines. Images Unlimited.

fore examining those strategies and tactics devised by the leadership to realize that vision of solidarity born out of the passion of the great HSM strike.

To begin with, the very fact that the new leadership of the strike was overwhelmingly Jewish suggests that initially, at least, Jewish workers were more likely to support the union and to participate actively in its formation. And this was unquestionably the case. While the Jewish workers had failed to establish a durable union before the ACWA, they had nevertheless conducted innumerable strikes over the previous twenty years. By 1900 the Jewish garment workers' strike had become an annual ritual. Although the unions left behind proved ephemeral, these cycles of industrial rebellion nurtured an extraordinary moral stamina, organizational inventiveness, and a fighting élan that was to prove invaluable later in the history of the ACWA. Furthermore, many Jewish immigrants (64 percent of all tailors migrating to the United States between 1900 and 1930 were Jews) brought with them from the old country not only a familiarity with industrial work but a tradition of industrial and political struggle. This was particularly true of the skilled artisans arriving after the great pogroms of 1903 and the revolution of 1905.[9]

These newer arrivals belonged to an artisanal culture undergoing decomposition that cast its shadow back into the handicraft past and forward into the industrial future. During the 1890s, this "preindustrial proletariat" erupted in a series of mass strikes and demonstrations in the Pale (the region in western Russia and eastern Poland to which Jews were largely confined by tsarist edict). These uprisings, partly conservative in nature, aimed at preserving what was left, and perhaps recovering some of what had been lost, of their social existence and identity as artisans. The class struggle in the Pale also looked ahead to the future and "aimed at instituting 'modern' relations between employers and employees, relations based on contract, not on habit and whim." New institutions of industrial and political struggle (the 'kassy' and the General Jewish Workers Union in Russia and Poland, better known as the Bund) thrown up by the mass movement became incubators of a new morality and character structure that promoted self-restraint, social solidarity, and a sense of mission and individual integrity and helped supplant the age-old resignation and apathy of the shtetl.[10]

Contemporary observers and historians of the Jewish labor movement have all remarked that the generation of immigrants fleeing to the United States after the 1905 revolution exhibited a capacity for self-organization, a political sophistication, a general level of literacy and individuation, and an ethos of self-improvement far in advance of earlier arrivals. The movements against political autocracy, the stigmata of caste and religion, national discrimination, and the economics of the sweatshop created intense interest in the dawning of a new civil order. Their ideology expressed the historic aspirations of the third estate—the rights of man and citizen, equality, democracy, and fraternity—that inspired the whole Jewish labor movement in its struggle to establish trade unionism in America.[11]

Of course, only a minority of Jewish garment workers were actually prepared to act consistently and militantly on behalf of these commitments. But it was a decisive minority bound by a shared heritage to the larger mass of more passive workers who, under the right circumstances, were prepared to follow the lead of the active minority. These shopfloor cadres were the union's most reliable organizers and shock troops during its formative years. Again and again, the leadership relied on the stamina and tenacity of these skilled work groups, especially the cutters, who had sustained independent organization for years under difficult conditions. They were often the first to respond to union organizing efforts and proved absolutely dependable in strike confrontations.[12]

Immigrants from southern Italy responded, in the main, quite differently. On the one hand, there was a quite similar—although much smaller—minority of skilled Italian tailors who displayed an analogous pattern of artisanal resistance and rebellion. They were also the first to show interest in unionization and supplied the ACWA with some of its early Italian organizers. More commonly, however, the mass of Italian factory operatives demonstrated a frustrating inertia. Frank Bellanca, who, together with his brother Augusto, was among the most important Italian leaders of the union, noted that most Italian immigrants learned the tailoring trade in America and that few knew anything about trade unions (and their knowledge of socialism was even less) when they arrived. Northern Italians familiar with urban life, acquainted with trade unionism and socialist politics, took up the work of educating their southern brethren, first through the syndicalist Italian Socialist Federation and later through the Italian sections of the Socialist Party.

But it was a daunting task. Many southern Italians continued to bear the legacy of seigneurial oppression and economic misery. If their Jewish artisanal co-workers imported the millenial enthusiasms of the Old World, Italian tenant farmers and day laborers brought with them the poverty, suspicions, and resignation that flourished in the desiccated provinces of the south.

Women homeworkers particularly were subject to a pervasive patriarchal pressure only slightly less omnipresent for those women who went to work in a factory. Even in cases where manufacturers actively cooperated with the ACWA in an effort to eliminate the destabilizing influence of homework, Italian women, along with their padrone-employers, clung tenaciously to the old ways. In fact, homework thrived until the advent of the National Recovery Administration in 1933, and the mass of older Italian women remained untouched by unionization until well into the 1930s.[13]

Among Italian males, however, the oppressive routines of factory work were just as likely to be punctuated by episodic outbursts of mass rebellion, analogous to the risings of the *fascio* in Sicily in the 1890s, that expressed long-accumulating hatreds with great energy. These outbreaks occurred sometimes under the auspices of the IWW or under the charismatic influence of free-lancing Italian anarcho-syndicalists but left few organizational traces. Frank Bellanca described the perennial rhythms of these industrial jacqueries:

> Italians are impulsives, are easy to enthusiasm, but they are also easy to mistrust. And those who know Italians know also that it is more difficult to keep the organization among the Italians than organize themselves. Often is easy to organize the Italians: to call them in strike; but for to keep them, believe me, is necessary constancy, sacrifice, honesty, and big moral and material power.[14]

Over the long term, however, the "Italian problem" for the union leadership was more often one of inactivity rather than this sort of hyperactivity. While Jewish garment workers resident in the United States for five years or more were most likely to belong to a union, southern Italians (along with Bohemians and Moravians) were least likely to.[15] In every market where they were important, local union cadre reported extraordinary difficulties in organizing Italians. In St. Louis, Italian inertia was reportedly the biggest obstacle, and in Cincinnati a combination of Italian sympathy for the IWW and a more general resistance to organization of any kind stymied local Italian organizers. Rochester remained unorganized until 1919, despite the support of the Jewish, Polish, and Lithuanian workers, mainly because the Italians in the coat trade and the Italian women were unreachable, especially those working for the Hickey-Freeman company, whose paternalist labor policies gave it a reputation as the "Paradise" of the industry. Philadelphia, another center of Italian workers, resisted organization until 1929, in part because Italian subcontracting padrones insulated female Italian homeworkers from union appeals, and because "the situation in the shops where the Italians are the dominant factor is bad."[16]

This culturally embedded resistance to the incentives of unionization quite naturally strained relations with the far more responsive Jewish rank and file. It exacerbated the prejudices of local Jewish organizers to a point where complaints from locals to their national offices about the "goim" were not uncommon. Italian-Jewish tensions in Philadelphia soured relations between the Jewish organizer, Lazarus Marcovitz, and his Italian equivalent, Phillip DeLuca, as the latter accused Marcovitz of not combatting Jewish charges that Italians were working for less. Instances of actual scabbing were of course most inflammatory: and although Italians more frequently were guilty of strike-breaking, resentment over previous infidelities could work both ways. Thus, Italians who resisted ACWA organizing efforts in Cincinnati in 1916 did so in part because they bitterly recalled that their Jewish co-workers had returned to work during a strike in 1913 while they held out.[17]

It was to be expected, furthermore, that managements would take advantage of such ethnocultural tensions. Hickey-Freeman foremen and lower echelons of management close to the shopfloor quite deliberately incited Jewish-Italian antagonisms to impede union organization. This was true as well of other leading Rochester manufacturers; and in Chicago, management tried to "play one race against another" in order "to keep up a bitter feeling."[18]

Socialists versus Syndicalists

Meanwhile, the union leadership was almost as frequently disturbed by that activist minority of Italian workers whose political proclivities represented a different kind of threat to the stability of the new union. As already noted, Italian anarcho-syndicalists first made their presence felt in Chicago in 1910. While IWW strength in Baltimore rested on the Lithuanian workers, the organization, with the assistance of Arturo Giovanitti, made a concerted and partially successful effort to win Italian adherents in the city's major clothing factories. Indeed, relations between the ACWA and the IWW were at their nastiest in Baltimore, where at times the IWW allied with the UGW to prevent the organization of the city by the ACWA. Wobblies continued to work when the ACWA struck two major manufacturers, and both organizations traded ethnic slurs, along with acid accusations of scabbing. Frank Bellanca reported early in 1916 that to woo Italians away from the IWW would require the creation of a separate Italian local; such a gesture would be required to allay their fear of Jewish retaliation. (Later that same year, in fact, the Italian IWW local joined the ACWA en masse as a new nationality local). For as long as the IWW remained influential in Baltimore, ACWA efforts to control the labor market were in jeopardy.

Similarly, in Philadelphia an independent union of 300 Italian anarcho-syndicalists agreed to provisionally support an ACWA strike in 1917 but otherwise refused, along with the city's 5,000 less politically articulate Italian tailors, to join the union. And the situation was even tenser in Rochester. There Augusto Bellanca conveyed news from two Socialist Party comrades that "conditions there were very bad, especially among the Italians; because a deep sentiment of race's antagonism blow among the people . . . " thanks to the "filthy, liar work among the Italians of the IWW against the Jews."[19]

Even after these syndicalist currents were incorporated within the union's formal structure, political tensions persisted, giving rise to a new set of organizational problems. Italian syndicalists often remained estranged from the union leadership by virtue of strong localist and nationalist as well as political sentiments. Thus, the most radical antiwar resolutions were introduced into union conventions by New York Italian syndicalists who demanded that the ACWA refuse to produce uniforms for the army. The leadership went to great lengths to squelch such sentiments for, despite its own strong ties to the socialist movement, it had come to rely on government support for collective bargaining to consolidate the union's position during the war.

Often what was ostensibly political opposition actually fed on deeper resentments about alleged or actual Jewish discrimination and domination. Thus, reports from Philadelphia regularly complained about the local business agents of the union not only because they were apparently both "grafters" and incompetents but because they openly discriminated against Italian workers. There was, as a consequence, enormous pressure to create separate all-Italian locals. Later on, when the union was wracked by factional divisions in the mid-twenties, these locals often emerged as centers of opposition to the union leadership, sometimes under the guidance of older syndicalist or nationalist figures, sometimes loosely organized by the Communist Party's Trade Union Educational League.[20]

Organizational tensions of course did not always emerge as full-blown political faction fights. Sometimes they simmered beneath the otherwise reassuring surface of union strength. Thus, even where unionization eventually succeeded, as in Baltimore, the results were often ephemeral, as Italian locals were soon nearly defunct or subject to rapid turnover or included a great number of members who simply refused to pay dues. More troubling still was the organizational behavior of ostensibly loyal Italian members who nonetheless seemed unwilling to adjust to the procedures of collective bargaining instituted by the ACWA, either because such procedures mistakenly assumed a familiarity with legal obligations and bureaucratic behavior or because some Italian workers were, on the contrary, all too familiar with forms of bureaucratic obfuscation and were determined to avoid them. Thus, Italian syndicalists in the union opposed not only the elaborate mechanisms of grievance mediation and impartial arbitration but any form of binding contractual arrangement covering wages, hours, and the conditions of work. Anarchist-inspired work stoppages in Boston and Rochester, nominally carried out under union auspices, occurred frequently. In Rochester, union president Sidney Hillman, lectured Italian collar makers and others on the question of sabotage.[21]

Frank Rosenblum, director of the union's midwest region, complained that the Cleveland rank and file lacked "the proper respect and appreciation for authority and discipline," and he feared that "the manufacturers will not stand some of the tactics of our people and can hardly be blamed for it because our people at times assume very impossible attitudes." Rosenblum was mainly concerned with the Italians. Although he and others in the union leadership were, on one level, committed socialists, their new responsibilities as conventional trade unionists took precedence while anticapitalist principles were reserved either for ceremonial occasions or for the political arena, where they did not directly aggravate relations with employers.[22]

Peaceful Coexistence

The strategy and tactics devised to solve these cultural, political, and organizational conundrums were as varied as the problems themselves. To begin with, the overriding historic difficulty posed by Italian inertia began to solve itself even before the ACWA officially announced its existence in 1914. This was in part due to the needle trades uprisings of 1909 through 1913. The Women's Trade Union League established an Italian Committee to organize Italian women and girls in the men's clothing industry and to reduce the incidence of Italian scabbing. The New York strike conducted by the United Brotherhood of Tailors (the ACWA predecessor in New York City) in 1913 was the first time Italians participated in substantial numbers in the periodic organizing efforts of men's clothing workers.

More fundamentally, the emergence of mutual aid societies and supralocalist associations like the Sons of Italy helped supplant the relatively more insular familial and village-centered relations of the Old World. Thus, although a middle-class-led organization, the Sons lent financial aid to the great 1913 strike in New York, and in fact remained reliable allies of the union until they split with the Italian socialists over their attitude toward Mussolini. Indeed, Italian socialist and ACWA cadre like the Bellanca brothers were quick to sense the opportunity and sought to ally with or to systematically infiltrate the Sons in order to establish a liaison with Italian tailors. In Philadelphia, the Sons gave the union access to their membership lists and enforced the organization's constitutional provision calling for the expulsion of scabs. The Sons actively aided the ACWA during the New York lockout following the war and in subsequent campaigns in Rochester, Buffalo, and Utica.[23]

Calling on the assistance of personalities and institutions highly regarded within the Italian community was not limited to the Sons. Thus, the danger of Italian scabbing was serious enough for the union leadership to ask for Fiorello LaGuardia's help. LaGuardia used his growing political prestige as well as his close ties to the New York union leadership to persuade Italian workers to refrain from strikebreaking.[24]

Such tactics, however, assumed the existence, at least to some limited degree, of a self-conscious Italian community. This of course was not everywhere the case, as the process of cultural transformation proceeded steadily but slowly. Not surprisingly, the union had its greatest success among the "young new Italian-American element." Group and associational life in the United States expanded considerably compared to the relative isolation of the family in the Old World, and this was particularly so among the second generation. More familiar with urban and industrial life, this generation was stirred by the nationalist agitation of the war and by the growth of Italian fascism which followed. But it only began to come of age in the mid-1920s.[25]

In the meantime, the union tried to turn traditional values and forms of behavior to its own advantage. Naturally, Italian organizers were assigned wherever possible, to organize Italians, especially during strikes and in preparation for strikes. Frank Bellanca fervently believed that the only way to reach the mass of Italian workers was through Italian organizers, Italian newspapers, and autonomous Italian institutions. Such organizers were encouraged to use village ties from the old country and the ethos of *la famiglia* and were careful to observe sexual and other cultural prohibitions. Union broadsides urged strikers not to "dishonor your name and that of your family by committing treason against your fellow workers" and painted a dim picture of the social ostracism that awaited any Italian scab. The union was furthermore careful to avoid inflammatory topics in its educational program, as for example "the late Mexican situation, the separation of Church and State, we were careful not to discuss, because while as a union we might approve of it, our Italian Catholics naturally would not."[26] Italian leaders like Augusto Bellanca at times deliberately cultivated a traditional brand of *personalismo* politics in order to more securely bind their ethnic brethren to the new union. With the full support of the national leadership, they dispensed a kind of informal patronage, providing both jobs and advice, helping newly arrived immigrants to adjust to the rigors and discipline of industrial labor.[27]

A United Leadership

While the Italian and Jewish leadership of the union made temporary concessions to ethnic sensibilities, they were prepared to go only so far in this direction. They were quite conscious of avoiding a problem prevalent throughout much of the Italian labor movement whereby self-interested labor bosses "saw to it that no general interlocking movement among Italian workers developed and that whatever leadership was created should remain regionalistic, clannish, and almost feudal in its antiquated form and function."[28] Thus, Frank Bellanca took the lead in trying to organize an Italian Chamber of Labor which, as an all-inclusive organization of Italian labor, was analogous to the United Hebrew Trades and similarly designed to provide Italian workers with a source of support and with a national ethnic self-confidence that the indifference of the AFL undermined.

All of these men (except for Augusto Bellanca's wife, who was born Dorothy Jacobs, and, briefly Mamie Santora and Bessie Abramovitz Hillman, the entire national leadership was male) shared a socialist or progressive commitment to the principles of internationalism that placed great emphasis on overcoming those particularist racial, ethnic, and religious rivalries that so frequently undermined broader working-class political unity. Moreover, the Italian component of this socialist elite grew in strength during and after the war. Italian radicals like Emilio Grandinetti, who had been a national secretary of the Italian Socialist Party during the period when Mussolini was still a loyal partisan of the Second International, and Anthony Capraro, once enamoured of the syndicalist vision of the IWW, now joined with the Bellanca brothers and other Italian socialists more committed to conventional trade union and political strategies. They helped overcome the suspicions of rank-and-file syndicalists and added a badly needed complement of experienced cadre to the union's national staff. The presence of such men in the national leadership also led the Italian affiliate of the Socialist Party to offer its assistance, especially in the form of trained organizers. (It is noteworthy that while the IWW was perhaps more vocal and visible during the 1910 strike, the Italian Socialist Federation had been proselytizing among HSM workers for some time before the strike.)[29]

Besides sharing an ideology and strategic perspective, members of this core group of Italian and Jewish leaders displayed a remarkable similarity in background and experience that furthered their collaboration in the ACWA. Born in the late 1880s and 1890s, they had come to America with some education, often as teenagers or young men with some training as tailors. Aldo Cursi, for example, born in 1881 in Iesi, Italy, was an apprentice tailor at age eleven; became a journeyman tailor in Rome, skilled enough to make clothes for the Italian nobility; and worked as a custom tailor for Rogers Peet in New York. Before joining the ACWA, he served as general secretary of the Italian branch of the ILGWU. Joseph Catalonotti's father was a skilled tailor in Sicily (a good number of the early cadre were from the south, including Capraro; Grandinetti, who came from a long line of socialist organizers; and Anthony Velona, who had been a socialist railroad worker in Calabria); and when Joseph arrived in America at the age of thirteen, he went to work in a New York custom shop. Like Frank Rosenblum, Dorothy Jacobs, and Joseph Schlossberg and others on the Jewish side, they were involved in early, pre-ACWA efforts to organize the needle trades. Many, like Marimpietri (formerly a journalist in Italy) were self-educated and pursued, as best they could, further education in night school in the United States, as did both Hillman and Marimpietri. Indeed, from the earliest days of the organization at HSM, Hillman and Marimpietri established the closest of working relationships; the latter actually donated a portion of his meager wage to allow Hillman to devote all his time to organizing. Finally, some like Schlossberg, Hillman, and J. B. S. Hardman among the Jewish leaders and Grandinetti, Bellanca, and Velona among the Italians were already heavily influenced by socialist politics before they arrived in America.[30]

They were a shrewd and practical group of men, committed to a set of ideals without being ideologues, thoroughly familiar with the workaday world of the garment industry, prepared to adjust their ideals if that was necessary to achieve tangible gains in organization and material well-being. For them, ethnic unity was not only a matter of political and moral principle but absolutely essential from the narrower standpoint of building an institution capable of stabilizing and standardizing labor conditions throughout a highly fragmented industry.

However, if the general strategy of the union leadership called for the muting and eventual dissolution of ethnic divisions, the tactics devised for accomplishing that purpose could range from the overtly coercive to the gently persuasive. For example, while it might be preferable to woo Italian workers with seductive appeals to their sense of family honor, when Italians refused to pay dues or join the ACWA at all, the union not infrequently "virtually forced the Italians to join" by means of closed shops and compulsory dues check-offs. Such rough tactics, however, were a last resort. More often, the union leadership sought other ways to encourage ethnic cooperation, ethnic integration, and what in some respects amounted to a process of Americanization.[31]

On the one hand, the leadership was prepared to accept, if only temporarily, the need for separate nationality locals. At HSM, for example, there were five language locals, including Local 270 for Italians, as well as locals for Bohemians, Poles, Lithuanians, and for those who spoke English. In Chicago, aside from the catch-all and therefore cosmopolitan Local 39, all the other ethnic locals had their own business agents. Even in the case of the large, multiethnic locals like 39, separate Italian-language branches were often created, in response to complaints of neglect and mistreatment by the local leadership. Similarly, where the language barrier was considered a serious enough obstacle to organization, as in Montreal, requests for separate Italian locals were granted. Even where mixed locals were established, different nationalities continued to meet separately, and differences were resolved by the locals' multiethnic executive committee.

Although only a few Italians could be counted part of the national leadership, a much wider circle of Italian cadre were part of the union's second tier of organizers. Men like Aldo Cursi, Joseph Catalonotti, Paul Arnone, Phillip LiCastro, and Anthony Ramuglia functioned as national Italian organizers, ready to move on a moment's notice from one center of Italian agitation and organization to another, depending on where the General Executive Board (GEB) felt they were most needed.[32]

Cultural Revolution

Clearly then, the leadership remained acutely aware of national sensibilities. But whenever the opportunity presented itself, they sought to dissolve foreign-language locals into mixed assemblies and to do away with other institutional and cultural hallmarks of ethnic exclusivity. Nationality locals could easily become pawns in local struggles for pelf and power so that, for example, for years in Chicago rival leaders would alternately champion or denounce the existence of separate ethnic locals, depending on which position would enhance their own power in the Chicago organization and win them credit from the national office. Especially in the early years when resources were in short supply, intense squabbles developed between Italian and Jewish locals over who most deserved their own business agent.[33]

Nationality locals were thus viewed as perhaps necessary but not desirable. However, attempts to force the amalgamation of locals could, rather predictably, result in prolonged and explosive factional battles. Considerable resistance could be anticipated where one ethnic group, the Italians in Chicago, for example, feared being subordinated to the Jewish plurality. In such instances, the leadership drew back and waited for a more propitious moment to attempt amalgamation. Ethnic integration remained, however, the consistent long-term objective. Thus, while the union supported, in 1922, as many as six foreign-language newspapers, the union leadership not only encouraged the rank and file to read the union's principal English-language organ, the *Advance,* but to write for it as well.[34]

The leadership undertook an even more deliberate program of cultural transformation that essentially aimed at replacing the multiplicity of cultural agendas articulated by each significant ethnic group with a unitary set of values, beliefs, and motivations that emphasized contractual obligation, economic self-interest, and the parliamentary practices of union and national politics. Thus, they insisted that only English be spoken at conventions and encouraged members to take out citizenship papers. While president of Local 39 in Chicago, Marimpietri, for example, as early as 1916 urged all tailors to subscribe to the English-language paper of the union and to move toward becoming citizens.

Finally, the leadership adopted a broad program of general education designed to acquaint the rank and file with the operating assumptions of American life as well as with the particular requirements of the ACWA's innovative and socially conscious form of collective bargaining, dubbed the "new unionism." A theme reiterated at every national convention was that the union was far more than an agency of economic protection and advancement. It was also intended as a kind of civilizing institution, a carrier of modern culture, and a school for the socialization of the oppressed and ignorant. The union educational program was no mere frill, but a serious and systematic effort at reeducation, with at least some modest success, which called upon a whole roster of progressive intellectuals and academics (including Charles Beard, Lincoln Steffens, Horace Kallen, A. Phillip Randolph, and James Harvey Robinson) and was designed to impart not only the elementary principles of trade unionism but to be so "all-embracing" as to include the sciences and arts, lectures on revolution, and studies of women's problems, the party system, and the role of the trade union movement in the political economy. Labor relations mediator and friend of the union, William Leiserson, valued the ACWA as a great agency of Americanization, and, with Italian as well as other immigrant workers in mind, noted that the union managed to replace the "traditional patriarchal clan leader" with the self-conception of the "independent citizen."[35]

Ultimately, the objective was to formulate a new shared language and ideology, including a concept of industrial justice, equity, and democratic participation, and a new set of motivations emphasizing economic self-interest, purchasing power, and mass consumption. In the long run this diligence in the arena of cultural reform and reeducation helped instill in the Jewish, and, to a lesser extent perhaps, the Italian rank and file, a dedication to the principles of social liberalism embodied later in the New Deal. But this was largely the cultural world of a second and third generation; moreover the American political economy would require rather fundamental transformations to make it permanent. During the formative two decades of the ACWA's development the process of ethnic cooperation and acculturation proceeded quite gradually and required great patience and much painstaking work on the part of the union leadership.[36]

The euphoric hopes that greeted outbreaks of workers' revolution and revolutionary nationalism throughout the world in the period immediately following the war strengthened the bonds of international solidarity within the union. Thus, when Joseph Schlossberg, the ACWA general secretary, delivered a stirring eyewitness account of the Italian factory occupations of 1920 to an

ACWA convention, "continuous and uproarious applause ensued for a period of three-quarters of an hour." During the same period the ACWA won the hearts of many Italian workers by its early and staunch campaign on behalf of Sacco and Vanzetti.[37]

No doubt all of this—revolutionary expectations, education in the rights and duties of industrial citizenship, exhortations to trade union and working-class solidarity, inventive organizational devices for integrating the membership—was of considerable value. But of even greater importance were those innovations of the new unionism that delivered tangible benefits while equalizing relations between ethno-occupational groups. Because they did inhabit very different segments of the industry's occupational terrain, Italians and Jews were divided not only by income levels but by their prospects for job security and upward mobility. Because Italians were heavily concentrated not only in semi- and unskilled factory jobs but also comprised the principal population among impoverished homeworkers, their incomes were conspicuously less than the earnings of their Jewish co-workers, often as much as 40 to 50 percent less. Even before the ACWA was firmly established in all the major markets, the leadership adopted a policy of demanding larger wage increases for the union's lowest-paid workers, thus closing a gap that had aggravated ethnic tensions.

At the same time, the leadership made repeated efforts to root out the homework system. In 1920, the organization established the Italian Joint Executive Board, whose principal purpose was to abolish the system of homework and to "enforce the production of the entire garment on the premises." The massive organizing campaign launched in Philadelphia in 1929 was perhaps the most successful such assault on the system. Although homework nevertheless persisted, and indeed became even more extensive with the onset of the depression, the leadership proved its determination to eradicate perhaps the most repugnant form of garment work, one that victimized Italian women particularly.[38]

Job insecurity and unemployment were other painful problems from which everyone suffered, though not equally. There was perhaps no industry as vulnerable to seasonal, cyclical, and utterly arbitrary oscillations—and therefore to frequent, unpredictable, and prolonged periods of unemployment—as was the clothing trade. In the slack season it was not uncommon for 75 percent or more of the industry's capacity to lie fallow and for countless numbers of petty entrepreneurs and contractors to cease business entirely. Such extreme insecurity was a principal reason that led the new unionism to pioneer in the creation of a system of unemployment insurance in the mid-twenties. But years before that system was installed, the ACWA leadership implemented a policy of work-sharing to distribute the hardships of unemployment more evenly. Cutters and other skilled workers were better able to weather cyclical downturns, especially since employers were more reluctant to dismiss experienced people, who might suddenly and without warning be needed again should a rush order transform enforced idleness into frantic activity. Thus, New York City cutters were on the average apt to lose two to three months of work each year, while tailors could expect to be idle from three to four months. The industry's less-skilled factory and tenement labor force was the most expendable and easily replaced, and this rather naturally fueled a certain resentment. Work sharing, while not applicable across the most basic lines of skill (it was simply not feasible to have a sewing machine operator assume the duties of a skilled cutter) did at least make some tangible contribution to easing the burden of the worst off and, perhaps more importantly, served as a visible token of the leadership's commitment to eliminating ethnic inequalities.[39]

By the mid-twenties, most of the sources of Italian-Jewish friction had been eliminated or were fast disappearing. However, the embers of ethnic resentment were briefly reignited by the factional battles between the union leadership and the Communist Party between 1924 and 1927. Political animosities also gave vent to long-accumulating ethnic grievances and insults; and particularly in places like Rochester and Toronto, Italian radicals were as apt to accuse the ACWA Jewish leadership of racial injustice as of being "labor lieutenants of capitalism." But even the Communist Party acknowledged that its most glaring weakness was a failure to establish deep and durable roots among the Italian workers; they could take advantage of Italian-Jewish antagonisms only temporarily. Most Italian insurgents kept their distance from the Party, and the alliance essentially proved to be both organizationally unreliable and politically ambiguous. By the end of the decade, the flames of political and ethnic civil war were extinguished.[40]

So far as the Italians were a problem, the only other real threat to union solidarity was the sympathy and support for Italian fascism that grew substantially throughout the decade. Thus, the head of the Cincinnati Joint Board informed the GEB about a large number of fascist sympathizers in the city, and the board debated how openly to associate its extra-union, anti-fascist activity with its customary work organizing the city's clothing shops.

In general, the leadership responded promptly to the fascist threat. As early as 1924, the ACWA convention adopted a strong anti-fascist resolution and called for the support of the Anti-Fascist Alliance of North America. At the 1926 convention, Arturo Giovanitti appealed to the delegates to support the anti-fascist paper, *Il Nuovo Mondo,* which was begun with help from the ACWA. And at the 1928 convention, Giovanitti delivered a passionate exhortation about the need to destroy fascism, while many locals introduced resolutions against the Fascist League.

Italian organizers anxiously pointed out that fascism was both a foreign and a domestic danger: members of the Fascist League were serving as shop chairmen and as heads of locals. Rochester became a focal point of anti-fascist activity. In 1929, the local chapter of the Anti-Fascist Alliance adopted a militant anticlerical and anti-fascist resolution on the occasion of the Concordat between Mussolini and the Vatican. It called on Italian workers not to repudiate the spirit of independence nurtured by Garibaldi and Mazzini, described the church as an ultrareactionary institution, and explained that the anticlerical, anti-fascist, and anti-monarchist movements constituted one indissoluble struggle.[41]

It is important to note, however, that the sources of fascist sympathy were varied and not necessarily threatening to the union. One local Philadelphia militant explained, "I was a fascist in Italy because I was drunk with the humanitarian ideas of Giuseppe Mazzini. I came to the United States and am no longer a fascist sympathizer especially after the split between the Fascisti and the Combattenti Nazionali [War Veterans]."[42]

The fascist problem did persist, indeed would grow, under the pressure of the Great Depression, it led, in fact, to violent encounters between fascists and anti-fascists on the shopfloor. But it rarely took on an anti-Jewish coloration. Indeed, by the time the depression presented the ACWA with a whole new set of problems, *landslayt* and *paesani* had learned to work well together. Credit is certainly due to a dedicated and ingenious leadership that found ways to make inter-ethnic solidarity possible. More impersonal forces, however, affecting the cultural transformation of the second generation, were also largely responsible. By 1929, both *landslayt* and *paesani* were becoming something else entirely—citizens of the factory and the marketplace. Their ties to ethnic-based kin, craft, and community had weakened considerably, and with them the jealousies and conflicts that had threatened the ACWA's formative years.

Notes

1. There is a considerable body of literature on garment unionism in this period. The following books are most useful: Matthew Josephson, *Sidney Hillman: Statesman of American Labor* (Garden City, N.Y: Doubleday, 1952); J. M. Budish and George Soule, *The New Unionism in the Clothing Industry* (New York: Ancon Publishing, 1920); Jesse Thomas Carpenter, *Competition and Collective Bargaining in the Needle Trades, 1910–1967* (Ithaca, N.Y.: Cornell University Press, 1972); Charles Elbert Zaretz, *The Amalgamated Clothing Workers of America: A Study in Progressive Trades Unionism* (New York: Harcourt, Brace and Howe, 1934); ACWA, *The Clothing Workers of Chicago, 1910–1922* (Chicago: Chicago Joint Board, 1922); Joel Seidman, *The Needle Trades* (New York: Farrar and Rhinehart, 1942).

There is an even more extensive literature on the Jewish labor movement, much of which deals to one degree or another with the needle trades. Among the most helpful books are Irving Howe, *World of Our Fathers: The Journey of the East European Jews to America and the World They Found and Made* (New York: Harcourt Brace Jovanovich, 1976); Melech Epstein, *Jewish Labor in the U.S.A.* (New York: Trade Union Sponsoring Committee, 1950); Nora Levin, *While Messiah Tarried: Jewish Socialist Movements, 1871–1917* (New York: Schocken Books, 1977); Moses Rischin, *The Promised City: New York's Jews, 1870–1914* (Cambridge: Harvard University Press, 1962).

Unfortunately, less has been written on the Italians and the Italian labor movement in this period, especially with regard to the men's clothing industry, but readers can consult Thomas Kessner, *The Golden Door: Italian and Jewish Immigrant Mobility in New York CIty, 1880–1915* (New York: Oxford University Press, 1977); Edwin Fenton, *Immigrants and Unions, A Case Study: Italians and American Labor, 1870–1920* (1957; New York: Arno Press, 1975); Robert F. Foerster, *The Italian Emigration of Our Time*; Humbert S. Nelli, *From Immigrant to Ethnic: The Italian-Americans* (New York: Oxford University Press, 1983); John W. Briggs, *An Italian Passage: Immigrants to Three American Cities, 1890–1930* (New Haven, Conn.: Yale University Press, 1978); Humbert S. Nelli, *The Italians in Chicago, 1880–1930: A Study in Ethnic Mobility* (New York: Oxford University Press, 1970).

"Minutes of the Joint Board of HSM Employees, 1912–13," ACWA Papers, Labor-Management Documentation Center of the Martin P. Catherwood Library of the New York State School of Industrial and Labor Relations at Cornell University (hereafter, ACWA Papers); "Call for Action," leaflet in possession of Beatrice Bornstein, Chicago; Howard Barton Meyers, "The Policing of Labor Disputes in Chicago; A Case Study" (Ph.D. diss., University of Chicago, 1929); *Chicago Daily Socialist*, 17 January 1911; *Chicago Tribune*, 17 November 1911.

2. *Documentary History of the ACWA* (hereafter *Doc. Hist.*), 1924–1926; ACWA Papers; Membership-Nationality file, ACWA Papers.

3. Steven Fraser, "Dress Rehearsal for the New Deal: Shopfloor Insurgents, Political Elites, and Industrial Democracy in the Amalgamated Clothing Workers," in *Working-Class America: Essays on Labor, Community, and American Society*, ed. Michael H. Frisch and Daniel J. Walkowitz (Urbana: University of Illinois Press, 1983); Howe, *World of Our Fathers*; Rischin, The *Promised City*, pp. 26, 45; Ezra Mendelsohn, *The Class Struggle in the Pale: The Formative Years of the Jewish Workers Movement in Tsarist Russia* (Cambridge: Cambridge University Press, 1970), 2–17.

4. Joseph Schlossberg to Nicholas Klein, 18 March 1916, ACWA Papers.

5. Rosara Lucy Passero, "Ethnicity in the Men's Ready-Made Clothing Industry, 1880–1950: The Italian Experience in Philadelphia" (Ph.D. diss., U. of Pennsylvania, 1978), pp. 160–64, 151–56; Fenton, *Immigrants and Unions*, pp. 463, 467–68; David Saposs, interview with Frank Bellanca, 29 March 1919, Box 21, David J. Saposs Papers, Wisconsin State Historical Society; Foerster, *The Italian Emigration*, pp. 347–48; Kessner, *The Golden Door*, p. 56; *Doc. Hist.*, 1920–1922.

6. Steven Fraser, "Combined and Uneven Development in the Men's Clothing Industry," *Business History Review* 57 (Winter 1983): 522–47.

7. *Garment Worker,* August 1901 and August 1903; David Saposs, interview with B. Schweiter and Ephriam Kaufman, 31 March 1919, Saposs Papers.

8. Fraser, "Dress Rehearsal for the New Deal," pp. 212–55; Josephson, *Sidney Hillman,* chap. 2.

9. Mendelsohn, *Class Struggle in the Pale,* pp. 6–17; Howe, *World of Our Fathers;* Henry Tobias, *The Jewish Bund in Russia from Its Origins to 1905* (Stanford, Calif.: Stanford University Press, 1972).

10. Rischin, *The Promised City,* pp. 26, 45; Mendelsohn *Class Struggle in the Pale,* pp. 6–17, 59, 64, 82, 85; Howe, *World of Our Fathers;* Levin, *Jewish Socialist Movement,* pp. 219–39; Budish and Soule, *The New Unionism,* pp. 51–52; Arthur Liebman, "The Ties That Bind: Jewish Support for the Left," *American Jewish Historical Quarterly,* 1976, p. 294; Tobias, *The Jewish Bund,* pp. 7–8; David Lane, *The Roots of Russian Communism* (University Park: Pennsylvania State University Press, 1968), 167; Epstein, *Jewish Labor in the U.S.A.,* vol. 1, pp. 305, 350; Will Herberg, "The Jewish Labor Movement in the U.S.," *American Jewish Year Book,* 1952, pp. 15–16.

11. Rischin, *The Promised City;* Howe, *World of Our Fathers.*

12. Fraser, "Dress Rehearsal for the New Deal."

13. David Saposs, interview with Frank Bellanca, 29 March 1919, Saposs Papers; Passero, "Ethnicity in the Men's Ready-Made Clothing Industry," pp. 151–56, 305–6, 314, 319; Fenton, *Immigrants and Unions,* pp. 462–63, 469; Foerster, *The Italian Emigration,* pp. 347–48; Barbara Klaszynska, "Why Women Work: A Comparison of Various Groups in Philadelphia, 1910–1930," *Labor History* 17 (1976): 84–85; Jacob Loft, "Jewish Workers in the New York City Men's Clothing Industry—Report of a Preliminary Study," *Jewish Social Studies,* January 1940, p. 63; Case Records of the HSM and Chicago Boards of Arbitration, ACWA Papers.

14. Eugene Miller and Gianno Panofsky, "Radical Italian Unionism: Its Development and Decline in the Chicago Men's Garment Industry, 1910–1930" (Paper presented at 100 Years of Organized Labor in Illinois, 1881–1981 Conference, Chicago, October 1981); Fenton, *Immigrants and Unions,* pp. 16–18, 510–14, 467–68; Passero, "Ethnicity in the Men's Ready-Made Clothing Industry," pp. 315–18; Chicago Arbitration Board Records; Frank Bellanca to Joseph Schlossberg, 12 February 1914, ACWA Papers.

15. "Immigrants in Industry," Parts 5–7, vol. 73, Senate Documents, Committee on Manufacturers.

16. Ibid., Jacob Potofsky to Emilio Grandinetti, 19 January 1921, Box 4, Emilio Grandinetti Papers, Immigration History Research Center Archives, St. Paul, Minnesota; A. Bellanca to Schlossberg, 6 September 1915, ACWA Papers; Aldo Cursi to General Executive Board, 1917, A. Bellanca to Schlossberg, 1915, and F. Bellanca to Schlossberg, 6 January 1915, 4 and 12 February 1915, and 7 March 1915, all in Sidney Hillman Papers, Cornell University; Paul Arnone to Schlossberg, 9 June 1917; Artoni to Schlossberg, 1918; Valenti to Schlossberg, 16 September 1917; Cursi to Schlossberg, 23 August 1917, all in Hillman Papers; Grandinetti to Potofsky, 20 September 1916, Jacob Potofsky Papers, Cornell University.

17. Sander Genis to Hillman, 14 July 1915, Hillman Papers; Philadelphia Joint Board file, 1923, ACWA Papers; Grandinetti to National Office, 28 September 1916, ACWA Papers.

18. Abraham Shiplacoff to National Office, 15 June 1916, Shiplacoff file, ACWA Papers; Schlossberg to Hillman, 16 September 1915, Schlossberg file, ACWA Papers; David Saposs, interview with Sam Levin, 26 December 1918, Saposs Papers.

19. Minutes, Joint Board of Baltimore, 1915–1916, ACWA Papers; A. Bellanca to Schlossberg, 6 September 1915, ACWA Papers; *Doc. Hist.,* 1914–1916 and 1916–1918; A. Bellanca to Schlossberg, 1915; F. Bellanca to Schlossberg, 6 January 1915, 4 February 1915, and 7 March 1915; F. Bellanca to Hillman, 15 June 1919, Hillman Papers; *Scabs and Scab Agencies: Proven Facts of the Scandalous Scabbism of the*

IWW, Hillman Papers; Mandanick file, 1916, 21 January 1916, 23 February 1916, ACWA Papers; Baltimore Joint Board meeting, 12 April 1916, ACWA Papers; Valenti to Schlossberg, 16 September 1917 and 28 December 1917, and Gillis to Hillman, 15 July 1917, all in Hillman Papers; A. Bellanca to Schlossberg, 12 February 1914, ACWA Papers.

20. *Doc. Hist.*, 1914–1916; GEB Minutes, July–August, 1924, ACWA Papers; Paul Arnone to Schlossberg, 9 June 1917; Artoni to Schlossberg, 8 May 1917, ACWA Papers.

21. Frank Rosenblum to Hillman, 6 December 1916; ACWA Papers; "Official Souvenir of the 4th Biennial Convention, 1920," Boston local history, ACWA Papers; David Saposs, interview with David Wolff, 1 March 1919, Saposs Papers; Hillman, talk to shop chairmen, 1919, Hillman Papers.

22. Fraser, "Dress Rehearsal for the New Deal," pp. 225–27; Rosenblum to Potofsky, 3 September 1920 and 27 September 1920, both in ACWA Papers; Hillman to Schlossberg, 19 February 1915, ACWA Papers.

23. Fenton, *Immigrants and Unions*, pp. 487, 520, 530; Foerster, *The Italian Emigration*, pp. 347–48, 381; A. Bellanca to Hillman, 10 July 1916, ACWA Papers; *Doc. Hist.*, 1916–1918, 1918–1920, and 1920–1922; Artoni file, 1917, ACWA Papers; GEB Minutes, June 1921; Anthony Capraro Papers, Immigration History Research Center Archives, St. Paul, Minn.

24. Extract of Fiorello LaGuardia's report to New York Joint Board meeting, 19 February 1916, ACWA Papers.

25. Nelli, *From Immigrant to Ethnic*, pp. 114–15; Briggs, *An Italian Passage*, pp. 94, 97, 109, 159; John Horace Mariano, *The Italian Contribution to American Democracy* (New York: Arno Press reprint, 1975), 19–29; John Diggins, *Mussolini and Fascism: The View from America* (Princeton, N.J.: Princeton University Press, 1972), 21, 80, 87, 88–89, 116, 421.

26. David Saposs, interview with F. Bellanca, 29 March 1919, Saposs Papers; Mary Shipman, interview with ACWA Research Director M. Friedman, 7 March 1930, Saposs Papers; "The Man without a Friend," Grandinetti Papers, Folder 11, Box 4, Capraro Papers; this leaflet by a contrite ex-scab describes the social ostracism he faced in his Italian community.

27. A. Bellanca to Anthony Capraro, n.d., Box 6, Capraro Papers; Foerster, *The Italian Emigration*; Fenton, *Immigrants and Unions*, pp. 509–10.

28. "What Is and Why an Italian Labor Council of America?" Box 1, Capraro Papers.

29. Fenton, *Immigrants and Unions*, pp. 547–48; Grandinetti Papers, Folder 14; Rochester Joint Board file, 1918, ACWA Papers; Capraro to Potofsky, 16 June 1922, Box 3, Capraro Papers; Potofsky to Grandinetti, 19 January 1921, Folder 2, Grandinetti Papers.

30. Anunzio Marimpietri, "From These Beginnings," Chicago Joint Board, Chicago file, 1911–1914, ACWA Papers; Fenton, *Immigrants and Unions*, pp. 506–7; Biographical file, ACWA Papers; includes sketches of Marimpietri, Catalonotti, Cursi, Ullise de Domincis, Rosenblum, Jacobs, and Hardman; Josephson, *Sidney Hillman*.

31. David Saposs interview with David Wolff, 1 March 1919, Box 21, Saposs Papers.

32. *The Clothing Workers of Chicago*, pp. 3–4; Illinois file, ACWA Papers; Stephen Skala, "The Story of the Great Organizing Campaigns in Chicago, 1915–1919," unpublished manuscript, ACWA Papers; "The Reminiscences of Jacob Potofsky," Oral History Collection of Columbia University (OHCCU); Chicago Joint Board to Schlossberg, 14 December 1917, ACWA Papers; Montreal Joint Board file, 1920, ACWA Papers; David Saposs, interview with David Wolff, 1 March 1919, Saposs Papers.

33. Aldo Cursi to Schlossberg, 23 August 1917 and 25 September 1917, ACWA Papers; Valenti to Schlossberg, 6 September 1917, ACWA Papers; and Potofsky to Schlossberg, 4 September 1916 and 11 September 1916, Levin to Hillman, 7 July

1916, Rosenblum to Hillman, 6 December 1916 and 26 December 1916, and Rosenblum to Schlossberg, 26 December 1916; the last seven are in the Hillman papers.

34. *Doc. Hist.*, 1916–1918 and 1920–1922; Rosenblum to Hillman, 15 June 1916, ACWA Papers; GEB Minutes, February 1917, ACWA Papers.

35. *Doc. Hist.*, *1916–1918* and *1920–1922*; "Chicago Local 39 file," 1916, ACWA Papers; William Leiserson statement in Michaels-Stern injunction case, 20 September 1920, ACWA Papers; David Saposs also noted that the union "substituted the labor leader for the clan leader. . . . The first step in the assimilation of the immigrant . . . is to weaken the old national tie." Saposs also optimistically observed that "as soon as the immigrant has acquired a working knowledge of the English language, his connection with a union based on nationality ends and he enters a union based on occupation." This Americanization process advanced even further because, "the Amalgamated initiates its members into the mysteries of self-government," Saposs Papers.

36. Fraser, "Dress Rehearsal for the New Deal," pp. 240–41.

37. Folder 14, ACWA Clippings, 1915–1917, Grandinetti Papers; *Doc. Hist.*, 1920–1922.

38. Fraser, "Dress Rehearsal for the New Deal," pp. 230–31; GEB Minutes, 20 March 1920, ACWA Papers.

39. "Immigrants in Industry," pts. 5-7, vol. 73; Fraser, "Combined and Uneven Development in the Men's Clothing Industry," pp. 522–47; Fraser, "Dress Rehearsal for the New Deal"; *Doc. Hist.*, 1922–1924.

40. Fraser, "Dress Rehearsal for the New Deal," p. 238; Daniel Bell Collection, Tamiment Library, New York University.

41. GEB Minutes, May 1927, ACWA Papers; *Doc. Hist.*, 1922–1924, 1924–1936, and 1926–1928; "Rochester Local 63," Box 1, Capraro Papers; *New York Times*, 13 February 1927.

42. Clinton Golden to Schlossberg, 23 December 1923, Box 4, A. Bellanca Papers, Immigration History Research Center Archives, St. Paul, Minnesota.

ALLEN SEAGER

Class, Ethnicity, and Politics in the Alberta Coalfields, 1905–1945

Industrial capital's thrust into the western Canadian frontier created a series of remarkable labor movements,[1] among them the multiethnic organizations of the coal miners in the province of Alberta. Not dissimilar from the American context that aroused such nativist alarms as F. J. Warne's *The Slavic Invasion and the Mine Workers,* the Alberta coalfields were rapidly populated, at the beginning of the twentieth century, by an immigrant and "foreign" working class—with the significant caveat that the region's newly formed mining communities had never attracted large numbers of native-born workers. The national census of 1911, the first to enumerate more than 1,000 coal miners in Alberta, showed that 88.5 percent of the work force, numbering just less than 5,000, were immigrants. As late as 1941, 53 percent of all Alberta's coal miners—whose numbers peaked at more than 8,000 in the census of 1921—had been born in continental Europe; another 15 to 20 percent were second-generation mine workers of European descent. Thus, the immigrant community would shape Alberta's miners' movement in its own image: first, within the ambience of specific ethnic associations and immigrant nationalism, and second, through trade union and political organizations that crossed ethnic boundaries, particularly in the "second generation."[2]

What follows is an overview of the rise, fall, and reconstitution of the labor movement in the Alberta coalfields between 1905 and 1945, with a focus on class, ethnicity, and politics in one Alberta coal town—Blairmore in the Crow's Nest Pass—whose experience illustrates the essential continuities of the immigrant milieu. Though located on the periphery of North America's labor world during the first half of the century, the coal miners were nonetheless touched by its major institutional developments, from the socialist and syndicalist challenge to the AFL to Communist collaboration in the "new industrial unionism" of the CIO. At every stage, however, the response of the immigrant to industrial capitalism was central. This paper first traces the early development of the miners' movement, inseparable from that of the Alberta-based western Canadian District 18 of the United Mine Workers of America, 1905–1919, and then explores the links between the socialist tradition of District 18 and the emerging communist movement that had a decisive impact on the mining community during the 1920s. The Communist Party, whose presence coincided with the cessation of significant immigration into the coal towns, first provided a relevant organizational and ideological framework for cooperative ethnic relationships in the mining communities. However, the latter 1920s were a period of defeat, disillusionment, and fragmentation of the miners' movement. The paper next examines the ambiguous phenomenon of "red" trade unionism during the depression, prelude to the more pragmatic orientation of the new industrial unionism of the late 1930s and early 1940s and concludes with a detailed examination of the matrix of social relations in the town of Blairmore, "red" stronghold par excellence, and emblematic of the often powerfully radical response of the Albertan coal-mining community.

From the United Mine Workers to the One Big Union

From modest beginnings during the Territorial period (1870–1905), Alberta coal mines increased their output tenfold in the period from 1900 to 1920. Local, central Canadian, American, British, and European investors fueled the mining boom that had made Alberta, by the end of the First World War, the leading coal-producing province in the Dominion: a terrifying honor for the mine workers. Between 1906 and 1945 there were slightly more than a thousand fatal accidents in the Alberta collieries. Shared experience at the workplace and in the community did much to foster a common sense of grievance among the miners, although, as this 1914 report of the aftermath of the greatest of Alberta's mining disasters at Hillcrest in the Crow's Nest Pass suggests, immigrant miners shared as well some delicate sensibilities:

> Interment took place in several trenches. Upwards of eighty of the Catholic faith were laid in orderly array. . . . In the next trench were buried members of the Anglican, Methodist and Baptist denominations, amongst whom five Welshmen were buried side by side. The Italian brothers [were] buried in one separate trench. The friendly societies, including the Masons, Odd Fellows and Orangemen, had their several burial spots, while Mr. Frank Pearson, president of the Hillcrest local, read the burial service on behalf of the U.M.W. of A. . . . [two] were sent back to Nova Scotia for burial. The Hungarian Society buried their comrades in Blairmore.[3]

Although its leadership was overwhelmingly English-speaking, the United Mine Workers represented the majority of Alberta's coal miners by 1914 through collective bargaining agreements with the Calgary-based Western Canada Coal Operators' Association. Hard lessons in the Pennsylvania anthracite fields and elsewhere had taught the union the necessity of mobilizing across ethnic lines, although solidarity was often honored more in the breach than in actuality. "I may say that there have been several quarrels recently amongst the Italians and English-speaking men," a corporal of the Royal North West Mounted Police reported from Frank, Alberta, in 1905, "and in several cases the White men [English-speaking miners] have been threatened, several of them saying they do not care to work in the mine, as they are scared of getting a pick in the back, when they were not looking." Union officials protested police intervention in the miners' internal affairs, arguing that they were best qualified to bring any miscreants to heel. "You are well aware that in the several matters between that organization and employees throughout the Crow's Nest Pass," wrote District 18's longtime solicitor on this matter, "the executive[s] have signally succeeded in effecting settlements and coming to agreements which have assured for a long time to come the existing prosperity of this rich and growing section of the Dominion." Moderation, temperance, discipline, uplift, and improvement—these were the values the first, British-born executives of the miners' union sought to inculcate among the polygot proletariat of the Alberta coalfields. "Mike and John," the proverbial Slavic and Italian miners, formed the backbone of the rank and file, in an uneasy alliance with their fellow workers that was cemented, trade union leaders agreed, not "by love" but by the "selfish idea" of collective bargaining.[4]

The mining unions had emerged most forcefully in the Rocky Mountain bituminous coalfield. Alberta's lignite mines, situated in scattered prairie localities, sustained a largely transient, partly rural, seasonal work force. The key to the organized miners' presence lay in the southern section of the bituminous coalfield, in the Crow's Nest Pass, including, in the course of development between 1897 and 1910, communities at Hillcrest, Frank, Coleman, Lille, Bellevue, and Blairmore. These mines, producing a specialized locomotive fuel for the Canadian Pacific Railway, engaged between one-quarter and one-third of the total provincial work force. Only here can an unbroken thread of socialist and communist political activity be traced throughout the period under review. Socialism, buttressed by the radical proclivities of not a few English, Scots, Welsh, and American immigrants, quickly emerged as an alterna-

A group of coal miners in the Crow's Nest Pass during the 1920s. These photographs were made into postcards, and the immigrant workers often sent them home to friends and relatives overseas. Photo courtesy of Allen Seager.

tive to the conservative philosophy of the UMWA's best-known turn-of-the-century spokesman, international president John Mitchell. Mitchell had taken a personal interest in the organization of the western Canadian coalfields in 1903, but labor radicalism here, as elsewhere, reflected the overall failure of collective bargaining and the larger project of labor reform. William Lyon Mackenzie King, future prime minister and then-deputy minister of labor, ideologist of Liberal reformism and confidante of John Mitchell, had played an instrumental role in arranging relations between the coal operators and District 18 in the years from 1905 to 1909. By 1911, Mitchell's strong hand had been removed from the scene of industrial relations, and King's dream of the western coal industry as a showpiece for the Progressive approach lay in ashes.[5]

Dominion legislation designed to foster conciliation over strikes proved spectacularly unsuccessful in the coal industry, as the record in District 18 between 1909 and 1911 attests. The ever-more belligerent stance of the organized operators completely undermined the moderate union leadership of district president Frank H. Sherman (1903–1909), while simple facts belied the claim that trade unionism forecast a new era of economic relationships in the coalfields. The benchmark of the wage scale in District 18—the rates paid skilled miners on day work—stood at \$2.75 to \$3.00 in

1903 to 1905. By 1914 it had advanced to a mere $3.30, a loss in real-dollar terms. Just to maintain this scale, and trade union rights, miners in Alberta's Crow's Nest Pass endured no less than twelve months on the picket lines in 1909 and 1911. In 1914, unemployment was so massive that most miners would have been happy to take a job "at any price," and violent outbreaks of popular unrest were widely feared.[6]

By the time of the national elections of 1911, the Socialist Party of Canada was polling between 30 and 70 percent of the popular vote in the Rocky Mountain coal towns. In 1912, a resolution in support of the party received minority support at the annual convention of District 18, but in February 1914 a similar resolution easily won delegate backing. The socialist position was reaffirmed in 1915 although it failed again, "by a very narrow margin," one year later. The Socialist Party spoke the Marxist language of the class struggle, in an imagery of "wage slavery" that was real enough to immigrant workers in the coalfields. Notably, socialist ideas were communicated in Finnish, Italian, German, French, and Slavic languages by the SPC's "foreign-language" organizers, among others, who planted their ideology firmly in the soil of the coal-mining community. Yet the party organization would be shattered by the outbreak of the First World War. An estimated 1,500 among 7,000 members of District 18 enlisted between 1914 and 1916. Socialist ideas were, in this period, "subversive" in the Canadian context. In the Alberta coalfields they became closely and fatefully intertwined with notions of revolutionary syndicalism. A Pinkerton agency spy interrogated two Italian coal miners in Alberta's Drumheller Valley in 1918; both were

> believers in the I.W.W. principles of just one big union of all the workingmen and that we shall all be brothers and shake hands no matter what nationality we are and that the day is near at hand when it shall be that way.[7]

Wartime militancy set the stage for postwar insurgency. Miners brought "the great Fight for Democracy" into the workplace in strike actions across the district in 1916. "When it comes to arguing with the miners on the basis of patriotism in these critical war times," a reporter for the coalfields daily, the *Lethbridge Herald*, discovered, "they simply point to the very large proportion of enlistment of miners in the most dangerous branches of the active service units . . . and say that they cannot be reproved for lack of patriotism." At the Galt Mines in Lethbridge in 1916 800 men were employed; less than a quarter (186) were classified as "English-speaking," while nearly two-thirds (499) had been former citizens of the Austro-Hungarian Empire. "I venture to say," wrote Lethbridge miner John Vaselenak, "that the majority of the so-called foreigners in our community are either Czechs or Slovaks," men and women who were vocal in their allegiance to the union, to the Empire and to the Czechs and Slovaks in the homeland who were now "recognized as a nation" by the Allies. Here, as in the industrial America surveyed by David Montgomery, immigrant nationalism was a powerful stimulant to working-class action. The miners deeply resented attempts by the press and anti-labor politicians to cast their job actions as the work of seditious enemy aliens. On 1 April 1917, demands for a "war bonus" to compensate for inflationary price hikes culminated in a full-scale district strike. The state capitulated after ninety days. District 18 was placed under a régime of national control by the federal Conservative government, under which the benchmark of the wage scale increased from $3.30 in 1916 to $7.50 in 1920. The union's power was never greater, but the miners' own complex agenda remained unfulfilled.[8]

Left-wing socialists and their syndicalist allies in western Canada correctly judged the timing for their own bid for power, after the European Armistice and the winter of discontent that followed. In March 1919 they convened the Western Labour Conference in Calgary, to launch the One Big Union (OBU) movement. The conference was attended by more than thirty miner-delegates, the majority of them British and English-speaking officers of the local unions of District 18, UMWA. A delegate from the Slavic community, Alex Susnar, successfully urged the adoption of a resolution condemning attacks on so-called aliens, "said alien enemies [who] have been true to labor's cause always." It was a landmark in radical solidarity; and police spies identified District 18, especially the Crow's Nest Pass, as one of the "principal centres of plotting" in the "pernicious" OBU agitation. It should be recognized, however, that the OBU movement in the coalfields had the open support of the established district executive, and tapped a long-standing alienation of the district organization from its international parent body. In some locals the OBU was known as the "Canadian"—as opposed to "American"—union, thus drawing on another wellspring of nationalist sentiment. The eclectic radicalism of the OBU movement in the coalfields is best captured in the personality of its foremost spokesman, recently elected district union president Phillip Martin Christophers, a Cornish immigrant, pro-war socialist, Labor town councillor in Blairmore, and future member of the Alberta legislature. In 1919, Christophers was politically astute enough to read the sentiments of his own militant constituency. Over 90 percent of the organzied miners canvassed in the OBU referendum cast their ballots in favor of affiliation.[9]

But before the OBU movement could consolidate its forces, the miners were swept up in the wave of sympathetic strikes set in motion by the Winnipeg General Strike of 15 May–26 June 1919—a one big union from below. Antonio Gramsci had no doubt that "in Canada, the industrial strikes have taken on the overt character of a bid to install a soviet regime," and the Canadian government agreed. The miners' walkout in District 18 would bring severe reprisals from the state, the employers, and the international office of the UMWA. The district officers, ousted from power by UMW president John L. Lewis, formally constituted the Miners' Section of the OBU, but the jurisdiction of the International was to be upheld in the union mines by a closed-shop agreement negotiated by federal Minister of Labor Gideon Robertson in December 1919. With the failure of the 1919 strike, blacklists of OBU men and pit-level activists were strongly and immediately enforced in most mines, with others following in 1920. Those lists which have survived in the records of companies operating at Coleman, Coalhurst, Brulé, and smaller Alberta centers suggest that the weight of discrimination fell equally upon the shoulders of English-speaking and Slavic-Italian militants. The red scare in the coal towns did not unleash, as some authors clearly hoped, a fury of ethnic strife. The radicalism of the immediate postwar period, however, had proven no match for the forces arrayed against it.[10]

Communist Movement and Ethnic Culture

The events of 1919 confirmed in the minds of moderate miners and their leaders the deadly error of entanglement with what John L. Lewis described as the "daydreamers and visionaries" of the Left. This view was not shared by rank-and-file militants or by crucial segments of the mining community, as the election of a still-unrepentant P. M. Christophers to the provincial legislature with 40 percent of the votes in the district of Rocky Mountain (Crow's Nest Pass) in July 1921 attests.[11] Electoral activity also confirmed that the OBU movement had owed as much to the socialists as it did the "I.W.W. principles" of some of its leaders and supporters. Neither the Socialist Party nor the OBU, however, would be rebuilt in the 1920s; instead, the larger part of the radical constituency turned further left. In 1930, 25 percent of the electors in the district of Rocky Mountain were disciplined Communist voters, the party's share of the vote in the mining towns of the Crow's Nest Pass ranging between 21 and 65 percent.[12]

The Communist Party's widest appeal was probably garnered before it engaged in direct electoral activities, in the early 1920s, a period of unprecedented economic and industrial crisis in District 18. The founding convention of the Alberta section of the fledgling Communist Party of Canada was held in early 1923, with mining delegates predominating. The so-called Rocky Mountain Labour Party had already voted to affiliate *en bloc,* but it was not the most important of adherents to the communist cause. Of key significance was the new allegiance of two foreign-language socialist organizations with cultural and ideological roots in parts of the former Russian Empire and a network of lodges and fraternal associations in the Alberta coalfields: the Finnish Organization of Canada, which supplied up to 50 percent of the actual membership of the Comintern's Canadian affiliate in the 1920s; and the Ukrainian Farmer-Labour Temple Association, a body that acquired a pan-Slavic complexion (with left-wing Poles, Slovaks, and Yugoslavs) in many Canadian communities. In addition, the Communist Party's "language locals" in the coalfields included French and Italian branches. If awkward in the eyes of Canadian party leaders, the CP's federated structure accurately reflected the needs of its still-unassimilated ethnic components. At the same time, rank-and-file militants who might otherwise have been indifferent to communism embraced the "fighting policies" of the CP. Diverse imperatives would have informed the idealistic Christophers's open declaration in favor of the Red International in 1923.[13]

The red-led opposition in District 18 was known as the Left Wing in the 1920s, the greater number of them former OBU men who had successfully fought for their reinstatement into the mines in 1921 and 1922. Industrial relations in the coal industry took a decided tack toward renewed confrontation in 1922, as the coal operators' association tabled demands for steep wage reductions to meet the challenge of postwar recession and competition. The Left Wingers claimed their share of the victory when 10,000 members in District 18 in Alberta and British Columbia fought the mine owners to a standoff in the course of a five-months-long strike. The Left Wing slate fared well in the first open union elections since the OBU débacle, held in the winter of 1922–1923. Former OBU Unit secretary Roddy MacDonald, of Blairmore, defeated former UMW international trustee Robert Livett, of neighboring Bellevue, in a symbolic clash between the left- and right-wing factions for the post of international board member. The "red phase" in the miners' history had only just begun.[14]

The communist slogan of the "united front" thus had a dual character, symbolizing both the trade-union program laid down by Lenin's dicta and the cultural program of melding ethnic identities into a true "proletarian" consciousness avowed by the party. The party's Toronto organ, the *Worker,* took an extraordinary interest in the miners' affairs, publishing hundreds of local reports on the activities of red-led community organizations and trade unions. The fact of "various races mixing on the floor" at a mine town dance, "a sight for sore eyes" in communities where union solidarity had long since coexisted with rigid social segregation, was deemed newsworthy by the *Worker*'s Trotskyist editor. Despite hard times in the mines, *Worker* fund-raising benefits in militant strongholds such as the Drumheller Valley elicited a genuine flowering of proletarian culture. The ethnic components of the red bloc in the Crow's Nest Pass were revealed in the program enjoyed by "a full house" at the Bellevue Theatre in 1923, featuring music by the Ukrainian Choir and the Watts Goodwin Quartet, solos by Primo Stella, Mrs. Stokaluk and Mrs. Mozanaski, a poetry recital by local socialist bard John Loughran and finally, for the rougher elements in the crowd, "five rounds of boxing by Comrades Kid Burns and Dick Marshal."[15]

Provincial authorities had reason to worry about the prominence of communist leaders from the Great War veterans' community, such as Nordegg's Dai Morgan, a fiery Welshman, or Drumheller's Lewis McDonald ("Kid Burns"), a Nova Scotian. But perhaps the most dangerously radical feature of the communist culture was the organization of the Women's Labour Leagues in a handful of mining towns. Their origin lay in the uniquely feminist orientation of Finnish-immigrant socialism; with only a few exceptions, all of the leading women's activists in the mining towns were Finnish immigrants. Intensely proud of their traditions of literacy and self-education, increasingly assimilated, and devoutly Communist, they leave a detailed record for the 1920s in the pages of both the Finnish-language weekly *Toveritar* (Female Comrade) and the English-language *Woman Worker.* Arousing the solidarity of a minority of Slavic, Italian, and English-speaking women, they aimed to take politics from the union hall into the home and school, where the "bourgeois influence" combined with traditional paternalism to create a condition for mining wives and children equally as oppressive as the "slavery" of the workplace.[16]

The fortunes of the working-class movement and culture, however, remained hinged on the fulcrum of the miners' workplace struggle. In 1924 and 1925, a series of grueling strikes and lockouts destroyed the once-mighty UMWA in District 18; it left behind a patchwork of "local agreements"—or shattered locals. The highest wage scale that emerged, and only in the Rocky Mountain bituminous fields, was based on a rate of $5.40, a 30 percent reduction. The "fighting" program had manifestly failed, the Left Wing dispersed, dissipated, and in some instances, betrayed by its own comrades. Critical perspectives were not lacking even among still-loyal supporters. "The Left Wing thinks they have a monopoly on brains," reflected Blairmore union leader Frank Leary in the autumn of 1925. "Let no man make the mistake of thinking that he or any group or any country have a monopoly on brains."[17]

Red Unionism and the War Years

Although these words had an explicitly political intent, their relevance within the cultural and ethnic context of the mining community was manifest by the recognition accorded Ukrainian-born John Stokaluk in 1926. Stokaluk, secretary of the former Coleman local of the United Mine Workers, was the first individual of non-British background to serve in the capacity of a district union officer when the independent Mine Workers Union of Canada (MWUC) was formed in Alberta out of the wreckage of District 18. The MWUC represented only a minority of the former membership of District 18—between 2,000 and 4,000 Alberta miners in the period 1925–1936—and was denounced by one of its own officers in the latter 1920s as "a Pack of Cards." Its presence, if not its power, nevertheless spoke to the continued existence of a hard, militant core of trade unionists and the district's radical traditions in the coalfields, vice-president Stokaluk being a well-known member of the Communist Party. American radical Scott Nearing, after a tour of the union's stronghold in the Crow's Nest Pass in 1927, drew a bleak portrait of the condition of the working class, "a sullen, inert mass of workers being slowly worn down and crushed by the 'system,' " but unerringly predicted that the miners would rise to fight again. The process began during the early years of the Great Depression.[18]

On the surface of politics, the depression had an immediate radicalizing effect on the laboring community. In 1931, the Communist Party persuaded the majority of the MWUC membership to ratify a new affiliation to the Workers' Unity League, whose militants defined their program in the language of the Comintern's "Third period"—the building of socialism and the installation of a workers' and farmers' government in the Dominion of Canada. Facts belied these pretensions.[19] The early 1930s were a period of widespread xenophobia and political reaction, not revolutionary promise. R. B. Bennett's Conservative Party, sweeping to national power in 1930, openly articulated the sentiment that "foreign" immigrants were the cause of the growing unemployment crisis and pursued the politics of repression and deportation in the face of the Communist challenge. From none of this would the mining community remain immune. However, judging from the practice of the so-called red union in the Alberta coalfields in 1930 to 1932, labor's own program was simply pragmatic. Girding itself against unemployment, the mining community in the Crow's Nest Pass, for example, demanded that union and management negotiate work-sharing agreements, whereby all members would take "turns" at work in a dramatically falling market. The operators' temporary aquiescence turned to opposition in 1932, sparking a struggle that would loom large in the folklore of the community, the Crow's Nest Pass strike of February to September 1932.[20]

The strike was centered in the historically militant Blairmore mines of West Canadian Collieries Ltd., described by their own managers as "la citadelle de l'O.B.U. dans le province" in 1920, and the "centre of power" of the left wing and its communist successor, the Workers' Unity League. Local management vowed, in the words of WCC's Georges Vissac, "to clean up the red element from our mines." And to achieve this aim it would have to break the solidarity of an unusually heterogeneous work force. Although the WCC payroll had dropped by 140 between 1928 and 1931, a detailed "list of nationalities" employed as miners, tradesmen and mine laborers at its two collieries at Blairmore and Bellevue is available in Table 1:[21]

Table 1 West Canadian Collieries Payroll, February 1932

	Blairmore	Bellevue
British/Canadian	89	99
Belgian	19	15
Bohemian	28	24
Finnish	10	8
French	18	5
German	2	15
Italian	68	43
Lithuanian	—	5
Polish	16	38
Rumanian	—	10
Serbian	2	—
Slovak	54	39
Swedish	7	2
Ukrainian/Slavonian	17	34
TOTAL	330	337

At its peak, between March and April of 1932, the strike movement embraced 1,400 Crow's Nest Pass miners; but in early May, two locals of the MWUC at Coleman collapsed, leaving the Blairmore-Bellevue miners to fight alone with scant material aid from the Workers' Unity League, whose nationwide membership numbered 23,000. With mass picketing and violent confrontations the order of the day, tensions escalated with the intervention of the right-wing Crow's Nest Pass Citizens' League, an organization spearheaded by the Blairmore business community that pledged that "no one who bends his knee to the red flag of Russia should be allowed to stand in Canada."[22] In the face of this kind of opposition the union's ranks wilted further. Ninety-six members (28.5 percent) of the Bellevue local drifted back to work on an open-shop basis, as did fifty-one members (15.5 percent) in Blairmore. The coal company's records underscore the ethnic bias of the back-to-work movement, which cloaked itself in the guise of anti-communism. Two-thirds of the scabs were British and "Canadian" (the latter category excluding the Canadian-born sons of non-British immigrants) workers, who comprised less than 30 percent of the total work force. The English-speaking community at Bellevue split 2:1 in favor of discontinuing the strike; at Blairmore it divided in half. Among a dozen or so other ethnic groups there was no consensus, except among the Finns and Ukrainians, not one of whom broke ranks with either their union or party affiliations. But on the whole, the ethnic communities stood like a rock behind the union: among 111 Italians, for example, only one crossed the Rubicon of the picket line.[23]

Alberta premier John E. Brownlee, at first supportive of the mine owners on behalf of his United Farmers government, interceded to negotiate a compromise agreement on Labour Day 1932. The only concession granted the strikers was a promise that previously published blacklists of men who would "never" be rehired would be destroyed. West Canadian Collieries general manager Vissac honored his pledge; the earlier blacklists have disappeared. However, the names of sixty-three men who had not been rehired as of December 1932 constitute a de facto list of employees judged to be reds by foremen at the Blairmore colliery. On it are the names of no less than sixteen Italians, nine Slovaks, seven Czechs, six Belgians, four each of British immigrants, "Canadians," and Frenchmen, three Finns, two Germans, two Poles, one Swede, and three others. The Communist Party claimed that "national lines were wiped out" among the strikers, and to an extent, this was indeed the case.[24] In February 1933 the red-led miners squared off against the bourgeois Citizens' League in a contest for local government in Blairmore. "Never in the history of any town in western Canada was such a degree of interest manifested in a municipal election," remarked the pro-Citizens weekly *Blairmore Enterprise.* The Citizens were defeated by a narrow margin, and a carefully constructed Workers' Slate, including English, Welsh, Scottish, Italian, Slavic, and Scandinavian representatives, seized the reins of power in this small community of 1,629 souls, 59 percent of whom (1931 census) were of non-English-speaking background.[25]

The Blairmore miners earn their footnote in Canadian history for one symbolic act of the red administration. In 1934, it renamed the town's main thoroughfare (now an anonymous Highway 3) Tim Buck Boulevard, in honor of the then-imprisoned leader of the Communist Party of Canada. In a ceremony marking his release from the penitentiary in 1935, Buck received the keys to the city from workers' mayor William Knight. Less well known is the fact that the labor administration, despite repeated attempts by the Citizens to unseat it during the 1930s, was never defeated at the polls. A segment of the electorate supported the left wing in local government, but not the party of Tim Buck. Its candidate in the 1935 provincial elections, strike organizer Harvey Murphy, received only 36 percent of local votes—and only 20 percent in the district of Rocky Mountain. By 1945, however, 54 percent of Blairmore's electors were casting ballots for the Communist Party in the national elections. A member of the Communist Party, Enoch Williams, served as Blairmore mayor from 1937 to 1952.[26]

Outside this local milieu, the party's fortunes showed no marked improvement during the 1930s. The red unions were dissolved in the name of the Popular Front in 1936, and the former locals of the Mine Workers' Union of Canada were merged once more with the forces commanded by John L. Lewis and the United Mine Workers—now following the flag of the Congress of Industrial Organizations. The CIO in 1936 and 1937 seemed to offer again the miners' elusive prize—industrial power—while the Communist leaders, such as John Stokaluk, parlayed their regional influence into nonelected staff positions in Lewis's revamped union. The operators yielded, one by one, to the demand for union recognition. By 1941, District 18 was a de facto closed shop for the UMWA. Not until 1943, however, did the miners use their potential bargaining leverage to demand the restoration of the wage scale that had obtained at the end of the First World War. In western Canada, the controversial wartime walkout of November 1943 was to be the last major demonstration of the coal miners' historic militancy. Technological change rapidly wrote *finis* to Alberta's coal-mining community in the late 1940s and early 1950s.[27]

As illustrated by the experience of the leanest years of the interwar period, the real strength of the miners' movement lay in local communities. Blairmore's example drew much attention, then and later. When the Canadian Broadcasting Corporation sent its reporter to investigate the situation in District 18 during the 1943 strike—which was continent-wide—he knew exactly where to look for answers. "I spent last week in the town of Blairmore here in Alberta," Herbert Mays told a national radio audience; he detailed the miners' grievances, praised their anti-fascist sentiments (ninety-eight townspeople were in uniform and the company's records indicate that the great majority of miners, from virtually all ethnic groups, enlisted after 22 June 1941); and gave an approving review of the achievements of the union-dominated local government. It was the community's ordinary citizens, however, that most impressed this visitor: "you can hear the accents of almost every nation in Europe. These miners come from Poland, Italy, Germany, Hungary, Czechoslovakia, and all of the British Isles. If ever there was a melting pot, Blairmore is."[28]

Class and Ethnicity in Blairmore

"Blairmore's stand," communist journalist Dorothy Livesay had written in 1936, "must rest upon something much firmer than having a Tim Buck Boulevard." It rested, in part, on a unique historical development that would have had significant importance to the collective consciousness of its worker community in the 1930s. For example, of the men who walked out of the pits at West Canadian Collieries to protest discrimination against their "red" comrades in February 1932, approximately 25 percent had been at the same mine in which they currently worked since the outbreak of the First World War. Nearly 40 percent had been members of their same local unions when they embraced the OBU in 1919. About 20 percent of the payroll in 1932 was comprised of the sons of these same men, integrated into the work force in the 1920s.[29]

Blairmore and its satellite villages of Bellevue, Lille, and Frank formed a single industrial-commercial enclave brought to life between 1898, the year of the completion of the Canadian Pacific Railway's Crow's Nest Pass line, and 1911, when the town of Blairmore proper won municipal incorporation. The commercial activities of the region were dominated by a community of native-Canadian and immgrant entrepreneurs (the majority of them English-speaking citizens); these made up the bulk of the "leading citizens" enumerated by a local directory published in 1922 (233 names among Blairmore's population of 1,552 in the 1921 census). Industrial capital, however, was represented by French and Belgian mining promoters who had been invited into the region on the most generous terms by the government of Sir Wilfrid Laurier between 1903 and 1908. Of the two pioneering companies, the Paris-based Canadian Coal Consolidated, which operated mines at Frank until 1918, fell by the wayside in an increasingly harsh and competitive economic environment. West Canadian Collieries (headquartered in Lille, France)—which at one time in 1910 produced no less than a fifth of all Alberta's coal—survived by the application of hard-nosed business practices after its original dreams of corporate grandeur had dissolved with the ending of the prewar settlement boom. The small industries it had sustained—cement and brick works, a lead-zinc smelter and the Blairmore Iron Works—were abandoned by the 1930s, while its plant and townsite at Lille, Alberta, were permanently shut down on the eve of World War I. Its two mines at Blairmore-Bellevue were, apart from a small sawmill, the only industrial employers after the closure of the Canadian Pacific Railway's local roundhouse in 1931. During the depression and after, the working class of the community was fighting a slowly losing battle for economic survival which underlay the militancy of that latter era.[30]

In 1911, the year that the socialists appear to have won over the support of a majority of enfranchised miners in the four towns (with 248 Socialist ballots cast), their combined population was slightly less than 2,000. According to the census that year (the first and last that yields such data for all of the West Canadian Collieries towns), the largest ethnic or national groups were the Italians (555); Austro-Hungarians (382); French and Belgians (381); Russians, most of whom were ethnic Finns (85); and Germans (69). The large number of West European immigrants, attracted by West European capital, is notable. Canadian socialists would have little difficulty garnering support in these milieux, while Catholic clergy routinely blamed "immigrants from mining areas in Europe" for spreading "communism, anti-clericalism and general disaffection" in the larger immigrant community—an interesting example of the convergence of ethnic traditions and working-class consciousness. Working-class leaders from the French and Belgian communities, for their part, warned against the baneful influence of native francophone organizations, whose conservative influence seems to have been nonexistent in the mining milieu.[31]

The rich tapestry of ethnic working-class organizations present in the Crow's Nest Pass in the years between 1910 and 1930 included the Finland Society, the Fiora d'Italia, the Belgian-Italian Co-operative Society, the Bohemian National Alliance, the First Slovak Mutual Benefit Society, the Polish Brotherhood, and its leftist rival, the Ukrainian Farmer-Labour Temple Association. Five of these associations (except the Poles and Ukrainians, headquartered in Coleman) had their local, or, in the case of the Slovaks, national headquarters in Blairmore or Frank. Together with the ubiquitous fraternal lodges sustained by British-born miners—the socialist leader P. M. Christophers is said to have been a prominent Mason—they formed a dense network of working-class association transcending the nexus of the union or political party. The relationship between the two, however, was increasingly blurred through time. The failure of the pivotal bloc of Italian miners to scab in 1932 may have had something to do with the constitution of the Italian society, which barred strikebreakers from drawing benefits! The anti-fascist stance of the Blairmore Slovaks, which led to their isolation from national Slovak organizations during the 1930s, was not unrelated to the status of the Communist Party in the local Slavic community.[32]

Potentially, there was as much basis for national antagonisms as for labor solidarity within these ethnic groups. In other mining towns in District 18, the outbreak of the First World War led to rank-and-file agitation, even strikes, to secure preference of employment to workers of Allied nationality. In a word, British and Italian patriots forged alliances against Slavs, especially the Ukrainians, who stoutly refused to side with either Czar Nikolai or the Emperor Franz Josef in 1914.[33] But the local experience in 1914 to 1918 was quite different; it fostered instead unprecedented pride and solidarity among the major ethnic groups as local spokesmen for labor, capital, and the middle class adopted an ideology of wartime unity and rejected the "enemy alien" cry.[34] French and Italian army reservists received enthusiastic send-offs in 1914 and 1915. In 1916, Blairmore was the center for the recruiting of a special regiment of miners and sappers, the 192d Crow's Nest Pass. William Archer, the delegate who had cast his vote in favor of socialist affiliation for District 18 on behalf of the Blairmore union local at the 1912 convention, is listed among the community's war dead. Of key importance was the mobilization of the bulk of the Slavic community by "loyal" Czechs and Slovaks. The Labour Day march in 1918 was appropriated by the Bohemian National Alliance, which orchestrated a celebration of national liberation joined by Czechs, Slovaks, and Poles.[35]

The postwar decade witnessed developments that were quite as important as brutal industrial conflict and the radicalism of the Communist Party. The emergence of a second generation of miners, who left behind the particularisms of their parents, heralded the true birth of the "new culture" of the Marxist Left. Not surprisingly, the "young miners" were at the cutting edge of the strike struggle in 1932. Men under 30 comprised one-quarter of the labor force at the Blairmore colliery, but 40 percent of the blacklisted "reds." WCC Chief Engineer J.-A. Brusset, for good reason, articulated his concern over "young men . . . supposed to be of more or less communistic tendencies," while manager Vissac pursued an atavistic vendetta against the oldest man on his payroll, Françoise Demoustiez, "Belge . . . rouge avec assez mauvais réputation."[36]

Union secretary Joseph Krkosky, Jr., a communist moderate called Merciful Joe, was one of the second generation. Born in British Columbia of Slovak parents, Krkosky was bred to the mines in Blairmore. His name was on the ballot for the first Workers' Slate in 1933—as well as on the blacklist of 1932—and in 1934 he won more votes than any municipal candidate in the history of the town. A slide of top coal in the Blairmore colliery ended his life of labor activism in October 1944, at age thirty-five. The mines in the whole district closed down on the occasion of his burial, and according to the *Blairmore Enterprise,* 3,000 witnessed his last, secular rites. Krkosky's parents had requested a Catholic burial, a request denied by the clergy. Merciful Joe Krkosky was apparently the second man of those on the 1932 blacklist to be killed in that colliery in 1944. In April, Georges Danscoine, of Pas-de-Calais, France, a twenty-five year veteran of the pit, lost his life there. His was also a church-ordered burial in the Protestant cemetery.[37]

Class consciousness, community-based solidarities, political ideologies, and ethnic identities are not easily sorted out and neatly compartmentalized in this history. Radicalism flourished in a relatively isolated industrial environment where worker communities enjoyed a substantial measure of cultural autonomy, and the working-class culture that sustained it was clearly an admixture of residual and emergent elements. Union Jacks flew proudly alongside red flags at Blairmore's famous May Day demonstrations during the 1930s, often marked by a mocking theater of charivari by the plebeian crowd—in 1934, one group were "all dressed as clowns, and played their parts exceedingly well"—as well as speeches, picnics, and sports. As anthropologists remind us, "The paradox of culture, which provides for continuity and change, holds for ideological systems also. . . . The 'death' or 'loss' of a culture is a myth, as is the notion of ideological purity, which has no more reality than the myth of a 'pure race.' " These are helpful reflections upon the process of acculturation as well as ethnic response in the mining community, and themes that might be noted carefully in future considerations on North American immigrant radicalism.[38]

Notes

1. For an overview see David J. Bercuson, "Labour Radicalism and the Western Industrial Frontier, 1897–1919," *Canadian Historical Review* 58, no. 2 (1977): 154–75.

2. F. J. Warne, *The Slavic Invasion and the Mine Workers* (Philadelphia: J.P. Lippincott and Company, 1904); Victor Greene, *The Slavic Community on Strike: Immigrant Labor in Pennsylvania Anthracite* (Notre Dame, Indiana: Notre Dame University Press, 1968); Michael Nash, *Conflict and Accomodation: Coal Miners, Steel Workers and Socialism, 1890–1920* (Westport, Conn.: Greenwood Press, 1982).

3. *District Ledger* (organ of District 18, United Mine Workers of America, Fernie, B.C.), 27 June 1914. For a survey of mining conditions see David J. Bercuson, ed., *The Alberta Coal Industry, 1919* (Calgary: Historical Society of Alberta, 1978).

4. Correspondence concerning District 18, UMWA, 9–14 June 1905, cited in Lewis G. Thomas, ed., *The Prairie West to 1905: A Canadian Sourcebook* (Toronto: Oxford University Press, 1975), 212–13; *District Ledger,* 10 July 1915.

5. Paul Craven, *'An Impartial Umpire': Industrial Relations and the Canadian State, 1900–1911* (Toronto: University of Toronto Press, 1980), 241–70; J. H. Harrington, "Struggle in the Crow's Nest Pass," *Western Clarion,* Vancouver, 15 April 1911.

6. Charles A. MacMillan, "Trade Unionism in District 18, 1900–1925" (M.A. thesis, University of Alberta, 1969); Department of Labour Records, Strikes and Lockouts Files, vols. 298–99; Public Archives of Canada (hereafter PAC).

7. Glenbow-Alberta Archives (Calgary), Frank Moodie Papers, "Detective Reports," f.4, 16 January 1919; on the Socialist Party and the miners see A. Ross McCormack, *Reformers, Rebels and Revolutionaries: The Western Canadian Radical Movement 1899–1919* (Toronto: University of Toronto Press, 1977), 53–76; Carlos Schwantes, *Radical Heritage: Labor, Socialism and Reform in Washington and British Columbia, 1885–1917* (Seattle: University of Washington Press, 1979), 163–83; Allen Seager, "Socialists and Workingmen: The Western Canadian Coal Miners, 1900–1920," *Labour/le travail* 16 (Fall 1985).

8. Quotations from *Lethbridge Herald* strike reports, 2 August 1916; letter from J. Vaselenak, *District Ledger,* 26 October 1918. The Galt Mines payroll can be found in the Glenbow Archives, Western Canada Coal Operators' Association Papers, f. 77; on the district strike of 1917 see Prime Minister Robert Borden's Papers, vol. 213, PAC.

9. Gerald Friesen, *The Canadian Prairies: A History* (Toronto: University of Toronto Press, 1984), 356–64; *Verbatim Proceedings of the Western Labour Conference,* pp. 61–63, Public Archives of Manitoba; Donald Avery, *'Dangerous Foreigners': European Immigrant Workers and Labour Radicalism in Canada, 1896–1932* (Toronto: McClelland and Stewart, 1979), 80–81; "Secret: Memorandum on Revolutionary Tendencies in Western Canada, Prepared by Assistant Comptroller, Royal North West Mounted Police," pp. 6–8, RG 24, Naval Service Intelligence, vol. 3985, 105-2-21, PAC; David J. Bercuson, *Fools and Wise Men: The Rise and Fall of the One Big Union* (Toronto: McGraw-Hill-Ryerson, 1978), 196–214.

10. Gramsci quoted in Gregory S. Kealey, "1919: The Canadian Labor Revolt," *Labour/le travail* 13 (Spring 1984): 33–34; John Laslett, *Labor and the Left: A Study*

of Socialist and Radical Influences in the American Labor Movement, 1881–1924 (New York: Basic Books, 1970), 228; West Canadian Collieries Ltd. Papers (hereafter, WCC Papers), strike memoranda, f.83, esp. "Grève 1919," 15 August 1919, Glenbow Archives; blacklists located in the same archive, Western Canada Coal Operators' Association Papers, f.82.

11. Melvyn Dubofsky and Warren Van Tyne, *John L. Lewis: A Biography* (New York: New York Times Book Co., 1977), 52; Tim Buck, *Lenin and Canada* (Toronto: Progress Books, 1970), 11–12.

12. The election returns, Rocky Mountain polls, were published in the *Lethbridge Herald,* 19 June 1930. The Communist candidate in these elections was a Yorkshire miner, "Rock" Sudworth from the Coleman local union, whose name is to be found on the 1919 blacklist cited in note 10.

13. See Ian Angus, *Canadian Bolsheviks: The Early Years of the Communist Party of Canada* (Montreal: Vanguard Publications, 1981), 92; *Worker,* 1 January and 1 February 1923.

14. See *Left Wing,* the monthly organ of the Trade Union Educational League of Canada, 1924–1926; "Keen Competition for UMW Offices," *Western Canada Coal Review* (Winnipeg), November 1922; Oscar Ryan, *Tim Buck: A Conscience for Canada* (Toronto: Progress Books, 1975), 104; *Worker,* 1 March 1923.

15. "Sight for Sore Eyes," *Worker,* 29 December 1923, the Christmas dance being attended by "English, Irish, French, Italians, Ukrainians and a small group of bonnie rebels from Fifeshire, Scotland" at Drumheller; Bellevue theatre events described in the 30 May issue; another *Worker* benefit at Hillcrest, reported in the 15 March number, was dominated by the "Italian comrades . . . singing revolutionary and operatic music with great gusto" long after everyone else had been exhausted.

16. "Strike Reports—1925," Attorney-General's Papers, 75. 126, Box 232, Public Archives of Alberta: "This is given as an example of the sway that [Kid Burns] has over the miners. The men had no intention of marching . . . but Burns had only to shout a couple of times for them to form up, about 3,000 men . . . headed by a number wearing returned soldiers' buttons." For the Women's Labour League see Joan Sangster, "The Communist Party of Canada and the Woman Question, 1922–1929" (Paper read at the Canadian Historical Association Annual Meetings, Vancouver, 1983), pp. 30–37; Varpu Lindstrom-Best and Allen Seager, "*Toveritar* and the Finnish Canadian Women's Movement, 1900–1930," in *The Press of Labor Migrants in Europe and North America,* ed. Christiane Harzig and Dirk Hoerder (Bremen: University Printing Office, 1985), 243–64.

17. Proceedings, Mine Workers' Union of Canada founding convention (typescript), p. 27, in "Strike Reports—1925," Public Archives of Alberta.

18. John Kolasky, *The Shattered Illusion: The History of Ukrainian Pro-Communist Organizations in Canada* (Toronto: Peter Martin Associates, 1979), 14; Proceedings of the Second Annual Convention, Mine Workers' Union of Canada (1926), "President's Report," p. 4, Department of Labour Library, Hull, Quebec, Canada, Scott Nearing, "Crow's Nest Pass," *Labour Monthly,* February 1927, pp. 102–3.

19. See Prime Minister R. B. Bennett's Papers, vol. 141, 93152-3, PAC; J. R. Smith, West Canadian Collieries Ltd., to Bennett, 27 June 1932, with enclosure, "Manifesto of the Communist Party to Miners of the Crow's Nest Pass," n.d.

20. Lita Rose Betcherman, *The Little Band: The Clashes between the Communist Party and the Political and Legal Establishment in Canada, 1928–1932* (Ottawa: Deneau Publishers, 1982); Howard Palmer, *Patterns of Prejudice: A History of Nativism in Alberta* (Toronto: McClelland and Stewart, 1982), 137–38; "Labour Situation" memoranda, 1931–1932, WCC Papers, f.101, Glenbow Archives.

21. Quotations from "Situation Ouvrière," 26 March 1920, WCC PApers, f. 83, "Our Future in District 18" (policy document), Coleman, 8 May 1925, Communist Party of Canada Papers 10C25155-7, and "Vissac to Head Office," 27 February 1932, WCC Papers, f. 101; list of nationalities, linked where possible to the manuscript register of employees of the Bellevue colliery, WCC Papers, f.174, WCC Papers.

22. William Peters, Jos. Krkosky, J. Price, J. F. Dugdale, G. C. Gaseoff, and Andrew Dow, "What We Are Striking For: The Stand of the Striking Miners of the Crow's Nest Pass" (copy of broadside of three-town pit committee), 18 April 1932, WCC Papers, f. 101; "Alberta Miner Reviews Strike," *Worker*, 25 June 1932; reference to the red flag in the words of Citizens League delegate J. E. Gillis, B.A., "Citizens League Hears Stirring Pleas, Blairmore," undated typescript, WCC Papers, f. 101.

23. Information on strikebreakers from "Distribution of Employees by Nationality," 22 July 1932, f. 101, WCC Papers; "Situation Générale aux mines," 27 September 1932 (Bellevue employees register), f. 103, WCC Papers. The most detailed accounting is from the relatively less militant Bellevue local, where strikebreakers were drawn from the following groups: British/Canadian (64), Belgian (4); Bohemian (4); French (2); German (3); Italian (1); Lithuanian (2); Polish (5); Rumanian (3); Slovak (4); others/not specified (3). Recognizing the bitter opposition that would have been aroused among all local factions by any attempt to break the strike with the aid of outsiders, the company relied instead upon political, economic pressure on their own employees. Single men who broke with the union received a special "relief" allowance of seventy-five cents a day—a dollar for married men. Those who surrendered under these terms were of course regarded as "filthy traitors" or "fascists," regardless of race or creed.

24. Vissac to Brownlee, 19 August 1932, and memorandum, "Grève, 1932," 2 September 1932, both in WCC Papers, f. 101; the blacklist is found in a letter, Jos. Krkosky, Jr., to Georges Vissac, 19 December 1932, WCC Papers f. 604; "Blairmore: A Union Camp," in the *Worker*, 9 June 1933, provides a Communist evaluation of the strike.

25. *Blairmore Enterprise*, 9–16 February 1933.

26. Ralph Allen, *Ordeal by Fire: Canada, 1910–1945* (Garden City, N.Y.: Doubleday, 1961), 323–24; Tim Buck reception reported in the *Lethbridge Herald*, 22 March 1935; 1935 election results from ibid., 28 August 1935; *Report of the Chief Returning Officer, Twentieth General Elections* (Ottawa: King's Printer, 1945), 707. Enoch Williams, running under the "Labor-Unity" banner in the 1944 provincial elections, district of Crow's Nest-Pincher Creek, garnered a record 1,812 votes (to 2,190 for the Social Credit incumbent) for the communist cause in the region.

27. Irving Abella, *Nationalism, Communism and Canadian Labour: The Communist Party, the CIO and the Canadian Congress of Labour, 1935–1956* (Toronto: University of Toronto Press, 1974), 3–5; Tom McEwen, *The Forge Glows Red: From Blacksmith to Revolutionary* (Toronto: Progress Books, 1974), 148–49; J. W. Pickersgill, *The Mackenzie King Record, 1939–1944* (Toronto: University of Toronto Press, 1960), 594–97.

28. Allen May, "CBC Reporter Visits a Mining Town," *Canadian Mineworker*, November 1943, pp. 3–5, 11; on enlistments see *Lethbridge Herald*, 10 November 1943, f. 201, WCC Papers.

29. Dorothy Livesay, "A Coal Camp in the Mountains," *Daily Clarion* (Toronto), 5 May 1936; employment histories from the Bellevue mine register, cited in n.21.

30. *Crowsnest and Its People* (Crow's Nest Pass Historical Society: Coleman, Alta., 1979), 75–85, 121–33; *Wrigley's Alberta Directory*, vol. 2 (1922): 91–94; Prime Minister Wilfrid Laurier Papers, 119548–51, PAC; West Canadian Collieries correspondence, PAC; "West Canadian Collieries—One of the Biggest Industries in Canada," *Blairmore Enterprise*, 8 September 1910; Directors' reports, f. 57, WCC Papers.

31. "Report of the (1911) General Elections," *Sessional Papers*, 1912, no. 18, pp. 476–77; Canada, *Fifth Census of Population and Agriculture*, vol. 2, pp. 162–65; church complaints voiced in M. B. Venini Byrne, *The Buffalo to the Cross*, excerpted in *Crowsnest and Its People*, p. 293. An article in the "News for our Foreign Brothers" feature in the UMW weekly, *District Ledger* (17 February 1913) noted that "Les journeaux Canadiens-français sont . . . les ennemis de la class ouvrière." On 22 May 1914, the *Blairmore Enterprise* announced the appointment of a Presby-

terian missionary" to work among French-speaking people in the Crow's Nest Pass. . . . The subject of his first address will be 'The Religion of the Future: The New Christianity, Social and Anti Clerical.'

32. Ferucio de Ceco, "The Italian Benefit Society," in *Crowsnest and Its People,* pp. 322–24 (and other entries for ethnic and fraternal associations); see also *Wrigley's Alberta Directory,* s. v. "Blairmore," vol. 1 (1920), p. 104; John Gellner and John Smerek, *The Czechs and Slovaks in Canada* (Toronto: University of Toronto Press, 1967), 99.

33. Helen Potrebenko, *No Streets of Gold: A Social History of Ukrainians in Alberta* (Vancouver: New Star Books, 1977), 135–36; Avery, *'Dangerous Foreigners,'* p. 67; "Opposed to Working with 'Alien Enemies,' " *District Ledger,* 12 June 1915.

34. A small number of German nationals were laid off from West Canadian Collieries in August 1914, but all had been rehired by November ("August Bogusch" biography, as told to Alice (Bogusch) Van Wyk and Florence E. Kerr, *Crowsnest and Its People,* pp. 423–24).

35. The recruitment of the 192d regiment, reported in the *Lethbridge Herald,* 25 January–29 March 1916, was especially significant; its commissions were carefuly divided between trade-union, company, and middle-class representatives. For the Slavic celebration see the *Blairmore Enterprise,* 30 August and 6 September 1918.

36. See "Blairmore Kids Mean Business" and other articles on local communist youth work in the *Young Worker* (Toronto), 21 July 1932; WCC Papers, Brusset to Vissac, 7 January 1932, f. 101, WCC Papers; Memoranda *re* Marc Piard case, 12 October 1932, f. 103, WCC Papers.

37. I am indebted to Charlie Drain, Anthony Patera, and John Krkosky for interviews they gave me during 1975 to 1979 at Blairmore, on their recollections of Joe Krkosky; see the *Blairmore Enterprise,* 28 April and 13–20 October 1944. The graves of the two miners are side by side in the Blairmore cemetery.

38. "Workers Celebrate May Day in Pass Towns," *Coleman Journal,* 8 May 1930; *Blairmore Enterprise,* 3 May 1934; see also Bryan D. Palmer, "Discordant Music: Charivaris and Whitecapping in Nineteenth Century North America," *Labour/le travailleur* 3 (1978): 57; quotation from Lydia Black, "The Nature of Evil: Of Whales and Sea Otters," in *Indians, Animals and the Fur Trade,* ed. Shepard Krech III (Athens: University of Georgia Press, 1981), 133.

Class and Nationalism

DAVID MONTGOMERY

Nationalism, American Patriotism, and Class Consciousness among Immigrant Workers in the United States in the Epoch of World War I

The aspirations of immigrants and their assimilation into urban America are matters as complex as they are essential to the history of the United States. Conceptions of changing mentalities which imply a single, direct line of development, such as "modernization," "Americanization," or the "transition from peasant to proletarian," tend to obscure both the active role of immigrants in shaping their own world and the impact on their aspirations of events and conflicts which at one moment opened up or at another foreclosed various visions of individual and collective opportunities. Such visions, whether fleeting or enduring, were important precisely because, as Julianna Puskás has written, "the decision to emigrate was made by those who, for whatever reason, refused to accept their lot, who had a strong desire for change. . . ."[1] But what changes did immigrant wage earners consider possible or even desirable?

Foreign-born workers and their children took part in a world war, in conflicts over the future of their native lands, and in the most intense and protracted strike wave in American history. They endured a veritable deluge of political propaganda. But they also had many occasions to express their own views, and they did so in ways that revealed not only the persistent force of their cultural traditions and familial needs but also widespread hopes for a future social life, in America and in Europe, which would be very different from that which they had experienced in the past.

When Lithuanian strikers crowded into St. Michael's Hall in Lawrence, Massachusetts, in April 1919, they opened their meeting by singing "The Internationale." Men, women, and children clamored for the floor to speak with bitterness about America. All agreed that they wanted to go home. And all responded with cheers to expressions of solidarity with Italians, Poles, Letts, Syrians, Franco-Belgians, Jews, and others who were then on strike with them for a 48-hour week (in defiance of the American Federation of Labor's United Textile Workers).[2] Here was the discourse of class consciousness and of internationalism, yet it was mingled with ethnic cohesiveness and with a desire to resume life on the land at home—and to do so under circumstances made better than those they had left behind through the wages earned in Lawrence, as well as through the new liberties which they thought were being achieved in the homeland. Nevertheless, this discourse was also spiced with Wilsonian and Gompersian rhetoric. Its diverse themes were underscored by frequent parades in which immigrants grouped by nationality physically manifested class solidarity while waving American flags.

The crushing defeats suffered by unions in mass production industries between 1919 and 1922, however, snuffed out dreams of collective power in American industry, which had flourished at the peak of the postwar strike wave; at the same time the news of grim conditions in Europe put to rest dreams of a new life in the old country. These immigrant dreams, so much alive in 1919, were crushed almost beyond recall.[3]

Evidence of what was being said to workers at this time is abundant. National causes, supporting various movements in the mother country, were vigorously picked up by the immigrant community and found extensive coverage in the foreign-language press. At the same time, authorities in Washington systematized their efforts to "Americanize" the foreign-born population, both through the suppression of "disloyal" elements and through the cultivation of patriotic attachments to the United States. Finally, the AFL expanded its membership dramatically by enrolling many immigrants in the cause of "American trade unionism" and collective bargaining.

It is the aim of this paper to describe and analyze the complex blend of peasant aspirations, ethnic cohesiveness, and class consciousness through which immigrant strikers of the war epoch translated the rhetoric of immigrant nationalists who espoused the cause of the mother countries, governmental demands for patriotic devotion to the United States, and trade union efforts to involve the workers in contractual bargaining relationships with their employers, into their own unique consciousness and discourse. They often used a vocabularly of citizenship, self-determination, and legal or contractual rights to express a sense of self that fit poorly with any of those concepts. They both applauded and confounded government officials, nationalist leaders, socialists, and union organizers alike. Both their behavior and their speech, however, betrayed aspirations quite different from those which had originally driven them from European villages to American factory towns.

Sources for the study of the immigrant workers' sentiments are scarcer and more difficult to interpret than those generated by governmental, nationalist, socialist, or trade union activities. Much can be learned, however, from the demands and behavior of strikers. Since the end of the depression of 1908 every period of relatively high levels of industrial employment had produced numerous strikes in the basic industries staffed by recent immigrants. Between 1916 and 1922 between one and a half to four million workers struck each year, in the most continuous strike wave in the history of the United States. Not only were foreign-born workers prominent among the strikers in the coal, steel, textile, clothing, oil, lumber, maritime, and other industries; their patterns of collective mobilization were also usually based on ethnic communities. The fact that strikes of the immediate postwar years tended to be not only larger but also longer on average than those of any other epoch in the country's history made the workers' reliance on family and community networks of support inevitable. Union strike funds, intended to sustain the tens or even hundreds of thousands who stayed off jobs for months on end, were meager at best. Immigrants thus responded publicly to the conflicting appeals for their loyalties.[4]

Moreover, the strikes were occasions for incessant public meetings (just as were the national and patriotic American movements). True, many of these meetings were tightly controlled, either from the platform to inhibit expression of the workers' own views[5] or by the police who made sure that the workers' cause was expressed in rhetoric acceptable to them.[6] Nevertheless, there were many meetings where immigrants did speak with contagious enthusiasm, especially within the halls of their own ethnic organizations.

They were also sometimes interviewed by sympathetic people. Three sets of interviews are of special value. One was undertaken by David Saposs and a team of assistants on behalf of the Interchurch World Movement's inquiry into the 1919 steel strike. Another was carried out several months earlier, also by Saposs, for a Carnegie Foundation study of Americanization. The third was collected during the 1919 strike in Lawrence, Massachussetts, by the strikers' relief committe and by organizer Anthony Capraro.[7] None of these interviews was recorded verbatim: all were preserved in the form of investigators' notes. With the possible exception of some of Capraro's interviews, the discussions were all conducted in English, rather than the mother tongue of the striker. Interviewers did, however, record expressive phrases in quotation marks ("My country no bosses," said Syrian-born Mrs. Bastyani).[8]

Above all, readers of these reports must be alert to the biases of the questioners. Capraro, an immigrant himself and an organizer on loan to the Lawrence strikers from the Amalgamated Clothing Workers of America, was concerned with promoting the cause of socialism. Saposs and his group were concerned with assimilation and with trade union rights in the context of the American republican tradition. Their investigation was guided by two preconceptions. One was the proposition that immigrants became receptive to unionization and supported a sustained strike only when they had committed themselves to remaining in the United States and had to some degree become imbued with "American ideals." From this vantage point, immigrants' nationalist causes were simply obstacles to union consciousness, and conversely, unionization was a badge of assimilation. The second, and closely related, preconception was that immigrant leaders were of two types: "clansmen" and "intellectuals." The former "would be a person accustomed to profit from the helplessness of his fellow countrymen," who led them "in accordance with his business ideals." The latter were "generally students and idealists," usually committed to social revolution.[9] When such "intellectuals" were invited by the AFL to speak to immigrants in their own languages, lamented steelworkers' organizer Edward Evans, they often took advantage of the union officers' inability to understand the speeches in order to "advocate I.W.Wism or Bolshevism and incite the workers against the A.F. of L."[10] Both these notions reflected the ideology of industrial union advocates in the AFL hierarchy. They obscure, rather than clarify, the views of the immigrant workers themselves.

Elites and Workers in Ethnic Communities

Urban immigrant communities nurtured an ethnic elite, which was constituted of clergymen, tavern and store keepers, bankers, shipping agents and professionals, as well as padroni and other labor agents. Their social ties pulled on them from three different directions: those defined by the American business community, by their countries of origin, and by the workers, who constituted the bulk of their fellow nationals in the area and their clientele. The pressures generated by these different connections could be painfully contradictory. They definitely restrained "clansmen" from leading openly "in accordance with . . . business ideals."

Take, for example, the case of Albert Mamatey of Braddock, Pennsylvania. Having been educated as an engineer in Austria-Hungary, Mamatey rose quickly through the ranks of the corporate and academic elite so carefully reserved by Anglo-Saxon America. In 1923, after twelve years of service as president of the National Slovak Society, he was appointed consul of the Czechoslovak Republic in Pittsburgh. His Society, which had become America's largest and most influential Slovak fraternal body by 1910, contributed heavily in money and soldiers to the American war effort and in moral influence to the formation of Czechoslovakia.[11] Most of its 40,000 members were workers, who relied upon it for insurance against accidents and sickness and for life insurance, as well as for educational and cultural activities and for the popular newspaper *Národné Noviny.* The Society's constitution had called for the expulsion of any member who scabbed during a strike, until a court ruling prohibited that provision.

Although *Národné Noviny* had always urged members of the Society to join unions (a matter of no small importance, given the heavy concentration of Slovaks in coal mining and steel), the great steel strike of 1919 found Mamatey and his fellow officers in a dilemma. As he explained to Saposs: "Judge Gary in behalf of the United States Steel Corporation donated a large sum of money to the Slovak red cross fund at the solicitation largely of the National Slovak Society. Now the Slovaks are fighting the Steel Corporation. This seems like ingratitude." Consequently, the newspaper avoided taking any stand at all on the great strike, while the Society's leaders warned immigrants that the strike was hopeless, that the American workers would betray them, and that the strike might be used to "usher in Bolshevism."[12]

Ruthenian journalists and clergymen found themselves in a similar dilemma, but not all voices of immigrant Pittsburgh were so reticent during the strike. Stephen Gyöngyösy, who edited the paper of the National Hungarian Workmen's Society, ardently supported the strikers and boasted that his readers were largely urban-born, skilled, and socialists.[13] The pastor of Braddock's Slovak Lutheran church contended that his congregation consisted of "church people," not Bolsheviks, and that they loved America (though a quarter of them would return home "as soon as the way is opened"); but he and they together supported the strike. The assistance offered the union cause by the Reverend Adelbert Kazinczy of Braddock's

St. Michael's Roman Catholic Church was so consistent that once the church itself was closed by police order. In response Father Kazinczy posted a notice: "This Church Closed by Activity of the J. Edgar Thompson Steel Company."[14]

Kazinczy's conversation with David Saposs revealed that he was more than a simple rustic prelate. In explaining his support of the strikers, Kazinczy pointed out: "Protestantism [and] Capitalism came into existence at the same time, and they are the ones that blocked the progress of our church. You destroy Capitalism, you destroy Protestantism."[15]

In a word, the behavior of the elites of the foreign-born communities cannot be explained simply in terms of "business ideals." It was influenced simultaneously by personal and institutional ties to the American business world, by association with national struggles in Europe, and by the rising level of self-assertion among working-class immigrants. Especially among Slovak and Yugoslav immigrants, whose nascent bourgeoisie in American cities was not so well integrated into the economic hierarchy as its German or Irish counterparts, the influence of the workers weighed heavily.

To be sure, the lure of personal success and the necessities of business and professional life in the new country linked the ethnic elite firmly to American banks, chambers of commerce, and professional societies. Stores, taverns, and rackets could not be operated without friendly police connections, which could be secured only through the dominant political party (usually the Republicans in mill towns). Moreover, to hold workers in a client relationship required helping them to find jobs. That, in turn, involved a relationship with the largest companies of the area, one that was clearly recognized by plant superintendents. United States Steel's A. H. Young advised all superintendents to "become personally acquainted with the individual boarding bosses, steamship agents, clergymen, and other influential agents with whom the immigrant maintains a close contact. These are his supply depots. . . ."[16]

These influences necessarily pushed immigrant businessmen and professionals toward close ties with the local power structure and toward an individualistic perspective on the world. However, as Scott Cummings and his collaborators have argued in *Self-Help in Urban America,* Slavic community development in the United States has been essentially collective. Community banks, stores, real estate agencies, savings and loan societies, and above all the fraternal orders were inherently mutualistic, nurturing ingrown, self-contained enclaves of group security. Within those enclaves elites exerted great influence, but the moral inhibitions imposed on them by their neighbors and clients tightly circumscribed the techniques and arenas of their personal pursuit of wealth and power. Only in New York or Chicago did the Slovak bourgeoisie enjoy an exclusive cafe and club life. In America's mill towns, reported the Hungarian correspondent Emil Zerkowitz to the imperial authorities in 1908, Slovak workers washed up "from head to toe in the evening, got dressed up, sat down at the richly laid table" of an elegant saloon ("such as they had never seen in the home country"), drank "unbelievably cheap" goblets of beer, smoked and conversed, "workers, engineers, inspectors" all together in "genuinely democratic promiscuity."[17]

The most important institution embodying this mutualistic ethic was the fraternal lodge. The insecurities of industrial life, intensified as they were by the high accident rates of the mills and mines and by the frequency with which illness struck even young peasant men and women in the squalor of urban America, made the need for insurance urgent. Rural Poles, Slovenes, Italians, and others had been accustomed to mutual benefit societies in the Old World, but it was in industrial America that the fraternals flourished, especially after a rash of statutes in northern states early in the 1890s made their legal foundations secure.

The ubiquitous presence of workers or ex-workers among the local administrators was of great importance to the fraternal orders. Handling large amounts of money, presiding over meetings, arranging (often sumptuous) funerals, and planning the parades, which became such an important immigrant ritual by the early twentieth century, lodge activists guided their communities' efforts to establish their identity and their financial security in a society hostile to both. Membership, in turn, seems to have been a badge of tenure in the new country, and in addition the fraternals were important agencies for the self-education of all their members.[18] As a Magyar Catholic priest in South Bend had complained in 1913: "At the monthly meetings of the benefit associations, they learn to put forward a proposal, to orate, to vote, to build and to destroy: they would like to see the same forces at work in parish affairs as well."[19] The values cultivated by the fraternals, however, were not those of individualism, but of family and community obligations. Croat organizations expelled members for revealing the societies' secrets, for slandering other members, and for divorce, while those of the Serbs considered adultery, drug use, venereal disease, conviction for felony, and "murder for profit" grounds for expulsion. Along with mutual insurance came mutual supervision.[20]

Patriotic Causes

The mutualistic ethnic enclaves in capitalist America proved to be hospitable to activities on behalf of the national aspirations of the countries of origin. Polish and Irish nationalists had shown by the end of the 1870s that a well-organized diaspora could not only support military operations against foreign rule of the homeland but also exert effective influence upon the diplomatic conduct of the U.S. government as well.[21] Public meetings, memorials to Congress, statues dedicated to national heroes, and speaking tours for the Kossuths and Davitts of many lands were familiar practices by the end of the nineteenth century. World War I brought to the surface a large array of immigrant community engagement which was, however, never independent of class interests and, depending on the international development, was either in accordance or at discord with the political aims of the United States. Volunteers were raised for the Balkan Wars, and after 1915 many Italians left to fight for their government, just at Poles and Czechs went to fight against theirs.[22] Some of this activity was sponsored by political conservatives, for example, the National German American Alliance, which supported the imperialist aims of the Kaiser.[23]

Enthusiasm for Italy's claims to Trieste, Fiume, and other portions of the Dalmatian Coast mustered the Italo-American elite solidly in support of Woodrow Wilson's policies before the Paris Peace Conference, and against him after Premier Vittorio Orlando marched furiously out of that conference. Among some other nationalities, however, national aspirations were advanced not by established elites but by insurgents. For example, important Slovene and Finnish socialists ultimately supported war against the Central Powers in the hope of promoting revolutionary republics at home.[24]

After April 1917, all such activity took place within the context of increasingly severe and effective suppression of dissent against the war and of the explicit encouragement of some national causes by the government's Committee on Public Information. Anti-war activity had been widespread through the summer of 1917 and had coincided with a strike wave of unprecedented scale, which peaked between July and September, and with widespread popular protest against the rising cost of living. Consequently, the Socialist Party, having firmly opposed the declaration of war, won very impressive numbers of votes in local elections of November. By early 1918, however, mass dissent had been effectively silenced. Factories were saturated with agents of military and naval intelligence; and War Industry Committees, made up of workers and foremen, staged patriotic rallies and combatted "slackers" on the job.[25] As Freda Maurer recalled those days in a Philadelphia hosiery works:

> We were getting good wages, buying bonds, giving a day's wages for the war chest, observing heatless, meatless, wheatless, and other days. As our boys left for camp we went to see them off. We laid down our tools and paraded with our boys to the railroad station . . . and took the afternoon off to show our patriotism. The next day we went back to show our patriotism. Didn't Uncle Sam need hosiery to help win the war?[26]

Prominent immigrants eagerly linked their national causes to the tide of American patriotism, wherever possible. Well-known Slovaks, Italians, Poles, and Ruthenians in the Pittsburgh area contributed their prestige and energies to Liberty Bond drives, recruiting efforts, and flag-raising ceremonies. Not until after the end of the war did many workers complain that those who had not shared in the enthusiasm had been threatened with discharge from the mills and that vocal foes of conscription (usually Finns) had been singled out for beatings and evictions.

Hungarian-, Croatian-, German-, and Sandinavian-language newspapers that had previously supported the Central Powers now fell silent or began to find promise in the Allied cause. In Cincinnati the *Westliche Blätter* admonished its readers:

> Protest and indignation meetings must absolutely cease. . . . We must follow the motto of the suffering Kaiser, "Learn to suffer without complaint." Whether we will or no, we must do our duty as American citizens. We owe it to the oath of allegiance which we took to the union, we owe it to our families.[27]

Priests in Rusyn, Slovak, and Moravian communities, who had once urged continued loyalty to the Hapsburgs, abruptly changed their stance with the American declaration of war. In Homestead, Pennsylvania, for example, Greek Catholic priests dedicated a new ninety-six-foot flagpole donated by U.S. Steel.[28] So effective was this mobilization of opinion that Italian anarchists, who called for a meeting in nearby Monessen to protest proposals to conscript foreign-born workers, could only lament: "notwithstanding the danger threatening us, the proletariat was not present."[29]

Especially important in this context was the work of the Committee on Public Information. This agency, headed by George Creel, was thoroughly dominated by Wilsonian reformers. They repudiated the repressive tactics through which more conservative agencies tried to coerce immigrants into shedding their national cultures and allegiances. Creel's explanation of the Committee's role summed up neatly the ideological continuity between prewar Progressive reform and war mobilization:

When I think of the many voices that were heard before the war and are still heard, interpreting America from a class or sectional or selfish standpoint, I am not sure that, if the war had to come, it did not come at the right time for the preservation and reinterpretation of American ideals.[30]

The task of reinterpreting American ideals (cleansed of class or sectional interests) involved a deliberate integration of immigrant nationalism into the American cause. A spectacular idea was to dedicate the Fourth of July 1918 to immigrant America. President and Mrs. Wilson themselves hosted representatives of thirty-three groups (Albanians, Armenians, Assyrians . . . Swiss, Syrians, and Ukrainians) on a pilgrimage to Mount Vernon aboard the Potomac riverboat *Mayflower.* Wilson used the occasion to stress the decisive place of self-determination and a league of nations among his war aims.[31]

Immigrant elites of the Pittsburgh region responded enthusiastically to the call for the Fourth. In Homestead a planning meeting attended by representatives of churches, clubs, and fraternal orders of Poles, Slovaks, Hungarians, Slovenes, Rusyns, Lithuanians, and Romanians decided that steelworkers would be grouped by nationality for the parade; would carry the banners of their ethnic societies or churches; would attend in national costume, if possible; and would march together with units of soldiers, boy scouts, Civil War veterans, schoolchildren, and even the nativist Junior Order of American Mechanics. The program for the public meeting at the end of the parade reveals both the alliance of patriotic causes and the dominant role of the steel corporation and of anti-Bolshevik Slavs in providing the political content of that alliance.[32]

Loyalty—to the United States, to the homeland, to U.S. Steel! These themes blended smoothly with warnings against Bolshevism and class agitation. Nevertheless, there is evidence that many immigrant workers did not fuse their own loyalties in the same way.

Working-Class Nationalism

Italian immigrants acquired a reputation for ardent patriotism and enthusiastic contributions to war relief and bond drives. A closer examination of their enthusiasm, however, reveals both diversity of opinion and independence of behavior. The *prominenti* of Italian-American communities overwhelmingly supported the participation of both Italy and the United States in the war and urged Italy's territorial claims upon the Wilson administration. In turn, the Committee on Public Information not only brought distinguished Italians to the United States to promote the war effort, but also tried the much more formidable task of stimulating war enthusiasm over there. In December 1918 a delegation of pro-war Italian labor leaders, all of whom had been expelled from their unions or from the Socialist Party of Italy, visited the United States. They were welcomed by an impressive committee that included Fiorello LaGuardia and Samuel Gompers. Nevertheless, the visitors were roundly denounced by the Italian Socialist Federation and by all the Italian officers of the Amalgamated Clothing Workers, the International Ladies Garment Workers, and the Hotel and Restaurant Workers, in addition to half a dozen Italian-American workers' papers. The critics savagely attacked the visitors as the king's socialists (*Ai Socialisti del Re*).[33]

This is not to say that Italian immigrants were immune to patriotic appeals. Quite the contrary. But their patriotism sprang from communal solidarities that often defied the efforts of *both* the socialists and George Creel to guide them. At times it assumed a rather militant outlook that openly threatened war production.[34] The style of patriotism widely encountered among Italo-American workers was evident, for example, in a wartime strike at the Jones and Laughlin Steel works in Aliquippa, which gave the AFL its first beachhead among steelworkers in the Pittsburgh region. Only about one-tenth of the mill's 25,000 workers took part in the walkout of September 1917. With the help of AFL organizers, however, the strikers formed a union and remained out for eight days. Federal mediators, who rushed to the scene and headed off a general stoppage by negotiating with the company a wage increase and a pledge not to discharge union members, found that virtually all of the strikers were Italians. Their main grievance was the open animosity of the mill's supervisors toward them. The strikers claimed not only that were they forced to contribute to the Red Cross in order to keep their jobs but also that the superintendent consistently gave the better jobs to "Austrians." Evidently the bloody confrontation between Italian and Croat soldiers around Caporetto had roused hatreds in the Aliquippa mills, which the strikers directed against the company. Although the evidence suggests that national feelings were strong among both Italian and Croat workers, this response bore little similarity to the stage-managed parades of Independence Day.[35]

To cultivate loyalty to the United States and to its business leaders with the help of European national aspirations, therefore, was to traverse an ideological minefield. This was also experienced by Budimer Grahovac, editor of the Yugoslavian *Amerikanski Srbobran* in Pittsburgh, who told Saposs he had taken the job "to help hold the Serbs here in line for the U.S." His task was formidable. He found Serb workers not only "on strike and good union men" in 1919, but also pro-Bolshevik. Grahovac tried "to indirectly keep as many Serbians from striking as possible" by "appealing to them not to go back on the United States after what it did to help Serbia. . . . " Serbs had the highest return rate of any Yugoslav immigrants, so Grahovac confidently advised his readers "to be content with conditions no matter how bad for the short period that they remain here" and not to "waste their savings" by striking.[36]

In one important respect Grahovac was right: immigrant workers had not abandoned their concern for the homeland or their desire to return to their native villages. Immediately after the armistice a large number of immigrant steelworkers of the Monongahela Valley cashed in their Liberty Bonds and other war savings in order to buy tickets for a voyage to Europe. The government's requirement that each person wanting to depart apply for permission, as well as the lack of civilian shipping, aroused great anger in the valley. By the summer of 1919 the immigrant inspector for western Pennsylvania tried to ease the tension by waiving clearance requirements for all but enemy aliens, only to be overruled by the regional U.S. district attorney. At the time the Federation of Russian Workers was leafletting meetings of the National Committee to Organize Iron and Steel Workers and other gatherings of workers, calling for a general strike to force the government to grant permits for a return to Europe.[37]

The longing for home was expressed time and again in Lawrence. Typical is the record of Mary Gurska's conversation with the strike relief committee:

> Came to America because it was "a fine place"—could earn more, go to school longer. Does not like America. Have to work so hard here and have nothing to show for it. Wants to go back [to Poland].[38]

Mary Grinka, a Lithuanian striker and self-proclaimed Socialist, said she was "crying all the time to go back home, but has no money." In Lithuania one could enjoy fresh air and "better eats" from one's own farm: "A bad way here, running to the store for everything."[39]

Anxiety over the fate of relatives in war-torn areas and hopes that a more just society was being created in the homeland intensified this desire to return. The same motives inspired the Amalgamated Clothing Workers, a union unique in its responsiveness to the wishes of immigrants, to involve itself heavily in money transfers, relief, and even industrial investments in revolutionary Russia. Moreover, the solicitude toward immigrants encouraged by the Committee on Public Information seemed to have evaporated as soon as the war was over. Saposs found special bitterness among immigrants who had returned from service in the U.S. Army only to find that the better jobs had been occupied by others and that they were again despised as "foreigners." Rose and Grace Santora said that in Lawrence, Italians had dared to "speak" to foremen about grievances during the war, but no longer. "The bosses then called all Italians 'American people.' Now they are 'foreigners.' "[40]

Socialists and Nationalism

The ideological minefield of national loyalties was as perilous for socialists to traverse as it was for Slavic elites or for George Creel. The Socialist Party of America had declared its "unalterable opposition to war" as the keynote of its 1916 campaign. It had designated the militarization of America as the most ominous menace facing the country's workers, and it had singled out American imperialism for special attack (especially as it functioned in Central and South America). At its April 1917 Emergency Convention the party's majority resolution denounced "the declaration of war by our government as a crime against the people of the United States and against the nations of the world" and urged its members to combat conscription, restrictions of civil liberties, the militarization of social life, and the export of food, while they demanded price controls and the immediate "socialization and democratic management" of all industries related to the supply of food "and other necessaries of life."[41]

The tight repression locked into place by the government and local associations of volunteer patriots by the end of 1917, coupled with the elaborate efforts of the government to defuse industrial disputes through mediation, wage and hour concessions, and the promotion of shop committees, pushed Socialist opposition to the war well out of public view by the summer of 1918. Although the animosity to the war tended momentarily to close the party's ranks, it ultimately drove many native-born Socialists out of the party, intensified the divisions between those who remained and their foreign-born comrades in the language federations, and seriously weakened the party's influence in the union movement. Most party members who held high union offices dropped out. Only James H. Maurer, a Socialist and President of the Pennsylvania Federation of Labor, persistently embarrassed Gompers's effort to manifest a unanimous patriotic enthusiasm among the leaders of the AFL.[42]

A closer look at some immigrant locals and foreign-language federations of the Socialist Party reveals that divisions over the war, and especially over issues roused by immigrant nationalism, ran through the ranks of the socialists themselves. There was no clear-cut confrontation between nationalism espoused by immigrant elites ("clansmen") and internationalism championed by socialists ("intellectuals"), such as the Report of the Interchurch World Movement might have suggested. Each turn of events in Europe could have a profound impact on the thinking of socialists, as two officers of New York's Ornamental Iron Workers' Union revealed to Saposs. Before the war, the German and Austrian members of the union had been primarily reformist socialists, while the Jewish and Italian artisans had sustained a revolutionary industrial unionist bloc. Both groups had opposed American participation in the war, until the Treaty of Brest-Litovsk, after which the Jewish members ardently supported war against Germany as a way of supporting revolutionary Russia.[43]

Questions of war, revolution, and the future of the homeland had special urgency for the members of those of the party's language federations whose homelands were under the rule of the Russian, Austro-Hungarian, or German empires. Among them were the South Slavic and Finnish federations, two of the oldest and strongest language groups affiliated with the party. The fortunes of war divided the Yugoslavs and united the Finns, but both cases illustrate the powerful influence of sentimental and personal ties to Europe on immigrant communities and on the American workers' movement. They also help us understand why the strike militancy of 1916 to 1922 failed to produce a cohesive workers' political movement.

The Yugoslav Socialist Alliance grew from 982 members in 1911 to 2,112 in 1916; and despite wartime secessions, when it joined the Communist Party in 1919, the enrollment stood at 2,200. It was deeply rooted among the Slovene and Croat coal miners of Pennsylvania, Ohio, and Colorado, where immigrants tended to be settled with their families, but where local ethnic elites were virtually nonexistent. It was weaker among the highly transient Serbs in large urban areas, that is to say, in communities where established Yugoslav merchants, saloon keepers, and professionals held sway. Even in those areas, however, the socialist-led Slovene National Benefit Society and the secularist, pro-union Croatian Fraternal Union enjoyed sufficient strength to make them far larger than the Yugoslav fraternal orders linked to the Catholic church.[44]

The leading Slovene and Croat socialists were highly educated men, some of whom had been sent by the Social Democratic parties of Slovenia and Croatia for the express purpose of proselytizing the diaspora. Despite the fierce opposition they faced from the clergy and often from immigrant businessmen and professionals, they were remarkably successful, enjoying more influence among immigrants of peasant origins in America than they had among peasants at home. In America, after all, Yugoslavs from peasant villages toiled for wages in coal and iron mines and steel mills, alongside men of other nationalities; and they were often recruited by the United Mine Workers and the Western Federation of Miners, both of which had many socialists among their officers, or by the Industrial Workers of the World. In short, South Slavic enclaves of mutualism in capitalist America provided fertile soil for socialism, as well as for nationalism.

Originally the YSA had taken a strong stand against the war, but various events in the course of the fighting roused such profound (and often contradictory) feelings among its working-class constituency as to force its leaders to reconsider their position. By the end of 1915 the federation's members had developed nearly unanimous support for a federated Yugoslav republic, but they disagreed sharply among themselves concerning the best way to obtain such a republic.[45] While the Croatian newspaper *Radnička straža* and the majority of the delgates to the YSA's 1916 convention firmly supported the party's campaign against militarism, Etbin Kristan, the Slovenian leader, broke ranks. Through the pages of the newspaper *Proletarec* he appealed for revolutionary warfare to create a Yugoslav republic, denouncing in increasingly strident tones the "pacifism" of the YSA. From that point on, all energies of the Slovene sections were dedicated to supporting the successful American war effort and to a futile campaign to make the emerging Yugoslav state a federated republic.

Quite different was the course of the YSA. Left under firm control of anti-war Croats, the order aligned itself with the Third International. Its influence, however, had been greatly reduced, and its paper had been suppressed early in 1918. When tens of thousands of Yugoslav steelworkers and coal miners went on strike in the late months of 1919, there was no socialist paper in a Slavic language left to support their cause.[46]

If conflicts over the homeland divided the Yugoslav socialists and served to minimize the impact of the YSA in the expression of American workers' aspirations after the war, they had the opposite effect among Finnish socialists. The difference may help account for the extraordinary prominence of Finns in the Communist movement of the 1920s and for the persistence of left-wing influence among the Finns in later years. More than 10,000 members made the Finnish federation by far the largest language group affiliated with the Socialist Party in 1916. That membership represented 15 percent of the adult Finns in America, and Michael Karni has estimated that the press and activities of the federation reached 25 percent to 30 percent of the Finnish immigrants. All of its leading figures had been prominent in the Revolution of 1905 and had come to the United States after its defeat.

The popularity of the IWW among Finnish miners and among the numerous activists educated at Work People's College in Duluth by Leo Laukki and his staff, led to a bitter schism between the "opportunists" and the "industrialists" in the Finnish federation by 1916. Its effects could still be felt during the organizing drive of the Committee to Organize Iron and Steel Workers on the iron range in 1919, when "opportunist" organizers working for the AFL encountered fierce hostility among the Finns.[47]

By that time, however, events in Finland were already healing the breach in the Finnish-American socialist leadership. Finnish independence was declared in December 1917 by socialists, and immediately the country was plunged into civil war, with armed German intervention on the side of the Whites. A whirlwind campaign on behalf of the Finnish republic supported by members of the Socialist Party broke through official censorship, in part by sheer audacity among the Finnish workers who took up the cause and in part by offering loud support to America's war against Germany. The socialists were quite able to make the conservative Finnish-American Loyalty League, which the Committee on Public Information had nurtured, appear to be pro-German. A May 1918 rally in New York's Carnegie Hall, addressed by Santeri Nuorteva, Morris Hillquit, and John Reed in support of revolutionary regimes in Finland and Russia was certainly the largest public activity of the Left that year (at least until the armistice). In short, Finland's bloody civil war united the leadership of the Finnish federation, provided it with public prominence when other radicals were being silenced, and moved it inexorably toward the federation's ultimate (1921) merger with the Workers' (Communist) Party, where it provided 45 percent of the total membership.[48]

Nevertheless, the interviews Saposs conducted on the iron range in July 1919 suggest that ideological consensus had developed more quickly among Finnish socialist leaders than it had among the miners at large. Leo Laukki, on bail pending appeal after his conviction in the Chicago IWW trial, spoke of the need for "an independent industrial union" and even claimed he "had never joined the I.W.W. and is opposed to it not on principle but because of its lack of business sense. . . . " Nevertheless, he added, "At present the Finns are active I.W.W.'s and if a strike took place the Finns might swing the foreign element to accept I.W.W. leadership."[49]

The Drive to Organize Unions

The statement of Laukki suggests that neither the craft union practice of the AFL nor the revolutionary unionism of the IWW enjoyed the unequivocal support of the immigrants who participated in the great strike wave of 1919. Both currents of the labor movement were visibly present in the immigrants' struggles, and both of them left an imprint in the way in which immigrant strikers expressed and acted upon their own aspirations. Neither one, however, can be identified as the immigrants' movement, let alone as the Voice of the Working Class.

Workers of southern and eastern European origins were well aware that the AFL's leaders, and most "American" workers (those of northern and western European ancestries), regarded them with suspicion at best, and with contempt at worst. In the minds of most craft unionists, the recent immigrants could be organized into unions only if they were "Americanized," a prospect they considered hopeless. The head of the Federation's New York office, J. E. Roach, for example, explained to Saposs that "the foreigners . . . chase after isms," being easily swayed by "highbrows" like Hillquit, and that unions that preached an end to capitalism could not expect employers to deal with them. Moreover, immigrants had to learn English and had no right to expect union activity to be conducted in their languages, Roach added. He had been born in Ireland, but he had no use for Gaelic. He was an American.[50]

Quite different was the attitude of the National Committee to Organize Iron and Steel workers and of A. J. Muste and his fellow leaders in the Lawrence strike. They believed that immigrants could be assimilated through unionization, provided the unions operated on an industrial (rather than craft) basis and made special efforts to reach immigrants in their own languages and through their own societies. Nevertheless, the task was a delicate one, involving both reassurance to the "American" workers that the "foreigners" would not run amuck and carefully managed direction and education of the immigrants. As Director Edward Evans of the Chicago District of the National Committee to Organize Iron and Steel Workers explained the point:

The organizers have constantly been met with the following argument from the English speaking workers. We will join you but we are afraid of the foreigners, as they are hotheads and will want [an] immediate strike which may lead to rioting and blood shedding. The Committee feels that they have convinced the English speaking workers that they have the situation sufficiently in hand to be able to avoid such an occurrence. The Committee is, however, not so confident as they make themselves out to be, since . . . [it] was only by pleading and threatening that they have controlled them [the immigrants] so far. It seems that the foreign workers regard the union as all powerful and [do] not understand its aims, demand the immediate discharge of all foremen under whom they are working, as well as other action which the Committee does not feel itself competent to carry out.[51]

This cautious attitude was evident in the committee's consistent policy of confining discussion at its rallies to speeches from the platform and in its well-known reluctance to give union buttons to those who joined (for fear of fights between workers with buttons and those without them). It also underlay a secret but incessant war waged by the Committee against the IWW, especially in the Chicago region. Evans himself testified that he had "got the managers" of the Pullman works "to discharge these I.W.W.s," and subsequently made "as good headway [there] as elsewhere."[52] His colleague F. H. Dietrich used a police escort to break up a meeting of 400 Poles, Croats, and Serbs who had joined the Workers' International Industrial Union (the "Detroit I.W.W.") in Indiana Harbor, and subsequently persuaded their employer to sign a closed shop contract, compelling all the workers to join the AFL's Boiler Makers.[53] In short, it was not only among the Finns of the iron range that Foster's organizing committee fought a war on three fronts: against the steel corporations, against immigrant nationalists, and against a significant IWW, or other revolutionary union, presence. Here was the basis of the Committee's conception of "clansmen" and "intellectuals" in the world of the immigrants.

The influence of radical organizations, fragmented though they were, upon the strikers of the postwar era was not simply a figment of conservatives' overheated imaginations. In some textile and munitions centers they openly led the workers' struggles, often as coalitions of many different left-wing groups. The Workers' Eight Hour Day Conference of Paterson, New Jersey, for example, involved delegates from the Workers' International Industrial Union; the Industrial Workers of the World; the Russian, Lithuanian and Passaic County locals of the Socialist Party; the Passaic County Socialist

Labor Party; the Paole Zion; three branches of the Workman's Circle, and the Sons of Italy. In defiance of the AFL's United Textile Workers, that alliance organized the strike of 1919.[54]

Because the Communist Party was formed by language federations, its original program reflected the diversity of radical initiatives that impinged upon the lives of the federations' members. The program denounced the AFL as "a bulwark of capitalism" and called for "the construction of a general industrial union organization, embracing the I.W.W., W.I.I.U., independent and secessionist unions, militant unions of the A. F. of L., and the unorganized workers, on the basis of the revolutionary class struggle."[55] Nevertheless, the new party was in no condition to realize its ambitious progam.

Paradoxically, the importance of revolutionary organizations in strike activity rose as the general level of strike participation subsided after 1922. The remarkable series of maritime and loggers' strikes demanding freedom for "class war prisoners" between May and July 1923 and the subsequent strikes of New York's garment workers (1926), textile workers in Passaic (1926), New Bedford (1928), and Gastonia (1929), not to mention the Colorado miners' strike to save Sacco and Vanzetti, were all led by Communists or Wobblies. Although the crushing defeats suffered by unions in mass production industries during the depression of 1920–1922 and the grim reports of European conditions sent back to America by immigrants who had returned to their homelands had abruptly deflated immigrants' hopes and directed their efforts of the 1920s inward toward their family and community lives, they had evidently also left behind in their wake a strong awareness of pan-immigrant solidarity (most sharply manifested in the defense of Sacco and Vanzetti and in the appeal of Al Smith's campaign for the presidency) and a significant radical presence within many immigrant communities. The ebb tide of labor militancy had stranded noteworthy clusters of highly politicized workers on the barren beach of the Coolidge Prosperity.[56]

Even in the midst of the 1916–1922 strike wave, however, it was clear that both the Left and industrial unionists had made an indelible mark upon the rhetoric of immigrant strikers and reinforced their suspicion of craft unions. Six months after the collapse of the steel strike, Saposs's investigators found intense loyalty to Foster personally and to his vanquished Committee among immigrants who had taken part in the strike and their families. Both the loyalty of Homestead's former strikers and the lesson they had drawn from their experience were made clear by Mrs. John Hriciak. Having managed the borough's strike commissary, she found herself half a year later visited incessantly by workers asking for news of the union. Although they were again afraid to speak publicly and were "generally disgusted," she said, the workers were "not sorry that they had struck" and "would not hesitate going on strike again if the Americans decided to come out, but the Americans must lead."[57]

One expression, repeated time and again by immgrants at their own meetings, as well as to outsiders, sums up the aspiration in which men and women alike concurred. "Our people ain't never goin' to stop," said a Slovak woman in Youngstown, "until our fathers can be home sometimes and not be just like a horse—take out of the stall and put back in the stall."

A Pole took the floor at a union meeting in the Monongahela Valley to use the same words:

> Mr. Chairman—just like a horse and wagon. Put horse in wagon, work all day. Take horse out of wagon—put in stable. Take horse out of stable, put in wagon. Same way like mills. Work all day. Come home—go sleep. Get up—go work in mills—come home. Wife say, "John, children sick. You help with children." You say, "Oh, go to hell"—go sleep. Wife say, "John, you go town." You say, "No"—go sleep. No know what the hell you do. For why this war? For why we buy Liberty bonds? For the mills? No, for freedom and America—for everybody. No more horse and wagon. For eight-hour day.[58]

The chorus in which this aspiration was expressed blended diverse and even discordant melodies. It drew heavily upon the ideology of citizenship, of rights, of self-determination. Those patriotic (if you will, bourgeois democratic) themes were mixed with the language of class consciousness, of solidarity, and of internationalism. Both commitment to trade unionism and a heavy sprinkling of revolutionary rhetoric were easy to detect. Apocalyptic visions mingled with clearly articulated programs and demands. Through it all, an idyllic image of life on the land, back home, provided a still irrepressible counterpoint. Intense nationalism, anxiety over the fate of loved ones across the sea, and hopes that a new day was dawning in the old country, as well as in the new, added special poignancy to those themes.

Notes

1. Julianna Puskás, *Emigration from Hungary to the United States before 1914* (Budapest: Akadémiai Kiadó, 1975), 63.
2. Lithuanian Mass Meeting, report in Anthony Capraro Papers, Box 8, Immigration History Research Center, St. Paul, Minn. (hereafter ACP).

3. On the 1916–1922 strike wave, see David Montgomery, "The 'New Unionism' and the Transformation of Workers' Consciousness in America, 1909–1922," *Journal of Social History* 7 (1974): 509–29; P. K. Edwards, *Strikes in the United States, 1881–1974* (Oxford: Basil Blackwell, 1981), 1–51, 84–133.

4. Edwards, *Strikes*, pp. 2–22, 254–56.

5. Edward J. Evans, interview, 27 December 1918, in David J. Saposs Papers, State Historical Society of Wisconsin, Box 21 (hereafter DSP).

6. Matthew Pluhar, interview, 3 April 1919, Box 21, DSP; U.S. Post Office Files, R.G. 28, National Archives (see, e.g., files of *Avanti* and *Elore Kepes Folyoirat*); David Montgomery, " 'Liberty and Union': Workers and Government in America, 1900–1940," in *Essays from the Lowell Conference on Industrial History 1980 and 1981*, ed. Robert Weible et al. (Lowell, Mass.: Lowell Conference on Industrial History, 1981), 145–57; editorial, *New York Call*, 17 April 1921.

7. Saposs' interviews are at the State Historical Society of Wisconsin. Capraro's papers are at the Immigration History Research Center, University of Minnesota.

8. Mrs. Bastyani, interview, 1 April 1919, Box 8, ACP.

9. Interchurch World Movement, *Public Opinion and the Steel Strike* (New York: Harcourt Brace and Howe, 1921), 230–31. On Capraro, see Rudolph J. Vecoli, "Anthony Capraro and the Lawrence Strike of 1919," in *Pane e Lavoro: The Italian American Working Class*, ed. George E. Pozzetta, (Toronto: Multicultural Historical Society of Ontario, 1980),3–27.

10. Edward J. Evans, interview, Box 21, DSP.

11. Frank H. Serene, "Immigrant Steelworkers in the Monongahela Valley: Their Communities and the Development of a Labor Class Consciousness" (Ph.D. diss., University of Pittsburgh, 1979), p. 84; Thomas Čapek, Jr., *The Čechoslovaks* (New York: Czechoslovak Section of America's Making, 1921), 89; Monika Glettler, *Pittsburgh-Wien-Budapest: Programm and Praxis der Nationalitätenpolitik bei der Auswanderung der ungarischen Slowaken nach America um 1900* (Vienna: Verlag der Österrichischen Akademie der Wissenschaft, 1980), 40–47.

12. Albert Mamatey, interview, n.d., Box 24, DSP.

13. Stephen Gyöngyösy, interview, n.d., Box 24, DSP.

14. Rev. C. V. Molnar in Interchurch World Movement, "Testimony" (typescript), pp. 77, 82, Box 24, DSP; Serene, "Immigrant Steelworkers," p. 219. Molnar charged "the Americanized 'Hunkies' " with *opposing* the strike ("Testimony," pp. 80–81).

15. David J. Saposs, interview, at Pennsylvania State University (typescript), Box 26, DSP. Saposs also told of two Irish Catholic priests in Harrisburg who introduced themselves to him through IWW literature. It is noteworthy that the Interchurch World Movement's report studiously avoided discussing the Catholic church.

16. A. H. Young, "Employing Men for the Steel Mill," *Iron Age* 98 (16 November 1916): 1108. Useful discussions of immigrant elites may be found in Joseph J. Barton, *Peasants and Strangers: Italians, Rumanians, and Slovaks in an American City, 1890–1950* (Cambridge, Mass.: Harvard University Press, 1975); Timothy L. Smith, "New Approaches to the History of Immigration in Twentieth Century America," *American Historical Review* 71 (July 1966): 1265–79; John W. Briggs, *An Italian Passage: Immigrants to Three American Cities* (New Haven: Yale University Press, 1978); Anna Maria Martellone, *Una Little Italy nell'Atene d'America: La Communità italiana di Boston dal 1880 al 1920* (Naples: Guida Editori, 1973); John J. Bukowczyk, "Steeples and Smokestacks: Class, Religion and Ideology in the Polish Immigrant Settlements in Greenpoint and Williamsburg, Brooklyn, 1880—1929" (Ph.D. diss., Harvard University, 1980).

17. Glettler, *Pittsburgh-Wien-Budapest*, pp. 296–99. The quotations are on pp. 297–98 (my translation). On Rovnianek, see ibid., pp. 29–32, 40–43, 71.

18. Scott Cummings, ed., *Self-Help in Urban America: Patterns of Minority Business Enterprise* (Port Washington, N.Y.: Kennikat Press, 1980), 125, 168, 124, 138. For a discussion of fraternal orders in ethnic communities see, for example, John Bodnar, *Immigration and Industrialization: Ethnicity in an American Mill*

Town, 1870–1940 (Pittsburgh: University of Pittsburgh Press, 1977), 87; Bodnar, "Immigration, Kinship and the Rise of Working-Class Realism in Industrial America," *Journal of Social History* 14 (Fall 1980): 45–65.

19. Quoted in Puskás, *Emigration from Hungary*, p. 178.

20. See Cummings, ed., *Self-Help in Urban America*, pp. 125, 138, 168.

21. Cummings, ed., *Self-Help in Urban America*, pp. 117–22; Charles C. Tansill, *America and the Fight for Irish Freedom, 1866–1922: An Old Story Based upon New Data* (New York: Devin-Adair Co., 1957).

22. E.g., Bodnar, *Immigration and Industrialization*, p. 118; *Iron Age* 97 (8 July 1915): 79; Serene, "Immigrant Steelworkers," pp. 153–55; Čapek, *The Čechoslovaks*, pp. 43–48.

23. Carl Wittke, *German-Americans and the World War (With Special Emphasis on Ohio's German Language Press)* (Columbus: Ohio State Archaeological and Historical Society, 1936), 23, 64.

24. John B. Duff, "The Italians," in *The Immigrants' Influence on Wilson's Peace Policies*, ed. Joseph P. O'Grady (Lexington: University Press of Kentucky, 1967), 240, 246; John P. Diggins, *Mussolini and Fascism: The View from America* (Princeton, N.J.: Princeton University Press, 1972), 87.

25. James Weinstein, *The Decline of Socialism in America, 1912–1925* (New York and London: Monthly Review Press, 1967), 119–76; James R. Green, *Grass-Roots Socialism: Radical Movements in the Southwest, 1895–1943* (Baton Rouge and London: Louisiana State University Press, 1978), 345–95; David Montgomery, *Workers' Control in America: Studies in the History of Work, Technology, and Labor Struggles* (Cambridge and New York: Cambridge University Press, 1979), 113–38; Stephen Meyer III, *The Five Dollar Day: Labor Management and Social Control in the Ford Motor Company, 1908–1921* (Albany, N.Y.: State University of New York Press, 1981), 175–93; U.S. Department of Labor, *U.S. Employment Service Bulletin*, (Washington, D.C.: Government Printing Office, 22 October 1918), 5; George Creel, *How We Advertised America* (New York and London: Harper and Brothers, Publishers, 1920), 85.

26. Gladys L. Palmer, *Union Tactics and Economic Change: A Case Study of Three Philadelphia Textile Unions* (Philadelphia: University of Pennsylvania Press, 1932), 150.

27. *Westliche Blätter*, Cincinnati, 4 February 1917, trans. and quoted in Wittke, *German-Americans*, p. 123.

28. Robert E. Park, *The Immigrant Press and Its Control* (New York and London: Harper and Brothers, Publishers, 1922), pp. 201–10; Serene, "Immigrant Steelworkers," pp. 152–54.

29. *Il Proletario*, 14 July 1917, as translated by Post Office censor. File 47457, R.G. 28, National Archives.

30. Creel, *How We Advertise America*, p. 105.

31. Ibid., pp. 200–207.

32. Serene, "Immigrant Steelworkers," pp. 155–57.

33. Creel, *How We Advertise America*, pp. 299–301; *Ai Socialisti del Re* (New York, 1918; copy in ACP, Box 2, file Azeffa, La Bolgia).

34. Franco Andreucci and Tommaso Detti, eds., *Il movimento operaio italiano: dizionario biografico, 1853–1943*, 5 vols. (Rome: Editori Riuniti, 1975–1979), 2:167–69; Gino Castagno, *Bruno Buozzi* (Milan: Edizioni Avanti, 1981), 28–29. Cf. David Corbin's analysis of the role of patriotism in the class consciousness of West Virginia's coal miners (*Life, Work, and Rebellion in the Coal Fields: The Southern West Virginia Miners, 1880–1922* [Urbana: University of Illinois Press, 1981], 176–252).

35. U.S. Department of Labor, Federal Mediation and Conciliation Service File 33/2849, R.G. 28. National Archives. Fiorello LaGuardia echoed the sentiments of the Aliquippa workers during the 1920 election campaign, when he asserted that "any Italo-American who votes the Democratic ticket this year is an Austrian bastard" (Duff, "The Italians," p. 133).

36. Budimer Grahavoc [*sic*], interview. Park calls the *Amerikanski Srbobran* a republican journal (*The Immigrant Press*, p. 305).

37. Serene, "Immigrant Steelworkers," pp. 161–62; Interchurch World Movement, "Testimony," pp. 27–28, 62. The Federation of Russian Workers remains unstudied, but its members seem to have been largely Rusyn and Ukrainian and its ideology a blend of anarchism and socialism. See Bruce B. Schubert, "The Palmer Raids in Connecticut: 1919–1920," *Connecticut Review* 5 (1971): 53–69.

38. Mary Gurska, Individual Stories, Box 8, ACP.

39. Mary Grinka, interview, 2 April 1919, Box 8, ACP. Cf. Peter J. Maczkov's nostalgic poem about the Carpathians in Paul R. Magocsi, *Rusyn-American Ethnic Literature* (Cambridge, Mass.: Harvard Ukrainian Research Institute, n.d.), 509:

> There is where you can drink clean water morning and evening,
> There is where clothes are made at home;
> There is where there are no factories, mines, dust, smoke,
> There is where every peasant is the "lord" of his own household.

But see also interview, Antonette Bolis, 2 April 1919, Box 8, ACP, where the hardships of women in Lawrence and Lithuanuia offer little choice.

40. Rose Santora and Grace Santora, Statement concerning Wood Mill of the American Woolen Company, 24 April 1919, Box 8, ACP; Waslaw Stafanski [*sic*] and C. C. Robinson, interviews, and "Chat on the Curbstone with Five Lithuanians and One Italian," Box 26, DSP. On the contributions of the ACWA, see Joseph Schlossberg, *The Message of Internationalism* (New York: Amalgamated Clothing Workers of America, 1923). The ILGWU made contributions to Polish and Jewish Unions. Louis Levine, *The Women's Garment Workers: A History of the International Ladies' Garment Workers' Union* (New York: B. W. Huebsch, 1924), 339.

41. Alexander Trachtenberg, *The American Socialists and the War* (New York: Rand School of Social Science, 1917), 39–43. The quotations are on pp. 42, 43.

42. David Brody, *Steelworkers in America: The Nonunion Era* (Cambridge, Mass.: Harvard University Press, 1960), 180–230; Alexander M. Bing, *War-Time Strikes and Their Adjustment* (New York: E. P. Dutton, 1921); Weinstein, *The Decline of Socialism*, pp. 119–76; Frank L. Grubbs, Jr., *The Struggle for Labor Loyalty: Gompers, The A.F. of L., and the Pacifists, 1917–1920* (Durham, N.C.: Duke University Press, 1968); C. Roland Marchand, *The American Peace Movement and Social Reform, 1898–1918* (Princeton, N.J.: Princeton University Press, 1972), 297–318; John H. M. Laslett, "End of an Alliance: Selected Correspondence between Socialist Party Secretary Adolph Germer, and U.M.W. of A. Leaders in World War One," *Labor History* 12 (1971): 570–95; Cecilia F. Bucki, "Dilution and Craft Traditions: Bridgeport, Connecticut, Munitions Workers, 1915–1919," *Social Science History* 4 (1980): 105–24; Levine, *The Women's Garment Workers*, pp. 320–28; James H. Maurer, *It Can Be Done* (New York: Rand School Press, 1938), 223–34.

43. Harry Jones and Sol Broad, interviews, 23 January 1919 and 6 March 1919, Box 22, DSP.

44. Joseph Stipanovich, "Immigrant Workers and Immigrant Intellectuals in Progressive America: A History of the Yugoslav Socialist Federation, 1900–1918" (Ph.D. diss., University of Minnesota, 1977); Cummings, *Self-Help in Urban America*, pp. 160–76; Smith, "New Approaches"; Charles Pogarelec, interview, 10 July 1919, Box 21, DSP; Theodore Draper, *Roots of American Communism* (New York: Viking Press, 1957), 189. The membership figures for the YSA are from Stipanovich, "Immigrant Workers," p. 147.

45. Trachtenberg, *The American Socialists*, p. 22; Stipanovich, "Immigrant Workers," pp. 213–19; George L. Prpic, "The South Slavs," in *The Immigrants' Influence*, ed. O'Grady, pp. 173–203; my account of the debates within the YSA relies heavily on information in Ivan Čizmić, *Jugoslavenski iseljenički pokret u SAD i stvaranje Jugoslavenske države 1918* (Zagreb: Sveučilište u Zagrebu—Institut za Hrvatsku Povijest, 1974). I am deeply indebted to Professor Ivo Banac for translat-

ing the relevant chapters for me and also for bringing to my attention Stjepan Lojen, *Uspomene jednog iseljenika* (Zagreb: Sveučilište u Zagreb—Institut za Hrvatsku Povijest, 1963). My interpretation of the information in Čizmić differs somewhat from his, by stressing the impact of these divisions on the American working class.

46. Čizmić, *Jugoslavenski iseljenički*, pp. 155–63; Stipanovich, "Immigrant Workers," 219–20; Frank Graff, interview, Homestead, Box 24, DSP.

47. Federation membership figures in Stipanovich, "Immigrant Workers," p. 147; Carl Ross, *The Finn Factor in American Labor, Culture and Society* (New York Mills, Minn.: Parta Printers, 1977), 141–56; Michael G. Karni, "Yhteishyvä—Or, For the Common Good: Finnish Radicalism in the Western Great Lakes Region, 1900–1940" (Ph.D. diss., University of Minnesota, 1975), p. 92; M. G. Karni, Matti E. Kaups, and Douglas J. Ollila, eds., *The Finnish Experience in the Western Great Lakes Region: New Perspectives* (Turku: Institute for Migration, 1975); S. Allanne [*sic*], interviews, n.d., Box 21, DSP.

48. Karni, "Yhteishyvä," pp. 194–217; Ross, *The Finn Factor*, pp. 154–61; S. Allanne [*sic*], interview. The Russian Red Guard of Chicago took the same position on the war in 1918 as the Finns and appealed to President Wilson to aid the revolutionary governments (Park, *The Immigrant Press*, pp. 199–200). In Canada, Finns provided two-thirds of the Communist Party's members in 1921. See *Polyphony: The Bulletin of the Multicultural History Society of Ontario* 3 (1981): special issue, *Finns in Ontario*, ed. Varpu Lindström-Best.

49. Lauki, [*sic*], interview. On Laukki and the IWW, see Karni, Kaups, and Ollila, eds., *The Finnish Experience*, pp. 169–70; Joseph R. Conlin, *Big Bill Haywood and the Radical Union Movement* (Syracuse, N.Y.: Syracuse University Press, 1969), 194–99.

50. Dave [Saposs] to Bill [Leiserson], 22 January 1919, Box 1, DSP; J. E. Roach, interview, 17 February 1919, Box 21, DSP.

51. Evans, interview. Good accounts of the Committee's strategy can be found in William Z. Foster, *The Great Steel Strike and Its Lessons* (New York: B. W. Huebsch, 1920); and Brody, *Steelworkers in America*. For Muste's role in Lawrence, which included the imposition of a strategy in nonviolent struggle, see Abraham J. Muste, *The Essays of A. J. Muste* (Indianapolis: Bobbs-Merrill Co., 1967), 57–83.

52. Evans, interview. Union button conflicts in Chicago had often taken the form of racial encounters. See William M. Tuttle, Jr., *Race Riot: Chicago in the Red Summer of 1919* (New York: Atheneum, 1970), 134, 147, 153–56.

53. John Howard and F. H. Dietrich, interviews, 3 July 1919 and n.d., Box 21, DSP.

54. *Press Guardian*, Paterson, N.J., 3 January 1919. I am indebted to David Goldberg for this information.

55. Communist Party of America, *Manifesto and Program. Constitution. Report to the Communist International* (Chicago: Communist Party of America, 1919), 17. See also the anonymous pamphlet issued jointly by the Communist Party, the IWW, and the One Big Union, probably early in 1920: *The Rank and File vs. The Labor Skates, with Official Statements of the Communists and I.W.W. and the One Big Union Advocates in Regard to Industrial and Political Action in America* (n.p., n.d.).

56. Insightful portrayals of immigrant life and aspirations in the 1920s can be found in John Bodnar, Roger Simon, and Michael P. Weber, *Lives of Their Own: Slovaks, Italians, and Poles in Pittsburgh, 1900–1960* (Urbana: University of Illinois Press, 1982); John Bodnar, *Anthracite People: Families, Unions, and Work, 1900–1940* (Harrisburg, Penn.: Pennsylvania Historical and Museum Commission, 1983); Tamara K. Hareven, *Family Time and Industrial Time: The Relationship between the Family and Work in a New England Industrial Community* (Cambridge and New York: Cambridge University Press, 1982); Hareven and Randolph Langenbach, *Amoskeag: Life and Work in an American Factory-City* (New York: Pantheon Books, 1978); Louis Adamic, *My America, 1928–1938* (New York and London: Harper and Brothers, 1938); Adamic, *Dynamite: The Story of Class Vio-*

lence in America, rev. ed. (New York: Harper and Brothers, 1934); Ewa Morawska, "The Internal Status Hierarchy in the East European Immigrant Communities of Johnstown, Pa., 1890–1930's," *Journal of Social History* 16 (1982): 75–107. On the strikes of 1923 to 1929, see David Montgomery, "Immigrants, Industrial Workers, and Social Reconstruction in the United States, 1916–1923," *Labour/Le Travail* 13 (1984): 101–114; John S. Gambs, *The Decline of the I.W.W.* (New York: Columbia University Press, 1932); Fred Thompson, *The I.W.W.: Its First 75 Years* (Chicago: Industrial Workers of the World, 1981); Irving Bernstein, *The Lean Years* (Boston: Houghton Mifflin Company, 1960).

57. Slavish Blast Furnace Laborers, interviews, McKeesport, n.d.; Mrs. Lapag, Homestead, n.d.; Frank Wierneckie, Pittsburgh, n.d.; Mrs. John Richick [*sic*], Homestead, 17 July 1920, Box 26, DSP. John Hriciak of Homestead was often named in local newspapers as a union activist (Serene, 219, n. 13.) See also interviews with Mr. and Mrs. Frank, Homestead, n.d.; Mrs. Swab, "Slav of Homestead," n.d., Box 26, DSP.

58. John A. Fitch, "The Closed Shop," *Survey* 43 (8 November 1919), 91.

The Contributors

James R. Barrett teaches at the University of Illinois, Urbana-Champaign. He is coauthor of *Steve Nelson, American Radical* and has just completed a book dealing with the experience of "new immigrants" and Black migrant workers in mass production industry and big city neighborhoods. His interest in the problem of class formation among ethnically and racially diverse populations derives as much from personal as from professional experience: "I grew up in an ethnic working-class neighborhood on the West Side of Chicago inhabited largely by second generation Italian- and Polish-American workers and their families. Blacks were not welcome north of Lake Street, and it was not difficult to appreciate the fact that race and nationality could and often did divide people who otherwise had a great deal in common. Too often labor historians have cited the very existence of racial and ethnic diversity as an explanation for the relative weakness of class consciousness in the United States. Yet native, immigrant, and Black workers sometimes did identify with one another and successfully organize along class lines. Even when such attempts failed, it is important to understand why, not in abstract terms but rather in terms of how the failures were experienced by those involved. Investigation of these questions will frequently lead one from the national or even community level to the microscopic level of household or work group. But it is important that these small pieces be placed back eventually into the broader picture of the developing American political economy."

David Brundage is an assistant professor of community studies at the University of California, Santa Cruz. Until quite recently, Irish-American working-class radicalism had drawn little notice from historians. Students of immigration, focusing on issues of social mobility and cultural assimilation, had little to say about Irish workers or about social conflict within the Irish immigrant community. And labor historians, despite their growing concern with the complexities of working-class life and thought, gave little attention to the Irish. This situation has changed dramatically since the mid-1970s: "My essay, which is drawn in part from earlier work I did on working-class radicalism in the Mountain West, reflects this new concern. I was originally interested in the question of the role of the Knights of Labor in the shaping of an American working-class culture. It was apparent, however, that the Knights did not spring from thin air. In Denver the Land League and Irish radicalism had prepared the way. In New York City the Henry George campaign clearly did represent a watershed in the history of Irish-American working-class radicalism. But the problem that remains is what happened to this radicalism after the 1880s, after the decline of the Land League and the Knights. This question represents the focus of my present research. I am now working on a study of the role played by Irish working people in the powerful western Populist movement in the 1890s. It should help us to understand the full legacy of the Land League."

Steven Fraser is a senior editor at Basic Books, held a fellowship at the Woodrow Wilson International Center for Scholars in 1984–1985, and is presently at work on a biography of Sidney Hillman. His interest in the history of the labor movement sprang from a long-standing concern with the possibilities of radical political change: "Such concerns were part of the political culture in which I grew up and were enhanced during the period of my own political activity in the civil rights, anti-war, and socialist movements of the 1960s. It did strike me that one avenue of explanation for the putative failure of the U.S. labor movement to develop a durable socialist consciousness and organization might lie with the experience of that hybrid form of socially conscious trade unionism which simultaneously expressed a reformist impulse while neatly avoiding a direct challenge to the political economy of industrial capitalism in the U.S. There is perhaps no better example of this kind of 'social' if not quite 'social democratic' trade unionism, than the Amalgamated Clothing Workers of America: During the era of World War I the most celebrated example of the 'new unionism' and later the foremost advocate of the New Deal and its political alliance with the CIO. One of the reasons the union and its president, Sidney Hillman, attracted such extraordinary attention was their remarkable success in building a coherent and stable organization out of a multiplicity of first generation immigrants. This was not an easily accomplished task."

Donna Gabaccia teaches history at Mercy College, Dobbs Ferry, New York, and is a Fulbright Lecturer, 1985–1986, at the University of Bremen. "I began my undergraduate studies by working with a social theorist; thereafter, for ten years, I alternated between American and European residences. Predictably, perhaps, most of my research has taken a comparative and interdisciplinary approach. My dissertation focused on changing immigrant family life and ideals; I called myself a family historian and I hoped I was writing history from 'the bottom up and the inside out.' While I taught first at a German university and thereafter at a small American college with open admissions, my view of my own research changed. As I wrote *From Sicily to Elizabeth Street,* I found that I could no longer separate family from political history. My current research examines the intertwined histories of transatlantic migration and 'labor' movements for social and economic change. The project appealed to me because of the many geographical and 'specialty' boundaries it promised to transcend. Here was a way of writing both European and American history, ethnic and labor history, family and economic, 'new social' and 'old political' history. For the past three years, I have focused mainly on the Sicilian and South Italian experience; exploring the German, Irish or Scandinavian variations seems an exciting and important possibility."

Michael G. Karni serves as editor of *Finnish Americana* and is both an editorial supervisor in the Department of Independent Study and a member of the Department of Scandinavian at the University of Minnesota. In 1979 he was appointed Fulbright Professor of American literature to Finland. Until the late 1960s, he had taught English at the Buffalo State University College in New York: "I assumed I would eventually earn a doctorate in English literature. Instead, the emergence of a totally different consciousness that was due to the war in Asia and the advances being made by Black and Native American minorities at home turned me toward a different discipline. I enrolled in the Ph.D. program in American Studies at the University of Minnesota and began working at Minnesota's Immigration History Research Center. While there, I came to the realization that I really knew nothing of the history of my own ethnic group. At about the same time, many other descendants of Finnish immigrants with similar attitudes became interested in Finnish migration to North America. Together we have held major conferences on Finnish ethnic history in the United States, Canada, and Finland; and we have published widely and have begun exchanges with scholars from Finland."

Hartmut Keil, presently a research fellow at the Smithsonian Institute, was director of the Chicago Project on German immigrant workers. His interest in American history was awakened through personal contact with American society when he was an exchange student in Concord, N.H. "My unreflected, youthful enthusiasm of the late 1950s and the Kennedy years was soon tempered, however, by a more scholarly approach that gradually discarded many of the myths about American history and society, as they were taught at German universities. It was not only a coincidence that my dissertation dealt with the 'American Dream' and that McCarthyism caught my interest at a time when civil and personal liberties were very much at issue in the Federal Republic of Germany in the 1970s. My selection of a collection of congressional hearings, published in 1979, tried to draw parallels by concentrating on occupational groups and institutions who were affected by McCarthyism in the United States in the postwar years in similar ways to those in comparable situations in Germany two decades later. In recent years, I have pursued the question of the transfer of German radicalism to the United States in the second half of the nineteenth century and, more generally, the role of German workers in the development of the American working class. Together with several colleagues and encouraged by Herbert Gutman, I conducted a large research project on the social history of German workers in Chicago from 1850 to World War I, their work and culture and their interaction with other ethnic groups."

Paul Krause teaches at Duke University, Durham, N.C., where he has held a fellowship from the Andrew W. Mellon Foundation. He studied Russian as an undergraduate at Haverford College and then worked as a newspaper reporter and editor for seven years. "Three routes took me to the study of Homestead. First, I grew up in Pittsburgh, not far from what then were the busy furnaces of the Homestead Steel Works; and my parents and immigrant grandparents owed their livelihoods to it and to the other mills of the Monongahela Valley. Second, my experience as a newsman in Philadelphia, in small cities in the Berkshire Mountains and the Mississippi Delta, and in the industrial heartland of the 'New South' led me to questions about the nature of political power that could not be addressed in the world of daily journalism. Third, graduate study convinced me that such questions are best approached through the interpretation of culture, and not exclusively by way of class analysis. Homestead seemed to provide ample material to test this conviction as well as to explore my political questions and personal origins.

"This essay points to a theme I am developing in a larger work: that in Homestead, and indeed throughout the Pittsburgh district, a blend of 'residual' and of 'emergent' currents of thought and behavior marked the initiatives of workers determined to construct an alternative to industrial capitalism in the Gilded Age."

Bruce C. Levine is the director of research and writing at the American Social History Project and a Senior Research Scholar at the City University of New York's Graduate Center. "This study of immigration, class, and politics in the Civil War era reflects three general interests that have engaged me for several years: the transition from precapitalist to capitalist society and social relations, the multiclass democratic revolutions that have often accompanied this transition, and the interrelation between class and ethnicity. My approach to these themes shows the influence of European scholars as well as Americans like Herbert Gutman, Eugene Genovese, and David Montgomery. Reading in nineteenth-century U.S. history convinced me that all three subjects could be combined in a reexamination of the 1840–1860 period."

David Montgomery is Farnam Professor of History at Yale University and co-editor of *International Labor and Working Class History.* "Native-born and immigrants, men and women participated in the militancy of the 1910s. They frequently voiced aspirations for fundamental social change; yet they did not produce even a cohesive reformist class movement, let alone a revolutionary one. On the contrary, the Socialist Party disintegrated, the trade union movement itself was ultimately reduced to its prewar size, and a wave of urban race riots coincided with the peak of the strike wave.

"Working-class behavior during these years seems to defy labor historians' favorite categories of explanation. Decisive elements of its context can be identified: the new role of the state, corporate capitalism's restructuring of both the world economy and power relations within the workplace, the dense concentrations of population in manufacturing cities, the recomposition of the working class itself, and the working people's own intellectual ferment and diverse forms of self-organization. Knowing what these workers imagined, however briefly, to be within their grasp might contribute to our understanding not only of the impulses that drove labor's workplace and political organizations into action during these years but also of those organizations' failure to absorb and build upon those impulses."

Gary R. Mormino and **George E. Pozzetta** teach in Florida. Mormino, who is at the University of South Florida in Tampa, has lectured at the University of Rome as a Fulbright Scholar. He is the author of a forthcoming book on Italian immigrants in St. Louis. Pozzetta, at the University of Florida in Gainesville, has served as President of the American Italian Historical Association. "Both of us have maintained an interest in immigrant cultures and groups throughout our professional careers. As with many immigration historians who have come to the discipline during the past fifteen years, we began with examinations of our own ethnic group. The motivations directing us along this path were both personal and professional: in part they were a search for 'roots' and in part a recognition of beginning advantages of language and cultural sensitivity that such a choice bestowed. During the past several years we have been drawn more and more to the recognition of the need for a comparative and interactive dimension to the study of American immigration: Much of the ethnic experience in this nation has consisted of the by-products that have resulted from the coming together of different groups in common urban settings. This perspective mandates a move beyond the focus of a single group and calls for an examination of the wider pattern of conflict and accommodation that occurred within the immigrant world."

Richard Schneirov is presently engaged in a project on the origins of Chicago's industrial working class, 1850–1873. With Tom Suhrbur, he coauthored a history of the carpenters' union of Chicago, 1863–1983. "My interest in Czech lumbershovers and Czech socialism stems from a paper I wrote under the direction of Professor Alfred Young in 1975 analyzing the 1877 Great Upheaval in Chicago. At that time I was particularly interested in the relationship between organized socialism and the semi-organized crowd actions of workingmen. I concluded that socialism had little influence on the 1877 strikes and riots, except in the case of the Czechs. Meanwhile, I attempted to explain the militancy of workingmen in 1877 by demonstrating that outdoor laborers of all nationalities had a propensity to resort to riots during strikes. Since then, my interests shifted to class relations and local politics in Chicago and to the Anglo-American-Irish branch of the labor movement, whose nonsocialist political traditions I examined in my dissertation. I continued, however, to be perplexed by the riddle of the Czechs: how could their adherence to socialism be explained?"

Allen Seager is associate professor of history at Simon Fraser University, Burnaby, British Columbia. "Writings in Canadian labor history," he writes, "have become increasingly sensitive to the regional and local contours of working-class experience. Any exploration of working-class culture in the Canadian context must confront the realities of ethnic communities and immigrant nationalisms. It must also confront the organizational outreach from the United States, from the 'international' unions. In my own work, centered around the little-understood phenomenon of 'red' unionism and communist political action among western Canadian workers in the 1930s, I have been convinced of the necessity for an approach that integrates these diverse themes. My study of the institutional development of the Mine Workers' Union of Canada was begun in the 1970s, when many of the principal participants were still available for interview research, thus evolved into a major consideration of the Albertan coal-mining community from 1905 to 1945."

Maxine Schwartz Seller teaches at the State University of New York at Buffalo. Her research on a nineteenth-century Jewish leader who worked simultaneously for the Americanization of Jewish immigrants and for the perpetuation of a distinctive Jewish community in the United States introduced her to the complexity of issues of Americanization, assimilation, and ethnic identity. "I also learned that ethnic leaders do not necessarily speak for the rank and file. A decade of teaching American history and 'American Minorities' and of exploring ethnic community life in the Philadelphia area during the late sixties and early seventies led to my writing a college text in which I tried to portray immigrants as subjects rather than objects, as an integral part of American life rather than occasional 'contributors' to it. While recognizing the reality of problems and discrimination, I also wrote about the reality of ethnic Americans as problem solvers; as builders of churches, schools, unions, organizations, and charities; and as creators and consumers of newspapers, literature, music and theater. The revival of feminism and the growth of women's history as a field of study confirmed what I had already learned while negotiating my way through academia as a married woman with young children—that women's experiences were different from men's. Applying this to immigration history, I asked questions specifically about women, their motives for immigrating; strategies for survival, education, and Americanization; work inside and outside the home; self-help networks and organizations; family lives; and political activities. I found that, contrary to the popular stereotype, many immigrant women had interests and commitments beyond the traditional sphere of home and family. Many played important, but often unheralded, roles in the American labor movement."

Index